ASSYRIAN

GREEK

CAROLINGIAN

LATE MEDIEVAL

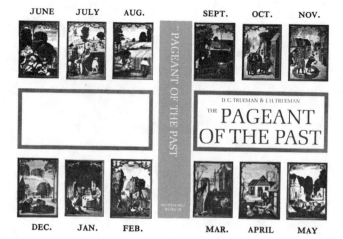

JUNE JULY AUG. SEPT. OCT. NOV.

D. C. TRUEMAN & J. H. TRUEMAN

THE **PAGEANT OF THE PAST**

DEC. JAN. FEB. MAR. APRIL MAY

THE COVER

The monks of the Middle Ages had a regular schedule of religious exercises. Pious laymen also practised their devotions faithfully. Some wealthy individuals commissioned artists to design their personal *Books of Hours*, elegant little prayerbooks containing daily inspirational readings and rich illuminations. The illustrations reproduced on the cover are from the da Costa *Book of Hours*, which was produced about 1515 by Flemish painters for a Portuguese prince. These vividly naturalistic scenes, depicting man's familiar round of activities throughout the twelve months of the year (see the key above), form what amounts to a miniature picture-gallery of the world as the medieval man saw it. Each little illumination is complete with remarkably detailed realism. The April scene, for example, shows a farm in the bustling excitement of spring. The shepherds are busy with the lambs; a woman milks a cow; one maiden is industriously churning while another prods a cow out of the barn behind the house; a farmhand leads the bleating flock to pasture; and far down the road in the misty frame of budding leaves a carefree soul makes his way into the heart of spring. If you study these colourful pictures, so lovingly and exquisitely executed, you will learn a great deal about life as it was lived in northern Europe five centuries ago.

THE **PAGEANT OF THE PAST**

Illustrated by Vernon Mould

McGRAW-HILL RYERSON LIMITED
Toronto   Montreal   New York   London   Sydney
Johannesburg   Mexico   Panama   Düsseldorf
Singapore   Rio de Janeiro   Kuala Lumpur   New Delhi

DAWN CLINE TRUEMAN & JOHN H. TRUEMAN

THE PAGEANT
OF THE
PAST

14 EP 432

ISBN 0-7700-3110-2

Maps by Robert Kunz

A NOTE ABOUT THE AUTHORS

Dawn Cline Trueman is a graduate in Honours English of
the University of Toronto and the Ontario College of
Education. She taught in secondary schools in Hamilton
and London, Ontario, before marrying her co-author. John
H. Trueman received his B.A. and M.A. in History from
the University of Toronto, and his Ph.D. from Cornell
University. He has taught at Stanford University, in
secondary schools in Tillsonburg and London, and for the
Ontario College of Education. At present he is Professor
of History and Associate Dean of Humanities Studies at
McMaster University.

The Truemans' collaborative efforts include *The Enduring Past* (revised edition, 1964) and *Britain: The Growth
of Freedom* (expanded edition, 1964).

PREFACE

Did your grandfather know Julius Caesar? What a ridiculous question, you say. Yet when you were in Grade 2 you might have taken it quite seriously.

Since that time you have, of course, learned a great deal about the measurement of time, and can clearly distinguish between the near and the distant past. It is this consciousness of the passage of time on which you must draw for a meaningful study of history. The events of the past happened in a certain sequence, and we have tried as far as possible to keep to this chronological order in writing our book.

We hope, however, that we have provided more than an orderly and concise account of the chief events in the life of man from earliest times to the close of the Middle Ages. Unfortunately, history for the young student often seems to be little more than a collection of dry and mouldering bones, a dead past. In order to bring that past to life and to clothe those bones with flesh, we have incorporated into our book two features that we believe are unique. First, there are seven *Daily Life* chapters, one at the end of each Part. These are not merely figments of our imagination. They are accurate reconstructions of the lives of certain representative characters. Rekhmire, for example, really lived; the riot at the Olympic Games of 420 B.C. actually happened; the people whom you meet at Charlemagne's court are drawn from documents of the time. Secondly, we have concluded each Part with a section of *Source Readings*. In these thirty selections some of the most notable figures of the past are allowed to speak for themselves. You will hear Socrates defending himself at his trial, Cicero weaving a tight net of evidence around a provincial governor, the Emperor Trajan giving advice regarding the prosecution of Christians, Pope Urban preaching the Crusade to a milling throng of enthusiasts. History, you will find, can be very exciting when you discover that it teems with real people.

You will need no urging to linger over the photographs and drawings. We also hope that the many diagrams, charts, and maps—all specially designed for the young student—will prove helpful.

Nevertheless, no textbook, however well written or lavishly produced, can take the place of vigorous and informed teaching. Many of us trace our earliest interest in history back to some dedicated teacher who had that rare faculty of making printed words come to life. We hope that this book, in the hands of your teacher, will provide you with a living pageant of the past.

Hamilton, Ontario
May, 1965

D.C.T.
J.H.T.

CONTENTS

Preface v

Maps viii

MAPS

THE ORIGINS OF CIVILIZATION

PART I

THE ORIGINS OF CIVILIZATION

CHAPTER 1

In the Beginning

In the beginning . . . the earth was without form and void . . . GENESIS 1: 1, 2

Ours is the age of the exploration of space. Soon, very soon, man will be setting foot on new planets. Indeed, it is quite possible some of you reading this book may one day land on the moon. If you do—and live to tell the tale—what stories of strange and ghostly landscapes will you bring back to earth?

Now studying history is something like riding in a rocket. Only instead of penetrating space, you are exploring time. Supposing we could actually board a rocket ship that would travel *backward* in time, back, back some five billion years to the very beginnings of the earth. If we could circle around this strange planet of ours, what would we find?

❖ *Strange Life on a Strange Planet*　In those very first days we could not land our ship on earth, for in the beginning we would find that we had discovered only an eerie ball of vapour, a sort of globe of gas. These gases cooled very, very slowly, and as they did they condensed and congealed to form a rocky outer crust which became the earth's surface. Even then the earth was still too hot for water vapour to condense or clouds to form. This took hundreds of thousands of years more. Eventually, however, as the cooling continued, great banks of clouds built up, completely shrouding the earth. Rain fell, slowly at first, then in torrents until our planet's surface eventually cooled enough for the cycle of evaporation and condensation to slow up. Next the world was to be affected by its tremendous neighbour of fire, as the sun's rays began to warm its surface and produce local climates. Yet still earth was uninhabited, a lifeless planet spinning endlessly around the sun.

One day in 1879 a Spanish nobleman was exploring a cave near the village of Santillana del Mar when something caught the eye of his five-year-old daughter. "Papa, look!" she shouted excitedly. "Painted bulls!" The "bulls" were bisons, twenty of them (each approximately 5 feet long), painted on the ceiling of the cave of Altamira by Old Stone Age artists about 13,000 B.C. A pastel copy of one of them is reproduced here in all its amazing realism and grace.

The three dinosaurs portrayed here have probably come upon each other by accident. Ordinarily, *Brontosaurus* spends his time partially submerged so that the water will buoy up his immense bulk of 40 tons. His few peg teeth mark him out as a vegetarian. Three-horned *Triceratops* has just become dimly aware that he is not alone, while across the lagoon the toughly plated *Stegosaurus,* 30 feet long and weighing 10 tons, wants nothing more than to be left in peace to forage in the reeds by the water's edge.

At last it would begin to seem possible for our imaginary rocket ship to land on this solid mass. But it would be a landing full of hazards. For from time to time the crust of the earth was greatly disturbed. Volcanoes belched forth fire and lava, mighty earthquakes spit up mountains and forced open ravines, and great rivers of ice ground like tremendous bulldozers across the landscape, scouring the earth as they moved. Then, finally, after hundreds of millions more years had passed, a miracle

occurred: that mysterious thing called life, both plant and animal, sprang
up on earth.

One of these forms of life is familiar to all of you—the dinosaurs.
The earliest of these strange reptiles (the word *dinosaur* means terrible
lizard) would not completely terrify the well-armed explorer of time, for
the smallest were the size of a rooster, and the largest ranged from only
ten to fifteen feet in length. But if our ship landed later, some 170 million

Early life on earth

years before the 20th century, we would encounter a blood-chilling spectacle—dinosaurs that had developed into monsters 85 feet long and weighing over 40 tons, snapping off full-grown trees like matchsticks as they crashed about through the swamps in search of delicacies for their vegetarian diet.

Much of our fear, however, would be unwarranted. For, contrary to all the cartoons and movies, few of these immense creatures were ferocious. In fact most were as timid as sheep, and—again contrary to comic books—were certainly no threat to man because as yet there simply were no men in existence. Moreover dinosaurs, in their infinite variety of large and small, docile and fierce, vegetarian and carnivorous, had one thing in common: they were all stupid. Equipped with a brain less complex than that of a kitten, they were doomed to extinction.

As the earth's strange cycle of change once more lifted up mountains and made deserts out of the rich swamps where dinosaurs had happily lazed, these early cousins of the crocodile were deprived of the tremendous food supply they needed to sustain their enormous bulk. Poor, dull creatures that they were, they were unable with their pea-sized brain to figure out a way to adapt. And so they died off, their heavy skeletons sinking slowly into the ground until one day, over 70 million years later, scientists would laboriously excavate their bones and painstakingly piece them together to reconstruct not only their bodily shape but the story of their strange life on a strange planet.

❖ *A Day Is a Thousand Years* It is very difficult to grasp the immensity of the stretches of time which we have been discussing. Perhaps it will help you if we think of time in the way that one of our Canadian scientists has. He fits thousands of years into a week, beginning on Sunday, January 1st.

Let us imagine that our human time scale can be compressed so that one day represents 1,000 years. Thus our scientific history is written over a period of one week beginning on Sunday morning, representing 5000 B.C. Throughout all day Sunday, Monday and part of Tuesday no progress at all is evident. . . . By late Tuesday evening some stone and timber buildings are evident and the Pyramids have been built using human power. Bronze tools are being used on Wednesday and oxen are pulling wheeled carts. Iron tools, hardened by tempering, are ready Thursday. Some canals and reservoirs have been constructed and by nightfall an alphabet has been invented to simplify communication.

Friday morning geometry has been exploited to make accurate land surveys. The screw and pulley have been invented and the Romans are building aqueducts and highways. . . . On this same Friday the stone arch construction is becoming evident in large bridges, palaces and cathedrals. . . .

Saturday the acceleration is apparent. Algebra and trigonometry are available as scientific tools. Magnetism has been discovered; alchemy is flourishing and cast iron is being produced in quantity; sizeable boats are being built and the invention of the magnetic compass is of great importance to their navigation. But it is only on Sunday that things really start to happen. Just before midnight Saturday, an Italian sea captain had his western trip to Asia interrupted by America and by 3 a.m. mass migration was under way. The steam engine was invented at 7 a.m. and immediately applied to land and sea transport. The Bessemer converter announced at 9 a.m. made large quantities of steel available, followed quickly by Portland cement, rubber, and petroleum. Cheap aluminum was available by 9:30, man flew in an aeroplane before 10, Lindbergh landed in Paris at 10:25, supersonic flights were common by 11 and the first artificial satellites were in the sky before lunch.[1]

This book covers an even longer scale of time than that of our imaginary week. In fact, using the same scale of one day equalling a thousand years, the story of man begins a full year and a third earlier than the week of time that began in 5000 B.C. In other words, man has lived on earth for at least 500,000 years.

The chart on page 8 simplifies man's history even more by showing what has happened by "months." Notice how much has occurred since 50,000 B.C. Now we have to think of time in terms of days. Between January 2nd and 3rd you will notice that the word "Civilization" appears. But what does it mean to be civilized? What can historians tell us of the hundreds of thousands of years before man painfully evolved from a savage into a civilized human being?

❖ *Civilization* Though all of you think of yourselves as being civilized, how many of you know the original meaning of the word? It is derived from the Latin *civilis* meaning "relating to a citizen"; and the word "citizen" meant a member of an ancient city-state. To be civilized, then, is to have lived in a town or city. For this reason we date the civilization of man from the establishment of his first cities, about 3500 B.C.

---

[1]J. W. Hodgins, "Modern Engineering at McMaster," *McMaster Alumni News,* Vol. 28, No. 1 (March, 1958), p. 8.

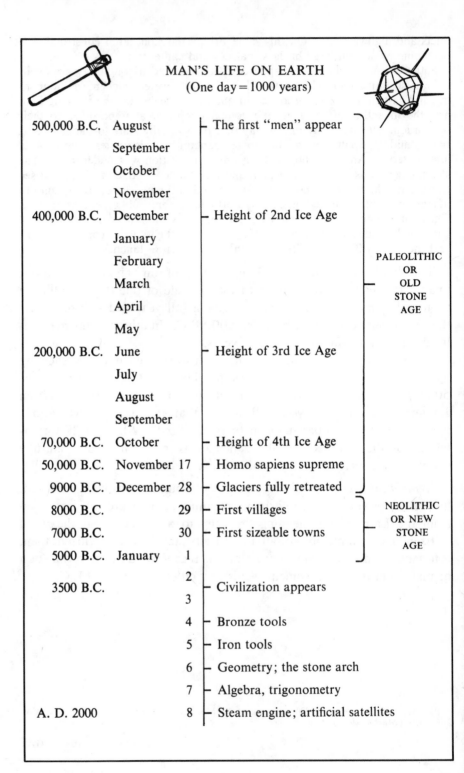

MAN'S LIFE ON EARTH
(One day = 1000 years)

500,000 B.C.	August	— The first "men" appear	
	September		
	October		
	November		
400,000 B.C.	December	— Height of 2nd Ice Age	
	January		PALEOLITHIC
	February		OR
	March		OLD STONE
	April		AGE
	May		
200,000 B.C.	June	— Height of 3rd Ice Age	
	July		
	August		
	September		
70,000 B.C.	October	— Height of 4th Ice Age	
50,000 B.C.	November 17	— Homo sapiens supreme	
9000 B.C.	December 28	— Glaciers fully retreated	
8000 B.C.	29	— First villages	NEOLITHIC OR NEW
7000 B.C.	30	— First sizeable towns	STONE AGE
5000 B.C.	January 1		
3500 B.C.	2 3	— Civilization appears	
	4	— Bronze tools	
	5	— Iron tools	
	6	— Geometry; the stone arch	
	7	— Algebra, trigonometry	
A. D. 2000	8	— Steam engine; artificial satellites	

CHAPTER 2

Man the Hunter

. . . no letters, no society, and, which is worst of all, continual fear and danger of violent death, and the life of man solitary, poor, nasty, brutish, and short.

THOMAS HOBBES, *Leviathan*

About 700,000 years ago[2] there was a radical change in our climate which transformed part of our globe into a world of ice. Cold air flowed southward from the north pole and glaciers descended to cover all of Europe down to the British Isles, while in North America Canada was completely covered by the ice cap. Then milder weather came again. In fact four times the ice moved south, and four times the climate warmed and the ice retreated. Today we are living in the fourth inter-glacial period which followed the retreat of the ice between 18,000 and 9000 B.C.

❖ *Master of the Earth* Up until quite recently, our oldest ancestor was presumed to be an ape-like man who once inhabited South Africa. Then discoveries were made that may eventually have the effect of drastically altering our picture of man's ancestry. For in April, 1964 a British anthropologist announced that he had discovered, in the Olduvai Gorge of Tanganyika, Africa, bone fragments of what he claims is a more advanced type of "man" than the South African ape-man. This "man" was 3½ - 4½ feet tall, walked upright, and had a small skull shaped much like modern man's. He probably had enough intelligence

---

[2]We cannot be definite about any date before 2000 B.C., since such early chronology is constantly being revised. Scholars are even in disagreement concerning some dates in Greek, Roman, and medieval history.

Recently scientists have come to the aid of historians in their attempt to fix the earliest chronology. They have found that all living matter, be it plant or animal, absorbs radioactive carbon (C^{14}). When this living matter dies it gives up its C^{14} at the fixed rate of 15.3 atoms per minute per gram of carbon. Hence by measuring the amount of C^{14} remaining in any sample, the number of years since the living matter died can be calculated within a margin of error of 200 or 300 years either way. This radio-carbon method of dating has a range of about 50,000 years. Scientists can also estimate geological dates much farther back by measuring the rate of decay of potassium in volcanic rocks.

In this book the dates quoted for rulers are those of their reigns. For others, life dates are given.

PREHISTORIC MEN

1. South African Ape-Man — skull of a child and remains of six adults, discovered from 1924 on. Adult weighed about 80 pounds and stood 4 feet tall; brain a little larger than ape's.

2. Java Man — skullcap, jawbone, and thighbone first discovered in Java in 1890. Larger than S. African Ape-Man and having a larger brain, though only half as large as modern man's.

3. Peking Man — remains discovered in a cave near Peking, China, from 1927 on. About the same size as Java Man but with legs more bowed.

4. Rhodesian Man — skull, shinbone, thighbone, etc., discovered at Broken Hill, Rhodesia, in 1921; heavy-boned adult standing 5 feet 10 inches and weighing about 160 pounds; brain about as large as modern man's. Another specimen found in Cape Province in 1953.

5. Neanderthal Man — first specimen found in Neander valley in Germany in 1856, and many others in various locations since. Stocky adults about 5 feet 4 inches tall with heavy bones, and a brain slightly larger, though less developed, than modern man's.

6. *Homo sapiens* ("Thinking Man") — part of a jaw discovered in Kenya Colony in 1932; other discoveries since near London, England, in 1935-36 and 1955, and at Fontéchevade, France, in 1947. A large brain set behind a high forehead, and a chin like modern man's.

Here is a "man" surrounded with mystery —*Zinjanthropus*. Was he a man? Or was he merely an ape-man? Did he make tools? Or was he killed by the tools someone else had made? Behind this shallow forehead was a brain little more than half the size of modern man's. Who was this creature, who lived some 1,750,000 years ago on the shore of a long-vanished lake?

to kill his stupid cousin, *Zinjanthropus,* whose skull Dr. Leakey had discovered five years earlier in an exciting archaeological find. Most startling of all the evidence concerning this Olduvai "man" is the possibility that he may be over three times as old as earliest man was previously believed to be! If this is the case, the time line on page 8 would have to start *four years* or more before the week beginning in 5000 B.C.

Much controversy still, however, surrounds the date of Olduvai man. The oldest men about whom there is certainty appeared in South Africa about 500,000 B.C. in the first interglacial period, and their descendants somehow survived the fluctuations of climate through hundreds of thousands of years. Yet fossil remains discovered in Java prove that at approximately the same time as the "ape-man" roamed South Africa, a more man-like creature was also managing an existence somewhere in the East Indies.

Java man

The scientific name of this Java man is *Pithecanthropus erectus,* "the ape-man who walks upright." He was like an ape in his shambling gait, his low sloping forehead, his prominently ridged brows, and his lack of chin. But Java man had a combination of special features which he shared to some extent with apes and monkeys. The difference was that he alone possessed all five in a fully developed form: erect posture, free-moving arms and hands, sharp-focusing eyes, a brain capable of judgment and perception, and the power of speech. With these five, man became master of the earth.

The bones of a number of the earliest men (usually parts of the skull) have been discovered, and from them reconstructions have been made to give us a rough idea of what Old Stone Age (or *Paleolithic*) men looked like. You can read brief descriptions of these men in the preceding table, which lists them in the order of their probable disappearance.

We would be mistaken if we thought that all of our first ancestors were hairy specimens like those shown in cartoons, who haul women around by the hair and wield immense clubs. In 1935-36 and 1955 three fragments of a skull were recovered from a gravel quarry a few miles down the Thames from London. The amazing thing about these bones is that although they are a quarter of a million years old, experts tell us they might in every way fit a modern head. Some modern type of man, then, lived in Britain at least a quarter of a million years ago! We call him *Homo sapiens* ("thinking man").

By 50,000 B.C. all the other human species had died out and *Homo sapiens* alone survived. Why had he survived when the others became extinct? Not because of superior physical strength. From the neck down he was little different either from other fossil men or modern man. But from the neck up both *Homo sapiens* and present-day man proved to be greatly different from the others: both had a high forehead encasing a large brain, and both had a lower jaw with a chin. It was probably this larger and more fully developed brain that preserved *Homo sapiens* for his role of the first modern man.

❖ *Thousands of Generations* We do not have to depend only on bits of skeletons to piece together what prehistoric men were like. Fortunately we have also been able to recover millions of their tools. These implements have been discovered in the trash piled up from generation to generation on the floors of caves, some of which had collected as much as fifty feet of debris to record the passing of thousands of generations of human occupants.

You may think of prehistoric man as a frightened creature who spent his days in the dark depths of the earth at the back of some gloomy cave. But this is not true. Instead he lived just within the cave mouth or on some adjoining terrace. He might even prefer the shelter of an overhanging cliff, much as the overnight camper does in the Canadian woods. Old Stone Age man stalked game and dragged it back to his home, littering the floor with the bones of the hunt. And what a variety of animals he managed to kill! — woolly mammoth, bison, reindeer, rhinoceros, antelope, wild horse, and cave bear.

Early man, of course, ate his meat raw. Until he could devise some better way to hunt and to prepare his food, then, he would not be able to accomplish anything that might be called progress. He would have no time to think of organizing families into a larger society, or of making laws, or even of working out some system of writing. To find and eat raw food would take up most of each day.

❖ *A Wonderful Discovery* In the early and middle Old Stone Age man fashioned some hand-axes or used broken bones to kill and dismember beasts. But towards the end of the Old Stone Age he gradually learned how to improve on his earliest tools. Weapons became many and varied. Man began to flake off flints to produce scrapers and crude knives, and eventually he evolved an elementary chisel with which to rough out other tools of bone, antler, or ivory.

At this stage man acquired a force more powerful and more terrible *Fire* than all his tools put together — fire. Probably Old Stone Age men "discovered" fire when they came upon an erupting volcano or a roaring forest fire. There is no evidence, at any rate, that the earliest men who had fire knew how to make it themselves: if it died out in one camp it would have to be obtained from another. It must certainly have made man's life much more bearable, for it kept him warm. And it did even more. It allowed him to cook his food so that bones could readily be broken and the marrow sucked out, while the fibres in both meat and roots could be broken down. Consequently the time taken up by eating could be reduced from most of the day to about two hours.

❖ *More than Survival* Even though early man depended for his life upon weapons and tools, there were apparently some who were beginning to think of life as more than mere survival. For in the caves of northern Spain and southern France archaeologists have discovered lifelike sculptures of bone and ivory, including the representation of the head of a woman who is wearing what is either an elaborate hairdo or some kind of head-dress.

Even more amazing is the fact that on the walls of the caves them- *Stone Age* selves, engravings and paintings of mammoths and reindeer may be *art* seen in all their wonderful profusion. Nor were the Old Stone Age artists who made these outlines by the light of small stone lamps any crude craftsmen. Whether it was a herd of passing reindeer, a stag pausing to drink, or a horse galloping by, the realism of these artists was strikingly successful. For a long time modern scholars thought that the paintings of the woolly mammoth were inaccurate — until an extinct mammoth found still frozen in Siberia proved the scholars wrong and the Stone Age artists right (see pages 36-39).

Over 15,000 years ago skilled Old Stone Age artists created marvellous pictures in the caves of western Europe. Working by the light of fat-oil lamps, the man at the extreme left is blowing powdered colour through a bone tube, while his companion draws with a "crayon" moulded of raw pigments. At the right, others grind the pigments in stone containers. The hunter in the foreground holds a primitive spear with a flint head, probably the type of weapon used to kill the bison being pictured on the wall.

The most impressive work of Stone Age artists is the series of multi-coloured murals to be found in such caves as those at Font-de-Gaume or Lascaux in France, or Altamira in Spain. The paintings were first etched on the limestone walls; then a strong outline of black was applied, followed perhaps by another of red; and finally rich browns deftly represented the hairy portions of the bison. The pigments were so perfect that today in the darkness of Altamira the colours are still brilliant—perhaps nearly as brilliant as when they were applied.

We can hardly believe that the average rude hunter would be capable of such fine work. Perhaps some few trained artists stayed home from the hunt while their neighbours roamed abroad in a pack to pursue big game. These artists would make their drawings as lifelike as they could, because they probably believed that they were thus somehow guarantee-

ing the success of the hunt. The more accurately the animal was portrayed, the more chance there was of its being killed. How did the artist achieve such realism? Perhaps he used dead models, or merely drew from keen observation; perhaps he took rough sketches with him back into the depths of the caves. We shall never know.

❖ *Dim Gropings* Man is different from all other animals in that, even from his earliest days, he has always puzzled over the strangeness of death. We can guess that he yearned over those gone and hoped to help the dead person on his way to some mysterious new world by the pathetic attempts he made to provide the corpse with what it might need in an after life.

Usually burials took place right in the home, beneath the cave floor and often near the hearth. The dead hunter, dressed in his finery and smeared with red ochre (perhaps in the hope of restoring blood to the pale corpse), was interred along with food and weapons. Thus primitive man did have the hope (or fear) of a life beyond death. Indeed, it is not too much to say that in his own childlike way Old Stone Age man was dimly groping towards a "religion."

There was another way in which man set himself above the animals: man alone developed the power of speech. Though the first men could not write they must have been able to speak, to exchange ideas through a language. Hunters must have told each other how to trap mammoths, artists must have compared sketches, and the survivors in a family must somehow have communicated with one another about their ceremonies for the dead. No one knows, of course, what kind of languages were used, or exactly how they developed. But a number of ingenious theories have been put forward to account for man's earliest speech.

HOW SPEECH MAY HAVE ORIGINATED[a]

1. The *bow-wow* theory —imitation of sounds, such as the barking of dogs.

2. The *oh-oh* theory —instinctive expressions caused by pain or other intense feelings.

3. The *dingdong* theory —harmony between sound and sense; for every inner feeling there is an outward expression.

4. The *yo-he-ho* theory —relief gained by letting out one's breath, and so making sounds, following heavy muscular exercise.

5. The *gestural* theory —imitation with the tongue of gestures already made with the body.

6. The *tarara-boom-de-ay* theory —humming or singing as the first and easiest way to give vent to one's feelings.

❖ *The Ice Retreats* About 20,000 years ago the last major climatic change came to the earth when the sun finally began to melt away the glaciers, causing them to retire slowly northwards for a fourth time. As the ice melted the sea levels rose. There was a retreat of tundra and a spreading of forest, and while the reindeer followed the tundra north, other mammals became extinct. Now bands of hunters equipped with bows and arrows and helped by dogs (all this we know from cave drawings) went forth from the scattered human settlements, sometimes hunting small animals and birds with tiny flints.

[a]Adapted from A. Montagu, *Man: His First Million Years* (Signet Books: The New American Library, revised edition, 1962), p. 103.

At the same time the vivid naturalistic drawings of animals disappeared and were replaced by geometrical designs. Why? Perhaps the artists lost faith in their power to help the hunter, and turned to abstract drawings when their lifelike pictures were no longer able to place a spell over the great beasts. For these animals had now migrated or become extinct.

Nevertheless man still depended on the hunt to provide him with his meals. He gathered his food wherever he was lucky enough to find it, and it did not apparently occur to him that he could grow it himself. But nature was to change all that. Beginning about 9000 B.C. there was a permanent change in the climate of southern Europe, brought on by the retreat of the ice. Huge areas of southern Europe and north Africa were left without rain, and simply dried up. Naturally the animal and human population that managed to survive now sought out the remaining rivers and oases. It was a process destined to convert man from a hunter to a farmer, a development which wrought such a change in the life of man that historians have not hesitated to label it a "revolution."

CHAPTER 3

Man the Farmer

When tillage begins, other arts follow. The farmers therefore are the founders of human civilization.

DANIEL WEBSTER, *Remarks on Agriculture*

At the beginning of the *Neolithic* or New Stone Age (8000-4500 B.C.), man was beginning to realize that he need not always bow to nature. Instead, he could make nature work for him. He began to observe how animals gathered at the water-hole and determined to corral them, and he cut the wild grasses about him and even attempted to cultivate some of them. Man was becoming a farmer; and when he began to develop his own sources of food instead of depending on luck to provide them, the population could increase more rapidly.

❖ *The Food-Producing Revolution* Where would you expect the first farming to grow up? In a region, you would say, blessed with both a

Man tills⟶More food⟶More people⟶Civilization spreads
the soil

warm climate and rich vegetation. Hence it follows that evidence for the first farms has been found in the oases or grassy uplands of Palestine, Syria, and western Iran and Iraq—the arc known as the Fertile Crescent. Polished tools used to reap grass have been discovered where perhaps huts were once built at an oasis. In time the old huts collapsed and new ones were built on top of them, so that a mound or *tell* was formed. Such tells are common in Israel and Iran, and by measuring the depths of the debris in them the age of an ancient settlement may now be estimated. Especially interesting are the tells discovered in the Fayum, a great depression in the Egyptian desert west of the Nile, where New Stone Age farmers were so advanced that they stored their crops in silos and used numerous pottery and stone vessels.

The first villages   The tells not only supply us with information about the first farmers. They also provide conclusive evidence that villages of 200 or 300 people existed, and that they carried on some sort of trade or barter; for shells have been found that could only have come from the Mediterranean or Red Seas. Further evidence of settled habits has been provided by the burial grounds. Here the villagers buried their dead individually or in groups, the bodies decked out with shell jewellery, stone ornaments, figurines, even linen grave clothing. Yet despite the occasional appearance of such an advanced craft as weaving, pottery was crude—usually simple open bowls made, of course, without the potter's wheel.

Jarmo and Jericho   In recent years two sites in particular have yielded rich information concerning man's earliest achievements in a settled mode of life: Jarmo in northern Iraq, and Jericho in Jordan. Jarmo is one of the earliest agricultural settlements known, and is interesting because here has been excavated the oldest definite evidence of the cultivation of wheat and barley, and of the domestication of animals. Perhaps even before 6500 B.C. the 150 or so citizens of Jarmo were keeping herds of sheeps and goats, reaping grain, and supplementing their diet by hunting. Jericho, however, dates back still further, for here a thriving town existed as early

This is the earliest individual ever to have his features faithfully preserved, someone who lived in Jericho 8000 years ago. The skull was solidly packed with clay. Then a layer of coloured plaster was moulded to the face and shells placed in the eye-sockets. This head was only one of seven found under the floor of an excavated house. But why had they been separated from their bodies? Did their enemies decapitate them? It seems unlikely. So skilfully is the plaster moulded into features, so lovingly and delicately has the dead one's face been formed that we think these early citizens wished to venerate their ancestors, and to somehow preserve some special power—perhaps their wisdom—for a life to come, or even for succeeding generations.

as 7000 B.C. Surrounded by fertile fields, Jericho's clay-brick houses covered some eight acres—which means that there were probably two or three thousand people living within the massive walls of this "oldest known town in the world." The houses were well built, too, even boasting plastered floors and walls. Strangely enough, however, these first town-dwellers did not have pottery at all. Instead they used dishes and bowls made of polished stone.

For various reasons the development of New Stone Age culture in Europe did not proceed at the same pace as that in the Middle East. In the Middle East it ended about 4500 B.C., but in Europe at a much later date. It is startling to realize that while New Stone Age farmers in Europe and Britain were slashing the forests and learning to keep cattle and pigs, haughty citizens stalked the streets of great Middle Eastern cities such as Memphis and Ur.

❖ *The Urban Revolution* The first villages and towns grew up, as we have seen, where man farmed in the arc that curved from Israel and Jordan, across Syria and the foothill zone of Turkey and northern Iraq, to Iran and the shores of the Caspian Sea. As we have also noted, it was no coincidence that farming first occurred there. These territories contained oases (as at Jericho) or grassy uplands (as at Jarmo), and for this

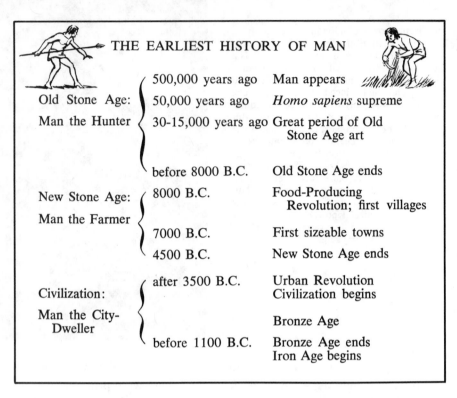

THE EARLIEST HISTORY OF MAN

Old Stone Age: Man the Hunter	500,000 years ago	Man appears
	50,000 years ago	*Homo sapiens* supreme
	30-15,000 years ago	Great period of Old Stone Age art
	before 8000 B.C.	Old Stone Age ends
New Stone Age: Man the Farmer	8000 B.C.	Food-Producing Revolution; first villages
	7000 B.C.	First sizeable towns
	4500 B.C.	New Stone Age ends
Civilization: Man the City-Dweller	after 3500 B.C.	Urban Revolution Civilization begins
		Bronze Age
	before 1100 B.C.	Bronze Age ends Iron Age begins

reason were more favourable to early food production than the great river valleys farther south where the climate was drier.

Despite Jericho's early date, it seems probable that the grassy uplands were more likely places for agriculture to begin than the areas around isolated oases. There were several reasons for this. The uplands had enough winter and spring rainfall to support wild grains, which in turn encouraged wild goats and sheep to pasture there. Some of these animals became domesticated—partly out of the human desire for pets, a desire easily satisfied where they roamed plentifully. Finally, the foothill zones also held metal ores, and any sizeable community must have metals. What more natural location, then, for man's first farms than the grassy uplands?

The growth of population As time went on, overpopulation spilled the farmers out of the hills and onto the plains. Peasant villages multiplied until, some time before 4000 B.C., the men of the plains began to move into the swamps at the head of the Persian Gulf or along the fringes of the Nile Delta. On little islands of dry land they pursued agriculture, using their domesticated plants and animals. The population still grew, and once more new land was required, land gained either by draining sections of the swamps or by moving farther upriver.

These earliest of pioneers discovered that the land upriver was extraordinarily fertile—but there was one major drawback. There was not enough rain. More water must be obtained somehow.

The answer was, of course, some form of irrigation. But irrigation was a collective enterprise. It would require organization, some central directing authority to mobilize the manpower for digging ditches or building canals and dikes. Only in this way could settled communities produce enough surplus food to allow some of their members to devote all their time to being craftsmen, miners, or merchants, or even to directing the work of the whole community as rulers, priests, or administrators. With the appearance of these full-time specialists would come the birth of cities. And this is just what happened. By about 3500 B.C. an *urban revolution* had occurred, that, is, mature cities had developed.

In one of the earliest of these cities, Uruk (modern Warka) on the Euphrates River, great temples were built, protected behind a wall 5½ miles long bristling with over 900 towers. But from ancient Kish, north of Uruk, comes an even more fundamental feature of city life: the earliest known example of writing, dated at 3500 B.C.

It took a thousand years—more than twice the length of time that *The first* separates us from Columbus—for the Persian Gulf and Nile communities *cities* to develop the full-fledged cities that were the pulse of Mesopotamia ("the land between the rivers") and Egypt. Taken together, the stirring changes of the Food-Producing and Urban Revolutions between 8000 B.C. and 3500 B.C. were more far-reaching than all those in the preceding half million years of man's life on earth.

Man was at last civilized.

CHAPTER 4

The Races of Mankind

There are no racial conditions to civilization. It may appear on any continent and in any colour.

WILL DURANT, *Our Oriental Heritage*

All of you know in what a marvellous variety of shapes and forms man has been created. Not only are no two individuals exactly the same, but there are certain combinations of features that divide the human family into separate groups. We call these divisions *races*.

No one is sure exactly how or when the so-called races of man originated, but of one fact we can be positive. There is no such thing as a pure race. According to certain anthropologists there are in the world today four main races. Although all men share the same basic features, they are marked off from one another by six differing characteristics: colour of skin, texture of hair, shape of skull, nose, and jaw, and stature. Somehow over hundreds of generations distinctive combinations of these characteristics came to mark off the four main races of man:

1. The Negroid
2. The Mongoloid
3. The Australoid
4. The Caucasoid

❖ *A Marvellous Variety* It used to be thought that these races first came from a common stock in one part of the world, and then separated as they migrated across the seas and continents during the past 50,000 years, that is, after the time when their common ancestor, *Homo sapiens,* became supreme. Now, however, fossil evidence proves that *Homo sapiens* is much older than was at first thought. Since he is at least 250,000 years old, the belief is growing that man's separation into distinct races also occurred some hundreds of thousands of years ago. You can see what the four main racial types look like from their pictures on the following page.

Negroids The Negroid race is perhaps the most striking in appearance. Its members have black woolly or kinky hair, and skin ranging in colour

CAUCASOID

WHITE

HOMO

BROWN YELLOW

SAPIENS

BLACK

AUSTRALOID

MONGOLOID

NEGROID

THE FOUR RACES

from dark brown to black. They are long-headed with a broad, flattish nose, small ears, thick lips, and a forward thrust to the jaw. Negroids are usually tall—though their stature can vary tremendously, as witness the pygmies of the Congo who average only 4 feet 6 inches in height. The Negroid race is scattered widely, inhabiting areas from Africa to parts of south-eastern Asia, and on to New Guinea and east across the Pacific to the Fiji Islands.

A complete contrast to the Negroid is the round-headed Mongoloid, *Mongoloids* with his straight, coarse black hair, yellowish skin, and "slanted" eyes (the upper eyelid has a fold which produces this impression). The Mongoloid's nose is moderately spread, he has strongly developed cheek bones, and he is short in stature. His race is to be found today in Tibet, China, and Japan, as well as in the Philippines and in North and South America. We in Canada should be particularly interested in the history of this race, because both our Eskimos and our North American Indians, though probably a mixture of races, are more Mongoloid than anything else.

Australoids   The members of the third major race, the Australoids, are long-headed and usually brown-skinned. They are very short in stature with a broad but prominent nose, short face, receding chin, and low forehead. Australoids are found in the Malay peninsula, and were the native race of Australia before Europeans arrived. These Australian aborigines still inhabit the north-eastern coastal fringe of the continent.

Caucasoids   The majority of Canadians belong to the last group—the Caucasoid or so-called "white" race. Caucasoids have characteristics that may vary greatly. They have every form of head shape; their hair may be wavy, curly, or straight (although never woolly as in Negroids or coarse as in Mongoloids); their skin may be anything from a pale pinkish shade to a light brown; and they range from under 5 feet to well over 6 feet in height. Almost the only fairly consistent traits are a generally narrow nose and thin lips. Early in their history the Caucasoids spread widely over Europe, North Africa, the Middle East, and India, and today are distributed over the entire earth's surface. In Europe, a differentiation has come to be made among a considerable number of Caucasoid "subraces," groups such as the Nordics (tall, long-headed, long-faced, and fairhaired), Mediterraneans (long-headed, slight, and dark), and Alpines (stocky, round-headed, and of medium complexion). Actually, however, these are not races at all in the technical sense, but merely convenient classifications of distinctive groups of Europeans.

❖ *The First Americans*   We must pause here to trace briefly the history of one special group of peoples, that of the first inhabitants of our own continent, North America.

It was not only in the Old World that Old Stone Age man made his appearance. At about the time when Paleolithic artists were decorating the caves of Spain and France, a band of hunters was making its way painfully eastwards across a low-lying plain that stretched from Siberia to Alaska. Today the plain is submerged by the water of the Bering

Strait, but this old land-bridge could still be seen if the sea level were to drop only 180 feet.

Though they could not know it, our band of hunters were to be the first Americans. Gradually more and more of them migrated from Asia, and they spread south and east, fanning out across North America. So widely did they scatter that their flint javelin heads and scrapers have been discovered not only in Alberta and Saskatchewan, but in Wyoming and Massachusetts, in New Mexico, Texas, and Alabama. Indeed, the most recent excavations have shown that there was human habitation in both British Columbia and Nova Scotia as early as 9000 B.C.

Like their contemporaries in the Old World, these first North Americans began as hunters. But as the mammoths and giant bisons on which their livelihood depended were gradually killed off, these hunters, too, learned that they must gather acorns, berries, and roots in order to subsist. The next stage was to cultivate their own food, and by 5000 B.C. a new cereal, corn, had appeared in New Mexico—a very different plant from our own twentieth-century one, as you can see by the illustration. During the next four thousand years it spread northwards into the Mississippi valley and eastwards to the Atlantic seaboard.

Still these Stone Age men pushed southward, until by at least 7000 B.C. they had reached the southernmost tip of South America. But as they moved they changed racially, for they became diluted by migrations of non-Mongoloid peoples, Causasoids, who must also have crossed from Siberia. The mixture of these two races resulted in those graceful brown-skinned people, the North American and South American Indians.

❖ *An Accident of Geography*
Race as such plays an insignificant role in history. This is why we have left this brief discussion of it until the end of our first Part. Just as there is no such thing as a

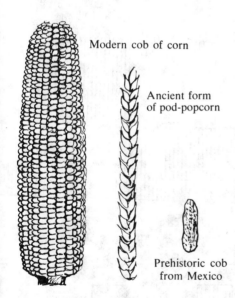

Modern cob of corn

Ancient form of pod-popcorn

Prehistoric cob from Mexico

THE DEVELOPMENT OF CORN
IN NORTH AMERICA

THE DISTRIBUTION OF RACES[4]

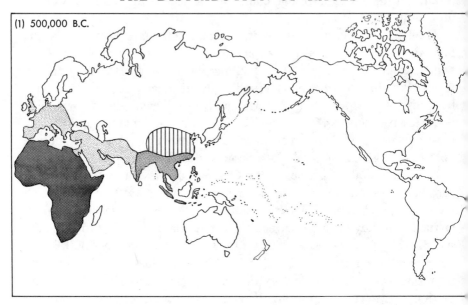

(1) 500,000 B.C.

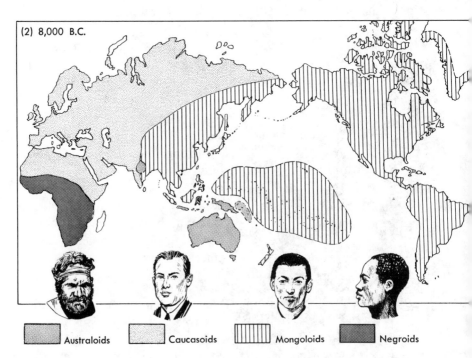

(2) 8,000 B.C.

| | Australoids | | Caucasoids | | Mongoloids | | Negroids |

[4]Adapted from C. S. Coon, *The Origin of Races* (Knopf, 1962), p. 659.

pure race, so also there is no evidence that there is any superior race, and we must be exceedingly careful of our classifications. As various races mixed and migrated they developed new languages and new ways of doing things. Yet languages, nations, and civilizations are in no way related to race. Nor is intelligence. Thus while it may be a useful textbook device to divide the world's population into various races, we should never forget that all racial classifications are to some extent artificial. Much more important than man's racial history is the story of man's rise from the animal level, the story of this distinct creature who very slowly and painfully created what we call civilization.

We should all be aware that it is merely an accident of geography that is largely responsible for the historic advances of the white and yellow races. Man, in his creation of civilization, made over his environment, and the Caucasoids and Mongoloids were especially fortunate in that they—and their descendants—occupied the most favoured geographical areas of the earth. As you can see from the accompanying maps, these regions were centrally located and had challenging climates. In such environments both Caucasoids and Mongoloids adapted and flourished. But any other races that had happened to inhabit these same lands would likely have been just as successful. It was geography, not any inborn excellence or racial superiority, that allowed the white man for so long to dominate the world.

❖ *The Birth of Languages*   There are two other classifications of peoples which will be referred to in this book, and which should be explained here. These are the peoples known as the *Indo-Europeans* and the *Semites*. These designations are, however, completely different from such terms as Mongoloid and Caucasoid in that they are linguistic, not racial, classifications. All Indo-Europeans, and all Semites, spoke languages derived from a common stock, though they might be peoples of entirely different nationalities.

The Indo-Europeans lived in the western Russian plains, and were the first people to train horses and to use the two-wheeled chariot. *Indo-Europeans* Perhaps this accounts for the wide sweep of their travels, for they surged out over the face of Europe and Asia (see the maps on pages 96 and 140) in two great waves—one (2000-1500 B.C.) during the Bronze Age, and another (1200-1000 B.C.) during the Iron Age. As you might expect, in the course of these migrations various groups developed, first individual accents, then completely different dialects, so that eventually the original Indo-European tongue broke down into a number of languages: Celtic, Germanic, Italic (Latin), Greek, Slavic, Persian, and Sanskrit (Indian).

Semites   The Semites, on the other hand, were children of the desert. These nomads moved out from the sands of Arabia into the surrounding fertile regions, and as they went their separate ways their tongue, too, evolved into several languages. As a result the Babylonians, Phoenicians, Hebrews, and Arabs all derived their language from Semitic stock.

We have seen man develop from a hunter to a farmer. We have seen how he was separated into four races, and how he came to speak an infinite variety of tongues. Now it is time to observe him as a city-dweller. Before we do, however, let us sum up human advances thus far by pausing for a day to see how a farmer of the New Stone Age lived and worked. They are advances that have nothing whatever to do with race.

CHAPTER 5

A Day in the Life of a New Stone Age Farmer

. . . something stupendous took place . . . the freeing of man from the limits of the natural supply of food.

WILLIAM HOWELLS, *Back of History*

Somewhere in the Middle East, five thousand years before Christ, the sun rose brightly on a small farming village of about 20 families. Houses of mud brick took on the reddish hue of its beams, and a dog barked noisily in the shadows. This dog is no household pet or barnyard animal. It is a vicious creature, part savage and part tame, who obeys the farmer's commands when he goes out to hunt some game to reinforce his supplies of meat on lean days.

It is not so many years since the farmer was a hunter, and the village did not exist. Indeed, it is only since Neolithic man discovered how to raise primitive crops that he *could* settle down and develop some skills; for the hunter must always be on the move. Nomadic tribes could hardly become civilized when they could not stay in one place long enough to set up substantial households. It is only with domestication that man could temper the tyranny of nature by *making* food grow, instead of going out and looking for it. Our Neolithic farmer has been fortunate enough to be born in a time when his forefathers have discovered the secret of a settled community: that man does not have to serve nature; it can be made to serve him.

Our farmer, who is known in the village as the Tall One, has already arisen and begun to make good use of the precious hours of daylight. For he has a large family to feed. It is not as it used to be when his forefathers were members of a roving band of hunters. Then the sick, the old, the maimed, sometimes even the newborn were ruthlessly abandoned so as not to impede the pace of the food-getters. His forefathers were not cruel; they simply had no choice. Nature is not a gentle master.

But the Tall One has been born in a new age, and so has to support his aging mother as well as his own family of eight. Yet their role, too, has changed. Now the children, instead of being a burden as in the days of his hunting forefathers, can assist with family chores. Even the toddlers help. His four-year-old daughter can do some weeding, and it is the job of his favourite son, the little Lame One, to frighten away birds and trespassing beasts from the crops. All the girls gather berries and nuts and ants' eggs in season, and snails when they can find them, and the younger boys herd the sheep and goats, chasing them into their rude corral at night.

The Tall One has been fortunate in his wife. She is stout and fairly obedient, and a good worker. Of course she has all the modern conveniences—a clay receptacle which serves as a hearth for cooking on, a sunken basin in the floor to rinse things in, and stone urns set in the ground for storing food. So why should she not hew wood and draw water, milk the goats, and grind grain with a rubbing stone? She also tends her vegetable garden of radishes and carrots, and the peas and lentils so important for protein. All told, with her work and her husband's as well as the children's little contributions, the family has an adequate, well balanced diet. Few cavities—and few toothaches—for these children!

There is magic in the Elder Mother's hands, and the Tall One is especially proud of her skill in weaving. She has made them good linen garments, garments much superior to the old-fashioned animal skins, which were so hot and clumsy for summer. The Eldest Daughter is also adept at the loom, and she and her grandmother are often asked for help and advice by the other village women when they gather together to weave and exchange gossip. The Wife-Mother has skilful fingers, too. She weaves baskets and mats for their house, and is learning to fashion pottery. The secret of firing earthenware has not yet been learned, and what she makes is a very elementary kind formed by rings of moist clay laid one on top of the other and let dry. But in another village not far away an important secret has been stumbled on, quite by accident. Someone dropped one of the baskets which was, as usual, plastered with clay to make it watertight, into the fire. It burned, of course. And lo! There lay a vessel as hard as stone, an ideal container both fireproof and waterproof—in short, a pot. Soon the secret would seep out and everyone would be firing their clay pottery. We must remember, however, that "soon" in the days of the New Stone Age Farmer might mean a few hundred years. In the meantime he had his stone bowls and jars (often very fine ones made of prettily coloured rock), and these must suffice.

The Tall One does not know there once was a day, although it is not so many generations past, when farming was considered woman's work. It may have been a woman who first grew some grain—perhaps pulling up weeds around a plant she knew bore food, or chasing birds away from it, or even bringing a few seeds home to the main camp and being amazed to discover that when they spilled and got covered up by soil they grew! If they could be made to grow, then why not *plant* some and have the food right at hand instead of having to go out and hunt for it? Better still, why not store small caches of cereals like wheat and barley in some safe place? And why not stay in a vicinity where you know they will grow well?

Such reasoning was sound; and so these early women set out to collect the seed of certain wild grasses like wheat and barley. When they had harvested these uncultivated grains they used to beat them with a stick so that the ripe, brittle heads would drop their seeds into the reaper's skin containers or baskets. This method meant two things: first of all, many of the seeds would spill and be lost, so that there was considerable wastage of grain. Secondly, in the plants that were not harvested, the brittle heads would split and cast their seeds on the ground, with the result that the plant reproduced itself by itself. When the idea came, then, of trying to plant some of these seeds in an enclosure where they could be watched over and cultivated, it was natural that the seed-gatherer should choose, not the brittlest heads that would drop their fruit easily, but the few wild plants that happened, by some quirk of nature, to have tough spikes that did not become brittle. These plants were ill-suited to reproduce themselves because the seeds did not fall out of the spikes; yet they were well suited to the farmer because they had intact heads which could be harvested by cutting down the whole grass plant in great swaths, fruit, stem, and all.

So you see man *selected* certain odd plants from the wild wheat, plants which did not drop their seeds and hence bred a species of domesticated wheat or barley that lost the ability to disperse its seeds, and hence to reproduce itself. In this way was bred a plant that became totally dependent on man, one whose grain could be harvested still in the spikes with no waste whatsoever, and whose straw, once threshed, was useful both for fodder for the Tall One's ox and stuffing for the Wife-Mother's mattresses. And at the same time as the wheat became dependent on man an ironic thing happened: man became the servant of his plants. Now his life had to revolve around them, around the seasons that produced and fostered them, around the Mother Earth whom he came to revere. Small statuettes of the Mother Goddess came to be fashioned and worshipped, and figurines of cattle and animals came to have magic properties.

Yet at first food-raising did not necessarily result in a settled existence. Probably the men of the family would cut down trees, and the women would go out with their flint hoes and digging-sticks and plant cereals in the rich soil around the stumps. This was much easier than trying to plant in the open plains, where the wild grasses would encroach on the little cultivated plots and choke out the grain. But soil that is repeatedly cropped loses its fertility. Was there any way of keeping it from being impoverished? Somehow they discovered that if the tree trunks were burned and the ashes strewn on the ground, some of the original goodness of the soil returned. Nevertheless this was still only a temporary measure. Eventually the farmer had to move on, to build himself a new hut in a new place and start his "slash and burn" pattern of cultivation all over again. At best he could remain settled no more than a few years.

Once again it was probably quite by chance that the ancestors of the Tall One discovered a secret that was to lead them out of this dilemma, a secret that enriched the soil and ultimately forced the men, and not their women folk, to work in the fields. As the years passed the hunter found his game becoming more and more scarce. It was logical, then, that he should try to conserve certain herds for himself, killing off the most troublesome and ferocious beasts when he had need of food, but

"They . . . could be harvested by cutting down the whole grass plant in great swaths,
fruit, stem, and all."

allowing, and even encouraging, the more docile animals to stay near
his settlement and his supply of water. One way to encourage them, he
found, was to let them graze on the stubble of his crops once they were
harvested. In so doing he accomplished two things: he managed to
domesticate such animals as goats and sheep, and later pigs and cattle,
guiding them to pasture and water and protecting them from fiercer
animals; and he learned that by allowing them to pasture on his fields
he was somehow enriching his soil. He had acquired valuable fertilizer,
so that the soil would bear crops indefinitely. Now he could stay in one

place permanently. Man the farmer had at last turned from a nomadic life and achieved a truly settled existence.

Once man had domesticated animals he no longer had to spend his days hunting them. Moreover, he discovered that an animal need not be dead to be useful to him. Meat, he found, keeps much better on the hoof than in a pantry, and he came to learn that the goat provides milk, the sheep (having been changed by selective breeding from a hairy animal into a woolly one) wool, and the ox power, all these without having to kill the animal to get them.

The last of these discoveries was the most important, and the one that made men take over—probably grudgingly at first—women's work in the fields. By the time our Tall One was born, men had learned to make an ox pull the plough which they (or their women) used to push themselves. Once they had tied a plough to an ox, often simply by attaching a rope to the animal's horns, they had tapped a whole new source of power. The spade, the hoe, and the foot plough could not compete with this new implement, inefficient though it was—sometimes simply a fallen tree trunk, and at best a roughly hewn piece of wood—and hence only suited to light soils. New Stone Age society was revolutionized. The plough stirred up fertile elements in the soil which a hoe did not reach, and with an ox a man could cultivate an area far larger than a woman could by hand. Now the woman gave place to the man, the plot gave way to the field, crops became larger, and population expanded. Men lived in settled villages and went out to their fields. Life for the first time became peaceful as they stopped fighting and started co-operating. After all, now that there was no cut-throat competition for game what reason was there to fight?

That is the way it has come about that it is now the Tall One's job to go out and work his plantings of emmer, einkorn wheat, and barley, while the little Lame One limps along beside the ox applying his goad liberally (and, I am sorry to say, with considerable enthusiasm) on the puny creature's thin ribs to keep it moving slowly along. Two other sons are herding the sheep in the nearby grasslands, and the Eldest One is repairing some tools. One of these tools is a most important one for Neolithic man: a fine ground stone, on the end of which he has polished a sharp cutting edge, hafted into the end of an antler to form a good axe. With this he can shape a timber, something his ancestors could not do with their hunting tools of chipped flint—arrowheads, knives, and scrapers. The youth is also sharpening sickles so that his mother can cut some rushes for baskets, as well as for a larger project which will soon be under way in the village. These sickles have been made of flint blades set in a row in a piece of wood or bone, and the flints must be kept sharp.

There are two plans on foot in the village that are creating great excitement and debate. One concerns the storage of grain. Ever since man learned that his food must last over the winter, that he must have a surplus, he has had to find some good place to put this surplus. It so happened that just after the winter rains ended this year one of the young men from the village was driving his flocks to spring pastures when he met a herdsman from another settlement. This herdsman lost no time in describing, with great pride, a grain storage bin which his fellow villagers had built last fall. They had made the structure more sub- stantial by lining it with straw basketry, and it had proved most satis- factory. Now the Tall One's village council has voted to attempt one too, and for this reason the Wife-Mother, along with all the other women, is already collecting rushes for the matting.

The second project is more controversial. The young men insist that their settlement would be safer if it were surrounded with a wall of stakes, a kind of palisade, and they say the wall should be begun when the spring planting is finished. Meanwhile the old men can grind and polish more stone axes, and the work of felling and stripping trees and sharpening stakes can be begun. But some of the elders protest vehemently. Why, there are fewer wild animals now than when they were boys, they say, and they are less apt to attack. And the men from the neighbouring villages are on the whole friendly, even if some of the nomads are not. So why build a wall? What is this younger generation coming to anyway? "We have lived all our lives without a wall," they argue. "Have we raised sons who are cowards?" "Why waste time on a wall," one gray beard asks plaintively, "when so many mud houses are falling down? Mine needs repairing right now. Who will make the clay bricks for new ones if everybody is busy whittling?" A few old men do not really approve of the silo either. All these new-fangled ideas, they grumble, will only result in a soft-muscled, soft-headed generation.

Nevertheless the Tall One, like most of his fellows, votes for the wall. Life, after all, is still precarious enough. He has his crops to rely on, it is true. He does not, like his hunting forefathers, have to risk his life for his prey, then having gorged himself one day starve the next. But the farmer has many other enemies—ones which he cannot fight back against with spear and bow. The surpluses he can store are never very large. A drought, a hailstorm, a blight may mean famine. Little wonder he worships the Sun, the Thunder, the Earth, and at all costs tries to keep in their favour. For this reason he sacrifices to them, practises magic rituals, and worships their images.

He has great need of some Guardian Spirit, for tragedy is never far away. The day has been hot, and he has worked steadily in the sun, assisted by frequent drinks brought most willingly to him by the freckle-faced Lame One. But how slowly the ox moves! And how quickly the sun runs its course when there is work to do! Lunch was ample: two of the children ran out to the field with some fish and some wild apples. But it is now nearly sunset and he is hungry again. Besides, the day has been full of frustrations. The clumsy plough has balked and needed repair, taking most of the afternoon, and the pigs have managed to get into some of his grain and root it up. He is tired and discouraged. And when he gets home there will be flies swarming over the food, the goat will keep borrowing bits of his supper, and probably the Small One will have broken their best pottery jar. Tomorrow it will be the same, and the next day, and the next. Life is a treadmill, with few events to distinguish one day from another.

He could not know, as he tethers his ox and throws himself wearily down on the ground, that there will be an event today which will be seared into his memory forever. Perhaps, he thinks doggedly, if he stops and eats the bowl of porridge his wife has sent with him he will be able to finish the field before suppertime. But the Lame One, who has already helped himself to some wild apples nearby, prefers to go into the woods to pick his mother a little bouquet for their supper table. For a moment all is peaceful, only the snorting of the ox and the whining of mosquitoes breaking the quiet. Then there is an agonized scream. The Tall One grabs up his axe and runs towards the woods, but it is too late. The wild boar has disappeared back into the bush, and the child lies blood-spattered and white, his beloved flowers still clutched tightly in his fist.

They took him back to the hut and hollowed out the grave that was to be found by archaeologists thousands of years later. Softly they laid him there, his small body in the attitude of sleep, gently flexed and lying on one side. His father painted him with red ochre, which he knew had the magical life-giving properties of blood, and his mother adorned him with her most beautiful stone pendant necklace. His brothers put some of their favourite toy tools beside him so that he could play with them in the next world, and his sisters placed a supply of food near his hand for the long journey that lay ahead of him. Then they covered the slab-lined grave and marked it with a circle of horns of mountain goats, their points stuck into the ground. The creative force of the beast had always been expelled through his horn points; perhaps the Lame One would be a strong, agile animal, running fleet-foot and free in the next world.

But the Tall One, having buried his son, cannot afford to linger in mourning. He has won his first round with Nature: he knows where tomorrow's meal is coming from. He has a settled home, and he lives in a co-operative community. Both plants and animals are his servants. But the world around his clearing is his enemy. Until the circumference of his security widens, he will walk daily with danger, and all too often with death.

SOURCE READINGS

(a)

In 1900 a Siberian tribesman offered to barter a MAMMOTH tusk which he said he had chopped off a "great hairy devil." A group of scientists proceeded to investigate his story, and made the amazing discovery that an extinct mammoth had been preserved for centuries by nature in her own deep freeze. The painstaking excavation is recorded in these extracts from the diary of the expedition's leader.

September 24—It was so warm today that the soil became loose and easily handled, and I was able to begin the work of excavation.

The mammoth lies a third of a mile from our tents and 115 ft. above the present level of the water, on the left bank of the River Beresovka. The body lies in a cliff that faces east and extends in a semicircle for a mile. . . .

According to the Lamut natives of the region, the head of the mammoth was exposed two years ago by the breaking away of a considerable mass of earth. The rest of the body was exposed only in mid-September 1900. . . .

To my great surprise I found well-preserved food fragments between the teeth, which proves that our mammoth, after a short death struggle, died in this very position. The fact that what we found was food, and not substance carried into the mouth recently, was later proved by comparing it with the stomach contents. . . .

I first gave orders carefully to remove the mound of earth about the mammoth, beginning with the soil which had been placed over the head. At a depth of 2 ft. 3 in., we found the left foreleg, still covered with hair on all sides up to the humerus. The epidermis had apparently completely rotted, but on account of the moist earth the hair still clung to the skin. We may perhaps succeed in getting it, frozen, to St. Petersburg.

So far as a preliminary examination can determine, the hair on the upper part of the fore-leg consists of a yellowish brown matted under-coat, 10-12 in. long, with a thick upper bristle-like coat, the hairs of which have ragged ends, are rust-brown, and from 4-5 in. long. The left fore-leg is bent, so that it is evident that the mamoth tried to crawl out of the pit or crevasse into which probably he fell, but he appears to have been so badly injured by the fall that he could not free himself.

Further excavation exposed the right fore-leg, which had become turned almost horizontally under the abdomen by the beast's fall. . . . Upon the left hind-leg I also found portions of decayed flesh, in which the muscular bundles were easily discernible. The stench emitted by this extremity was unbearable. We had to stop work every minute or two. A thorough washing failed to remove the horrible smell from our hands, yet we were obliged to perform part of our task with bare hands.

September 25—The right fore-leg was so placed as to indicate that the mammoth, after falling, had supported himself on this leg while trying to step forward with the left one. We concluded that while in this standing position he became exhausted and died on this very spot, and that he had by no means been washed there by the water from elsewhere. The presence of a thick wool shows that the animal was well adapted to endure cold, and it is improbable that he died from hunger, for a large quantity of fragments of food was in his stomach. . . .

October 4—The shed over the mammoth is nearly finished. As we proposed to build this structure below the upper wall of the skull, we removed the latter. We were then able to take out the remnants of food from between the molars on the left side. These remnants appear masticated and apparently contain not parts of pine or larch needles, but only bits of various grasses.

37

The imprint of the tooth crenations is well preserved upon the half-chewed food. There is also a small quantity of food upon the well-preserved tongue. . . .

October 18—In the afternoon we removed the left shoulder, leaving on it the tendon and muscular fibres.

The flesh from under the shoulder, fibrous and marbled with fat, is dark red and looks as fresh as well-frozen beef or horse-meat. It looked so appetizing that we wondered for some time whether we would not taste it. But no one would venture to take it into his mouth. . . . The dogs ate whatever mammoth meat we threw them.

October 21—The more the hind-quarters are freed the more difficult the work grows. . . . The flesh beneath the pelvis is still frozen as hard as stone, like the flesh about the shoulder-blades. Near the stomach there is a lump of ice which we must remove little by little. . . .

October 24—Snow fell today. Very soon we shall have to get away. . . .

M. Wheeler (ed.), *A Book of Archaeology* (Cassell, 1957), pp. 135-136, 137, 140, 142, 144, 145.

(b)

Compared to the frozen mammoth, the oldest MAN faithfully preserved by nature is relatively modern. This mysterious contemporary of Julius Caesar dates from the early Iron Age, about 2000 years ago, and was discovered in a peat-bog in Denmark in 1950. A Danish professor describes the find.

One of the best preserved and most thoroughly investigated bodies was brought to light in May 1950, in the course of peat-cutting in Tollund Bog in Central Jutland. While lecturing at Aarhus University, I received a telephone call from the police, who informed me of the discovery of a well-preserved corpse and requested me to investigate the matter, as they suspected an unsolved murder. A visit to the finding-place, however, a little elongated peat-bog surrounded by high, steep hills in a desolate heather-clad area, established that the crime, if crime it was, had taken place perhaps 2,000 years ago. It was an amazing sight to see this prehistoric man, his face so well preserved and as expressive as though he had but a moment ago fallen asleep. He lay in a contracted position as though sleeping, with wrinkled brow, closed eyes and mouth fast shut, with all the appearance of a strong personality. Only the dark, brown-leather colour showed his age. But this man of a bygone age had not of his own free will laid himself to sleep on this spot and been covered in the course of centuries by successive layers of peat. A rope formed of two smooth plaited leather thongs lay in a noose round his neck, pulled tight and choking, with the long, free end lying along his back. And he was naked. On his head he bore a skin cap, sewn together from eight pieces of leather with the fur inwards, and fitted with a chin-strap. But the only body clothing was a leather belt knotted in a noose over the stomach. It is obvious that this man, clothed only in cap and belt, had been hanged and then deposited in the bog. But why? It is improbable that a common criminal would have been treated in this way. . . .

In many ways the Tollund man causes prehistory to live before our eyes. His handsome countenance, fantastically well-preserved, makes a stronger and more real impression than the work of the best sculptor could give. The strange circumstances in which he was found give us a glimpse of a remarkable religion. Well may he have been an offering to the gods to bring fertility and fortune to his fellow-men. The old gods did at least not relinquish him to the scientists of today without exacting their price. They took man for man. While the Tollund man was being lifted from his desolate resting-place to be taken for investigation to the National Museum in Copenhagen, one of the helpers dropped dead, struck down by heart failure. . . .

Wheeler, *A Book of Archaeology*, pp. 149-150, 151.

BOOKS TO READ

1. EARLY MAN
    Baity, E., *America Before Man* (Viking)
    Baity, E., *Americans Before Columbus* (Viking)
    Dickinson, A., *The First Book of Stone Age Man* (Edmund Ward)
    Hibben, F. C., *The Lost Americans* (Apollo paperback)
    Howells, W., *Back of History* (Anchor paperback)
    Leechman, D., *Native Tribes of Canada* (Gage)
    Quennell, M. and C. H. B., *Everyday Life in Prehistoric Times* (Batsford)

2. HISTORICAL FICTION (subject matter in square brackets)
    Begouen, M., *Bison of Clay* (Longmans) [Old Stone Age artists]
    Hilliers, A., *The Master Girl* (Putnam) [Stone Age life]
    Perkins, L. F., *The Cave Twins* (Puffin paperback) [Stone Age life]
    Sutcliff, R., *Warrior Scarlet* (Oxford) [Bronze Age village]

CHAPTER 6

The Land Between the Rivers

The scattered people I gathered; with pasturage and water I provided them; I pastured them with abundance, and settled them in peaceful dwellings.

HAMMURABI

Modern Iraq was once called Mesopotamia, a name which means literally "the land between the rivers." Mesopotamia was indeed a country blessed by nature. It lay in the rich flood plain between the Tigris and Euphrates Rivers, at one end of that semi-circle of arable land known as the Fertile Crescent.

But some of Mesopotamia's fertility was bought at a price. It is a land that has always been subject to dry and rainy seasons, and during the Bronze Age a devastating flood, which must have seemed like the end of the world to the people in that valley, overwhelmed the city of Ur, leaving behind various deposits of rich clay from nine to twelve feet deep. It is not surprising, therefore, that Mesopotamian mythology contains a flood epic which reminds us of the story of Noah and his ark.

The various city-states of Mesopotamia based their economy on *Agriculture* agriculture, and farmers raised truly amazing crops of barley, wheat, millet, and at least sixty varieties of vegetables. Because of the seasonal variation in rainfall, the Mesopotamians became adept at irrigation, and by 3000 B.C. there was a general system of dikes and canals in Sumer, the lower section of the Tigris-Euphrates valley.

In this advanced civilization there were various craftsmen, such as *Industry* metal-workers in gold, silver, or copper, and weavers of woollens and linens, who formed themselves into groups which organized industry and regulated the wages of the workmen. The business world was no haphazard affair either; thousands of clay tablets have survived to show us the careful accounts kept by Mesopotamian businessmen.

The subject of the most famous piece of Egyptian sculpture is Nefertiti, sister and wife of the religious reformer Akhenaton. How lifelike she looks! The long slender neck, sensitive mouth, dreamy expression, and delicate colour and modelling of this limestone head illustrate the pharaoh's preference for naturalism, and are remarkably untypical of Egyptian art.

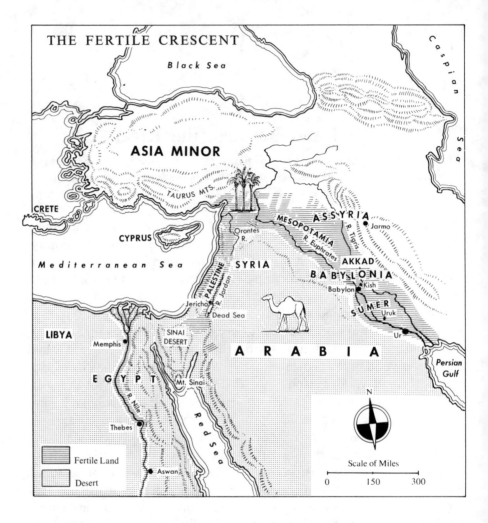

THE FERTILE CRESCENT

❖ *Kings and Invaders*   Little is known about Mesopotamia's first rulers. Ancient lists of kings merely show a series of civil wars between cities in the early part of the third millennium B.C. We do know, however, that about 2350 B.C. Semites from Akkad, the northern section of the great valley, rose under Sargon I to take over Sumer as well. Sargon thereby created the first empire in history. His grandson, Naramsin, extended his conquests and covered the country with temples and palaces.

About 2050 B.C. the Sumerian city of Ur conquered the Akkadians. Ur in its turn fell to other invaders, who were finally expelled by a new line of Semitic kings at the city of Babylon. The sixth and most famous, Hammurabi (1728-1686 B.C.), united the land as far north as Assyria.

Later, however, a succession of weak rulers left Babylonia prey to two Indo-European peoples, the Hittites from the north and the Kassites from the east.

❖ *Unequal Justice* From its earliest times—long before the strong government of Hammurabi—Mesopotamian society revolved around the city.

In any city the temple was the centre of government, and from here education was directed and landed estates were administered. Although much of the city was a squalid collection of adobe dwellings huddled on narrow, winding streets, the temple was a magnificent structure. The one at Ur was 200 feet long, 150 feet wide, and 70 feet high, constructed in the form of an artificial mountain or *ziggurat* with platforms or terraces on which flowers or trees might be growing. Perhaps it was on such a ziggurat that the hanging gardens of Babylon flourished, for it is almost certain such a temple inspired the story of the tower of Babel and of Jacob's ladder.

The well-to-do members of the priestly class were prominent in Mesopotamian society, as were the officers of the army. Both groups possessed hereditary land holdings. The workers on these estates might be slaves or tenant farmers—and in those days it was well to be the master rather than the servant. For although justice was available to every man, it was not, as we can see in the selections from the famous Code of Hammurabi in the Source Reading, equal to all. A legal

Hammurabi ordered his law code cut in this black stone pillar, which stands nearly eight feet high. At the top the sun god extends to the worshipping Hammurabi the rod and ring—symbols of his kingly authority—while below, in parallel columns, are inscribed the laws of the code.

distinction was made between nobles and common people, so that an offence committed against a noble was punished more severely than one against a freeman. On the other hand there was this much justice: if a noble committed a crime he was punished more severely than a middle-class transgressor.

❖ *Plaything of the Gods*   The Mesopotamian religion was primarily concerned with this world. Nature abounded in gods and in demons, and any natural phenomenon might be regarded as an omen. Man was the plaything of the gods. A dread of evil spirits pervaded his life; yet the gods did not protect him. Gods were to be feared, not loved; they asked much and gave little in return.

> A god, known or unknown, has oppressed me.
> A goddess, known or unknown, has brought sorrow upon me.
> I sought for help and none took my hand;
> I wept and none stood at my side;
> I cried aloud and there was none that heard me;
> I am in trouble and in hiding; I dare not look up;
> To my god, my merciful one, I turn myself,
> I utter my prayer.

This poignant cry of the Mesopotamian finds no answer, and the notions of a life after death were equally vague. The after-life was a shadowy existence in which the gods had no place or part. The living buried the dead properly only to ensure themselves against being haunted, not to open the way to hell or heaven.

The Mesopotamians, like the Hebrews later, had great religious epics such as the Epic of Gilgamesh. But this story of a legendary king who ruled for 126 years is hardly a moving moral tale. Gilgamesh was a tyrant and a bully who finally went in search of the mystery of eternal life.

> Gilgamesh, whither rovest thou?
> The life thou pursuest thou shalt not find.
> When the gods created mankind,
> For man they set aside death,
> Life they retained in their own hands.
> O Gilgamesh, fill thy stomach,
> Make merry by day and by night,
> Of each day make a feast of rejoicing,
> Day and night dance thou and play.

We find that Gilgamesh's idea of eternal life is of eternal youth, of an escape from death, and no more than that. Such religious annals served

Sumerian writing began as a series of crude pictures of common objects carved on stone (see tablet on left), which, as time went on, were gradually simplified into a number of lines. When, however, clay tablets came to be used instead of stone, it was found that "writing" could be done quickly and easily by pressing and turning the end of a square reed, which had been cut at an angle, into wet clay. Since the reed produced only short straight marks, all curved lines disappeared, and the resulting script of wedge-shaped characters is known as *cuneiform*.

to explain man's sad plight, how the world came to be what it is, and the manner in which the gods might be placated. Alongside the refined Hebrew versions of some of these stories, the Mesopotamian epics seem woefully shallow and crude.

❖ *The Cradle of Civilization* Mesopotamian architects developed some amazingly advanced principles of engineering. They knew how to build the arch and dome out of brick, and the long lines of their mighty ziggurats were curved to avoid the optical illusion of sag—a principle used later in the Athenian Parthenon of the 5th century B.C. Mesopotamians were also accomplished sculptors, being especially skilled in stone carving, while their metal-workers produced brilliant creations in gold, often inlaid with lapis lazuli.

Since the Mesopotamian civilization was one directed from the centre, from the temple administration, there had to be some efficient method of communication with outlying regions. A system of writing and notation was, therefore, essential. Such a system began with crude picto-

Cuneiform writing

graphs made in the wet clay by a square-tipped reed. But these eventually turned into a form of writing known as *cuneiform*, a series of wedge-shaped characters associated not with the thing pictured but rather with a particular sound.

Mathematics

There was also a fairly complex system of mathematics. It was based on both a decimal and a sexagesimal system, with a basic unit of 60. Division and multiplication could be easily handled, and the Mesopotamians devised the most complete of the early systems of measurement. An elementary form of algebra, too, was developed, although their system of geometry was very crude.

Medicine, astronomy, and geography

The earliest medical, astronomical, and geographical knowledge was, as you might expect, rooted in mythology and religion; hence these subjects were hardly what we would call scientific. Nevertheless the year was divided into 354 days, with 12 months of 29 or 30 days based on the phases of the moon, and an extra month added every three or four years to make the solar and lunar calendars coincide.

Almost 3500 years have passed since the civilization of Mesopotamia died out. Yet the Hittites adopted cuneiform writing, the Middle Eastern diplomatic language was Babylonian, Alexander the Great brought back the arch to Europe, the Hebrews adapted the epics of the Creation and the Flood, and the Mosaic Law borrowed from Hammurabi. Perhaps for these debts, which are considerable, Mesopotamia rightly deserves the title of the "cradle of civilization."

CHAPTER 7

The Gift of the Nile

All the world fears Time, but Time fears the Pyramids.

ARAB PROVERB

The Nile is Egypt's fount of life. Each year between June and October the mighty river rushes north out of the highlands of Ethiopia, surging over its banks in a great flood and leaving behind it water and fertile silt. The green gash of the Nile is Egypt's life-line, a valley some 14 miles wide slicing through the desert sands which stretch away to the east and

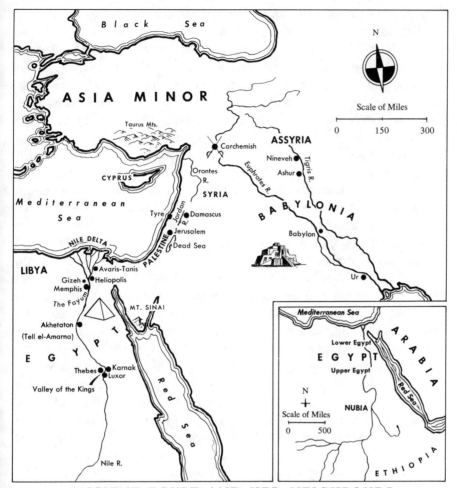

ANCIENT EGYPT AND HER NEIGHBOURS

west. In ancient times Egyptian life revolved about the Nile; in modern times it still does—as may be seen from the construction of the Aswan High Dam.

❖ *A Predictable Ally* One need only examine the language of the Egyptians to discover how profoundly the country was influenced by her environment. "To go north" was the same as "to go downstream"; "to go south" the same as "to go upstream." It was so unusual to be without a boat that a special word was coined to convey this meaning. The hieroglyphic sign for a "foreign country" was the same as that used for "highland" or "desert" because the deserts that fringed the Nile were both mountainous and foreign. Thus the influence of her geography was indelibly marked on both Egyptian life and thought.

The effect of geography on Egypt was, however, quite unlike its effect on Mesopotamia. Mesopotamia was, as we have seen, subject to invasion, and was therefore open to foreign influence. Nor were the consequences of dry and rainy seasons similar in the two countries. For while the Tigris and Euphrates, like the Nile, flooded each year, the time of their rising was not predictable. Consequently they were apt to go on the rampage without warning, drowning the country with such seas of water that they were impossible to control—yet at other times they did not provide sufficient water to prevent droughts. Hence nature seemed to taunt Mesopotamia, with famine following on the heels of both flood and drought.

The Nile Valley Contrast the situation in Egypt. There nature was benevolent, and the Nile was a predictable ally. No torrential rains turned the river into a raging curse. Daily the sun sailed across a cloudless sky, and yearly the benign Nile flood turned dead fields into a living carpet of green. It is not surprising that the Mesopotamians developed a pessimistic outlook on life, while the Egyptians were essentially optimistic.

The long sealed tube of civilization that is Egypt represents probably the first large territory to come under a single ruler in the ancient world. There were two reasons for this. The prosperity of the country depended to such an extent on the annual flooding of the river that the harvesting of crops could not be left to the whims of individual farmers. If famine was to be averted, state control was needed to make sure that water would be hoarded and food harvested, and to provide this state control there had to be a strong administration managing the economy on behalf of the whole country. Secondly, Egypt was fortunate in her early freedom from foreign invasion. For such comparative peace she had the desert to thank; it provided her with an insulation, and gave her relative isolation in which to develop her government.

❖ *The Double Crown* Much uncertainty surrounds Egypt's early history. The first records are inconsiderate enough of historians to name the years not for the rulers, but rather for those events which the particular chronicler considered most noteworthy—"the year of fighting and smiting the northerners," or "the year of the second enumeration of all large and small cattle of the north and south." More sense can be made out of Egypt's chronology once this inconvenient system of reckoning is replaced by a set of tables dividing the rulers of Egypt into 30 dynasties.

CHIEF DIVISIONS OF EGYPTIAN HISTORY

1. 2700-2200 B.C.—The "Old Kingdom" (Dynasties 3-6)
2. 2050-1800 B.C.—The "Middle Kingdom" (Dynasty 12)
3. 1570-1090 B.C.—The "New Kingdom" (Dynasties 18-20)

It was about 3400 B.C. that a race of newcomers began to penetrate Egypt along the eastern edge of the Nile Delta. Over the course of the next two centuries these conquerors set up two monarchies, one symbolized by the red crown of the Delta kingdom and one by the white crown of Upper Egypt. By 3200 these two monarchies had been fused into one, and a single king, the legendary Menes, came to wear the double crown of all Egypt as an absolute monarch and a living god.

Egypt's first two dynasties ruled for five centuries, and it was a time of peace and prosperity. Egyptians traded their stone pottery along the eastern Mediterranean coasts, mined copper in the Sinai peninsula, travelled to Byblos in Syria for timber and to Crete for wine and oil. From Mesopotamia they borrowed brick buildings, artistic decorations, the potter's wheel, and a theory of writing—borrowed and refined them until they far surpassed their Mesopotamian inspiration. By the time of the third dynasty Egypt had passed through adolescence and had entered upon the first of her three great periods of history, the "Old Kingdom."

❖ *Houses for the Soul* From the beginning the Egyptians were obsessed with the necessity of preserving the body after death. The reason for this obsession was a firm belief in man's immortality. The soul did not die. Instead it took the form of a bird, often a falcon, flying freely in the world but able to return to the dead body. How important, then, to preserve the body so that the roaming soul could recognize it.

As most of you know, the Egyptians developed a highly effective system of embalming. We have a description of this process, a rather crude account which has come down to us from a Greek historian: *Embalming*

First of all with a crooked piece of iron they draw out the brains through the nostrils. . . . Then with a sharp Ethiopian stone they make a cut along the flank and extract all the intestines, and after purifying and washing them with palm-wine, wash them once more with pounded spices. Then after filling the belly cavity with pure finely powdered myrrh, cinnamon, and other spices, except frankincense, they sew it up again. After this they put the body in salt, covering it with natron [salt] for seventy days; they must not leave it in the salt any

This cut-away drawing depicts the construction of the first and largest of the pyramids of Gizeh, the Great Pyramid of Khufu. The blocks of limestone were brought by boat from quarries across the Nile (1)—a method of transportation available only when the river was in flood. From the landing area the blocks were pulled on sledges by gangs of men along a stone causeway (2) and were finally hauled up a long brick and earthen ramp (3) which was removed when the pyramid was completed. From the entrance to the pyramid (4) a long corridor leads to the Grand Gallery (5), and thence to the King's Chamber (6). These rooms were even provided with air vents, as can be seen. There is also a Queen's Chamber (7), and an underground chamber (8) with a blind passage at its end. The pyramid originally rose 481 feet (as high as a forty-storey skyscraper); the base covers 12½ acres. The smooth white limestone casing, which was pilfered over the years for building elsewhere, is shown along one side (9), while at the top of the structure (10) workmen are fitting the huge blocks into place.

longer. When the seventy days are over, they wash the body and wrap it around from head to foot with strips cut from a sheet of fine linen, smeared with gum. . . . Then the relatives take it and have a wooden coffin made shaped like a man, and shutting the body up in it they place it in the sepulchral chamber, setting it upright against the wall.

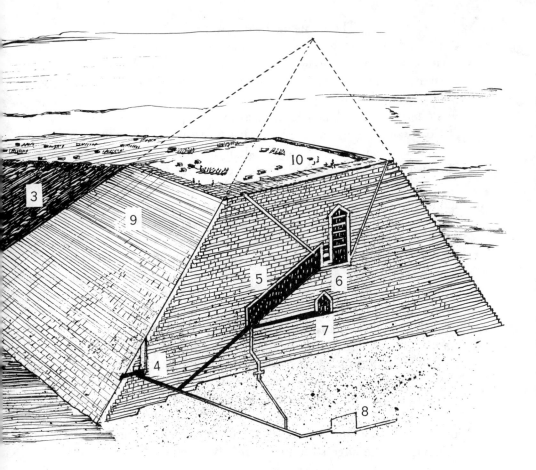

The preserved body, of course, required a home, and so, as you have just read, it was placed in a coffin. Then it was housed, along with the dead man's personal possessions, in a series of underground rooms excavated for that purpose. Finally a plain brickwork structure was erected above ground, gaily painted and adorned to suggest the home or palace of its late owner. As time went on these structures became more and more ornate, until eventually they developed into the immense stone memorials that have become the symbols of Egypt. "In sublime arrogance," writes a modern historian, "the royal pyramids dominated the Old Kingdom and sent their shadows down the ages."

The most famous Egyptian monuments are the Pyramids of Gizeh, *The* the elaborate tombs of three of the pharaohs of the Fourth Dynasty. *Pyramids* The largest of them, the Great Pyramid, comprises six and a quarter million tons of stone, with exterior casing blocks averaging two and a half tons each. These casing blocks were fitted with a joint of only one-fiftieth of an inch, while the whole tremendous mass of the pyramid was set on a rock pavement that had the unbelievably slight deviation from a true plane of .004%! Not only that, but the Great Pyramid was only partly built from local stone. The granite for the inner chamber was quarried more than 700 miles away.

How could these marvellous structures be built without modern machinery?—and when we say modern machinery we include the wheel. How was it possible to move these tremendous blocks of stone without wagons, and to lift them without pulleys or cranes? Apparently the immense blocks were hauled and levered up sloping brick and earth ramps greased with sand and gypsum. When certain Greek tourists came to Egypt to gaze at the Pyramids 2000 years later, they were told that it had taken 100,000 men 30 years to build the Great Pyramid.

A hundred thousand men—a hundred thousand straining, miserable bodies driven mercilessly in order that the last ounce of manpower might be extracted to gratify the vanity of one man. As a pharaoh's reign stretched out he might replan his pyramid, adding chambers and passages until its proportions were even more magnificent than its planner had at the beginning dared envisage. But magnificent monuments though they may be, it must not be forgotten that they are the symbols of ruthless absolutism and an unlimited supply of labour. "The groans of the slaves have been silenced, the Nile wind has swallowed up the whistle of the whiplash and blown away the harsh odour of human sweat. Nothing but the huge structures themselves remain."

❖ *Captive Conquerors* For a time the Fifth Dynasty maintained the vigour and originality of its predecessors; but bit by bit different areas broke away under independent princes, and gradually the central government of the Pyramid Age collapsed. The country was not united again until the reigns of the rulers of the Twelfth Dynasty.

During this "Middle Kingdom" period the capital was moved from Thebes to the Fayum, and the power of Egypt was again shown in such foreign ventures as raids north-east into Palestine and Syria, south into Nubia and west into Libya. In order to counteract the disruptive power of local princes, the middle classes—craftsmen, artists, scribes, government officials—were encouraged and promoted. Art and literature flourished, and for two centuries peace reigned in the land. Then a strange swarm of barbarian invaders inundated the country, and the state collapsed.

These new people who surged into Lower Egypt across the Delta of the Nile are known to history as the "Hyksos," a name which means "rulers of foreign lands." Probably they had been pushed south by the pressure of the Bronze Age Indo-European migrations, and once they had settled themselves in their adopted country they proceeded to take over the Egyptian system of administration, the royal style, and hieroglyphic writing. Thus they may have been the first—they were certainly not the last—people to be taken captive by those they conquered. But they gave as well as they received. They introduced a superior bow into Egypt, along with the horse chariot—a vehicle which the Egyptians were quick to adopt, and which they were to use against its originators. For the Theban princes of the Seventeenth Dynasty drove the Hyksos out of Egypt and themselves embarked on imperalistic conquests.

With the "New Kingdom," Egypt entered upon her golden age.

❖ *The Napoleon of Egypt* Thutmose III (1490-1436 B.C.) came to the throne with blood on his hands: he acquired the crown by murdering his stepmother. The reign thus begun in violence was to continue ruthlessly. Thutmose was determined to create a mighty empire, and to this end he waged seventeen campaigns in Asia, twice crossing the Euphrates. Everywhere his bowmen, axmen, spearmen, and charioteers trampled lesser peoples into the dust, then swept on, leaving governors and garrisons to keep the conquered in subjection. Here is an account of one of Thutmose's victories, won after a seven-month siege.

. . . they came out, pleading to My Majesty and saying: "Give us breath, Our Lord! The lands of Syria will never again rebel against thee!"
Then that enemy and the princes who were with him sent me great tribute, borne by their children: gold and silver, all the horses they possessed, their great chariots of gold and silver and painted, all their coats of mail, their bows and their arrows, all their weapons. With these had they come from afar to give battle to My Majesty, and now they were sending them to me as tribute, while they stood upon their walls, praising My Majesty and begging that they might be granted the breath of life.

Yet Thutmose was more than a mighty imperialist. He was also a painstaking administrator. No sooner was he back from a conquest than he hurried off on tours of inspection up and down the Nile, while the Vizier, as you will be finding out in the *Daily Life,* took charge in his absence. Before his campaigns were over, the boundaries of Egypt stretched to the Taurus Mountains and the Euphrates River. Tribute poured in from both Babylon and Assyria. Egypt ruled the East. To

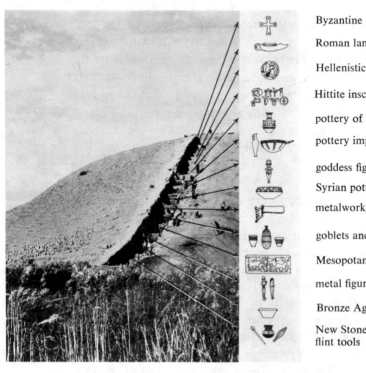

Byzantine bronze crosses

Roman lamps

Hellenistic coins

Hittite inscriptions

pottery of the "Peoples of the Sea"

pottery imported from the Aegean

goddess figurines

Syrian pottery

metalwork

goblets and drinking vessels

Mesopotamian cylinder seal

metal figurines

Bronze Age pottery

New Stone Age pottery and bone and flint tools

Over 5000 years of history were hidden in this one tell in Syria. The bone and flint tools found at the lowest level of the step-trench are traces of the earliest village life there (5500 B.C.), while the second highest level revealed Roman lamps from a community that flourished at the time of St. Paul (1st century A.D.).

celebrate the glories of his reign, Thutmose had certain obelisks set up to commemorate his accession to the throne, and four have survived to this day. The tourist may still marvel at them—but not in the sands of Egypt. They have been transported to Istanbul, Rome, London, and even Central Park in New York City, where they now tower proudly, mute testimonials to the greatness of Thutmose III.

❖ *A Religious Revolution*   Egypt reached her zenith under the grandson of Thutmose, Amenhotep III, who, unfortunately, could not or would not give his son any direction in wielding the great administrative machinery of the empire. Thus it was that when Amenhotep IV became co-regent with his invalid father, the young ruler was so preoccupied with building a new capital on the site of modern Tell el-Amarna, halfway between Thebes and Memphis, that he paid little or no heed to the calls for help from the weakly garrisoned provinces.

In some ways Amenhotep IV (1369-1353 B.C.) is one of the most remarkable of the pharaohs. The statue of him that is now in the Louvre in Paris shows us a flabby, effeminate young man who probably came to the throne when he was about twenty-five years of age. As a boy Amenhotep may have been a high priest of the sun-god Re, and as pharaoh he began to openly favour the purest form of the sun-god, the sun itself, which was called "Aton." He changed his own name to Akhenaton ("He Who is Beneficial to Aton"), and built a new capital called Akhetaton ("Place of the Glory of Aton"). The new city was rushed to completion in two years, and was designated as the sacred city of Aton.

Akhenaton believed that the sun-god should be worshipped above all other deities, and wrote a dignified hymn of praise to Aton:

When thou settest in the western horizon,
The land is in darkness like death. . . .
Every lion comes forth from his den;
All creeping things, they sting.
At daybreak, when thou arisest in the horizon . . .
Thou drivest away the darkness . . .
How manifold are thy works!
They are hidden from man's sight.
O sole god, like whom there is no other,
Thou hast made earth according to thy desire. . . .
Thou settest each man in his own place and thou carest for
    his wants. . . .
Thou didst create the Nile in the netherworld
And broughtest it forth according to thy desire
To maintain the Egyptians, even as thou hast made them
    for thyself, their universal lord. . . .
As for every distant land, thou hast provided their living also. . . .
Everyone beholdeth thee before him,
For thou art the orb of day above the earth.

The new religion has sometimes been called *monotheistic* (that is, believing in the existence of only one god) although strictly speaking this term is not correct because the pharaoh himself became a god along with Aton. At any rate the temples of other gods were closed and their property confiscated, while Akhenaton's agents busied themselves at hacking out the name of the former chief god, Amon, from inscriptions throughout Egypt and her empire. Surprisingly enough, there was apparently no revolt on the part of the priesthood and high officials at the passing of the old gods. Indeed it is doubtful how much attention the mass of the people paid to the new cult.

The mystic pharaoh's interest in religion and art left little time or inclination for statecraft. Small wonder that pleas for military aid from the governors of the Egyptian provinces went unheeded! But Egypt needed a ruler, not a philosopher. Akhenaton's last years were overshadowed by the defection of his beautiful and talented wife, Nefertiti, and the breakup of his empire. As the pharaoh's deputy wrote sadly from Jerusalem, "All the lands of the king have broken away. . . . If no troops come in this very year, then all the lands of the king are lost."

❖ *An Unrobbed Grave*　With Akhenaton's death his religious revolution collapsed. Indeed, the new pharaoh, Tutankhamon (1352-1344 B.C.) attempted to erase all memory of it by obliterating his predecessor's

Tutank-hamon

name from monuments and records. Akhenaton's name was stricken from the official lists of Egyptian kings, and Tutankhamon boasted of how he had restored the ruined shrines and temples of the gods and goddesses. Henceforth his devout predecessor was known as "the criminal of Akhetaton."

Strangely enough, we have come to know a great deal about this young pharaoh who undid Akhenaton's work. By a happy chance a tomb was discovered in 1922 behind a sealed doorway. The sealed door could mean only one thing to its English discoverer, Howard Carter: that unlike almost all the other tombs, this one had not been rifled by grave robbers. Actually Carter found on more careful investigation that this supposition was not quite correct. Robbers had skilfully opened and re-sealed the doors. But—most fortunately—they had not penetrated to the burial chamber. Best of all, the pharaoh's body lay undisturbed.

Who was he? The destroyer of Aton, the eighteen-year-old Tutankhamon.

There gleamed the gold inlaid furniture, the lavish jewellery, the nesting gold coffins. Underneath the glittering death mask reposed, in eerie serenity, the untouched body. Yet none of these impressed Carter as much as something he found nestled on the outermost coffin. Here, he writes,

[lay a] tiny wreath of flowers . . . the last farewell offering of the widowed girl queen to her husband. . . . Among all that regal splendour, that royal magnificence—everywhere the glint of gold—there was nothing so beautiful as those few withered flowers, still retaining their tinge of colour. They told us what a short period three thousand three hundred years really was—but Yesterday and the Morrow. In fact, that little touch of nature made that ancient and our modern civilization kin.

These two figures, carved on a parade stick found in the tomb of Tutankhamon, typify the ancient enemies of the Egyptians. The Syrian and the Negro are bound back to back for Pharaoh to trail in the dust.

❖ *From Empire to Province* With Ramses I (1319-1318 B.C.) the mighty Egyptian dominions of Thutmose III shrank to only Palestine. It was left for Ramses II (1290-1224 B.C.) to conclude a treaty of friendship with the fierce Hittites and marry a Hittite princess. But the empire was tottering. And although Ramses III (1195-1164 B.C.) was able to beat off attacks by groups of Bronze Age Indo-Europeans known as the "Peoples of the Sea", Egypt's Asiatic possessions did not outlive him.

As the power of the pharaohs declined, that of the priesthood of Amon increased, and during the Twenty-First Dynasty the kings were the high priests of Amon. Then followed a period when it was no longer Egyptians who wore the double crown. Foreigners ruled the land of the Nile as Lybians and Nubians ascended the ancient throne, until eventually Egypt went down before the Assyrians from the north-east. Finally in 605 B.C., defeated by the Assyrians' conquerors, the Chaldeans, Egypt lost her influence once and for all.

❖ *Of Mice and Gods* Egyptian religion was a conglomeration of cults. As well as the local city gods and goddesses there were many lesser gods and spirits, often portrayed in the form of animals. Nature deities, as one would expect in an environment where sky and sun and water were so important, were everywhere. The sun-god Re might travel in his barque or fly through the sky as a falcon; or in Upper Egypt he might be portrayed as a sun disk with outspread wings.

Ideas about life after death were equally confused. Trinkets and various types of food and drink were put in tombs to provide for the wants of the deceased, while inscriptions besought the passerby to utter a prayer that would help supply the dead man's wants. The *Book of the Dead* was a collection of magical spells which could be put inside

Life after death

THE GIFT OF THE NILE/57

the coffin in order that the departed one, having studied them at length, could recite to the king of the dead all the sins that he had *not* committed. You will find some passages from this book on page 90.

The Egyptians' preoccupation with death and the after-life might make you think they were a gloomy people. Far from it. Their literature, like most early writing, was mainly given over to religious themes. But there were exceptions, sheer adventure stories such as the tale of an Egyptian Sinbad entitled "The Shipwrecked Sailor," or the account of a roving political exile called "The Tale of Sinuhe." There were even cartoons lampooning the vast Egyptian civil service, or depicting the battles of pharaohs and their enemies as fights between cats and mice.

❖ *The Grandeur that Was Egypt*   Perhaps because the pyramids turned out not to be proof against grave robbers, Egyptian kings came to favour rock-cut tombs in the Valley of the Kings—though as a matter of fact these proved no safer. With the Pyramid Age over, immense temples such as those at Karnak or Luxor became the style. Like the pyramids, they overwhelm us with their sheer mass: the Temple of Amon at Karnak was planned on a scale large enough to contain not only the Maple Leaf Gardens, but the Montreal Forum, Madison Square Garden, and seven football fields as well!

Art   Egyptian art will look very odd to you at first, because the artist had an unusual aim. He was not concerned to make his portrayal of a person as lifelike as possible. He could have done this; but instead he preferred to pick out the most characteristic aspects of his subject and put them all together. The result was that he usually chose a full front view of the eyes and shoulders, but preferred a profile for the head and body. It should be emphasized that this was the way the Egyptian *wanted* to paint and carve. The distortion was deliberate, not the result of faulty technique, as can be proved by an examination of the perfectly proportioned clay figurines put inside tombs to help the dead hunt or fish or perform other tasks.

During the reign of Akhenaton Egyptian art did become more naturalistic, so that for a time the dignified and aloof statues began to look almost human. The pharaoh's sculptor certainly did not flatter him, and the magnificent painted sculpture of Nefertiti, while perhaps idealized, is amazingly lifelike. This trend to naturalism, however, represents only the influence of one pharaoh (who apparently admired realism in art) over a group of sculptors. It was hardly the Egyptian ideal.

These drawings show how the Egyptian word symbols (*hieroglyphs*) became simplified through the centuries (line 1: 4000 B.C.; line 2: 2500 B.C.; line 3: 700 B.C.). It is easy to understand why only trained scribes could master the complex Egyptian script.

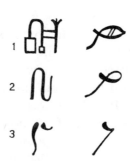

In science, too, Egypt demonstrated her ingenuity. The most outstanding scientific accomplishment was a yearly calendar of 365 days. It was based, like ours, on a solar year, which began when the star Sirius rose above the horizon, and coincided closely with the annual Nile flood. Both water clocks and sundials were used, and the day was divided into 24 hours. Aside from their calendar, however, the Egyptians' achievement in mathematics and astronomy was not spectacular. Mathematics was practical and primitive, using a numeration system that could deal equally well with the mathematical problems they might encounter in erecting the pyramids, or in everyday living. And their astronomical observations were little more than crude schemes bound up with religion.

Science

The Egyptians gained a high reputation in medicine. Many of their medical records have survived in written form on *papyri*, very durable scrolls of paper which they made by pressing together strips of the papyrus, a plant growing in swampy regions. Medical papyri from the Middle and New Kingdoms set forth a large collection of prescriptions for ailments, including the surgical treatment of wounds and fractures. Even so, anatomical and surgical knowledge was elementary. Magic was intertwined with medicine, and illness and disease were often blamed on demon possession. Yet, by virtue of their practice of mummification, the Egyptians gained important medical knowledge in dissection and anatomy. Furthermore, their preservation of bodies has enriched the history of medicine by bequeathing to us some corpses that show the actual ravages of ancient diseases.

Medicine

❖ *The Structure of Society*   The Egyptians were well governed. Since the pharaoh was both god and man, he was high priest as well as chief justice and commander-in-chief. Naturally much of his work had to be delegated, and his chief executive was a sort of prime minister called a *vizier*. Next in line came the ministry of finance, which was administered

Government

by various overseers who collected taxes and disbursed salaries. It is easy to see how the bureaucracy would become extensive by the time of the New Kingdom.

Local government was managed by nomarchs, independent princes who ruled the various provinces or *nomes*. Ability seems to have been rewarded, so that it was possible for a talented man of the lower class to rise to a position of authority. Such opportunity may explain the stability and long life of Egyptian society. "Put writing in thy heart," the young man was urged, "so that thou mayest protect thine own person from any kind of labour and be a respected official."

Egyptian society

The structure of Egyptian society, and of ancient Middle Eastern societies in general, is shown in the accompanying diagram.

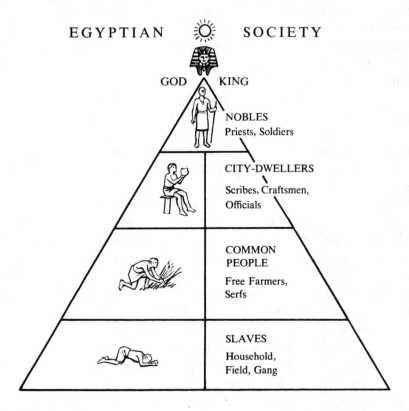

EGYPTIAN SOCIETY

GOD KING

NOBLES
Priests, Soldiers

CITY-DWELLERS

Scribes, Craftsmen,
Officials

COMMON
PEOPLE

Free Farmers,
Serfs

SLAVES
Household,
Field, Gang

In Egypt as in Mesopotamia, agriculture was the basis of economic life. And though many of the slaves had an unenviable lot, the small free farmers do not seem to have fared too badly, despite the fact that they were called upon for forced labour in mines and quarries and in irrigation and construction projects. Nevertheless, all land belonged to Pharaoh. It could be used only with his permission, and he collected an annual tax on it. The following description by an Egyptian scribe was probably not entirely typical; since tax collectors are never popular they are fair game for criticism, just or unjust. Yet the account does show how harsh life could be under corrupt administrators.

Dost thou not recall the picture of the farmer when the tenth of his grain is levied? Worms have destroyed half the wheat, and the hippopotami have eaten the rest; there are swarms of rats in the fields, the grasshoppers alight there, the cattle devour, the little birds pilfer; and if the farmer loses sight for an instant of what remains on the ground, it is carried off by robbers; moreover, the thongs which bind the iron and the hoe are worn out, and the team has died at the plough. It is then that the scribe steps out of the boat at the landing-place to levy the tithe, and there come the Keepers of the Doors of the [King's] Granary with cudgels, and Negroes with ribs of palm-leaves, crying, "Hand over the wheat!" There is none, and they throw the cultivator full length upon the ground, bind him, drag him to the canal, and fling him in head first; his wife is bound with him, his children are put into chains. The neighbours in the meantime leave him and fly to save their grain.

In the towns lived the labourers and merchants. Egypt carried on a flourishing commerce, importing raw materials — minerals from her mines in Arabia and Nubia and timber from Syria — and exporting such finished products as furniture and linen even as far west as Italy. The early Egyptians also discovered how to fuse copper and tin to make bronze, from which weapons and tools were manufactured for home and abroad.

❖ *History's First Strike* Egypt's decline under the New Kingdom was due in part to the pressing demands of war, in part to the passing of the Bronze Age. By the time of the Twentieth Dynasty the effects of the Iron Age were being felt—and Egypt had no iron. This meant that she had to buy from abroad the new metal that made harder and more durable weapons, and the consequent drain on her economy caused the price of grain at home to go up alarmingly.

Those who suffered most from the price rise were the workers on government projects, who were paid in grain. In fact it was they who staged the first strike recorded in all history, when the government fell behind two months in their wages. "On this day [occurred] the crossing of the five walls of the necropolis by the gang, saying: 'We are hungry!' . . . And they sat down at the back of the Temple." When they still did not have their grain two days later they invaded the temple and put their case to the officials in these words: "We have reached this place because of hunger, because of thirst, without clothing, without oil, without fish, without vegetables! Write to Pharaoh, our good lord, about it, and write to the Vizier, our superior. Act so that we may live!"

They were given their grain that day.

❖ *Glory in the Sand*   The coming of the Iron Age spelled disaster for Egypt. Its effects were aggravated by the increasing power of a nobility and priesthood who made Egyptian society even more top-heavy by stamping down the masses. Meanwhile, the Egyptian armies abroad could not stand up to new and powerful states. Foreign troops had to be hired to protect a country which had once united to expel the Hyksos.

Egypt averted her eyes from the whole unpleasant prospect and looked back on her long past. In doing so she ceased to be creative. On that note the glory of Egypt seems to have sunk slowly down into the sand.

What has she bequeathed to us? Later architects adapted her stone columns—but for new types of buildings. Greek mathematicians took over her clumsy arithmetical system—but had to refine it. Later religious thought received little or no inspiration from Egypt.

All told, then, Egypt passed on no very significant spiritual or intellectual heritage. Yet because her civilization lasted so long, later civilizations continued to regard her with worshipful awe. The fact remains that more than 1000 years of cultural stability is in itself no mean accomplishment.

CHAPTER 8

A Vast Subcontinent

Worn-out garments
Are shed by the body:
Worn-out bodies
Are shed by the dweller.

EARLY HINDU SCRIPTURE

While the Egyptians were building the pyramids and while Sargon I ruled Sumer and Akkad, a brilliant culture was flourishing far to the east of them. It had grown up in India. In the valley of the Indus River there existed a civilization that covered an area larger than either Egypt or Mesopotamia, an area stretching some 1000 miles from the Arabian Sea to the headwaters of the Indus.

❖ *White-capped Sentinels and Rolling Seas*   The geography of the Indian peninsula has played a major role in making that vast subcontinent, half as large as the United States, the mother of one of the world's most ancient civilizations.   Across northern India the rugged spine of the Himalaya mountains stretches for 1500 miles.   These white-capped sentinels—over 100 of which soar to 20,000 feet—have protected India against two invaders: man, and the dry winds that sweep across Asia.   These same Himalayas nurture the Indian plains.   The monsoons from the south have to rise to cross the mountains, and when they do they are cooled so that they drop their rain and snow on the thirsty land below.   In this way India's rivers are fed, and her fields are watered.

Yet no mountains have ever succeeded in permanently barring men determined to climb over them.   Eventually invading peoples did force their way through the tortuous Himalayan passes and across the deep, jungle-clad foothills.   Once across these barriers, they were able to fan out into the wide river plains of the Indus to the west and the Ganges to the east. Here they found land so fertile that today in most places it supports two crops a year, and here many peoples over many centuries have met and fused together in a veritable crucible of nations.

Farther south lie hills, forests, and a great central plateau called the Deccan, while along the east and west coasts the hills give way to narrow tropical plains.   All around this ancient peninsula roll her oceans, too wide to permit large-scale immigration from across the seas, but no lasting barrier to the merchants who were to flock to Indian shores to sample the mysteries of the East.

❖ *From Stone Tools to City Sewers*   India is one of the oldest homes of mankind.   Archaeologists tell us that man has lived there since at least 400,000 B.C., and if you look back at your Time Chart on page 8 you will see just how near the beginning of man's "time line" this is. Flaked tools 300,000 years old have been found in the Sohan valley, and by about 10,000 B.C. bone and flint implements made their appearance. After several thousands of years more, village life grew up.   Then some time after 3000 B.C. farmers from the Iranian (Persian) plateau, who had migrated eastward to the Indus valley, introduced an advanced civilization to India in part of what is today West Pakistan and northwest India.

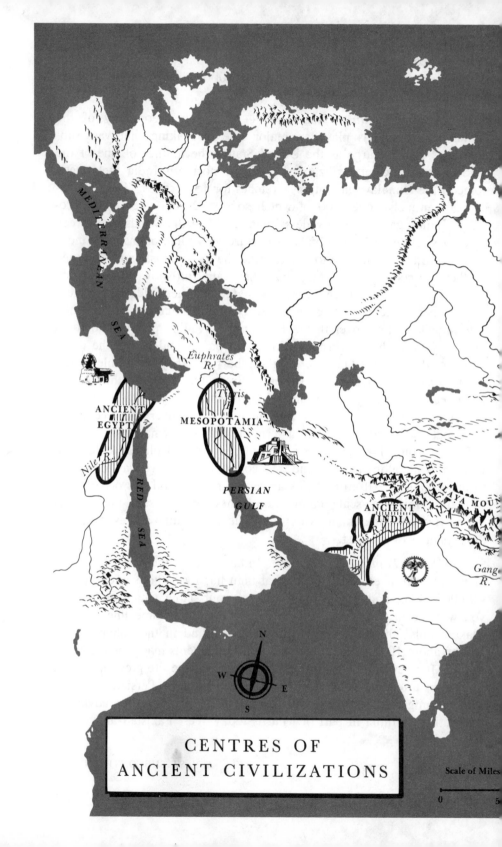

CENTRES OF
ANCIENT CIVILIZATIONS

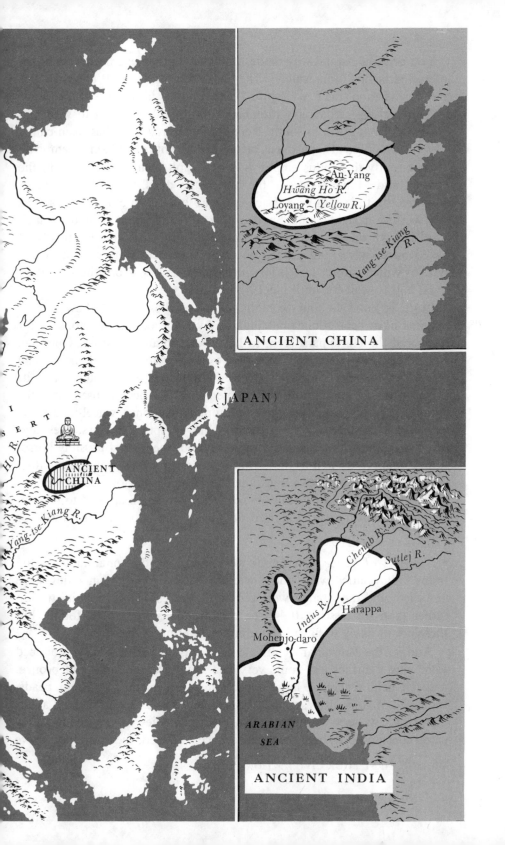

(JAPAN)

Ho R.

ANCIENT
CHINA

Yang-tse-Kiang R.

ANCIENT CHINA

An-Yang
Hwang Ho R.
Loyang (Yellow R.)

Yang-tse-Kiang R.

Chenab R.
Sutlej R.
Indus R.
Harappa
Mohenjo-daro

ARABIAN
SEA

ANCIENT INDIA

You can understand why modern archaeologists have been very much interested in this Indus valley. They have dug up over 70 ancient cities and towns, and their widespread excavations in recent years prove that an exciting civilization stretched 1000 miles from east to west and 500 miles from north to south. Here once matured what has been called "the vastest political experiment before the advent of the Roman empire."

The Indus Empire

Apparently this Indus empire had two capital cities: Harappa in the Punjab, and Mohenjo-daro ("the hill of the dead"), nearly 400 miles downriver to the south-west. Each city was laid out in blocks with streets intersecting at right angles, and each centred around a citadel which looked down on the city from an artificial hill. The houses, mostly of baked brick, were built around courtyards. There were even drainage systems which ran off into brick-lined street sewers—something modern India had to wait for until the 19th century.

The Harappans

Little is known about the inhabitants of these cities. Few human remains have been found, but judging by some of the skeletons so far recovered the Harappans seem to have been small in stature. One man was 5 feet 4½ inches tall, and two women were 4 feet 9 inches and 4 feet 4½ inches. We have, however, found out many interesting bits of information about both the implements the people used and the animals they domesticated. The Harappans fashioned wheel-made pottery, copper, bronze and silver utensils, knives, spears, arrows, axes, and razors; and they domesticated camels, buffalo, sheep, and possibly horses and elephants—as well as those traditional enemies, the cat and the dog. One day, in fact, these two must have been the despair of a certain brickmaker. For a clay brick has been recovered on which are still to be seen the footprints of a cat, followed at hair-raising proximity by those of a dog.

❖ *The Arts of Peace* As far as we know now, the inhabitants of the Indus valley cities were not a warlike people. Harappan cities were unwalled, and the citadels were probably centres of local administration rather than fortresses. It is true that weapons have been found, but these are as likely to have been used for hunting as for war.

And so the Harappans cultivated the arts of peace. They produced some clay figurines and some very fine sculptures in stone and bronze, and left behind them a large collection of bracelets, rings, and beads, fashioned of gold, silver, copper, bronze, and stone. From such an abundance of jewellery we might guess that the ladies of the Indus valley cared considerably about their appearance. Indeed, they were not above

Grain was a valuable commodity for the cities of the Indus Valley—not only as food but as "money", since it was the universal basis for barter. It was imperative, then, that grain storage should afford protection not only against floods but against thieves, and the State Granary at Mohenjo-daro, pictured here, was particularly fitted to ward off both human and natural menaces. The granary, which was a national bank and revenue department in one, was built on a massive mud-brick platform rising some 40 feet above the surrounding plain, so that the wheat and barley had to be hauled up on ropes to the granary floor above. The holes visible in the brick walls are the ends of ventilating shafts that allowed air to circulate beneath the grain. The carts, which are drawn according to models found in the ruins of Mohenjo-daro, look precisely the same as ox-carts used in West Pakistan today—some forty centuries later.

A VAST SUBCONTINENT/67

using tricks to improve it. Archaeologists have discovered that women resorted to rouge, lipstick, tweezers, and ear-piercing implements over 4500 years ago!

Many examples of Indus script have survived on seals and pottery-stamps, but as yet no one has discovered how to decipher them. Some religious objects have been unearthed, among them a three-faced figure in a sitting position which is probably the original Shiva, a primitive Hindu god. We know that certain animals, such as the humped bull, were revered, the fig tree was regarded as sacred, and bathing was a sort of religious ritual. We are still puzzled, however, as to whether some small clay animals had religious significance or were simply children's toys.

By 2500 B.C. the Harappans were being introduced to the outside world through trade with Mesopotamia. Probably such contacts were good for the Indus valley culture: foreign influence stimulates any civilization. Still, in art, in writing, and in plumbing the Harappans remained unique. Yet it was not these physical accomplishments of their civilization that were to be passed on to later ages. It was their gift of the spirit, their religion.

❖ *Fair-haired Invaders* Time finally wears away any civilization, and by 1500 B.C. the Indus valley cities had begun to decline. Then waves of Bronze Age Indo-European invaders crashed down over this peaceful, if somewhat puzzling, people, slaughtering them and scattering through the country. Across the plains in swift battle-chariots swept these fearful

The Aryans warriors—the tall, fair-haired, fair-skinned Aryans. Their war-god, they said, "rends forts as age consumes a garment," and the trail of death they left behind them can still be seen by the archaeologist. "The attackers left the dead lying where they fell. In one of the houses sprawled thirteen skeletons—men, women, and children—some wearing bracelets, rings and beads, and two of them with sword cuts upon their skulls."

The Aryans settled down along the banks of the Indus. They were an agricultural people (their word for "war" meant "a desire for more cows"), and with them they brought the plough, adapting it to the wet, heavy soils of the river valleys. Widespread cultivation of barley and rice now began, and iron-working was introduced. Cities eventually flourished, and by 600 B.C. there were some sixteen separate states. Yet for most of the people life must have gone on much as it had before the invaders seized their land.

Proud as they were, the conquerors were not above learning from their

This delicate 11th century bronze figure represents Shiva, the Indian god of destruction and creation. Shiva dances with one foot poised on a dwarf, which symbolized evil. The god's dance sets in motion the perpetual cycle of creation and destruction which eventually releases the soul.

captives. Some of the ritual and religion of the Indus peoples was destined to be adopted, and with the coming of the Aryans we can clearly see the early stages of Hinduism—one of the world's major religions, and hence our chief interest in early Indian history.

❖ *The Wheel of Life* The Aryans practised a sort of nature religion. This gradually merged with the Harappan beliefs, and the resulting mixture found expression in a series of hymns to the gods called the *Vedas* and the *Upanishads*. Here are recorded the origins of the basic Hindu beliefs.

The Vedas
and
Upanishads

According to the early beliefs of Hinduism man was destined to be divided by sharp class distinctions and a caste system. At the head of these classes stood the powerful priests, followed in descending order by kings and warriors, artisans, labourers, and finally the outcastes or "untouchables." Each man was born within a certain caste, and there he stayed—he, and his children, and his children's children. It was the will of the gods.

There was also a strong conviction that all living things were part of a world soul, Brahma, from which they came and to which, ultimately, they returned. If a man died before his soul was worthy of final release, the soul would be *reincarnated,* that is, would find a home in another body, before being reunited with Brahma. In fact a succession of rebirths, known as transmigrations of the soul, might be required before a final reunion with the world soul.

Thus death was not something to be feared. Life was a kind of wheel.

Never was there a time when I was not, nor thou . . . and never will there be a time when we shall cease to be. . . . Just as a person casts off worn-out garments and puts on new, so does the soul cast off worn-out bodies and put on others . . .

❖ *Achieving Nirvana* By the 6th century B.C. Hinduism had become extremely formal and ritualistic, and there were certain members of the noble class who wished to reform it. One young man named Siddhartha Gautama (567-487 B.C.), the son of a petty Indian king, became so dissatisfied with the Hindu religion and so oppressed by the suffering in the world that he felt he must go to any lengths to find the true meaning of life. So at the age of twenty-nine he left his wife and infant son, and for six years lived as a wandering beggar. Sometimes he deprived himself of food and drink; sometimes he inflicted tortures on himself; yet still he failed to find the truth. Then one day as he was sitting under a fig tree enlightenment came to him. Thenceforth for the next forty-five years Gautama, who is better known to history as Buddha, "the Enlightened One," was to preach his vision.

Buddha

The first sermon that the enlightened Buddha preached to his followers may be read in the Source Reading on page 90. Buddha believed that man did not have to remain chained to the ever-revolving wheel of life. It was man's desire for material things that shackled him there, and if he could conquer desire he could escape this repeated rebirth into successive existences. With desire conquered he could be absorbed into oneness with the Supreme Spirit, an exalted state called Nirvana. But Buddha had an even more revolutionary message: men, he declared, were born equal. The caste system was rejected; monks replaced the aristocratic Brahmins; and the many gods of Hinduism were renounced.

The eightfold path

Buddha proceeded to set down an eightfold path for his followers by which they could achieve Nirvana.

1. Right views, which meant a knowledge of Buddha's teaching, especially about misery.

2. Right resolve, which meant the resolution to resist desires, to bear no malice, and to do no harm.

3. Right speech, which meant to abstain from lying, slandering, and talking aimlessly.

4. Right conduct, which meant not to kill or steal or live immorally.

5. Right livelihood, which meant not to follow occupations such as slave-dealing, caravan-trading, butchering, dispensing liquors, and selling poisons.

6. Right effort, which meant the suppression of evil states of mind and the stimulation of good intentions.

7. Right mindfulness, which meant the achievement of self-mastery by self-knowledge.

8. Right concentration, which meant the ordering of thought so that, purified of desire, temper, sloth, fretfulness, and perplexity, the sense of duty done gave a feeling of peace and freedom.

Buddha considered compassion a prime virtue. "Never shall hatred cease by hating; by not hating shall it cease." He also preached non-violence and, since all creatures housed living souls, taught that the Buddhist should refuse to take life and should practise vegetarianism. Hence it is easy to see how later Hinduism, with its insistence on non-violence and the sacredness of all life, owes much to Buddhist teachings. In fact with the passing of years the gulf between the formal religion, Hinduism, and the reformed religion, Buddhism, narrowed, with each borrowing from the other.

It is important to note that Buddha did not consider himself to be anything more than a teacher. It was not until some centuries had passed that one branch of his followers began to revere him as a god and saviour of mankind.

Buddha's teachings did not spread widely until two centuries after his death. Ironically enough, today his religion abounds in every Asian country except India, where it eventually gave way to—or rather became merged with—Hinduism. Only half a million of the world's 155 million Buddhists now live where the Buddha himself taught. The rest are to be found in Ceylon, Burma, Thailand, Cambodia, Vietnam, Laos, China, and Japan.

❖ *A Strange Mixture*   We must not think that the world's great religions were always transferred to other countries without being changed. You have already seen how Buddhism and Hinduism mingled in India, and the introduction of Buddhism to Japan from China in the 6th century A.D. provides an even more interesting example of the mixture of old and new. The native religion of Japan was a form of nature worship   *Shintoism*

This immense Buddha towers 49 feet high over the worshippers in Kamakura, Japan. Cast in A.D. 1252, it is a world famous example of bronze sculpture. The contemplative pose of the brooding figure reflects the Buddhist's search for peace of mind, while the jewel in the forehead, made up of 30 pounds of silver, represents the radiance Buddha casts throughout the universe.

known as Shintoism, which, like most early cults, explained the wonders of nature by saying that the world was inhabited by many gods and goddesses, the most important of which was the sun goddess. It was a primitive, superstitious religion ("Shinto" means "Way of the Spirits"), with no official sacred scriptures but with many shrines.

When Buddhism was introduced to Japan, a strange thing happened. Instead of Shintoism disappearing it simply became a sort of background for the new religion. The people continued to believe in their many gods and superstitions, Shinto shrines were allowed to remain in

Buddhist temples, and Buddhist institutions were even protected by Shinto taboos. The emperor, whom Shintoism regarded as divine because he was supposed to be directly descended from the sun goddess, was still "the Son of Heaven." Gradually Shintoism became not so much a religion as a strong force in Japanese nationalism (although after World War II the emperor renounced his divinity, and Shintoism was prohibited by the Allies). What has really happened is that many Japanese, while remaining Shintoists, superimpose another faith on top of it. Most Japanese families still perform a simple daily rite before a Shintoist family shrine.

We have now observed how religions sometimes change as they are transplanted into new countries—Buddhism interacting with Hinduism in India, Buddhism becoming enmeshed with Shintoism in Japan. And the Japanese picture becomes even more complex, for along with Buddhism came two other Chinese faiths, Confucianism and Taoism, both of which we are about to examine. You see, then, how very complicated the mixture of religions can be.

CHAPTER 9

The Sleeping Giant

If there be righteousness in the heart,
there will be beauty in the character.
If there be beauty in the character,
there will be harmony in the home.
If there be harmony in the home,
there will be order in the nation.
If there be order in the nation,
there will be peace in the world.

CONFUCIUS

Napoleon called China "the Sleeping Giant," and right up to modern times she seemed to be just that—a far-off, mysterious, and isolated phenomenon as far as Westerners were concerned. Early China was almost cut off from the outside world. The only way contacts could be made with her was by caravan across 2500 miles of steppe and desert from Mesopotamia, or by ship around the long southward thrust of the

Malay peninsula. Nevertheless a few traders did penetrate the interior, and when they did they found an exotic and brilliant civilization.

❖ *The Floods that Feed*   Along the Yellow River (Hwang Ho) lies a flood plain much like those through which the Nile, Tigris-Euphrates, and Indus Rivers flow. Here, in this North China plain, yet another early civilization developed.

The Indian symbol for time is a wheel. The Chinese symbol is a pool —an apt one in a land constantly in danger of erosion. For the mighty Yellow River, bearing heavy yellow silt, gradually builds up its own bed with this silt until it brims over and floods viciously across the northern plains. Through the centuries, this river has posed an apparently insoluble problem. All of China's rulers have had to grapple with its ravages; none has tamed it. Yet because North China is normally dry, the floods, when not disastrous, supply much needed moisture. Obviously, then, some system of water control would have to be a first concern.

South China, on the other hand, has an ideal climate for agriculture. But its soils have been exhausted by thousands of years of extensive farming, and although most of the area can still produce two crops a year, China has to support a population four times as large as that of the United States on a cultivated area one-half the size. In the last 1800 years there have been over 1800 famines in China.

One of man's earliest ancestors came from China, as the table on page 10 indicates. Peking Man's skeletal remains, which are perhaps 400,000 years old, were discovered in a cave thirty miles from Peking. Then six years later a second cave yielded skeletons dating from about 20,000 to 10,000 B.C.

We know next to nothing about the life of these earliest Chinese. But we do know that in the New Stone Age people lived in North China in sunken pit-dwellings and raised pigs and dogs for food, and that there was a settlement at Yang-shao which goes back to 2000 B.C. For an entire village has been excavated there, showing that its inhabitants painted large earthenware pots with black geometric designs, sewed with bone needles, and used other tools of bone and horn. It is, however, *The Shang* only with the coming of the Shang dynasty about 1400 B.C. that any- *dynasty* thing in the way of a clear historical picture of early China emerges.

❖ *Bones and Bronze*   There have long been Chinese literary traditions concerning a Shang dynasty which for some three centuries ruled the

Here we see the remains of a Shang noble, along with his most precious possessions, his horses and his chariot, which were buried with him. Though the chariot itself has completely decayed, it has left a clear impression of its two wheels and of the heavy pole projecting behind them to support the chariot car in which the dead man was laid. You can also see the bead traces and tall bronze decorations that ornamented the horses.

relatively small area in the Yellow River basin that comprised ancient China. But many historians doubted that these stories were true. Then in the late 1920's something happened that changed their minds.

Strange bones with writing on them had for some time been turning up on the Peking market, usually to be ground up for medicinal purposes. When they were finally traced back to their point of origin it proved to be none other than An-Yang—the modern site of the ancient City of Shang. Archaeologists immediately became excited, and proceeded to dig up thousands more of these items, mostly shoulder-bones of cattle and under-shells of tortoises. They were found to date from 1400 to 1100 B.C., and bore the names of the traditional Shang rulers. So these rulers *had* existed, after all! Not only that, but there were also inscriptions in early Chinese characters. Why had they been put there? And what did they mean?

The strange discoveries, it turned out, were "oracle bones." These were devices used to predict the future. The oracle worked like this: a question was scratched on a bone; then heat was applied to it to produce cracks, and by interpreting the size and direction of these cracks the questioner received his answer. All sorts of inquiries were made—and all sorts of answers received. One bone, for instance, asks, "Will it rain tonight?" A later disgusted notation reads, "It really didn't rain."

Chinese writing

The Shang people lived over thirty centuries ago; yet they had 2000 different symbols, each one representing a word. These symbols were the ancestors of the later Chinese script with its 50,000 or more characters—a most complex system of writing.

The Chinese language is very complex because it uses a separate individual symbol for each object, whereas Western writing expresses words phonetically, that is, by sounds which can be repeated over and over in different combinations. Example (1) is the Chinese character for vehicle. It represents a two-wheeled Shang chariot drawn by two horses as seen from above (compare with illustration on page 75). Examples (2) and (3) are the pictographs for "tree", in Shang and in modern times respectively. Examples (4) and (5) are the pictographs for "sun", first in Shang and then in modern characters.

The discovery of such an advanced system of writing was amazing enough, but another discovery was unearthed which has imparted even more glory to the Shang dynasty. This was a collection of bronze weapons and of bronze vessels used in religious ceremonies. They are bronzes that have never been surpassed. Not even the superb craftsmen of the Italian Renaissance could match the Shang technique of casting bronze, with its patterns and lines formed by square—not rounded—grooves, perfect miniature trenches with perpendicular sides and flat bottoms. All of you should try some day to see a display of Shang bronzes in a good museum.

Both in their writing and their bronze-working the Chinese likely drew from the already existing civilizations to the west of them. But it was only the *idea* that came from the West. The execution of the idea was characteristically and exquisitely Chinese.

The Shang rulers probably exercised firm authority over much of the

North China plain, although they were frequently at war with neighbouring peoples. In their fighting the kings and nobles used a two-wheeled chariot which could be manoeuvred with great ease over the flat, open country. So highly esteemed was this vehicle that it was entombed, along with the charioteer and horses, with the An-yang rulers when they died. Even yet, as you can see from the illustration, a drawing of one of these chariots (viewed from above) forms the Chinese character for "vehicle" or "wheel."

The royal palace was large and imposing, built in a style which remains characteristic of modern China. Yet the common people still lived in the crude pit dwellings of Neolithic times. Life was precarious (we know, for example, that human sacrifice was practised), and the world for the Chinese was inhabited by all sorts of spirits. "Pray to grandmother Yi for rain," reads one of the oracle bones. Even after death the ancestors hovered near to affect the living.

❖ *Rule by Underlings*   Soon after 1100 B.C. the Shang dynasty fell before a confederation of tribes under the leadership of the Chou people. The Chou rulers, like the Shangs before them, found it a very difficult task to exercise authority over the many walled city-states of the North China plain, and they attempted to solve the problem by parcelling them out to relatives and allies. These deputies were expected to support the king with money and soldiers. Otherwise they were left free to govern their territories pretty much as they pleased.

The Chou dynasty

Below the Chou aristocracy, as below any ruling class, toiled the masses of peasantry, bound to the land for life. An old Chinese adage sums up their lot: "The superior man uses his mind; the commoner uses his body. He who uses his mind rules; he who uses his body is ruled. He who rules feeds on others; he who is ruled provides food for others." Little wonder that when a peasant died a hoe was buried with him.

The Chou dynasty, too, fell on evil days. A traditional story tells us that a Chou king of the 8th century B.C. had fallen into the habit of summoning his subject armies merely to amuse a certain court lady. The signal he used was a lighted beacon. Then in 771 B.C. disaster struck. Rude invaders swept in from the west. The fires were again lighted—but they had been lighted once too often. This time no armies came. The king was killed, his capital destroyed, and never again did the Chou rulers assert real control over their wide lands.

Nevertheless the later Chou period was an important one in Chinese history. Iron weapons now replaced bronze, the iron-tipped plough came into use, large-scale irrigation works were constructed, wealthy traders and merchants plied a lucrative business, copper coinage was developed, and chopsticks were in use. Mediterranean ideas and inventions at last flowed into China, speeded up by the Chinese adoption of horseback riding. Moreover, the hodge-podge of tiny semi-independent states now gave way to larger units as the Chou domains were expanded by the incorporation of border areas in the west and south.

Confucius

This age, which coincided with the period of the Hebrew prophets and Buddha, was also a time of vigorous intellectual activity. It produced the first, and the greatest, Chinese professional teacher on record —K'ung-fu-tzu (551-479 B.C.). We know him better as Confucius.

❖ *More Cruel than the Tiger* Confucius was a tall, homely youth with large ears, a flat nose, and buck teeth. He was a member of the lower aristocracy, and his great ambition was to achieve high political office. But the ambition was never realized. Confucius failed at politics and took up teaching as a sideline. His hobby made him, at least in the eyes of later generations, an outstanding success.

Confucius did not preach a religion. Rather he taught respect for authority, tradition, law, and custom. Yet, like the prophets of the Old Testament, he spoke out against the basic weakness of his society—the turbulent rule of petty monarchs who felt themselves above reproach. He taught that Chinese society must build on its past, and that the rulers must be an example to their subjects.

There is a famous story about Confucius which well illustrates his abhorrence of harsh tyranny. One day he came upon a woman wailing on a lonely mountainside.

"Why do you weep?" asked Confucius.

"My husband's father was killed here by a tiger, my husband also was killed by a tiger, and now my son has met the same fate."

"Then why do you dwell in so dreadful a place?"

"Because here," the woman answered, "there is no oppressive ruler."

Confucius turned to his disciples.

"Scholars," he said, "remember this: oppressive rule is more cruel than a tiger."

Although he was basically a conservative, Confucius was deeply concerned with reform. In this connection his courage should not be underestimated. Many of his sayings were addressed to men who would have tortured him to death as readily as they would have crushed an insect.

Confucius never claimed divine inspiration: it was his followers who eventually deified him. Nor was he outstandingly original in his thought, although we must recognize his fearless independence in the harsh age in which it was asserted. Once when he was attacked in the town where he was teaching he reassured his followers by saying, "Heaven has appointed me to teach this doctrine, and until I have done so, what can the people of Kwang do to me?" Perhaps one of the reasons that Confucius' advice for living came to be so popular was that he expressed his ideas in short pithy sayings that were easily remembered. These were collected after his death under the title *Analects*, some examples of which are given in the Source Reading on page 91.

The Analects

Confucius' teachings had little effect on Chinese society during his lifetime. Yet through his disciples, men of the pen rather than the sword, he was destined to have a profound and abiding influence. The conservative nature of Confucianism made it popular with the ruling classes, to whom it became a code of gentlemanly behaviour. Thus, in a vastly overpopulated country where great masses of people were forced to live close together, Confucianism buttressed both the state and the family. So enduring was the need for some rules to make life in China at all bearable that only in our own century, under the impact of Chinese communism, has the Confucian system come to be seriously questioned.

❖ *The Way of Serenity*   There is an old Chinese fable that Confucius once visited another famous philosopher. After talking with him for some time he came away respecting this strange old man, yet completely baffled by him. "Of birds," Confucius told his disciples, "I know that they have wings to fly with, of fish that they have fins to swim with, of wild beasts that they have feet to run with. For feet there are traps, for fins nets, for wings arrows. But who knows how dragons surmount wind and cloud into heaven? This day I have seen Lao Tzu. Today I have seen a dragon."

Lao Tzu is a mysterious figure in Chinese history. We do not know when he lived; there is considerable doubt that he lived at all; and we do not even know his name. Lao Tzu simply means "the Old Fellow." He was a philosopher who did not preach, who did not organize a church, who simply wrote a few pages entitled *Tao Te Ching*, "The Way and Its Power," and then, discouraged by man's failure to cultivate the natural goodness he believed to be the key to serenity, rode off to Tibet on a water buffalo. The contrast with Buddha, who travelled India's highways and byways for forty-five long years, or Confucius,

Taoism

THE TREE OF CIVILIZATION

NEOLITHIC

PALEOLITHIC

Egypt
Mesopotamia
India
China

HOMO SAPIENS

Neanderthal Man
Rhodesian Man
South African Ape-Man
Java Man
Peking Man

who strove valiantly for thirteen years to translate his philosophy into political reforms, is almost ludicrous. Yet Taoism ("The Way"), as the philosophy of Lao Tzu came to be called, has rivalled Confucianism in its influence on Chinese philosophy and life.

Confucianism and Taoism are like two halves of life. Confucianism stresses social responsibility and concentrates on man and his morality. Taoism rejoices in spontaneity and naturalness, looks to something beyond man, and rejects formal restrictions on him. As the Chinese say,

80/THE FIRST FOUR CIVILIZATIONS

Confucius roams within society; Lao Tzu wanders beyond it. Confucius was concerned to give men rules to live by, and to help organize their government properly. Lao Tzu believed that the supreme goal in life was to be passive. Let nature take its course. Over-government was society's gravest impediment. "The greater are the number of laws and enactments, the more the thieves and robbers there will be."

The "Three Jewels" of Taoism were Compassion, Moderation, and Humility. Yet not even Chinese scholars can fully agree on this mystical doctrine. It is more a point of view than a religion, and one which has had a profound effect on Chinese life and character. Taoism brought placidity and grace to the Chinese. It asserted that all values were relative, that even good and evil were not absolute, and that death was not to be feared but is a thing of peace. Men should be strictly pacifist. "Heaven arms with compassion those whom she would not see destroyed."

> In time of war men civilized in peace
> Turn from their higher to their lower nature.
> But triumph is not beautiful.
> He who thinks triumph beautiful
> Is one with a will to kill.
> The death of a multitude is cause for mourning:
> Conduct your triumph as a funeral.

Taoism never became a dominant religion in China—and certainly its founder never intended it to be a religion at all. But it exerted a great influence, and coloured Chinese Buddhism, which it resembled. Its lessons of simplicity and unaffectedness have been the source of tranquil living for millions of Chinese.

It is easy to see how the Taoists would regard the formality of the Confucianists as pomposity, and Taoist literature loves to make fun of them. One story tells of two men strolling over a bridge one day and looking into the water.

"See how the minnows dart hither and thither at will," observed the Taoist. "Such is the pleasure fish enjoy."

"You are not a fish," replied the Confucianist. "How do you know what gives pleasure to a fish?"

"You are not I," was the prompt retort. "How do you know I do not know what gives pleasure to fish?"

CHAPTER 10

A Day in the Life of a Bronze Age Vizier

Look after the office of vizier and watch over everything that is done in it, for it is the constitution of the entire land.

THUTMOSE III'S INSTRUCTIONS TO HIS VIZIER, REKHMIRE

". . . The fresco must also include a portrait of my wife and children," dictated the rather nasal voice with the ring of authority. The scribe, sitting cross-legged with his roll of papyrus on his knee, made a note of this instruction while his master strode about the open courtyard. The heat of the Egyptian sun would soon force this hard-driving executive to take an afternoon rest; but meanwhile every moment, he hoped, would be used to plan the details of his tomb.

A servant entered, prostrated himself, and announced the arrival of an architect. Then he left as noiselessly as he had entered, his short white kilt in sharp contrast with his naked brown chest. The scribe, too, wore the kilt, and all were clean-shaven as was the custom with Egyptians. Only the master was dressed in a long white linen robe. He frowned now at having once again to put aside the plans for his tomb, and the heavy black wig that framed his face gave it a sombre dignity.

It was this wig that marked the man out as a high official, for only men of rank wore wigs. And this was indeed a man of rank, no less than the vizier of Upper Egypt, the pharaoh's right-hand man, "the supporting post of the entire land," as Thutmose III once called him. As he conducted a brief conference with the architect he was acting in only one of the multitude of his capacities, that of Superintendent of Works, the supervisor of the artisans who were employed by the government and the temples of the capital. The state project under discussion at the moment was the great portal of the temple of Amon at Karnak, and even the bricks for it must be manufactured under his supervision. Pharaoh was no haphazard worker himself, and he expected nothing less than perfection of those beneath him. Only the *best* of bricks, made by mixing the moistened Nile mud with sand and chopped straw, could go into the mighty portal. There was never any problem of manpower—Egypt had that in abundance. It was the foremen whom Rekhmire had to keep hounding.

The architect concluded his report, bowed low again, and departed. But no sooner had he gone than a man who from his mode of dress was obviously a foreigner was ushered in. Thutmose III was the greatest of warrior pharaohs, and his armies had marched as far as the Euphrates in the north-east and had conquered the Nubians in the south. This man — an artist — was one of the many foreign captives whom the pharaoh had brought back to his capital. Thebes was now experiencing new dimensions of culture, and foreign princes were being brought up at the royal court. Some Egyptian noblemen had even married foreign wives!

"I have just been dictating some instructions on the frescoes I want," Rekhmire began, already unrolling the sketches that the artist has submitted to him. "Ah!" Obviously the great man was pleased. "Just what I want. I intend that every phase of my life shall be depicted in my tomb. But where is the one of my favourite sport?" Like many busy men, Rekhmire was proud of the fact that he was good at physical recreation. His "game of golf" was spearing fish in the Nile, and he intended, through the pictures in his tomb, to enjoy it in the afterlife, too.

At this point Rekhmire interrupted the interview with the artist briefly to go and look at the toy boat his nine-year-old son was working on. It was a rich child's toy, for it was made of wood; and wood was so scarce in Egypt that no timber could be felled without the vizier's permission. Today was a holiday from the temple schools, and the lad was enjoying his freedom to the utmost. Rekhmire could sympathize with him. He remembered only too well his own schooling, the hours spent before an old scribe in a windowless classroom, sitting cross-legged and laboriously copying out exercises on scraps of pottery. Little did he or the other boys know how much work they were making for future archaeologists who would find these pieces and spend years trying to decipher an almost impossibly difficult ancient language made even more complicated by childish mistakes in grammar! But learn he must, and master the difficult art of writing he must, if he was ever to hope to rise to high administrative rank—indeed, if he was to hold any government job.

Rekhmire smiled to himself as he patted his son's head and prepared to return to his interview. How well he remembered the exercises he had had to learn by rote, many of them admonishing him to be a good boy, but *all* praising the profession of a scribe and harping on the dangers and unworthiness of other callings. How did that one go about the baker? . . .

When the baker standeth and baketh and layeth bread on the fire, his head is inside the oven, and his son holdeth fast his feet. Cometh it to pass that he slippeth from his son's hand, he falleth into the blaze.
But the scribe, he directeth every work that is in the land.

And how could he ever forget that other one—the one that described so neatly what happened to boys if they did not behave themselves. Even his own son, he knew, would not be exempt from the rod.

Fortunate is a scribe that is skilled in his calling, a master of education. Persevere every day; thus shalt thou obtain the mastery over it. . . . Spend no day in idleness, or thou will be beaten. The ear of a boy is on his back, and he harkeneth when he is beaten.

It was fortunate that the great man did not return to the courtyard too promptly, for the artist, having observed his departure with secret annoyance, was taking this opportunity to get rid of some pent-up bad humour.
" 'Every phase of my life' he says!" grumbled the fellow, mimicking the vizier's voice. Then, having looked cautiously around to make sure no one was watching, he spat contemptuously on the stones. "Here I am planning pictures of Rekhmire receiving his food-offering, Rekhmire supervising his farms and estates, Rekhmire entertaining his guests at a banquet. Now I'm to add Rekhmire spearing fish in the Nile, and one of him and his family. What more does he want?" He looked at his sketches ruefully. "Why, this man has duties without number. He confers with the pharaoh every day when he's in the capital; he hears all cases in the Vizier's Court; the Chief Treasurer reports daily to him; he makes tours of inspection and supervises the local authorities. (I wouldn't want to be one of *them*. The old vizier's a fussy one!) He's the minister of war, of agriculture, of irrigation — he has just now ordered the cutting of another canal. He administers the estates of the temples and examines the offerings to see if any priests are making off with the funds. He regulates the traffic of the Nile, appoints a door-keeper to the judgment hall, manages the king's bodyguard and royal expeditions, checks up on arrears of taxes, on grievances of local governors, robberies in the provinces, quarrels, changes in boundaries of the nomes. By the gods, he's a second pharaoh! He looks after all the details of administration: he *is* the administration. His power is all-reaching. . . . And he expects me to depict all *that*?" The man looked

". . . the vizier, like most Egyptians, enjoys the warm circle of his family life. . . ."

up to the heavens in despair, but since just at that moment the vizier returned, he had quickly to attempt to appear as if he were looking at a pigeon that was fluttering by.

The artist received only a few more hurried instructions, because now several civil servants had arrived and were waiting their turn to see Rekhmire. The last of these was a District Inspector (there were four in each province), a stout little man who had journeyed here, full of importance, to give the vizier a census list. Only too often did the tribesmen drive their cattle into the uplands to escape the census and hence evade taxes! These inspectors were the royal officials who acted as a check on the local officers of the province. Rekhmire, like the pharaoh himself, was most anxious that no local princeling get too much power and consider himself independent.

The District Inspector was an affable fellow who would have liked nothing better than to have prolonged his visit by a discussion of current events (and, incidentally, of what a good job he was doing on the census), had the great man been so disposed. He was not. In fact the good inspector was treated so curtly that he worried all the way home about how he must have displeased the vizier. The simple truth was, however, that Rekhmire was tired. His job was a most arduous one. He had just returned from a long journey of inspection up the Nile to find that Pharaoh was away—*again*—on an expedition, so that once more the vizier was virtually ruler of the country until the king's return. Yesterday he had received ambassadors from Punt, from Crete, from Syria and Nubia, sitting for hours on a gilded chair attended by his retinue while tribute was borne past him. Tomorrow he would preside in the Hall of Judgment as Lord Chief Justice, "dispensing justice impartially," he was having the walls of his tomb record, "and seeing to it that the two litigants are contented, judging between poor and well-to-do alike, no petitioner weeping because of him. . . ." But as the wrangling goes on and on, his wig will grow heavy on his head, and his shoulders, so formally rigid, will ache; and he will decide to insert a surprisingly frank phrase in his tomb inscription:

Lo, as to the position of Vizier, lo, it is not pleasant at all; *no, it is bitter as gall. . . .*

Yet if Thutmose should die tomorrow, how long would he remain Vizier? Rekhmire's eyes hardened. There was no use killing himself with work. Today he had been busy since dawn, and there were still people waiting to see him. Let them wait. He was ready for his siesta.

Tonight Rekhmire planned to show off his house, for tonight he was giving a feast. He looked proudly around him as he walked toward his bedroom. Like all upper-class Egyptians he spent most of his indoor hours in this walled courtyard where he held his audiences, and, weary as he was, he was loath to leave its silent pool and its trees and flowers of every kind. Perhaps it was because they lived in the midst of desert that ancient Egyptians cared so tenderly for their flowers. Rekhmire's courtyard also boasted a large tank of ornamental fish, this display being both decorative and useful because the fish ate the mosquitoes.

The vizier's house was anything but attractive from the outside, as even he would admit. The visitor who approached found himself gazing at high, blank walls, sightless except for very small windows at the top. Like all Egyptian dwellings, except temples, it was built of the ever-available mud-brick blocks. (Why use other material when this one was so cheap? And besides, in Egypt it never rains.) But the almost shabby exterior was deceiving. He who proceeded on through the single narrow entrance discovered a mansion—and "mansion" is the correct word, for it comprised sixteen rooms instead of the usual Egyptian's four to six. There were columned reception halls, dining-rooms, bedrooms, the harem quarters, the servant quarters, the kitchen, and store rooms. In front of the house bloomed a garden; behind it lay a large patio; in the centre was the courtyard. Unlike the Westerner's home which faces on the street, the Egyptian's, then as now, looked inward. The courtyard is the centre of the plan: it is the centre of life in this torrid country.

Rekhmire's walls were adorned with delicate frescoes of plants and birds painted in vibrant colours. Even his bedroom was pleasingly decorated, and it was with relief that he stretched out—assisted by ever-present slaves—on his high-rising bed with its cord-matting mattress. A manservant adjusted his wig around the semicircular wooden head-rest, shaped to fit under the neck and near the ears. Then he departed, and quiet descended.

For a few moments Rekhmire lay awake thinking—and they were pleasant thoughts, for they were about tonight's party. His Chief Wife, Meryet, will be at his side, beautiful in her clinging robe of sheerest linen, her finger- and toe-nails dyed red, her large eyes emphasized by turquoise eye-paint. Women in ancient Egypt enjoyed a position of dignity, and it was wise to treat them with deference since all property was inherited through them. Even the pharaoh was king only by virtue of having married a queen, which explains why so many of them married their sisters or even their daughters. Meryet has brought Rekhmire a handsome inheritance, but it will go to her daughters, not to him, if she predeceases him. She pleases him well; and besides, although divorce is easy there is a heavy fine for it. Moreover the vizier, like most Egyptians, enjoys the warm circle of his family life, and he boasts about his three daughters and four sons. Tonight, he has decided, the two youngest children will be allowed to stay up for the party for a little while. Why shouldn't they? And why shouldn't his guests see what beautiful offspring he has?

It will be a delightful evening. Everyone will wear garlands of flowers, presented to them by the handmaidens, and flowers will also adorn many small tables which will groan with good things—roast beef, chicken, duck, pigeon, vegetables, many kinds of bread, and great quantities of wine. The guests will eat with their hands (they will use a knife only to cut the meat), and slaves will pour water over their hands at the end of the meal. Dancers, among them his favourite from the harem, a Nubian girl, will entertain the men and bore the women, and nearly everyone will get drunk. It is the custom. Outside the porters will sit cross-legged on the pavement, waiting by their chariots to drive the revellers home.

In the warm glow of that African evening, as he relaxes in one of the handsome chairs reserved for the highest-ranking guests (the rest sit on straw mats or cushions on the floor), Rekhmire cannot but think that this 15th century B.C. is a good one in which to live. The oil alabaster lamps will cast a flattering glow over the slim-waisted women, making their dark eyes sparkle and their jewelled bracelets and neck-laces dance with light. Even the furniture, gorgeously inlaid with gold and silver, red carnelian, and blue lapis-lazuli, will take on a breath-taking beauty. As long as there are evenings like this, life is worth living. And when he dies he will lie in a rock-cut tomb not far from the tombs of the pharaohs. He will rest in a handsome sarcophagus, and the priests will not neglect to bring food-offerings to him. Perhaps that is the greatest reward for the crushing weight of his office—an honoured place in the halls of the dead, and the assurance that the name Rekhmire will live forever.

SOURCE READINGS

(a)

HAMMURABI (1728-1686 B.C.) of Babylon gathered together and organized all the laws and customs of his lands into a code of over 300 laws. This code was cut in a stone shaft nearly eight feet high (see illustration on page 43) which was discovered in our own 20th century. Codes of earlier rulers have also been discovered, but Hammurabi's is the most famous.

6. If a man has stolen goods from a temple, or house, he shall be put to death; and he that has received the stolen property from him shall be put to death.

14. If a man has stolen a child, he shall be put to death.

25. If a fire has broken out in a man's house and one who has come to put it out has coveted the property of the householder and appropriated any of it, that man shall be cast into the self-same fire.

48. If a man has incurred a debt and a storm has flooded his field or carried away the crop, or the corn has not grown because of drought, in that year he shall not pay his creditor. Further, he shall post-date his bond and shall not pay interest for that year.

141. If a man's wife, living in her husband's house, has persisted in going out, has acted the fool, has wasted her house, has belittled her husband, he shall prosecute her. If her husband has said, "I divorce her," she shall go her way; he shall give her nothing as her price of divorce. If her husband has said, "I will not divorce her," he may take another woman to wife; the wife shall live as a slave in her husband's house.

195. If a son has struck his father, his hands shall be cut off.

196. If a man has knocked out the eye of a noble, his eye shall be knocked out.

198. If he has knocked out the eye of a freeman or has broken the limb of a freeman, he shall pay one mina of silver.

199. If he has knocked out the eye of a noble's servant, or broken the limb of a noble's servant, he shall pay half his value.

200. If a noble has knocked out the tooth of a man that is his equal, his tooth shall be knocked out.

218. If a surgeon has operated with the bronze lancet on a noble for a serious injury, and has caused his death, or has removed a cataract for a noble, with the bronze lancet, and has made him lose his eye, his hands shall be cut off.

229. If a builder has built a house for a man, and has not made his work sound, and the house he built has fallen, and caused the death of its owner, that builder shall be put to death.

G. H. Knoles and R. K. Snyder, editors, *Readings in Western Civilization* (J. B. Lippincott, revised edition, 1954), pp. 3-7, slightly adapted.

(b)

THE BOOK OF THE DEAD was a collection of magic spells which the Egyptians believed the soul could use in making its confession before Osiris, the god of the Nile, in the judgment hall of the dead. These "negative confessions" were composed about 1500 B.C.

1. I have not acted sinfully towards men.
2. I have not oppressed the members of my family.
3. I have not done wrong instead of what is right.
4. I have known no worthless folk.
8. I have not domineered over servants.
10. I have not filched the property of the lowly man.
12. I have not vilified a servant to his master.
13. I have not inflicted pain. . . .
14. I have not permitted any man to suffer hunger.
15. I have not made any man to weep.
16. I have not committed murder. . . .
17. I have not given an order to cause murder.
18. I have not made men and women to suffer calamities.
21. I have not carried off the cakes of the dead.
27. I have not added to the weights of the scales [to cheat the buyer].
30. I have not driven away the cattle from their pastures.
31. I have not snared the geese in the preserves of the gods.
34. I have not made a cutting in a canal of running water.
46. . . . I have not played the eavesdropper.
49. . . . I have not spoken treasonably about the king.

Knoles and Snyder, *Readings in Western Civilization,* pp. 26-27.

(c)

BUDDHA (567-487 B.C.) preached his first sermon in a park outside the city of Varanasi (modern Benares). It was delivered to five of his former associates who had left him in disgust when he gave up trying to find wisdom by practising self-denial, and outlines to them the enlightenment he had gained while sitting under a fig tree at Gaya. In the following extracts you will find three of Buddha's basic rules for living: the Noble Eightfold Path, the Middle Way, and the Four Noble Truths.

There are two ends not to be served by a wanderer. What are these two? The pursuit of desires and of the pleasure which springs from desire, which is base, common, leading to rebirth, ignoble, and unprofitable; and the pursuit of pain and hardship, which is grievous, ignoble, and unprofitable. The Middle Way of the Buddha avoids both these ends. It is enlightened, it brings clear vision, it makes for wisdom, and leads to peace, insight, enlightenment, and Nirvana. What is the Middle Way? . . . It is the Noble Eightfold Path—Right Views, Right Resolve, Right Speech, Right Conduct, Right Livelihood, Right Effort, Right Mindfulness, and Right Concentration. This is the Middle Way. . . .

And this is the Noble Truth of Sorrow. Birth is sorrow, age is sorrow, disease is sorrow, death is sorrow; contact with the unpleasant is sorrow, separation from the pleasant is sorrow, every wish unfulfilled is sorrow—in short all the five components of individuality are sorrow.

And this is the Noble Truth of the Arising of Sorrow. It arises from craving, which leads to rebirth, which brings delight and passion, and seeks pleasure now here, now there—the craving for sensual pleasure, the craving for continued life, the craving for power.

And this is the Noble Truth of the Stopping of Sorrow. It is the complete stopping of that craving, so that no passion remains, leaving it, being emancipated from it, being released from it, giving no place to it.

And this is the Noble Truth of the Way which leads to the Stopping of Sorrow. It is the Noble Eightfold Path—Right Views, Right Resolve, Right Speech, Right Conduct, Right Livelihood, Right Effort, Right Mindfulness, and Right Concentration.

W. T. de Bary, editor, *Introduction to Oriental Civilizations: Sources of Indian Tradition* (Columbia University Press, 1958), pp. 101-102, slightly adapted.

(d)

CONFUCIUS (551-479 B.C.) was not accepted as a great teacher during his lifetime, except by a small band of disciples. But slowly his teachings gained influence until, by the 2nd century B.C., Confucianism was declared the state creed of China, and all scholars and statesmen were expected to study it. The chief source of Confucian philosophy is the *Analects*, 20 chapters and 497 verses recording his activities and conversations. They were written after his death. Here are a few selections.

Confucius said: "The young are to be respected. How do we know that the next generation will not measure up to the present one? But if a man has reached forty or fifty and nothing has been heard of him, then I grant that he is not worthy of respect."

Someone inquired: "What do you think of 'requiting injury with kindness'?" Confucius said: "How will you then requite kindness? Requite injury with justice, and kindness with kindness."

Confucius said: "He who sins against Heaven has none to whom he can pray."

Confucius said: "Were any prince to employ me, even in a single year a good deal could be done, and in three years everything could be accomplished."

When Confucius was travelling to Wei, Jan Yu drove him. Confucius observed: "What a dense population!" Jan Yu said: "The people have grown so numerous, what next should be done for them?" "Enrich them," was the reply. "And when one has enriched them, what next should be done?" Confucius said: "Educate them."

Tzu Kung asked about government. Confucius said: "The essentials are sufficient food, sufficient troops, and the confidence of the people." Tzu Kung said: "Suppose you were forced to give up one of these three, which would you let go first?" Confucius said: "The troops." Tzu Kung asked again: "If you were forced to give up one of the two remaining, which would you let go?" Confucius said: "Food. For from of old, death has been the lot of all men, but a people without faith cannot survive."

Tzu Kung asked about the gentleman. Confucius said: "The gentleman first practises what he preaches and then preaches what he practises."

Tzu Lu asked about the worship of ghosts and spirits. Confucius said: "We don't know yet how to serve men, how can we know about serving the spirits?" "What about death?" was the next question. Confucius said: "We don't know yet about life, how can we know about death?"

Tzu Yu asked about filial piety. Confucius said: "Nowadays a filial son is just a man who keeps his parents in food. But even dogs or horses are given food. If there is no feeling of reverence, wherein lies the difference?"

Confucius said: "I won't teach a man who is not anxious to learn, and will not explain to one who is not trying to make things clear to himself. If I hold up one corner of a square and a man cannot come back to me with the other three, I won't bother to go over the point again."

Confucius said: "At fifteen, I set my heart on learning. At thirty, I was firmly established. At forty, I had no more doubts. At fifty, I knew the will of Heaven. At sixty, I was ready to listen to it. At seventy, I could follow my heart's desire without transgressing what was right."

W. T. de Bary, editor, *Introduction to Oriental Civilizations: Sources of Chinese Tradition* (Columbia University Press, 1960), pp. 22-35, slightly adapted.

BOOKS TO READ

1. GENERAL
    Milliken, E. K., *The Cradles of Western Civilization* (Harrap)
    Mills, D., *The Book of the Ancient World* (Putnam)
    White, A. T., *Lost Worlds: The Romance of Archaeology* (Random House)

2. MESOPOTAMIA
    Carrington, R., *Ancient Sumer* (Chatto and Windus)
    Chiera, E., *They Wrote on Clay* (Phoenix paperback)
    Cottrell, L., *Land of the Two Rivers* (World)
    Kramer, S. N., *History Begins at Sumer* (Anchor paperback)
    Pike, E. R., *Finding Out About the Babylonians* (Muller)

3. EGYPT
    Cottrell, L., *Land of the Pharaohs* (World)
    Green, R. L., *Ancient Egypt* (Weidenfeld and Nicolson)
    Mellersh, H. E. L., *Finding Out About Ancient Egypt* (Muller)
    Montet, P., *Everyday Life in Egypt in the Days of Ramesses the Great*
        (Arnold)
    Sheppard, E. J., *Ancient Egypt* (Longmans)
    White, J. M., *Everyday Life in Ancient Egypt* (Batsford)

4. INDIA, CHINA, AND JAPAN
    Battistini, L. H., *Introducing Asia* (John Day)
    Dilts, M. M., *The Pageant of Japanese History* (Longmans)
    Fitzgerald, C. P., *Finding Out About Imperial China* (Muller)
    Kidder, J. E., *Ancient Japan* (Weidenfeld and Nicolson)
    Pike, E. R., *Ancient India* (Weidenfeld and Nicolson)
    Spencer, C., *Ancient China* (Weidenfeld and Nicolson)

5. HISTORICAL FICTION
    Beck, L. A., *The Splendour of Asia* (Collins) [Buddha]
    Coolidge, O., *Egyptian Adventures* (Houghton) [twelve stories of life
        in ancient Egypt]
    Grant, J., *Winged Pharaoh* (Methuen) [First-dynasty Egypt]
    Morrison, L., *The Lost Queen of Egypt* (Lippincott) [wife of Tutankhamon]

CHAPTER 11

Assyria Crushes Her Neighbours

Nineveh is laid waste: who will bemoan her? . . . For against whom has not her malice continually gone forth?

NAHUM 3: 7, 19

Anyone who reads the newspapers of the second half of the 20th century must be aware of the importance of the area called the Middle East. The modern states of Israel, Lebanon, Jordan, Iraq, Iran, Egypt, and Syria are in the headlines regularly.

If there had been newspapers in the Iron Age, the same areas would have made front-page news. But they would have had different names: they were called Assyria and Persia then. Occasionally, too, buried back in the inner pages, you might have found a brief dispatch dealing with another people, the Hebrews. Let us turn back three thousand years and find out what these nations did to make themselves newsworthy.

On the upper Tigris River, in the north-east corner of the Fertile Crescent 300 miles north of Babylon, lies a triangular rolling plateau of land which for centuries was a prey to invaders. As early as 3000 B.C. one of the first invading forces, the ancestors of the Assyrians, settled down on the banks of the Tigris River to form the city-state of Ashur. Ashur was in a strategic position: it could hold up caravans and command the great east-west highway along the Crescent. Only constant warfare or constant preparedness for warfare could hold this bridge-head. From it the ambitious Assyrians could strike out against their neighbours such as the Babylonians, and in 1247 B.C. they sacked and razed to the ground the ancient city of Babylon.

Assyria was getting ready to step on to the stage of world politics, and the times were ripe for her. For by 1200 B.C. the power situation in

---

Lion-fighting for the Assyrian kings, like bull-fighting for the Cretans, was a ritual, a kind of compulsory ceremony in which the king of men killed the king of beasts. This limestone carving from Nineveh shows Ashurbanipal tackling a lion released for the royal sport. It has been said that Assyrian art reached its highest expression in scenes of bloodshed—particularly, it might be added, when the blood shed was that of a wounded animal.

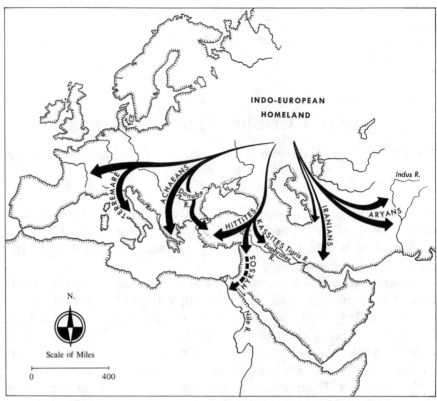

Indo-European Homeland

Indus R.

ACHAEANS

Danube R.

TERREMARE

HITTITES

KASSITES

Tigris R.

Euphrates R.

IRANIANS

ARYANS

HYKSOS

Nile R.

N.

Scale of Miles

0   400

BRONZE AGE INVASIONS (2000-1500 B.C.)

the Middle East had altered drastically. How had this happened, and what were the results?

❖ *A Valuable Secret*   The most important change in the Middle Eastern picture, as far as Assyria was concerned, was that by 1200 both the Kassites and the Hittites had suffered the fate they had inflicted on others when they went down before stronger forces. The fall of the Hittites was especially important, since it was largely responsible for the spread of the Iron Age. Before 1200 B.C. the Hittites had enjoyed a monopoly of iron. They had tried to keep the knowledge of smelting and forging this crucial metal a secret, and valued their iron so highly that on one occasion they suggested to the Egyptians that a fair purchase price for it would be an equal weight of gold! By 1200, however, the Hittites were no longer able to monopolize either the process or the iron ores. The secret was out.

As the Hittite power dwindled, another great empire was also passing away. Egypt was slipping into a decline, and the eclipse of these two mighty empires provided a lull of three centuries during which a number of small independent nations could prosper. Two in particular are worth noting.

❖ *Enduring Exports* First there were the Phoenicians. The Greek word *phoinix* means "red," so that Phoenicians really means "red men." This name does not refer to their skin colour but to their most celebrated product, a deep red or purple dye. The Phoenicians lived on a narrow strip of coast about 100 miles long and 30 miles wide at the eastern end of the Mediterranean. From this meagre coastline they took to the sea with a will, spreading their sails from such ports as Gebal, Beyrut, Sidon, and Tyre, founding trading stations along their routes, and exploring the Atlantic coasts of Europe and Africa—even getting as far as Britain in their search for tin.

THE DEVELOPMENT OF THE ALPHABET

1. Egyptian hieroglyphs for *aleph* (ox), *beth* (house), *nun* (snake) 2. Sinaitic			3. Canaanite 4. Phoenician	5. Archaic Greek 6. Latin alphabet	
1.	2.	3.	4.	5.	6.

As with many other trading nations in history, the Phoenicians were not so much innovators as imitators, carriers of other peoples' civilizations. In their ships the ideas of the entire Middle East were borne to Greece, Italy, Spain, and North Africa. There is, however, one original creation of theirs from which we have greatly benefited: their alphabet. The Phoenicians began by using a primitive Egyptian hieroglyphic "alphabet," and went on to work out a true alphabet of their own with twenty-two letters, all consonants.

This alphabet was a vast improvement over the older methods of writing. The cuneiform, hieroglyphic, and Minoan scripts (see page 135)

The Phoenician alphabet

were all *syllabic,* that is, the individual signs represented syllables rather than single letters. Consequently there had to be literally hundreds of signs—as many as the language had syllables. The new Phoenician alphabet, on the other hand, could express all the syllables and all the words with a scant twenty-two letters. No longer did businessmen need the services of specially trained scribes, nor rulers have to depend on a whole scribal class who jealously guarded their learning and their privileged position within the state. Henceforth almost anyone could, with a little instruction and practice, learn to read and write. By 850 B.C. Greek merchants in Cyprus or Syria had taken over the Phoenician alphabet and added vowels. From the Greeks it passed to the Romans, and so to us. The fact that you can now read these words is your greatest debt to the nomads of the sea, the Phoenicians.

The Aramaeans
The second people we will mention are the inhabitants of another small trading nation to the east of the Phoenicians, the Aramaeans. From their chief city, Damascus, long strings of camels plodded to the bazaars of the Middle East, exporting something infinitely more enduring than bundles of wares. For the Aramaeans adopted the Phoenician alphabet, and passed it on to the Hebrews, Persians, Arabians, and other Asians. Along with these letters they passed on their own language, with the result that Aramaic became a standard tongue in the Middle East and displaced Babylonian as the language of diplomacy.

On these small nations, enjoying a brief Indian summer after the season of great empires, the chilling Assyrian wind was soon to blow.

❖ *Building an Empire* The first Assyrian king to bring order out of chaos by systematically defeating his neighbours was Tiglath-pileser I (1114-1076 B.C.). Here was a man of action. He chased sharks, hunted lions, and conquered cities, nay, states, forty-two of them—or so he boasts in his records. But with his death Assyria's rise to power was temporarily stalled. It would take another 350 years for her to reach her peak.

Tiglath-pileser III
The Assyrian Empire was really founded by Tiglath-pileser III (745-727 B.C.), who made himself king of Babylon and reduced the Hebrews to vassalage. It was Tiglath-pileser III who began the Assyrian practice of deporting rebellious peoples to other parts of his empire: in the next twenty-five years over 200,000 captives were to suffer this fate. Sargon II (722-705 B.C.) went on to crush the petty Palestinian kingdoms, as did his successor Sennacherib (705-681 B.C.). Sennacherib besieged Jerusalem in 701 B.C., and twelve years later shocked

his world by annihilating the proud old city of Babylon and sowing the site with salt.

The kings of Palestine tried to protect their tiny country by playing off Egypt against Assyria, a policy that only egged on the Assyrians to greater conquests. Sennacherib's son, Esarhaddon (681-669 B.C.), invaded Egypt, and surprisingly enough rebuilt the Babylon his father had destroyed. It was under Ashurbanipal (669-633 B.C.) that the Assyrian Empire achieved its greatest extent when it stretched from Babylon to Thebes.

Finally, despite all her ferocity, Assyria lost control of her empire. In the summer of 612 B.C. the New Babylonians, or Chaldeans as they came to be called, succeeded in destroying the Assyrian capital of Nineveh. "I turned the hostile land into heaps and ruins," writes the Babylonian king. Archaeologists can still poke in the ash heaps and calcined sculptures which bear evidence as to how completely the great city was destroyed. None of the surviving records mourn its passing.

❖ *A Policy of Terror* Assyria organized the most powerful military machine the world had yet known. The army was a model of its kind, armed with bows, pikes, and swords, while iron-tipped battering-rams and siege towers on wheels pummelled enemy cities. How terrified the inhabitants of a city must have been to see the Assyrians pitch camp outside their walls! The Assyrian reputation for ruthlessness preceded them, and their chroniclers seemed to delight in describing the treatment meted out to a conquered city.

I slew one of every two. I built a wall before the great gates of the city; I flayed the chief men of the rebels, and I covered the wall with their skins. Some of them were enclosed alive within the bricks of the wall, some of them were crucified with stakes along the wall; I caused a great multitude of them to be flayed in my presence, and I covered the walls with their skins.

Probably the Assyrians purposely exaggerated their country's reputation for frightfulness in the interests of propaganda. They believed that terror would squelch revolts in the empire. Moreover Ashur, the national god, ordered his representative the king to begin these wars, and was pleased with profuse bloodshed on his behalf.

As might be expected, the Assyrian government was a military despotism. Even so, the inhabitants of the various city-states had self-rule, and the middle class of city-dwellers (bankers, merchants, carpenters, weavers, and metal-workers) was usually exempt from military service. Some of the slaves captured in warfare were employed in government *Assyrian government and society*

This Assyrian spearman, like the archer Dagan in the *Daily Life,* is a member of one of the first armies to be extensively equipped with iron. It was, in fact, the abundance of iron ore in the mountains of northern Mesopotamia that allowed the Assyrian kings to provide weapons for such large armies—virtually the entire male population in time of emergency.

building projects and fared no better than those who sweated on the Egyptian pyramids. Many, however, were employed in handicraft industries, in which case they lived a life little worse than the agricultural serfs. Not that the lot of these serfs was enviable. They were forced to hand over part of their produce and to work on the crown lands or to serve in the army.

❖*Preservers of Culture* It may surprise you to learn that, despite their brutality, the Assyrians were preservers of culture. Their military annals are important literary and historical works, and their great royal libraries show how much they valued education. Indeed the most cruel of the Assyrian kings, Ashurbanipal, had such a genuine interest in culture that his reign marks the golden age of Assyrian art and literature. Under him a huge library was set up at Nineveh—although it is true much of its contents consisted of copies of Babylonian cuneiform tablets rather than original Assyrian literature. From this library alone 22,000 tablets have been recovered.

It was in the palace of Ashurbanipal that Assyrian art reached its *Art* highest point of development. The portrayal of the lion-hunt in bas-relief there (which you may see in the photograph on page 94) excelled all earlier works in the faithfulness with which it copied every little detail of this cruel royal sport. To begin with, Assyrian art was little more than an imitation of Babylonian art. But its animal sculptures developed in vividness and realism until they were bursting with life. Artists were unable to equal them until the days of the Roman Empire.

In science, these ingenious people combined fact with superstition. *Science* Although astronomers made systematic reports of observations to the court it was mostly for astrological purposes, and it was the practice to examine the livers of sacrificial goats or sheep in order to foretell the future. As might be expected in a civilization that put great stock in a healthy army, the use of medicines was increased. Over 500 drugs were catalogued—including 11 to cure the effects of drunkenness, which medical opinion considered to be a form of poisoning.

Although the Assyrians modelled their religion on that of Babylon, *Religion* they placed their god Ashur above all others. Unlike most Orientals they did not respect other peoples' gods, and even went so far as to carry off the idols of foreign gods as booty.

In many ways, then, Assyrian civilization may be characterized as more than a brutal militarism, and despite all their inhumanity the Assyrians contributed to the progress of mankind. They succeeded, to a greater extent than any power before, in uniting the city-states and tribes of the Fertile Crescent and giving that region a larger measure of order and prosperity than it had ever enjoyed before. The success of their empire was short-lived because its methods were too harsh. Nevertheless it served as a model for a more gifted and humane people, the Persians.

❖ *Marble Magnificence* When Assyria fell in 612 B.C. the balance of power in the Middle East was destroyed. New Babylonia and Egypt now vied for the role of leader, until in 605 B.C. New Babylonia (that is, the Chaldean Empire) came out the victor when her king, Nebuchad-rezzar, or Nebuchadnezzar as he is sometimes called, decisively defeated

Egypt at Carchemish. Now the Babylonian king took over Assyria's former position of power. In due course all Syria and Palestine fell to him, as is well known from the Biblical story of the captivity of the Jews in Babylon. The magnificence of that ancient capital must have dazzled its rustic Jewish captives as they walked along the streets paved with marble and gazed in awe at the three- and four-storey houses, the imposing temples and palaces, the city walls 85 feet thick. Nebuchadrezzar was surely a masterly builder.

The new lords of the East had some fairly advanced scientific accomplishments to their credit. Chaldean mathematics was sufficiently developed to allow more exact astronomical calculations than had been possible under Old Babylonian science. The lunar calendar was brought into agreement with the solar year, and accurate observation and prediction of eclipses was undertaken. Yet astrology, even if a more refined form than that of the Assyrians, still went hand in hand with astronomy. When we "thank our lucky stars" we are reverting to a superstition as old as the Babylonian civilization.

Babylonia's bid for power was, however, destined to be brief. Nebuchadrezzar's successors were weak men, and in 539 B.C. the gorgeous capital fell to the mightiest conquerors the world had yet seen, the Persians.

CHAPTER 12

The Persian Empire

All the inhabitants of Babylon as well as the entire land of Sumer and Akkad, princes and governors included, bowed to Cyrus and kissed his feet, jubilant and with shining faces. . . . Happily they greeted him as the master by whose help they had come back to life out of death and had been spared disaster, and they worshipped his very name.

CYRUS THE GREAT

During the Bronze Age, Indo-Europeans known as Iranians had begun to move southward and eastward from the Caspian Steppes. By the 9th century B.C. these invaders had split into two groups, the Medes and the Persians. The Medes established an empire in what is today Iran, with a captial at Ecbatana (modern Hamadan), while their subjects the Persians made their home in south Media east of the Persian Gulf.

But the subjects were not to remain underdogs forever. A local *Cyrus* prince, Cyrus of Anshan, united these Persian tribes and led them against *the Great* Media in 549 B.C. Nor did he stop there. He went on to defeat the fabulously rich Croesus of Lydia in western Asia Minor, a victory that ultimately brought the Persians face to face with the Greeks. Then he looked covetously at the Chaldean Empire.

For the Babylonians the handwriting on the wall was all too plain: "The kingdom is divided, and given to the Medes and Persians" (*Daniel* 6: 28). Cyrus could boast that Babylon fell "without fighting a battle." In twenty years Cyrus the Great (549-529 B.C.) had conquered the civilized world from the Indus to the Dardanelles, from central Asia to the borders of Egypt.

❖ *A Strange Conqueror*   The conqueror behaved strangely. There were no deportations. Cities were not destroyed. A subject people was not deprived of its religion, and the Jewish exiles were even allowed to return from Babylon to Jerusalem. Cyrus had the good sense and shrewd statesmanship to mobilize all his propaganda and put himself forward to the conquered Babylonians first as "king of Babylon," and only then *Darius I* as "king of the lands." When Cambyses II (529-522 B.C.) succeeded his father, he managed to annex Egypt to the empire. Cambyses died, however, on his way back to Persia, whereupon the throne was seized by the gifted Darius I (521-486 B.C.).

First of all Darius the Great had to suppress a series of revolts—and in this he, too, was capable of cruelty. Then he mounted new offensives to extend the Persian Empire both east and west, and he is chiefly remembered today as the would-be conqueror of the Greeks. But it is his efficient administration that ought to be his main claim to fame. He issued a law code, established a system of uniform weights and measures and an imperial currency, completed a canal connecting the Nile and the Red Sea, and even built a fleet that sailed down the Indus to the Indian Ocean and thence on a two-and-a-half-year voyage to Egypt. Under Darius, Aramaic became the international language of diplomacy and commerce.

When this powerful Persian ruler decided to build a royal palace at

In the immense royal palace at Persepolis (begun by Darius I in 512 B.C.) the Persians, with their plentiful supply of limestone, made striking use of graceful columns. Sculptural reliefs along the grand stairway (foot of page) portray a stately procession of representatives from the vast Empire at a New Year's festival, their crisply chiselled details exhibiting a dignity and courtliness in sharp contrast to the dynamic realism of Assyrian art. Darius's majestic palace graced Persepolis until the city was captured and partly destroyed by Alexander the Great in 330 B.C.

one of his capitals, Susa, he determined to impress the whole world. For this purpose he summoned the varied resources of his vast empire:

The cedar timber was brought from a mountain called Lebanon. The Assyrians brought it to Babylon; from Babylon the Carians and the Ionians brought it to Susa. The yaka wood was brought from Gandara and from Carmania. The gold wrought here was brought from Sardis and from Bactria. The precious stone wrought here, lapis lazuli and carnelian, was brought from Sogdiana. The turquoise wrought here was brought from Chorasmia. The silver and the ebony were brought from Egypt. The ornamentation with which the wall was adorned was brought from Ionia. The ivory wrought here was brought from Ethiopia and from Sind and from Arachosia. The stone columns wrought here were brought from a village called Abiradu, in Elam.

The stone-cutters who wrought the stone were Ionians and Sardians. The goldsmiths who wrought the gold were Medes and Egyptians. The men who wrought the wood were Sardians and Egyptians. The men who wrought the baked brick were Babylonians. The men who adorned the wall were Medes and Egyptians.

Over this "community of nations" presided Darius, one of the greatest organizers of history. At his death his empire stretched from India to Macedon—about as far from east to west as from Toronto to Vancouver. This "King of Kings" immortalized his achievements in an impressive inscription, some extracts from which are in the Source Reading on page 129. The ancient Middle East had come to Europe.

❖ *An Able Administration* The Persians made two outstanding contributions to the ancient world: the organization of their empire, and their religion. Both of these contributions have had considerable influence on our western world. The system of imperial administration was inherited by Alexander the Great, adopted by the Roman Empire, and eventually bequeathed to modern Europe. The Zoroastrian religion passed on much to the Hebrews and, through them, to Christianity.

In their empire, the Persians turned the conquered kingdoms into provinces (*satrapies*), each under a governor (*satrap*). They were both wise and benevolent rulers, and the distinction between a ruling and a conquered people was gradually reduced so that a unified empire of many nationalities was built up. Excellent roads enabled the Persian king to keep in close touch with his extensive empire, and an imperial postal system was operated which was so dependable in its service that a Greek wrote: "Neither snow nor rain nor heat nor gloom of night stays these couriers from the swift completion of their appointed rounds." Roads were so good that there could be communication between Sardis and Susa (a distance of 1500 miles) in one to two weeks. Over these roads could also travel the king's agents—"the eyes and ears of the king"—to report lapses of duty on the part of his satraps.

The widely scattered Persian society was held together by its remarkable army. The archers were drawn from the peasantry; the cavalry was formed by the nobles (who could afford horses). War for the Persians entailed an all-out effort, and when it was declared all able-bodied males between the ages of fifteen and fifty were drafted. There was even a story—and it may be no more than that—of a father of three sons who petitioned the king to exempt one of them from military service. All three were executed.

Persian society

The fate of Persia's conquered peoples presents a marked contrast to that suffered by Assyria's. The private life of the citizens of the empire was not dislocated by the conquests because the separate satrapies were allowed to retain their own language and religion. Moreover, the Persian kings willingly adopted the royal style of the conquered peoples: in

COMPARATIVE EMPIRES

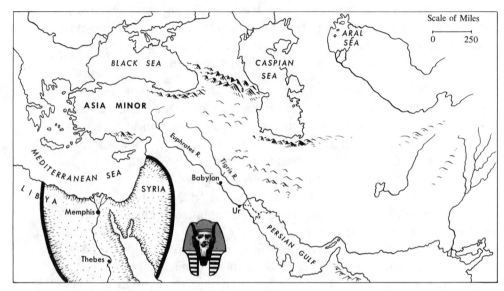

EGYPTIAN NEW KINGDOM (about 1400 B.C.)

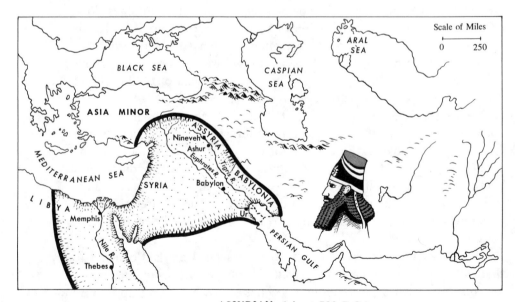

ASSYRIAN (about 700 B.C.)

COMPARATIVE EMPIRES

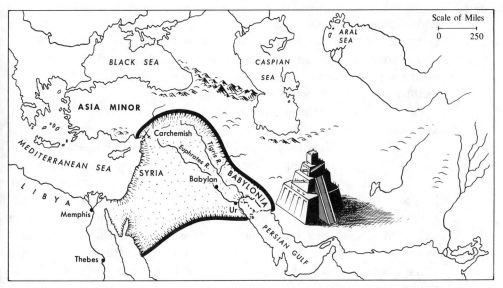

BABYLONIAN (about 550 B.C.)

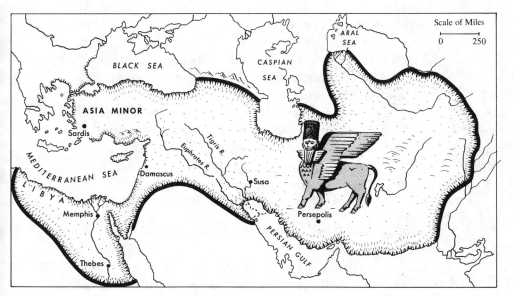

PERSIAN (about 500 B.C.)

Babylon the god Marduk ordained the Persian king; in Egypt the alien monarch became the son of Re.

Products of empire
Naturally such a vast empire boasted a wide variety of products. Fruits and vegetables, wheat and barley were cultivated in the fertile valleys and oases. Irrigation of small areas was practised (our word "paradise" comes from the Persian word meaning "a well kept park"), and in the northern plains horses, cattle, goats, and sheep were raised. Mining and metal-working were both important industries.

Of course the provinces were taxed; but it was not a burdensome tax, and various districts had greater opportunities to develop themselves economically because they enjoyed the benefits of the steady administration and open communications of the empire. The introduction of a uniform coinage and a uniform system of weights and measures also proved a great boon to their development. Eventually the fact that local authorities were thus encouraged to run their own economic affairs, as well as the decrease in the number of native Persians in the army, tended to disrupt the empire. Even so it lasted for two centuries; and then it succumbed, not because its peoples rebelled, but because a world conqueror overcame it.

❖ *Light versus Darkness* In the towering Behistun inscription (see page 129) Darius wrote these words: "On this account Ahura-Mazda brought me help . . . because I was not wicked, nor was I a liar, nor was I a tyrant, neither I nor any of my line. I have ruled according to righteousness." Who was this Ahura-Mazda who demanded righteous living of his followers, and who was in large measure responsible for the justice and humanity of Persian government?

Zoro-astrianism
To begin with, Persian religion, like other Semitic polytheisms, was full of primitive deities and sacrificial ritual. Then in the 6th century B.C. a prophet called Zoroaster rebelled against such practices.

> The false gods, have they been good masters?—
> I ask it of those who, in their worship,
> Behold the sacrificer and his attendant deliver the
> ox to fury;
> And the chief magician cause him to yield up his life
> with groans . . .

Zoroaster proclaimed a new and noble doctrine, one quite different from and far superior to any which had preceded it. He said that there was only one god, Ahura-Mazda (Ahura = lord, Mazda = wise), the lord of all knowledge and the creator of the world. Ahura-Mazda required of man not ritual or sacrifice (Zoroaster allowed neither temples nor idols), but assistance in the constant struggle against evil by righteous living and pure thought. Life was a battleground against evil, which was personified in Ahriman, the principle of evil and darkness. It was Ahriman who had created all the plagues of life—serpents, vermin, locusts, winter, darkness, crime, and sin. The man who fought the good fight faithfully and lived a life of piety and truth need not fear death, for he would escape the punishments of purgatory or hell which unfortunate sinners must endure, and be finally rewarded for his service to Ahura-Mazda. The day of the Last Judgment would see the triumph of righteousness and the resurrection of the dead.

Zoroaster was one of the greatest of all religious prophets, but his religion, this brightest star of the Persians, was destined to fade. Most branches deteriorated into polytheism and finally succumbed to Islam (see pages 362-366), although during the 8th century A.D. tiny groups of faithful Zoroastrians fled to India, where their descendants are known today as Parsees. Nevertheless, we can still trace the Zoroastrian influence on another great monotheism. The mighty drama of a struggle between good and evil, light and darkness, deeply affected Jewish thought.

CHAPTER 13

The Hebrews and Their God

Israel is a hunted sheep driven away by lions. First the king of Assyria devoured him, and now at last Nebuchadrezzar king of Babylon has gnawed his bones.

JEREMIAH 50: 17

Thus says the Lord, your Redeemer . . . of Cyrus, "He is my shepherd. . . ."

ISAIAH 44: 24, 28

At one end of the Fertile Crescent, in an area called Palestine, a rather insignificant band of nomads took up an uncertain abode. This small land found itself straddling a great highway for military conquest, trade, and the transmission of ideas. Caught in the currents of strife between ambitious neighbours, Palestine was often able to win an uneasy truce by balancing these powers off against one another. But never was she able

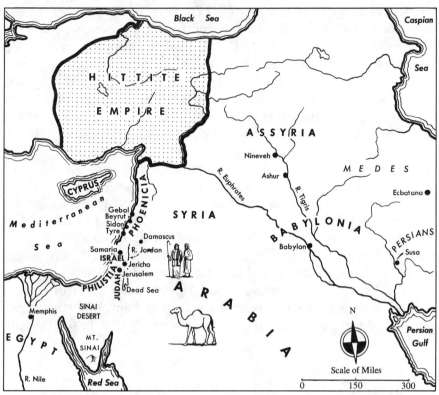

ANCIENT PALESTINE AND HER NEIGHBOURS

to maintain any prolonged political independence. First one power, then another, crushed her, until Egyptian, Babylonian, and Persian elements all became blended into her civilization.

The land of Palestine, in ancient times an area 400 miles long and 80 miles wide, had no fewer than forty different climatic and geographic units. This great variety of environments produced many tribes, and a marked division both in culture and ideals between the wandering hill people and the settled dwellers of the plains.

❖ *A Band of Nomads*   From the 20th century B.C. a group of people called *Habiru* or *Hapiru* (meaning "nomad" or "bandit" in Babylonian) are mentioned in Middle Eastern documents. Some of these were probably the Hebrews, who seem to have come out of the general area of Ur and who lived for a time in the north-west section of the Babylonian Empire. Eventually a group came to inhabit the land called Canaan or Palestine. What was their society like?

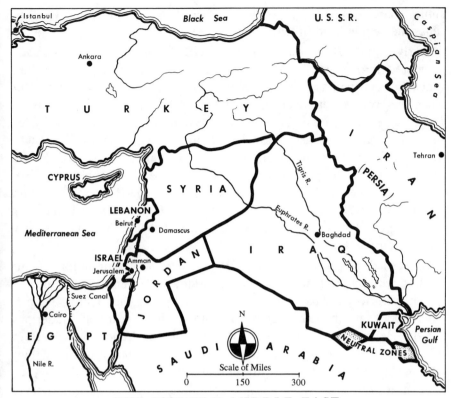

THE MODERN MIDDLE EAST

A vivid picture of a Hebrew band of metal-workers has been found on the wall of an Egyptian tomb of about 1900 B.C. Both men and women wear woollen tunics, and they carry the tools and baggage of their profession: simple weapons, a lyre, and bellows. Donkeys are their beasts of burden, for the camel was not domesticated for another eight centuries.

Abraham and his people

Although these Hebrews visited Egypt a century before the time of Abraham (1800-1750 B.C.), they probably looked and dressed much like later generations of Palestinian nomads. Abraham was a patriarch, that is, the ruler of his family group or closely-knit tribe. He and his family lived a frugal and insecure life among other bands of roving shepherds, always seeking out new grasslands, always on the move. No wonder there are so many references in the Old Testament to green pastures and still waters! As time went on and the Hebrews settled in Palestine, the tribal chiefs came to live in fortresses, to which their subjects could come in the winter or when danger threatened. At other times the people lived in tents or huts.

The Exodus Early in the 17th or late 16th century B.C. a group of these nomads wandered into Egypt. This was at the time the Hyksos were ruling that land, and perhaps Joseph became an administrator for them. But when the Hyksos were overthrown the lot of foreigners in Egypt was no longer an enviable one. They were enslaved and forced to work under brutal overseers. At last one of the Hebrews' own people was brought up by an Egyptian princess in the court. His name was Moses. Moses finally was able to persuade the pharaoh to let his people go. But Pharaoh changed his mind and sent soldiers after the Hebrews. The Old Testament vividly describes how the fleeing Hebrews made good their escape or *exodus* by the miraculous crossing of the Red Sea in the early 13th century B.C.

Moses led his people to Mount Sinai. There he withdrew for a communion with his God, and finally brought down the Ten Commandments which were to be a pattern of righteous living for the Hebrew people. Thereupon, says the Old Testament, followed forty years of wanderings for the Hebrews in their search for the Promised Land, forty years in which the rigorous desert life hardened them and prepared them for their conquest of a "land flowing with milk and honey."

At last they were ready, and the Hebrew tribes, some 6000-7000 strong, invaded Palestine a second time.

❖ *A Dynasty and a Temple*　The Hebrews had reached their Promised Land—but they had to wrest it from its inhabitants. And so they stormed Jericho under Joshua and the walls fell down, possibly because of an earthquake. This second Hebrew conquest of Palestine was a long drawn-out affair. Indeed, it may have gone on for from two to four centuries, the confusing years celebrated in the Old Testament books of *Joshua* and *Judges* when "there was no king in Israel; every man did what was right in his own eyes." The Hebrews swept down from the hills into the plains inhabited by the Canaanites, gaining control of the land by slow infiltration and intermarriage as well as by military conquest.

Yahweh But the new, soft life corrupted the rugged individualism of the hardy desert tribes. As time went on they adopted laws and local customs from neighbouring peoples. Elders dispensed justice by the town gate, and many even forgot their desert God and worshipped the local divinities of the towns called *Baals*. Not so in the back country. In the hills and on the frontier the desert ideals were preserved, and the Hebrews were still faithful to their God *Yahweh*.

Now that the Canaanite power had collapsed in Palestine, the Philistines and other "Peoples of the Sea" who had earlier been turned back at the Nile Delta saw their opportunity to invade the country. This danger forced a national unity on the Hebrews. They needed a capable military commander, and so they chose a king, Saul (1020-1005 B.C.), to lead them in war against the invading Philistines. Under Saul the nucleus of a standing army was formed, and the usual weapons seem to have been javelins, darts, and slings—as who that reads of David's encounter with Goliath can forget! Saul did not, however, succeed in building up a strong central government or in preventing the many tribes from warring amongst themselves. *Saul*

David was a shepherd boy who became such a successful warrior that he was made Saul's military chieftain. But the moody, insecure king became so jealous of David's growing popularity that he committed suicide after a Philistine defeat. The throne then passed to David, who, succeeding where Saul had failed, managed to weld the tribes into a permanent nation and to found a dynasty which ruled for over four hundred years. Jerusalem was made the national capital of a united Israel. *David*

Few men have been more fortunate than David. His rise to power about the year 1000 B.C. coincided with the decline of the Middle Eastern kingdoms. David inherited the advantages of this political power vacuum, which gave him and his successor Solomon much needed time to build up an administration. Power was centralized. Population increased, and about four hundred towns were joined together in a national federation. The army was made into a professional body under the king's command, and the chariot was introduced as an engine of war.

But the passionate, unpredictable king died before all his projects could be completed. It was his son Solomon (965-925 B.C.) who pushed David's plans to their ultimate realization. *Solomon*

Solomon's most famous work was the Temple, which made Jerusalem the religious as well as the political heart of Israel. Craftsmen from Phoenicia, great imports of wood, forced labour, crushing taxes—all were necessary to build the Temple. Trade boomed. Solomon's ships and caravans could be seen throughout Egypt or in the land of the Queen of Sheba in southern Arabia. Solomon married foreign princesses and established altars for the deities of his alien wives. He was a sort of sultan, surrounded by opulence.

Solomon in all his glory impoverished his country so that he might
live in luxury. His very drinking vessels were of gold: "none were of
silver; it was not considered as anything in the days of Solomon." Under
Solomon's son the kingdom split: Jerusalem was thenceforth the capital
of a southern kingdom, Judah, while Samaria became the capital of a
northern kingdom called Israel.

Now, about the middle of the 9th century B.C., Assyria moved in to
decide the political fate of the two Hebrew kingdoms. When she reduced
both states to vassalage Hebrew intrigues began (as we have noted)
with other Assyrian satellites—now Egypt, now Babylonia—to throw off
the foreign yoke. Finally a coalition of Middle Eastern states destroyed
first the Assyrian, then the Egyptian power. But the Hebrews were still
at the mercy of their neighbours. The crowning disaster came when
Nebuchadrezzar, the Babylonian, shipped off approximately one-third
of the population of Judah (mostly artisans and the ruling class) to
exile in Babylon in 597 B.C.

The two Hebrew kingdoms were at an end.

❖ *A Nation Apart*   As years went by and two generations of Hebrews
lived in exile, they gradually settled into an influential role in the Babylonian economy. At the same time, back in Judah chaos reigned, and
the old religion of Moses and the prophets dropped into disuse. There
the whole story of the Hebrews might have ended—but it did not. The
exiles ought to have been completely assimilated into the attractive
Babylonian culture—but they were not. A small remnant remembered
Moses and studied the prophets, and gave expression to their longing for
the homeland in the Biblical books of *Ezekiel* and *Isaiah*. The faithful
in Babylon still congregated to worship and be instructed in religious
traditions, probably in synagogues (the Greek word *synagogue* means a
"bringing together"). Stubbornly they kept themselves apart. They
did not intermarry with their captors. Above all they did not forget
their homeland, as Psalm 137 poignantly shows.

By the waters of Babylon,
  there we sat down and wept,
  when we remembered Zion.

On the willows there
  we hung up our lyres.
For there our captors
  required of us songs,
and our tormentors, mirth, saying,
  "Sing us one of the songs of Zion!"

How shall we sing Yahweh's song
  in a foreign land?
If I forget you, O Jerusalem,
  let my right hand wither!
Let my tongue cleave to the roof
  of my mouth,
  if I do not remember you,
if I do not set Jerusalem
  above my highest joy!

Thus it came about that when the New Babylonian Empire fell, and Cyrus of Persia issued an edict of liberation about 538 B.C. giving some of the Hebrews permission to return to Jerusalem to rebuild their Temple, a small group straggled back to the Persian province of Judaea.

These Judaeans, or Jews as they were henceforth known, had a long uphill struggle to re-establish their community. During this unsettled time two institutions became very important to them: their priesthood and their Law. The high priest became the real leader of the nation, and the Law of Moses was elevated to a supreme position. Thus the Jews and their religion were inseparable. They had become, as they termed it, a "nation of priests."

❖ *Religious Geniuses* The religious records of this "nation of priests" form a remarkable heritage, for the Hebrews were both literary and religious geniuses. Their *Old Testament* consists of a whole library of books—history, proverbs, songs, prophecy—composed in Hebrew between the 10th and 2nd centuries B.C. The name Old Testament was invented by Christian scholars of the 3rd century A.D. when they compiled an additional collection of books which they called the *New Testament*.

The Old Testament

The oldest Hebrew manuscript of the entire Old Testament dates only from the 10th century A.D. But there are much older manuscripts of individual parts of it. In 1947 biblical scholars around the world were electrified by the discovery of the "Dead Sea Scrolls," scrolls found in a cave in Palestine overlooking the Dead Sea. They were unrolled with great care, and from their script and an examination of the cave and the pottery jars in which they were sealed, experts have concluded that these scrolls must be earlier than the middle decades of the 1st century B.C. The most impressive of them is a complete Hebrew text of *Isaiah,* which has been dated in the second half of the 2nd century B.C.

❖ *God's Chosen People* Let us trace the steps by which the Hebrews developed the loftiest monotheism of all time. During the wanderings in the desert, Moses had had an experience which convinced his people that they had been granted a direct personal encounter with God. Moses met Yahweh on Mount Sinai, and this exalted experience was sealed by the Covenant, a sort of contractual agreement. It was not the first agreement the Hebrews had made with their God. Back in the time of the desert wanderings Abraham had made a pact with his God that the tribe would give him their exclusive obedience and trust in

The Covenant

This is the majestic and awesome peak which tradition says was Mount Sinai. On this mountain, according to the book of *Exodus,* Moses received the Ten Commandments from God. Doubtless the shepherd in the foreground looks much like the Hebrews who entered into the Covenant here 3200 years ago.

return for his favour. Now, by the Covenant, the whole of Israel vowed to become God's chosen people.

And Moses went up to God, and the Lord called him out of the mountain, saying, "Thus you shall say to the house of Jacob, and tell the people of Israel: You have seen what I did to the Egyptians, and how I bore you on eagles' wings and brought you to myself. Now therefore, if you will obey my voice and keep my covenant, you shall be my own possession among all peoples; for all the earth is mine, and you shall be to me a kingdom of priests and a holy nation. These are the words which you shall speak to the children of Israel."

The Laws   Moses passed on to his followers a new concept of God. Perhaps he even brought with him from Mount Sinai some sacred stones which, enclosed in a wooden coffer called the Ark, represented the presence of the new God on the field of battle, or in the temple or tent that sheltered the Ark. At any rate he brought down from the mountain the Laws, which are recorded in *Exodus*, chapters 21, 22, and 23. In them, the Hebrews adapted the customs of other peoples and refined them for their own use. The fact that this law was associated with the dictates of a living God gave it a divine as well as a human authority.

As you already know, the absolute authority of Yahweh was soon to be challenged by false gods. When the Hebrew tribes came to Canaan they encountered the Baals of a religion based on nature worship. Many went over to Baal worship, or in some way practised it and associated the various festivals with Yahweh. But the old faith of the desert would brook no compromise with mere nature gods. When King Ahab of Israel (869-850 B.C.) and his queen Jezebel fostered Baal worship, Elijah summoned the Israelites to Mount Carmel and there bested the "four hundred and fifty" prophets of Baal, proving the superiority of his God by slaying all the false prophets.

Yet if Yahweh could speak to Elijah out of the fire, he could also call him with "a still small voice." Gradually the Hebrews were spiritualizing Yahweh through their experiences with him. Probably the fact that they had lost their Ark to the Philistines in battle and it had eventually been returned minus its sacred stones had encouraged them to think of Yahweh as a holy spirit quite apart from any material image.

❖ *Watchmen of Yahweh*   Times were hard for the lower classes after the days of Solomon. When the rate of interest rose to 25% in rich and powerful Assyria, how much must money-lenders have charged in the poor country of Israel? But no matter how the peasants and artisans suffered, the kings seem to have been powerless to effect sweeping social changes.

Under such conditions, strange ecstatic men who heard voices and saw visions began to feel it was their duty to be the conscience of the Hebrew people, to fearlessly point out to them and their kings their mistakes and backslidings. They were no lovers of the priesthood, and they were little heeded by the king, who often kept his own band of "prophets" to echo his wishes. Yet they persisted in lashing out against the rich in their concern for social justice, and often saw the hardships that their people suffered under such powers as Assyria and Egypt as punishment for infidelity to Yahweh. Out of their messages came matchless Old Testament poetry which constitutes the special glory of Israel.

The prophets emphasized two fundamentals: the Covenant and the Law. If Israel did not prosper it was because she broke the Covenant, the compact made with God. God must be worshipped both in the letter and the spirit of the law if the Covenant was not to be violated. Moreover since the Jewish law code had no separate privileges for various classes, surely it ought not to countenance such wide gaps between the rich and the poor. God's laws were to be obeyed, not only in the Temple but in the heart. By doing nothing less could Israel be saved. So reasoned the prophets.

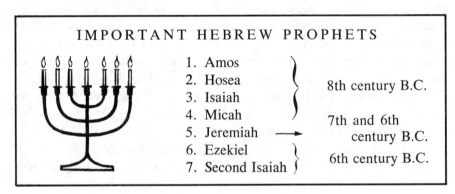

IMPORTANT HEBREW PROPHETS

1. Amos
2. Hosea
3. Isaiah   } 8th century B.C.
4. Micah
5. Jeremiah ⟶ 7th and 6th century B.C.
6. Ezekiel
7. Second Isaiah } 6th century B.C.

❖ *Foundations of Monotheism*   Very few details are known about the careers of the major prophets of the Hebrews. The prophet Amos lived in the time of Jeroboam II of Israel (786-746 B.C.). Amos was a shepherd from the south, an alien in northern Palestine who was shocked by the injustice and dishonesty of the courts, the economic inequalities of the market-place, and the degeneracy and corruption of the court and the holy places. Amos did not want to prophesy, but the Lord laid hold of him and he was compelled to. In a ringing denunciation which he must have delivered throughout the northern kingdom, Amos told his appreciative audience of the punishment to be meted out to all of Israel's powerful and wicked neighbours.

Amos

But his message reached a terrifying climax. He prophesied the doom awaiting Israel herself for breaking the Covenant, and when Assyria and Egypt were portrayed as the instruments of Yahweh's wrath in chastising His people Israel, the prophet's sedition went too far. Jeroboam ordered Amos to return to Judah.

Hosea

About a decade after Amos thundered his warnings, a contemporary of his, a man named Hosea from the northern kingdom, began to prophesy. The fortunes of the Israelites were now on the wane, and Hosea's own unhappy marriage seemed to him to be an allegory of the faithlessness of Israel to Yahweh. Instead of seeking the help of Yahweh Israel had sought the help of men. She had turned to Egypt for aid against Assyria.

In the time of *Judges*, Yahweh had been thought of as a great warrior whose armed might could save his people. Hosea was going far beyond this idea when he preached spiritual weapons rather than the use of force. He also had harsh words for Baal worship, bull worship, and the like that were practised in his day. What did Yahweh desire? Simply "steadfast love and not sacrifice, the knowledge of God rather than burnt offerings." Amos' God was a stern moralist; Hosea's was compassionate as well. Both prophets made more of God than a fickle, cruel, and jealous deity.

The first of the major prophets was Isaiah. When King Ahaz of Judah *Isaiah* (735-715 B.C.) was faced with a coalition of Israel and Syria, it was in vain that Isaiah put forward a policy of isolation. Ahaz appealed to the Assyrians for help. But things turned out much as Isaiah had predicted they would: Assyria ended by taking over Judah. Later Israel fell to Assyria, and when the armies of Sennacherib besieged Jerusalem in 701 B.C. Isaiah saw the invaders as the punishing arm of Yahweh— but in order to be Yahweh's instrument they also must be under his control. Then was Yahweh the God of the Assyrian too? Was there only one God for everyone? The Hebrews were approaching monotheism.

Even if the salvation from Assyria were only temporary, and were followed by fresh and greater disasters, Isaiah was convinced that a remnant of disciples would survive to form the nucleus of a new nation. To lead this remnant, Isaiah prophesied that God himself would provide a ruler, an anointed one, a *Messiah*. For, said Isaiah,

to us a child is born, to us a son is given; and the government will be upon his shoulder, and his name will be called "Wonderful Counsellor, Mighty God, Everlasting Father, Prince of Peace." Of the increase of his government and of peace there will be no end, upon the throne of David, and over his kingdom, to establish it and to uphold it with justice and with righteousness from this time forth and for evermore. The zeal of the lord of hosts will do this.

Micah　　　The last of the 8th century prophets was Micah. He, like Amos, concentrated on social injustice, and he expressed the prophetic position with great simplicity:

> And what does the Lord require of you
> But to do justice, and to love kindness,
> And to walk humbly with your God?

❖ *The Climax of Prophecy*　　The prophetic movement reached its climax
Jeremiah　with Jeremiah (641-586 B.C.), and with Ezekiel and the Second Isaiah of the period of the Babylonian exile. Like Isaiah, Jeremiah found himself caught in the cross-currents of Middle Eastern empires, and like Isaiah he preached that Israel should trust only in Yahweh. Indeed his advice to his countrymen not to resist the invading Chaldeans was what today might be called high treason.

When the Israelites were carried off to Babylon, Jeremiah counselled them to reconcile themselves to their sojourn in exile—for it was to be a long one—but not to forget Yahweh. Jeremiah's God knew all, saw all, heard all, was omnipresent. What was most important to Yahweh was the right mental and moral attitude. Perhaps it was because of Jeremiah's emphasis on personal faith that a later Jew, Jesus of Nazareth, admired him most of all the prophets.

Ezekiel　　　The exile transformed prophecy. Ezekiel, a priest at Jerusalem, was taken captive to Babylon in 597 B.C. and so had the unusual experience of worshipping Yahweh both in Israel and in a foreign land. Because of this experience, he was to realize that Yahweh was not just a national God who remained in Palestine, for after the destruction of Jerusalem by Nebuchadrezzar there was not even any homeland toward which to look with longing. God could enforce his laws anywhere and at any time. Yet even for Ezekiel He was peculiarly the God of Israel, of an Israel that was really the centre of the world.

Second　　About the year 540 B.C.—two years before Cyrus of Persia's edict
Isaiah　of liberation—an anonymous prophet whom scholars have called "the Second Isaiah" foretold Cyrus's restoration of Israel and enthusiastically proclaimed that Yahweh was responsible for it (*Isaiah,* chapters 40-55). For the Second Isaiah, Yahweh had become lord of the Persian as well as the Hebrew, and all gods of wood or stone or metal were nothing, "empty wind" (see Source Reading on page 130). Here was a far cry from the exclusively Hebrew God of Moses. At last monotheism was an accomplished belief.

According to the Second Isaiah, God must be universal. But Israel

TIME CHART FOR THE ANCIENT EAST

DATE (B.C.)	EGYPT	PALESTINE	MESOPOTAMIA	INDIA	CHINA
8000		Earliest Jericho			
7000		Jericho a sizeable town			
5000			Jarmo		
4000	Farming villages in Delta		Farming villages at head of Persian Gulf		
3500			City-states such as Uruk		
3400	Invaders from east				
3200	Unification of Egypt				
3000	Old Kingdom			Farmers enter Indus valley	
2700	Pyramids of Gizeh		City-state of Ashur		
2600					
2500				Indus civilizaton	
2300			Sargon I creates first empire in history		Yang-shao
			Ur conquers Akkad		
2000	Middle Kingdom	Abraham			
1700	Hyksos		Hammurabi in Babylon		
1600		Hebrews in Egypt	Hittites and Kassites		
1500	New Kingdom			Aryan invaders	Shang dynasty
1400	Thutmose III			Earliest *Vedas*	
1300	Akhenaton		Rise of Assyria		
1200	"Peoples of the Sea"	Moses and Joshua			
1100		Hebrew conquest of Canaan	Tiglath-pileser I		Chou dynasty
1000		Saul and David			
		Solomon			
900		Amos, Hosea, Isaiah, Micah; Assyrian conquest		*Upanishads*	Competing states
700		Jeremiah	Sennacherib	Competing states	
600	Battle of Carchemish	Babylonian Captivity	Ashurbanipal; fall of Nineveh; Median empire		
		Ezekiel and Second Isaiah	Nebuchadrezzar; Persian conquests of Cyrus and Darius		
500	Persian conquest	Liberation of Jews	Zoroaster	Buddha	Confucius

is to be "a light to the nations." Since she alone has true knowledge of God she may undergo all manner of humiliation and torture, yet must do so gladly on behalf of others as the "Suffering Servant" of Yahweh. It is not hard to see the roots of that strength which has enabled Judaism to survive the first and all later dispersions.

❖ *A Unique Legacy*   Why do we take as much space for the story of a politically insignificant people living in a land half the size of Nova Scotia as for the thousands of years of Egypt's history? Because the legacy of the Hebrews is unique, and lies at the heart of Western civilization.

Although the Hebrews lived in a land that was the natural meeting-place of great nations and great ideas, their religion did not fit into the general pattern of other Middle Eastern religions. What they took over they refined and elevated. The result was that they became unique vehicles for the proclamation of the glory of God.

We are all in their debt.

CHAPTER 14

A Day in the Life of an Iron Age Soldier

The voice of man, the steps of flocks and herds, and happy shouts of mirth—
I put an end to them. . . .

ASHURBANIPAL

A vulture circled high above, waiting, as the first red streaks of dawn bathed the camp in blood. The round tents of the Assyrians were bunched on the plain, but many of the soldiers had slept in the open. It was spring, and already the first hot breath of the fearful Babylonian summer could be felt.

A youth stirred, looked sleepily around, then closed his eyes again. He was still in his battle dress of the day before, a short-sleeved tunic falling just below his knees, a kind of mail shirt made up of small iron plates sewn on linen, and high boots laced in front. Beside him lay his pointed iron helmet, his bow, and his saddle-cloth (the Assyrian substitute for a leather saddle). This clean-shaven youth was a member of Sennacherib's mounted archers. Unlike the members of the cavalry, who fought with a lance on horseback, he discharged his arrows either when his horse was standing still or after dismounting, and had for his extra protection a short, flat-bladed dagger and a convex shield.

All was deathly quiet. Dagan looked at the soldier sprawled next to him, a seasoned veteran as one could tell from the square, curly black beard. Here was a man who had survived many a campaign. Even in his slumber he looked cruel and proud, for he was one of the "strong ones," the shock troops known as the *qurâdu*, a bodyguard of seasoned warriors who were responsible for the monarch's personal safety. How many dripping heads, Dagan wondered, had he carried to the king to be counted? The lad shivered slightly. Skilled rider and archer that he was, the ways of war were still fairly new to him. When he had been conscripted as part of his village's obliged contingent he had accepted his fate philosophically. For after all, was not the Assyrian born to fight? Did not the god Ashur himself command the wars that Senna-cherib undertook, and was he not appeased by the sacrifices of massacre and torture which followed? Like the others, Dagan tried to serve his god well.

He raised himself on his elbow and looked at the king's tent, far to the left, with its movable canopy which could be adjusted to fend off the wind or the sun. Oh mighty Sennacherib! How cunning and powerful were his ways. At the end of his reign his scribes were to boast that he had sacked 89 cities and 820 villages, captured 7200 horses, 11,000 asses, 80,000 oxen, 800,000 sheep, and 208,000 prisoners. Before he ever invaded a country, men said, his spies went throughout the land, drawing maps, ferreting out information, feigning friendship, building up a fifth column, undermining the loyalty of the people. And when his warriors moved down on their prey, like wolves on a fold, they moved in the confidence that they were led by the greatest of kings. They had no compunction about their calculated aggressions: Assyria regarded the countries on her borders as a variety of storehouses to be plundered at her pleasure, and their populations as fodder for her work gangs and her armies.

The efficiency of Assyria's war machine was unmatched. Her infantry, archers, engineers, mounted lancers, and artillery supported the lightly equipped auxiliaries who fought sometimes with only clubs and slings. Swift as the wind were her chariots, drawn by small, fleet horses; yet these ancient "jeeps" were most limited in their mobility because they were incapable of sudden changes of direction. Many a time Dagan had seen one charge fiercely at its prey, the driver cursing his horses on at top speed while the archer poised to shoot, and then the whole affair turn into a comedy when the victim noted his predicament and avoided extermination by the simple expedient of stepping aside. Woe betide the charioteer who found himself, too late, an irresistible force confronted with an immovable object!

Dagan closed his eyes again, and suddenly he seemed to be back in the heat of the battle. Fighting for the Assyrians was no haphazard mêlée, but an occupation whose strategy and tactics were well planned and whose object was clearly defined: to harass and confound the enemy with rapid movements and piecemeal attacks. War was a business to be engaged in for profit, filling Assyria's coffers with spoils and her cities with slaves. Was not Sennacherib to boast that he had gladdened the hearts of his people by establishing a capital without equal at Nineveh? Who but he had opened squares to let the crowded streets breathe, had brought in spring water from hills 30 miles away by the first aqueduct known to man, and had created farms in the suburbs where men experimented with new plants such as cotton? And where would the manpower for his experiments come from without slaves? True, he was brutal; but terrorism was a "surgical necessity" to cut out rebellion and cement discipline.

And so, protected by Ashur, Sennacherib led his vanguard of nobles proudly into battle, his splendid chariot announcing the royal presence by its gloriously embroidered canopy. Like a lion he raged against the wicked enemy, his dark beard thickened by false curls, his person protected by a coat of mail and an iron helmet with a characteristically sharp point, bow in hand, javelin in fist, ready to cut the throat of any opponents so that "their gullets and entrails run down upon the wide earth." History would show how strong his state had been. Egypt's symbol might be a disk scattering rays benignly; Athens would advertise her wise men by the symbol of an owl; Rome would be remembered by a she-wolf because she was the nurse of civilization. But Assyria, Assyria took as her symbol the war god as archer.

The strange thing, thought Dagan, was that terror did not seem to squelch opposition; it only bred it. He thought of the siege of Kutu, whence the army had come in answer to the pleas of the Assyrian commander-in-chief here at Kish. The river at Kutu had been full of soldiers swimming on their inflated goatskins, while the chariots and baggage wagons crossed either by a makeshift bridge or on light craft. The king watched from a nearby bank while activities got underway, the sappers making an efficient job of undermining the enemy's wall until its timber underpinning could be set on fire and the whole structure would collapse, sometimes on friend and foe alike. Meanwhile the men swarmed up the walls on ladders, and the battering ram—a mighty beam slung underneath a scaffolding by means of ropes—swung rhythmically backwards and forwards, its iron tip biting relentlessly into the enemy battlements while the defenders bestowed stone missiles, torches, flaming naphtha, and burning pitch (to say nothing of a species of so-called "stink pots" designed to discomfit, if not befuddle, the enemy) on the besiegers and attempted to stop the merciless hammering by entangling the ram in chains.

But Kutu was doomed from the start. For all the men knew that the king would not even set out on an expedition if the soothsayers and the auguries had not pronounced the time and place auspicious. And so the battle raged on, the mounted cavalry shooting their arrows while more foot soldiers prepared to scale the walls, protected from the defenders' hail of ammunition by the high, curving Assyrian shield—so immense that it required an extra man to carry it for the fighter. In due time the inevitable (according to Assyrian records) breach was made in the walls, and the men streamed into the city.

Dagan did not remember much after that beyond the heady excitement of plunder and bloodshed. He was swept along with the tide of it, killing to keep from being killed. There were, he realized, two great incentives for staying alive. No Assyrian was in any hurry to descend to the after-world, that dark, dust-shrouded, airless abyss whose only comfort was the sustenance of funerary offerings. If a body lay forgotten on the field, remembered by no man, then the spirit would have to return to earth to plague the living and snatch such miserable scraps as it could find from the refuse heaps. Then, too, there was a general rule in the Middle East that all captives in war might be either enslaved or slain. A warrior got his reward for every severed head he brought from the field, and scribes stood by to count the number of prisoners taken or killed in order to apportion the booty accordingly—being sure, if they valued their lives, *never* to minimize the number! It was always to be hoped that the inhabitants had not had time to bury too many of their precious possessions, for Assyrian greed for gold and silver knew no bounds.

Finally, when the count was finished, the king's throne was set up

"He was swept along with the tide of it, killing to keep from being killed."

before the gates of the city and the prisoners were paraded before him. This was the time when it was well for the captive to be born of humble blood. If there was food enough, or the campaign was nearly ended, the wretched prisoners might be granted the doubtful blessing of being spared for slavery; if they were likely to be a danger and a nuisance to the army they were quickly executed. But the town's ruler, the nobles, even their children were often reserved for the most exquisite of tortures while their wives and daughters were destined for Assyrian harems.

Dagan sat up and stretched. It was little wonder he was weary. Sennacherib's forces had been hurried from Kutu to Kish, and last night that city too had been put to the torch and another pile of bloody heads had been heaped up on the safer side of the river where the king had watched the proceedings. Now the sun's red had turned to gold, and noises began to come from the camp—but sounds of peace, not of war. Some soldiers set to work cutting up a sheep, another fanned a fire, another brought wood for the enormous stewpot, still another plucked some ducks he had caught on the river. The mutton would be for the king, the fowl for the men; for meat was an Assyrian rarity except among the highest classes.

Dagan rose and flexed his cramped muscles. It was time for the horses to be groomed. He walked a few steps toward the river, then paused. For there were other sounds of peace, and to these, try as he might, he could not close his ears. There were the murmurs of women's voices and the cries of little children. Someone was weeping inconsolably, and a man's voice could be heard trying to hush the sobs. Almost against his will Dagan turned and looked at the pathetic hodge-podge of captives who had been huddled together along with their possessions on the river bank. The men, suddenly bent with the terrible weight of captivity, were handcuffed in pairs and loaded with skins of food and water for the endless, bitter trek to their new homes. The women stood uncertainly, waiting to be herded into ox-carts or put on mules. One mother was holding out a water-skin for her children to drink from; another tried to soothe the pain from a tiny blistered heel; another enveloped her little girl in the comforting folds of her robe in a vain attempt to shut out the memory of a father kneeling before his murderers. Another father was more fortunate. Sennacherib had noted his massive shoulders and decided he would make an excellent draught animal. Soon, very soon so as to beat the fury of the Assyrian summer sun, the group would be shunted along as fast as it could move—the men driven like cattle by blows from the soldiers—to far-off Nineveh.

"And thus," thought Dagan, "thus my mother came to Assyria." Dagan's mother had been branded as a slave and bought by Dagan's father's legal wife to be his "secondary wife"; for this woman was childless and feared that her husband would take a concubine who was not to her liking. Dagan's mother lived in the miserable position of a servant to the first wife, obliged to treat her with the greatest respect, to carry her chair when she went to the temple, and to assist her in making herself beautiful. "But try as she might," Dagan smiled to himself, "she could never be as beautiful as my mother." The legal wife herself, like all Assyrian wives, was little better than a piece of property, acquired and treated without sentiment by her husband. But at least she had the privilege of wearing a veil. That was the distinguishing mark of a free woman and a woman of moral character. Dagan's mother was considered neither.

Gradually, especially after Dagan's birth, the second wife came to be greatly preferred to the first. She was pampered by her master, persecuted by her mistress. It was a relief to everyone when Dagan's father died. Indeed it was more than a relief: it was a signal for great thanksgiving. Assyrian law said that at any time any slave, even a "second wife" like Dagan's mother, could be sold; but at her owner's death she and her children should be free. Free! But for Dagan the freedom could not last. There was no escape from military obligation in Assyria. Even had he been a slave he would have been conscripted: the army took both slave and freeman.

Dagan went down to the river to wash. The grime of battle still clung to his face, and he began to remove it with the slender remnant of the soap his mother had sent with him. It was soap she herself had made from oil, pure clay, and ashes, and a good abrasive cleanser it was too. A soldier splashed triumphantly past him carrying a fish for his breakfast, and another even more triumphantly cradled a fistful of locusts, delicacies which he intended to dry and skewer. A veteran was sitting on a boulder nearby oiling his hair and beard in an attempt to smother vermin. In the distance Dagan could see a captive mother giving her child the main sustenance of many Assyrians, small strips of a bread-like substance something like a pancake.

Dagan fished out some onions which he had been lucky enough to salvage. He felt a sharp pang—which he would have been ashamed to call homesickness—as he suddenly thought of his home behind the tall, blank walls of the village, the roof-top where he used to sleep next the stars, the morning kiss exchanged by all the members of the family, and particularly of his favourite dish, a thin and delicate barley bread made by pasting dough on a jar containing a hot fire of thorns or charcoal. His mother used to hide pieces of this bread where she knew her small boy would find them, in the pottery strung up on cords beyond the reach of rats and mice. . . .

Even as the tents were being rolled up the vultures hovered lower. Soon the drums would signal the start of the long march home. Then the musicians would begin to play their several instruments, and the ungainly procession would shudder into motion. The king would be borne in triumph, the bearded veterans would swing along rhythmically, and the auxiliaries would follow in casual disorder. Last of all would come the animals, human and four-footed, ready for the market. And among them would be another dark-eyed maiden who would bear another son who would serve another Assyrian monarch. So the circle of massacre, defeat, brutalization, and deportation would repeat itself until, sapped by civil and foreign wars, her army weakened by alien conscripts, her subject peoples alienated by her heavy hand, Assyria would herself be destroyed. Until then the Dagans would gradually become the hardened veterans, and the world would cringe at the blare of an Assyrian trumpet.

SOURCE READINGS

(a)

DARIUS I of Persia (521-486 B.C.) had to put down many revolts during the first two years of his reign. He describes his successful wars and his other accomplishments in an inscription carved 300 feet on a rock cliff. This Behistun inscription is near Ecbatana in modern Iran, and was carved in the three imperial languages. Some translated passages from it follow.

1. I am Darius the Great King, King of Kings, King in Persia, King of countries. . . .

4. Saith Darius the King: VIII of our family there are who were kings afore; I am the ninth; IX in succession we have been kings.

5. Saith Darius the King: By the favour of Ahuramazda I am King; Ahuramazda bestowed the kingdom upon me.

6. Saith Darius the King: These are the countries which came unto me: by the favour of Ahuramazda I was king of them: Persia, Elam, Babylonia, Assyria, Arabia, Egypt, those who are beside the sea, Sardis, Ionia, Media, Armenia, Cappadocia, Parthia, Drangiana, Aria, Chorasmia, Bactria, Sogdiana, Gandara, Scythia, Sattagydia, Arachosia, Maka: in all, XXIII provinces.

8. Saith Darius the King: Within these countries, the man who was excellent, him I rewarded well; him who was evil, him I punished well; by the favour of Ahuramazda these countries showed respect toward my law; as was said to them by me, thus was it done.

52. Saith Darius the King: This is what I did by the favour of Ahuramazda in one and the same year after that I became king. XIX battles I fought; by the favour of Ahuramazda I smote them and took prisoner IX kings. . . .

58. Saith Darius the King: By the favour of Ahuramazda and of me much else was done; that has not been inscribed in this inscription; for this

reason it has not been inscribed, lest whoso shall hereafter read this inscription, to him what has been done by me seem excessive, and it not convince him, but he think it false.

67. Saith Darius the King: If thou shalt behold this inscription or these sculptures, and shalt destroy them and shalt not protect them as long as unto thee there is strength, Ahuramazda be a smiter unto thee, and may family not be unto thee, and what thou shalt do, that for thee may Ahuramazda utterly destroy!

68. Saith Darius the King: These are the men who were there at the time when I slew Gaumata the Magian who called himself Smerdis; at that time these men co-operated as my followers. . . .

69. Saith Darius the King: Thou who shalt be king hereafter, protect well the family of these men.

70. Saith Darius the King: By the favour of Ahuramazda this inscription in other ways I made. In addition, it was in Aryan, and has been made on leather. In addition, this inscription as a whole has been confirmed by the impression of a seal. And it was written, and the written document was read off to me. Afterwards this inscription was sent by me everywhere among the provinces; the people universally were pleased.

W. C. McDermott and W. E. Caldwell, editors, *Readings in the History of the Ancient World* (Rinehart, 1951), pp. 58-64.

(b)

THE SECOND ISAIAH wrote the following prophecies shortly before Cyrus the Great of Persia took Babylon in 538 B.C. These passionate words, addressed to the exiles in Babylonia, seek to reassure them that Yahweh (the Lord) will care for them, and that he rules the world.

Get you up to a high mountain, O Zion, herald of good tidings; lift up your voice with strength, O Jerusalem, herald of good tidings, lift it up, fear not; say to the cities of Judah, "Behold your God!" Behold, the Lord God comes with might, and his arm rules for him; behold, his reward is with him, and his recompense before him. He will feed his flock like a shepherd, he will gather the lambs in his arms, he will carry them in his bosom, and gently lead those that are with young.

Who has measured the waters in the hollow of his hand and marked off the heavens with a span, enclosed the dust of the earth in a measure and weighed the mountains in scales and the hills in a balance? . . . All the nations are as nothing before him, they are accounted by him as less than nothing and emptiness.

To whom then will you liken God, or what likeness compare with him? The idol! a workman casts it, and a goldsmith overlays it with gold, and casts for it silver chains. He who is impoverished chooses for an offering wood that will not rot; he seeks out a skilful craftsman to set up an image that will not move.

Have you not known? Have you not heard? Has it not been told you from the beginning? Have you not understood from the foundations of the earth? It is he who sits above the circle of the earth, and its inhabitants are like grasshoppers; who stretches out the heavens like a curtain, and spreads them like a tent to dwell in; who brings princes to nought, and makes the rulers of the earth as nothing.

Scarcely are they planted, scarcely sown, scarcely has their stem taken root in the earth, when he blows upon them, and they wither, and the tempest carries them off like stubble.

To whom then will you compare me, that I should be like him? says the Holy One. Lift up your eyes on high and see: who created these? He who brings out their host by number, calling them all by name; by the greatness of his might, and because he is strong in power not one is missing.

Why do you say, O Jacob, and speak, O Israel, "My way is hid from the Lord, and my right is disregarded by my God"? Have you not known? Have you not heard? The Lord is the everlasting God, the Creator of the ends of the earth. He does not faint or grow weary, his understanding is unsearchable. He gives power to the faint, and to him who has no might he increases strength. Even youths shall faint and be weary, and young men shall fall exhausted; but they who wait for the Lord shall renew their strength, they shall mount up with wings like eagles, they shall run and not be weary, they shall walk and not faint. (40: 9-12, 17-31)

The Holy Bible: Revised Standard Version (Thomas Nelson & Sons, 1953), pp. 749-750.

BOOKS TO READ

1. ASSYRIA

   Contenau, G., *Everyday Life in Babylon and Assyria* (Arnold)
   Saggs, H. W. F., *Everyday Life in Babylonia and Assyria* (Batsford)

2. PERSIA

   Lamb, H., *Cyrus the Great* (Bantam paperback)
   Pike, E. R., *Ancient Persia* (Weidenfeld and Nicolson)

3. PALESTINE

   Grollenberg, L. H., *Shorter Atlas of the Bible* (Nelson)
   Heaton, E. W., *Everyday Life in Old Testament Times* (Batsford)
   Jones, J., *David, Warrior of God* (Association Press)
   Smith, J. W. D., *Bible Background* (Methuen)

4. HISTORICAL FICTION

   Davis, W. S., *Belshazzar* (Collier-Macmillan) [capture of Babylon by
      Cyrus the Great]
   Wilson, D. C., *Prince of Egypt* (Pocket Books) [Moses in Egypt]

PART IV

THE GLORY OF GREECE

CHAPTER 15

Crete Dominates the Mainland

There is a land called Crete in the midst of the wine-dark sea, a fair land and a rich, begirt with water, and therein are many men innumerable, and ninety cities.

ODYSSEY, XIX

Perhaps because his climate was more rigorous, European man did not progress as rapidly as Middle Eastern man. While the citizens of Mesopotamia and Egypt were enjoying the fruits of an advanced civilization, the peoples of Europe still lived in an era of Stone Age culture. Eventually, however, the introduction of copper into Europe produced the more complex culture of the Bronze Age, which made its first appearance in Greece and the lands bordering on the Aegean Sea by 2000 B.C.

❖ *Digging Up the Past*   We owe much of our knowledge of this unique civilization which grew up around the cities of Troy and Mycenae to the excavations of a German named Heinrich Schliemann. His work, along with that done by Sir Arthur Evans on Crete, has built up a fairly complete picture of the oldest European civilization, and forms one of the most spectacular chapters in the science of archaeology.

Schliemann went to Hamburg as a youth in 1841, and signed up as a cabin boy on a ship bound for Venezuela. The ship, however, was ill-fated. It sank off the Netherlands, whereupon the cabin boy became a clerk in an Amsterdam office. In a cold attic room he managed to teach himself Greek and began reading Homer. As his fascination grew, Schlieman developed a passionate belief that the Troy and Mycenae of Homer's epics were no mere poetic inventions as many scholars insisted. They had existed as surely as Amsterdam, and somewhere, somehow he would find proof of that existence.

Heinrich Schliemann

This temple to Apollo the Helper was built about 420 B.C. by the city-state of Phigalia to commemorate relief granted from an epidemic during the Peloponnesian War. Riding high among some of the highest mountains of the Peloponnesus, this beautiful shrine seems to reach halfway to heaven in an attempt to entice its god to come down to earth.

133

The dream did not disappear with manhood, and when Schliemann made a fortune in Russian oil he retired to use it for his own private detective work on Homer. Eventually his persistence was rewarded. In 1871 he discovered the ruins of Troy—no literary fiction but a real city!—and those of Mycenae in 1876.

Sir Arthur Evans Schliemann's archaeological ambitions went even further. He planned to begin excavations on the island of Crete. But he died before he could do so, and the task was undertaken by the English scholar, Arthur Evans. Evans was the direct opposite of Schliemann: he was a professor who had been educated at English and German universities, whereas Schliemann was a self-educated, talented amateur. But both men were great archaeological pioneers, and between them they discovered a whole civilization. Since it surrounded the Aegean Sea, this civilization they uncovered is known as "Aegean" civilization. It is usually, however, separated into what is called "Minoan," that part centering on the island of Crete, and "Mycenaean," that part centering on Mycenae, a city on the Greek mainland.

When Evans unearthed this long-buried civilization on Crete in 1900 he called it "Minoan," a name which he derived from the legendary king Minos. He divided the civilization into three main periods:

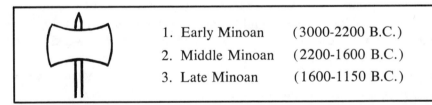

1.	Early Minoan	(3000-2200 B.C.)
2.	Middle Minoan	(2200-1600 B.C.)
3.	Late Minoan	(1600-1150 B.C.)

❖ *An Almost Modern Civilization* It is important to note that the Cretans were not Greeks. Rather they came overseas from Asia Minor during the New Stone Age, as early as 5000 B.C. As time went on and more immigrants brought a knowledge of copper and bronze from the lands in the south and east, the Cretans entered the Bronze Age. In this Early Minoan period a metal industry was established, and there was even some trade with Egypt. Pottery styles varied widely from one part of the island to the other, as did architecture, religious ritual, and burial customs. Political power seems to have been in the hands of local princes, whose palace-temples became the centres of prosperous towns.

Middle Minoan civilization The Middle Minoan period was the great age of the palaces at Knossos and Phaestos. Now Minoan civilization had become mature, and uniform-

These are the Minoan-Mycenaean signs of the archaic Greek word for tripod. Each sign stands for a syllable rather than, as in English, a single letter.

ti   ri   po

ity was established over the whole island. Cretan houses were remarkably modern in their appearance, two-storeyed dwellings of wood, brick, or stone, with windows either shuttered or covered with some sort of transparent panes. Cretan craftsmen achieved highly artistic creations in pottery and bronze, and a system of writing emerged. Until recently Minoan records could not be deciphered, but in 1952 an exciting discovery was made when a young English scholar succeeded in deciphering one of the types of Minoan script—a discovery which is revolutionizing our knowledge of early Greek history. We now know that a form of Greek was written in Crete and on the mainland a full six centuries before the Greeks adopted the Phoenician alphabet!

Then, some time after 1700 B.C., calamity struck the island when some mysterious disaster, possibly an earthquake, destroyed the palaces of Crete. But the destruction was followed by such energetic restoration that a golden age of Minoan civilization ensued. The new cities of this late Middle Minoan period were unfortified, and the rulers of Knossos—a city of 100,000 people—dominated the whole island. Apparently their palaces were both commercial and governmental centres, for the kings kept the surpluses of grain and olive oil in their basements in huge pottery jars over six feet high.

This sunny island must have been a place of happy prosperity. The chief crops were barley, flax, olives, grapes, figs, and dates, while goats, sheep, and cattle were pastured on the hillsides. Pottery manufacturing, metalworking, and shipbuilding flourished, and in their sleek seventy-foot masted ships the Cretans exported olive oil, wine, bronze utensils, vases, jewellery, and cameos, or imported marble, ivory, tin, and precious metals. Some southern Greek cities were definitely under the influence of Crete, and Cretan vessels journeyed so widely that trading posts and colonies were established from Cyprus to Sicily. No wonder the Cretan idea of death was of a last long voyage—an appropriate symbol for a civilization whose life was the sea.

These prosperous and contented islanders seem almost modern in their love of athletics, the fashions of women's clothes and their many hats, the sewage systems for their streets and palaces, their bath tubs and their flush toilets. Moreover they were less autocratic than their Oriental neighbours. The kings mingled with their subjects, there were no royal harems, and women took part in athletic contests and worked side by side with men in the "factories." It is an interesting fact of history that great sea powers usually seem to be more democratic than great land powers.

❖ *From Myth to History*   You will probably have read the famous Greek myth about Theseus and the Minotaur. Theseus was brought up by his mother far from Athens and in ignorance of his father's identity. Finally he was sent to King Aegeus in Athens, and here he was found to be none other than the king's son. One day he saw the Athenians sorrowing as the time approached for their tribute to King Minos of Crete. It was a dreadful tribute—seven maidens and seven youths to be devoured by the Minotaur, a frightful monster half bull and half man who lived in a labyrinth of halls and passageways built for him on Crete. Theseus insisted on being one of the sacrificial youths. Then he proceeded to woo and win Minos's daughter, who helped him kill the monster, find his way out of the labyrinth, and return to Athens.

The Palace of Knossos   Before Evans made his excavations this story was regarded as pure fiction. Today we are not so sure. Frescoes of the strange Cretan sport of bull-leaping have been discovered in Knossos. And the royal palace has been found to be a veritable maze of small rooms and corridors. Could it have been the labyrinth?

❖ *A Wild Spring Day*   It is known that the Late Minoan period saw a slow decline, but exactly what was the final fate of the island is a puzzle. Certain it is that there was some cataclysmic disaster.

. . . in the last decade of the fifteenth century on a spring day, when a strong South wind was blowing which carried the flames of the burning beams almost horizontally northwards, Knossos fell. . . .

The final scene takes place in the most dramatic room ever excavated—the Throne Room. It was found in a state of complete confusion. A great oil jar lay overturned in one corner; ritual vessels were in the act of being used when the disaster came. It looks as if the King had been hurried there to undergo, too late, some last ceremony in the hopes of saving the people. . . .

Crete had fallen and henceforth she was to be a mere satellite of the world centring round Greece, gradually drawing nearer until she was absorbed in the general Hellenic culture which she herself had done so much to found.

For centuries the palace lay deserted except for the ghosts of its departed glory mournfully wandering down the empty mouldering stairways. . . . With that wild spring day . . . something went out of the world which the world will never see again: something grotesque, perhaps, something fantastic and cruel, but something also very lovely.

We have been able to figure out just what the Cretans' sport of bull-leaping was like by studying their wall frescoes and carvings. As the bull charges, the athlete grabs its horns. The bull then tries to throw the man by tossing its head back, propelling him over its shoulders in somersault fashion. As the man goes over he lets go of the horns and lands feet down on the bull's back, and from this precarious standing position leaps to the ground to complete the feat. Both men and women practised this sport, such a dangerous one that modern acrobats and rodeo performers say it is virtually impossible. The Cretans, however, appear to have mastered it.

The legend of Theseus' slaying of the Minotaur probably enshrines a folk memory of the control Mycenae won over Crete. At any rate, after 1400 B.C. Crete is not mentioned in Egyptian records, and the island likely paid tribute to Mycenae. From this time on until the fall of the Roman Empire, mainland European civilization was to dominate the Mediterranean.

CRETE DOMINATES THE MAINLAND/137

CHAPTER 16

The Mainland Dominates the Mediterranean

Like frogs around a pond, we have settled down upon the shores of this sea.
PLATO

Mycenae was the chief city on the Greek mainland, and had been settled as early as 2500 B.C. by peoples who came overland from Asia Minor. Then about 1900 B.C. new Indo-European invaders seized the hilltop at Mycenae. These settlers are called Achaean Greeks.

❖ *A Glamorous Civilization* Unlike the pleasant, open cities of Crete, Mycenae was strongly fortified, and by 1350 B.C. had been rebuilt on a grand scale. Around its fortified hilltop (*acropolis*) were cemeteries with vaults or shafts for the bodies of the dead, although the princes themselves later came to be buried in beehive-shaped tombs.

You all know the story of the Trojan horse. Pottery discovered in the 7th layer of the ruins of Troy (where there are at least nine layers of cities built one on top of another!) has given us a new version of that famous 13th century B.C. siege. Probably it was no noble attempt of the Greeks to recover a kidnapped queen; probably it was not even an attack to free the Dardanelles from Trojan ships who patrolled it and imposed levies on intruders. Most likely it was merely a "wholesome exercise" in pillaging which these warlike mainland Greeks were enjoying under the leadership of Mycenae.

Golden Mycenae The culture of the mainland Greeks owed much to Crete. The Minoans passed on to them their athletic contests, their devotion to music and the dance, their artistic creations, even, perhaps, their dependence on a navy. But the Greeks also availed themselves of certain aspects of northern culture: their language, wheel-made pottery, and a northern style of architecture which the Mycenaeans added to their palaces in the *megaron*. This oblong building had a hearth in the centre of the floor, a porch supported by pillars, and a sloping roof—a structure much better adapted to Greece's cold, rainy winters than the flat-roofed houses of the Minoans.

What a picture of massive strength this Lion Gate, the main entrance to the citadel of Mycenae, must have presented to any foe! Its lions guarded the formidable palace-fortress from which the lords of Mycenae dominated the centre of Greece. Probably Agamemnon passed through this very gate on his way to Troy.

Schliemann and later excavators found such a wealth of weapons and ornaments in the shaft graves at Mycenae that the adjective "golden" is quite aptly used in speaking of Mycenaean civilization. But this glamorous civilization, too, collapsed. In the 12th century B.C. Mycenae fell to the Dorian Greeks, a rougher people from the north with iron weapons and scant appreciation of the culture they destroyed.

❖ *Displaced Persons* The Dorian Greeks were a part of the second wave of Indo-European invaders, that shattering expansion of Iron Age peoples in the two centuries following 1200 B.C. which you read about on page 95. As the Dorians filtered down from the north they destroyed

Greek migration

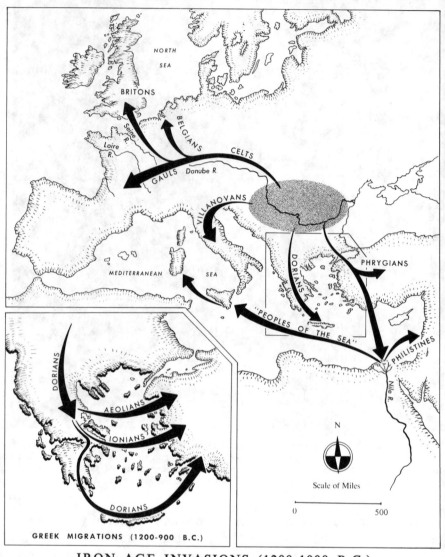

NORTH SEA

BRITONS

BELGIANS

CELTS

Seine R.

Loire R.

GAULS

Danube R.

VILLANOVANS

DORIANS

PHRYGIANS

MEDITERRANEAN SEA

"PEOPLES OF THE SEA"

PHILISTINES

Nile R.

DORIANS

AEOLIANS

IONIANS

DORIANS

GREEK MIGRATIONS (1200-900 B.C.)

N

Scale of Miles

0   500

IRON AGE INVASIONS (1200-1000 B.C.)

palaces, wrecked cities, and ravaged the countryside. Some bands settled in Thessaly and Boeotia, but the majority bypassed Athens and pressed on through Corinth down into the Peloponnesus. This influx shunted the displaced inhabitants eastward, and the resulting shifts among the peoples called Aeolians, Achaeans (who became the Ionians), and Dorians may be seen on the map above.

With the Dorian invasions, the old official Achaean class and its cumbersome Minoan script disappeared. Greek literacy gradually collapsed; but this result, though in many ways lamentable, was not all loss. Since people could not read they made up poems for themselves which were passed on by word of mouth from generation to generation. Finally, when the Greeks adopted the Phoenician alphabet, this "folk poetry" was written down for the first time. Such was the process by which the poems of an Ionian Greek from Chios, a man called Homer, were recorded. They were to become the Bible of the ancient Greeks.

Who was this Homer? A blind poet, a solitary figure who probably *Homer* lived in the 9th century B.C. What did he write? Whether he created both the epics, the *Iliad* and the *Odyssey,* is a matter not yet settled; a good case has been made out for a later authorship of the *Odyssey.* Why are these poems important? Because Homer, like Shakespeare, made the settings of his stories (which were supposed to have taken place centuries earlier) reflect his own day and age. Thus when he tells a story of Mycenaean civilization, the background for the tale is actually a description of Homer's own 9th century B.C. society.

Homer gave us a picture of *all* Greeks, not just the Greeks of a particular city. Before we look at that picture, however, let us see in what manner of country these Homeric characters dwelt.

❖ *Poverty's Foster-Sister* When we speak of the "Greeks," we are calling them by the name the Romans gave them; the Greeks called themselves Hellenes, and their land Hellas. This land of Hellas, which constitutes the southern projection of the Balkan peninsula, was very tiny—about the size of the provinces of New Brunswick and Nova Scotia combined. Even so, most of Greek history was enacted on a still smaller stage, the southern part of Hellas, which has only the area of New Brunswick alone.

Greece's temperate, bracing climate seems to be her only physical advantage. Hers is a poor land of low mountain ranges whose limestone absorbs rainfall and will not hold topsoil. The valleys are small and the coastline heavily indented: no place is farther than seventy miles from the sea. Less than a third of the country can be cultivated, and what little arable land there is is sealed in small plains where grain, wine, and oil can be produced; the rest is covered with scrub vegetation. The rainy season lasts from October to March, making the rivers quite unnavigable—torrential in winter, dry gulches in summer. And there are relatively few minerals.

Greece has undoubtedly become poorer than it was in ancient times, yet even then the usual dinner consisted of only one staple, porridge. Aside from the arable plains, the country is fit for little more than goat- and sheep-raising—and that in summer. Truly, in the words of the 5th century B.C. historian Herodotus (484-425 B.C.), "Hellas and Poverty have always been foster-sisters."

From the beginning, Greece's harsh geography shaped her history. Her lack of natural resources and the difficulty of overland communications combined to prevent the growth of large states. Moreover, Greece was almost cut in half by the Corinthian and Saronic Gulfs. This meant that the districts near the Isthmus of Corinth were strategic, because here land and sea routes converged.

Yet if the land divided Greeks, the sea united them. The whole country looked east—east to their "Greek lake," the Aegean Sea, around whose shores were to be found all the best harbours. Scattered across the sea like stepping-stones were innumerable islands, so many that the sailor was rarely out of sight of land. As long as the sea was open and free, the Greeks could use it as a safety-valve to work off some of the tensions born of a crowded existence in a stark terrain.

❖ *Homeric Society*　With the Dorian invasions and the introduction of iron, a new era of civilization began in Greece. This is the society in which Homer lived, and which is reflected in the pages of the *Iliad* and the *Odyssey*. Homer's Greece lacked Crete's political unity. There was a sort of heroic monarch—not a despot, but one first among equals— who ruled each city. Agamemnon of Mycenae was one. This king, like the oriental monarch, combined in his person the functions of commander-in-chief, supreme judge, and high priest. But neither the kings of Mycenae nor later Greeks could weld the mainland together; indeed right up until the days of Alexander the Great the inhabitants of Greece could not manage to create a unified nation. Hence Greek history is really the history of a number of Greek cities.

Homer's society was strangely primitive. One of the chief means of making a living was by warfare and plundering; wealth was measured in flocks and herds; and commercial transactions were carried on by barter. The religion contained both Mycenaean and Asiatic elements. The gods were all too human—jealous, playing favourites among men, and living in glory on Mount Olympus. Immortality was vaguely believed in. The body was cremated and the soul somehow survived in Hades, a land of shadows where the dead were like a swarm of bats fluttering and screeching in the hollows of a great cave. "I had rather," said Achilles, "be a slave of the meanest landless man on earth than be king in Hades." Morals had grown out of folk custom, hospitality being, as in the desert, the supreme virtue.

This early society was an aristocratic one in which the rich nobles formed a council of advisers to the king. As the upper class grew more powerful in the 9th and 8th centuries B.C., the various kingships disappeared, leaving these men of wealth to rule the state. Nevertheless all citizens were still felt to have an equal right to express themselves in the mass meetings.

The villagers found it wise to settle permanently around the foot of their acropolis. It gave them protection; it was easier than living in isolated country hamlets far from the hill-fortress; and it provided a meeting place for religious festivals. Most important of all—even more important to the Greeks than the need for defence—was the fact that here was a centre where political and public affairs could be discussed and justice dispensed.

There was an absolute necessity for such a centre; for the Greeks *City-states* refused to accept the idea of a state in which the farthest point from the capital was more than a day's walk away. Any larger state could not be governed by a direct democracy. It would require government by representation because there would simply be too many citizens for a fair proportion of them to come together in one place. There ought, then, reasoned the Greeks, to be no larger political unit than the city-state.

The Greek city-state included not only the city but its surrounding territory. Nevertheless, Athens, with 1000 square miles, was one of the biggest city-states, while the total area of four or five put together might not exceed several hundred square miles. In fact, since many Greek states must have had a population of not more than 10,000-15,000, we today would call them towns rather than cities.

The smallness of these city-states meant, as we have seen, that all citizens could participate in public affairs. But because each state was independent of its neighbours—often separated from them geographically by the mountains or the sea—each developed its own peculiar personality. Greeks were united by only three things: their language, their religion, and their games. Hence Greek separatism was counteracted by the meeting of all Greeks around the council table or at some universal religious or athletic festival, held at such sites as Delos or Delphi or Olympia.

(N.B. Though the shaded portions indicate the general areas of colonization, the names of only a few representative colonies are given.)

❖ *Land for the Starving* With the end of the 8th century B.C. Greece was a sorry land. She lay in the grip of a severe economic depression, one which is vividly portrayed by the Boeotian farmer Hesiod in his *Works and Days.* Hear his grim advice to the hard-pressed peasant:

Get a house first and a woman and a plowing ox—a slave woman—not a wife—who might also follow the oxen: and get all gear arrayed within the house, lest thou beg of another and he deny thee and thou go lacking, and the season pass by, and thy work be diminished. Neither put off till the morrow nor the day after. The idle man filleth not his barn, neither he that

144/GREECE

THE COLONIES OF THE GREEKS

Areas of Colonization

Danube R.

CRIMEA

Byzantium

BLACK SEA

MACEDON

TIC SEA

apolis

Tarentum

Corinth

AEGEAN SEA

Ephesus

Miletus

ASIA MINOR

MAGNA RAECIA

IONIAN SEA

Athens

RHODES

CYPRUS

Salamis

Sparta

CRETE

Sidon

use

A   N

Cyrene

S   E   A

Tyre

Naucratis

Nile R.

putteth off. Diligence prospereth work, but the man who putteth off ever wrestleth with ruin.

The population was starving; yet every day there were more mouths to feed. What were the Greek city-states to do? In the 7th and 6th centuries B.C. they thought they had discovered a solution: colonization.

At first the founding of colonies was a haphazard affair, but as time went on parent cities consulted the Delphic Oracle for guidance and chose their site with care. Although the colony was politically indepen-

Greek colonies

dent it was bound to its parent city by the strongest of ties—sentiment, reinforced by trade. Soon Greek colonies dotted the shores from the Black Sea and the Crimea to modern Gibraltar. So active, indeed, did the business of colonization become that one of the Ionian Greek cities of Asia Minor, Miletus, was reputed to have founded at least eighty colonies by herself, and even secured a foothold in the Nile Delta. Thus, on the wings of the colonies, Greek ways and ideas travelled far beyond the confines of the little city-states.

At first colonization had a therapeutic effect on Greece. It bolstered her ailing trade and industry as raw materials from the colonies were exchanged for manufactured goods from the mother cities. Crimean wheat, northern furs and gold, western timber, hides, and wool flowed into Greece in return for fine textiles, jewellery, metal utensils, arms, and pottery. Yet industry still developed on only a small scale. Most manufacturing was done in family shops; a shield "factory" employing 120 workmen was considered to be a large enterprise. Often prisoners of war worked as slaves in industry, where some might eventually buy their freedom. But it was a different story in the mines. There the most desperate characters were sent down shackled, day after day, to work endlessly and hopelessly.

It was natural that shipbuilding should flourish. No longer, as in the time of Hesiod, did Greeks go to sea only in the summer. By the 6th century B.C. they voyaged from spring to fall, often out of sight of land, and war galleys over 100 feet high were built to convoy the large Greek cargo vessels. Scholars are still not certain exactly what these galleys called *triremes* looked like, but in all probability they had three banks of rowers, with each man pulling one oar. A wood and bronze beak gleamed on the prow, ready to ram enemy vessels.

Up until this time Greece, like all ancient countries before her, had carried on business transactions by means of barter, usually oxen, or by using metal bars for currency. The economic transformation brought about by colonial expansion soon made this old system hopelessly cumbersome. Now the whole Greek world adopted the use of coinage from Lydia and the Ionian cities of Asia Minor, and with far-reaching effects. Gradually the man who had a great deal of portable wealth became more powerful than the one with noble birth or much property. He could buy out the poorer man who, having lost his land, was often enslaved for debt. Artisans and sailors swelled the ranks of the discontented in the cities.

Thus in the end colonization had given the city-states new economic problems for old—and the new ones were just as severe. What was needed was a reform of the city-state government. The old wealthy aristocracy who had succeeded the kings could have little concern for the problems of the ordinary man in this new money age. Someone should be put in power who would rule in the interests of the *people* (the *demos*). To get such reform the Greeks turned to tyrants.

❖ *The Age of Tyranny (650-500 B.C.)* The word "tyrant" did not have the sinister connotation for the Greeks that it has for us today. Indeed, at first it had quite the opposite meaning: the Greek tyrant was the man who ended the oppression of the masses by overthrowing the old government of the nobles. The weakness of one-man government, however, is obvious. To whom was the tyrant responsible, and how could he be removed? Ultimately he was responsible only to the people. Only a revolution could remove him. Hence the way of the tyrants led inevitably to violence. The independent Greek spirit was more content under the system of an *oligarchy* (rule by the wealthy few) or a *democracy* (rule by the many). We may trace these two types of government in the histories of Sparta and Athens, oligarchy and democracy.

CHAPTER 17

An Oligarchy and a Democracy

. . . a state exists for the sake of a good life, and not for the sake of life only.

ARISTOTLE

"The government of the Athenians . . . I do not approve of," wrote a crusty old Greek of the 5th century B.C., for "in choosing it they chose that scoundrels should become better off than decent citizens." To a present-day North American such words come as a shock. Is not democracy the best possible form of government? And did not the Greeks gain immortality by forming the first democracies?

The following chapters show us how the Athenians attained their form of government, and why it did not immediately meet with the approval of all the Greeks—particularly the Spartans.

❖ *On Top of a Volcano*   The principal city of the Peloponnesus (as the southern peninsula of Greece is named) was Sparta.   It was situated in the heart of Laconia, a district boasting the best agricultural land of the Peloponnesus.   Dorian invaders overran Laconia about 1000 B.C. and divided the population into three distinct layers of society:

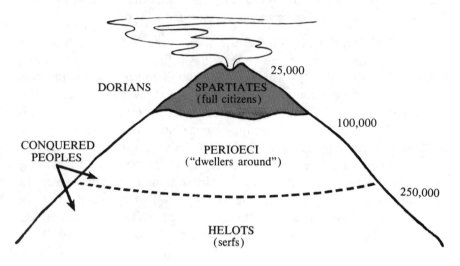

THE SPARTAN VOLCANO

The perioeci were left free to live in their own mountain and coastal towns which lay in a ring around Sparta. They could engage in industry and trade, but they lacked political rights, were heavily taxed, and were liable to military service. Helots were slaves in every sense of the word, except that they could not be sold or killed by their Spartan masters. They were owned by the state, had no political rights, and worked the land in permanent subservience.

Sparta had a unique means of relieving her economic hardships. Most Greek cities, as you have learned, sent out colonies to remedy the situation at home. But Sparta sent out only one. The main remedy she followed was to annex her western neighbour, Messenia, and by the end of the 7th century B.C. to reduce the Messenians to the status of helots. Henceforth the Spartiates were even more in the minority than they had been before. How, then, could they maintain themselves as the dominant group? A permanent standing army was the only possible safeguard against a Messenian revolt. Therefore society had to be organized to one purpose: the production and maintenance of the professional soldier.

Lycurgus

The name of Lycurgus is usually associated with the far-reaching reforms which were instituted in order to make Sparta into a military society, though little is known about this semi-mythical 9th century law-giver. (Indeed it has been said that he was not a man but a god.) When you realize that there was only one Spartiate to every 10 or 15 non-citizens, you can appreciate the problem faced by Lycurgus. The Spartan overlords must have felt as if they were living on top of a volcano.

Plutarch, a Greek historian of the 2nd century A.D., says that Lycurgus' reforms included the early abolition of "the unnecessary and superfluous arts"; henceforth Spartan artisans were to be "freed from useless tasks." In earlier times the Spartans had been noted for arts and manufactures. Architecture, pottery, music, poetry, and a busy trade with foreign ports were all known in Sparta in the 8th and 7th centuries B.C. But for the sake of the army all this was now renounced. The Spartan ideal became a military one with no room for culture or individuality, and no time even for the "laconic" (from the word "Laconia") inhabitants to indulge in flowery speech.

The training of boys

No Spartan boy could enjoy the carefree days of childhood for long. At the age of seven he was taken from his mother and put into barracks to begin his education (well described by Plutarch in the Source Reading on pages 215-216. Until he was twenty he was drilled and disciplined to be a self-reliant, tough, unthinking soldier. At twenty, adult military training began, and although the citizen was expected to marry he was to spend most of his time on active service and to visit his wife only by stealth. The troops ate in common messes—a visitor entertained in one of them is reputed to have said that he now understood why Spartans did not fear death!—and from thirty (the age of full citizenship) to sixty the Spartans could be drafted for military service. The army was made up of regiments of heavy infantry. With such rigorous and continuous training, it is little wonder that the Spartan heavy-armed *hoplite* (infantryman) was about as formidable a soldier as the world has ever seen.

The training of girls

Spartan women were expected to be hardy mothers. Girls were given physical training and were indoctrinated to expect their sons back from battle either carrying their shields or being carried on them. As might be expected, in order to preserve such a rigid system it was felt necessary to exclude foreign ideas and foreign travellers from Sparta, and Spartans ordinarily were forbidden to leave the country—possibly to prevent their desertion from the army. Moreover, a secret police was organized, a kind of commando corps of picked youths who were at the service of the state to murder any helots whom they suspected of plotting rebellion.

Spartan government

Spartan government included some early Greek ideas in that the two monarchs, who ruled simultaneously, exercised priestly and judicial as well as kingly functions. After the 7th century B.C., however, the real power rested in the hands of the five overseers or *ephors,* who presided over both the legislative bodies: the Assembly and the Senate (see diagram). The 30 members of the Senate, who served for life, prepared legislation for the Assembly and were advisers to the kings. The Assembly, it should be noted, did not initiate legislation or debate; it only voted to accept or reject what had already been put before it by the ephors. Nor was there any tedious business of counting ballots: the faction that the ephors decided had shouted the loudest carried the day.

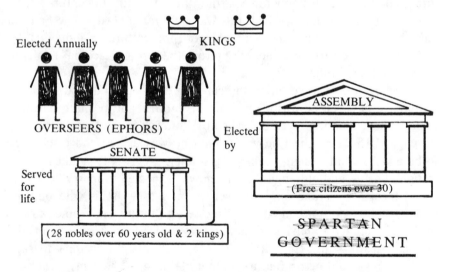

Thus the five ephors really controlled both kings and Senate, and were, in addition, responsible for maintaining order and discipline within the Spartan state. It was not, however, this peculiar constitution that marked Sparta off from other Greek states. It was her totalitarian and militaristic organization of society, an organization which guaranteed Sparta the military leadership of Greece.

The Pelo-ponnesian League

In the 6th century B.C. a league of states was organized in the Peloponnesus with Sparta at the head. Stability and singleness of purpose had made Sparta a first-class military power, and now she bent her energies to creating a centralized Greek military machine. It was thanks to Sparta that the Peloponnesian League was ready for the Persians when they came in the 5th century B.C.

❖ *Two Archons and the Law*   While Sparta was winning leadership in the Peloponnesus, Athens was a second- or third-class power. But she was to achieve her special glory, Athenian democracy, and in this four men are outstanding:

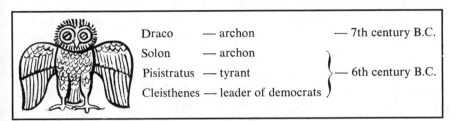

Draco	— archon	— 7th century B.C.
Solon	— archon	
Pisistratus	— tyrant	— 6th century B.C.
Cleisthenes	— leader of democrats	

In the beginning, Athens had an aristocratic government whose real head was a supreme judge or magistrate called an *archon,* and in 621 B.C. a man named Draco was elected archon. Draco is famous for the codification and publication of Athenian law, a law that was very harsh ("draconian") because it was designed to end blood-feuds and to make the state responsible for punishing those guilty of homicide. *Draco*

But times were hard, and all these legal reforms did not help the small farmer who had been unable to make his farm pay, had lost his land by defaulting on a mortgage to some noble, and had ended by being sold into slavery. A revolution was imminent—unless someone could accomplish a wholesale redistribution of land in Attica. With great foresight, the Assembly in 594 B.C. elected a remarkable man as the new archon having supreme power: Solon—poet, merchant, traveller, and statesman. *Solon*

Solon was no radical. He did not redivide the land, but instead reduced debts and freed all who had gone into slavery on account of them. Most important of all, he decreed that in future no one could be enslaved for debt. This meant that the whole population had achieved the status of citizens; there would be no Attic helots. *Oil and pottery*

Solon also did great things for Athenian trade and industry. He fully realized that Athens could not grow enough food to feed herself; she would always have to import grain. But what could she export in exchange for grain? Solon knew that Attica was one of the best olive-growing regions in all Greece. Accordingly he forbade the export of any agricultural products except olive oil. If exporting olive oil was the way to make money, farmers would grow olives. The result was that Attica soon became a leading producer of olive oil. Henceforth Athenian olive oil bought grain for Athens.

Olive-growing, however, did not require as many labourers as grain-growing. What work could be found for the additional unemployed? Once again the answer centred around the olive grove. Oil was transported in pottery containers; hence more of these would now be needed. To speed the manufacture of these jars foreign craftsmen were encouraged to settle in Athens in return for Athenian citizenship, and thanks partly to them and partly to the good beds of reddish-brown clay near the city, the pottery industry boomed. Soon the craftsmen of Attica were excelling their rivals in other city-states and had gained a virtual monopoly of the pottery business. Their beautiful jars, originally designed solely as containers for olive oil (and later for wine and honey), were the tin cans of the 6th century B.C. Now they grace many a museum.

Solon's political and legal reforms

Under Solon's rule four classes of Athenians were recognized on the basis of wealth. The first three were composed of the large and small landowners; the fourth consisted of the poor, the *thetes,* landless men who worked for hire. The first three classes already had the privileges and responsibilities of citizens. It was the fourth class that now won certain political rights which included membership in the Assembly.

Solon reorganized the laws of Athens and created a popular court of appeal, of which all citizens were entitled to be members. He increased the number of magistrates or archons to nine, and these were chosen annually by the Assembly from men of the two upper classes. After their year of office they became members of a Council of Elders, which functioned as a court to try those accused of crimes against religion or of plotting to subvert the constitution.

You would expect that such changes would give the lowest class a voice in the government. In theory they did; but in practice such was hardly the case. Since there was no pay for jury service or Assembly duty it is probable that few thetes could afford to attend, and that in practice both the juries and the Assembly were dominated by the propertied classes. Hence Solon did not end class strife, and the dissension was to be aggravated further by a war with a rival city-state, Megara.

Pisistratus

❖ *An Able Tyrant* The hero of the war with Megara was a young soldier named Pisistratus. Pisistratus was bent on making himself tyrant

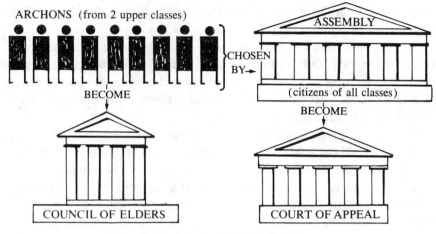

ARCHONS (from 2 upper classes)

CHOSEN BY→

ASSEMBLY

(citizens of all classes)

BECOME

BECOME

COUNCIL OF ELDERS

COURT OF APPEAL

SOLON'S REFORMS

of Athens, but as leader of a coalition of peasants, herdsmen, and miners ("Men of the Hills") he found himself opposed by the nobles with estates in the best farming districts ("Men of the Plains") and the wealthy traders and manufacturers ("Men of the Shore"). Pisistratus seized power in 560 B.C. Twice he was overthrown; but finally, backed by armed force and aided by his own masterly trickery, he consolidated his tyranny in 546 B.C.

. . . The people he deprived of their arms in the following manner. Holding a review of the citizens under arms at the Theseum, he attempted to address them, but spoke in a low voice; and when they declared they could not hear him, he bade them come up near the gateway of the Acropolis in order that his voice might sound louder. While he was passing the time making his speech, persons appointed to the task took the arms and locking them in a building near the Theseum, came and made a sign to Pisistratus. He finished his speech and then told them about the arms, bidding them not wonder or be dejected but go and attend to their private affairs, as he would himself manage all public matters.

Such was the origin of the tyranny of Pisistratus and such were its vicissitudes. . . .

Pisistratus drove many of the wealthy landowners into exile, confiscated their land, and divided it up among the landless. He then proceeded to levy an income tax on the first three classes, and to furnish employment for the city poor by undertaking extensive public works. He also encouraged greater production of olive oil and wine for export,

AN OLIGARCHY AND A DEMOCRACY/153

negotiated treaties to increase trade, and built a navy to protect the grain route. By so doing he was at least partly responsible for launching Athens on the road to empire.

Pisistratus was an outstandingly able tyrant and an enlightened ruler. Under his regime sculpture and vase-painting flourished, and it was his policy to encourage recitals of epic poetry and to promote performances of tragic drama. Pisistratus transformed Athens from a small country town into an international centre.

Yet, tyrant though he was, Pisistratus prepared the way for democracy. He strengthened the whole of the Athenian populace, both high and low, by improving the lot of the small peasants who now became independent farmers, the merchants who were now able to compete with those of Miletus and Corinth, and even the landed aristocracy who found more profit in producing oil and wine for export than in growing grain for home consumption. Above all, Pisistratus destroyed the strong political influence of the noble families.

❖ *Democracy Triumphs* In 527 B.C. Pisistratus was succeeded by his two sons, Hippias and Hipparchus. But their hold on Athens was soon weakened, and in 514 B.C. Hipparchus was assassinated. Four years later his brother was expelled from Athens.

Hippias and Hipparchus

This beautiful piece of pottery, created in Attica about 550 B.C., had a very practical purpose. It is an *amphora*, a general storage jar used for wine, grain, oil, or honey. The amphora was made with an opening large enough for a ladle to be inserted and, as you might expect, had a cover to protect the contents. The Greek craftsman painted his figures on the natural red clay in a velvety jet-black glaze, after which the details were etched with some hard pointed instrument so as to expose the red beneath. Sometimes white and purple pigments heightened the decoration. Here we see Achilles and Ajax (two of Homer's heroes) absorbed in a close game of draughts—so close, the inscription tells us, that the score is four to three.

In the forefront of those opposing Hippias had been an ambitious *Cleisthenes* noble named Cleisthenes. Cleisthenes now set about reorganizing the electoral system of Athens so that the political influence of the powerful old noble families was greatly reduced. Ten new electoral districts, each of which included a complete cross-section of Athenian society, replaced the four old groupings which had been drawn up according to wealth. Henceforth the individual counted for more than the family in Athenian politics.

In addition a new Council of Five Hundred (*Boulê*) was instituted. *The Boulê* It was chosen annually by lot from citizens over thirty years of age, and since each person served only once it was likely every citizen would get the chance to serve on it during his lifetime. This new body had power to draft legislation, to deal with foreign affairs, and to supervise the entire administration. The result was a vast increase in actual participation in government by the general populace. Amateurs ruled the politics of Athens, and probably every male Athenian citizen had some public service to his credit. For example, any man who could command attention could address the Assembly. A leather merchant who criticized a military campaign found himself elected general and told to finish it off!

The Athenians devised a unique method of preventing a return to *Ostracism*

tyranny. It was called *ostracism*. By this process, votes were recorded on broken pieces of pottery called *ostraka*. If at least 6000 people scratched on their ostraka the names of men whom they wished banished, then the citizen with the greatest number of votes cast against him had to leave Attica within ten days and remain in exile for ten years, although he did not lose his citizenship, property, or revenues. By means of this unpopularity contest the Athenians got rid of unwanted citizens without resorting to violence. Even this system, however, was abused. It seems that even an ostrakon box could be stuffed!

Jury duty

About a generation after Cleisthenes the old Court of Appeal was revamped in such a way that 6000 jurors were selected by lot to serve each year. So large were the juries (they numbered from 201, in some cases to 1001 or even 1501) that although justice was meted out by amateurs, it was a sufficiently large number of amateurs that it was quite impossible to either browbeat or bribe them.

The foundations of Athenian democracy had been securely laid. Solon had placed the administration in the hands of the aristocratic well-to-do, hoping that they would govern the poorer classes with wisdom. But by the time of Cleisthenes, the merchants and manufacturers from these poorer classes had risen in the scale to the point where they wanted to govern themselves—and did so, by means of an alliance with the landed peasants.

The meaning of "democracy" to the Greeks

Democracy did not, of course, mean to the Greeks what it means to us. Women, slaves and non-Athenians had no vote. Even so, no other state we have so far studied granted political rights to such a high proportion of its citizens despite the fact that the 43,000 adult males who

ATHENIAN MALE CITIZENS

WOMEN, CHILDREN, SLAVES, NON-ATHENIANS

THE ATHENIAN FRANCHISE

did have the vote made up only approximately one-seventh of the total Athenian population. Moreover, on any single occasion at least one in every 50 Athenians probably took an active part in the assembly. When we consider that 265 members of parliament represent 19,000,000 Canadians, then only one in about every 72,000 Canadians ever takes part directly in our national government. By modern standards of representation, then, the Athenians certainly took an active part in politics.

But we must be careful to understand fully the meaning of democracy for the Greeks. In Athens the landless thetes outnumbered all the rest of the citizens, so that Athenian democracy became almost synonymous with control of the state by the poorest class. This fact explains why most Greek writers tended to use the word "democracy" as a term of abuse. Such a critic was the Old Oligarch, whose bitter condemnation of Athenian government opened this chapter and whose further censures may be read in the Source Reading on page 217.

CHAPTER 18

Repelling the Persians

Our cause is now balanced on the razor's edge: whether we are to be free or slaves. . . .

THE IONIAN GREEKS

So far fortune had smiled on the Hellenes. In the 8th and 7th centuries B.C. they had been given a period of comparative calm during which they could establish a fringe of Greek colonies in Ionia along the Asia Minor coast without interference from Assyria or Babylonia. But in the 6th century B.C. the situation changed. Croesus of Lydia managed to gain control of this coast and most of the Ionian cities. When he was conquered by Cyrus of Persia in 546 B.C. these Greek cities found themselves part of the Persian Empire.

These Asia Minor cities were important to Persia as sources of revenue and as naval bases. Hence they prospered. But their rule by tyrants with Persian backing hardly measured up to Greek ideals of government by discussion, and a revolt led by Miletus broke out in 499 B.C. Sparta refused to help the rebels, but Athens and Eretria rallied to their assistance. The famous account of the wars recorded in Herodotus' *Histories* vividly describes Darius's reaction to the news:

He took no notice of the Ionians—they would not escape punishment, but "Who," he said, "are the Athenians?" On being told, he asked for his bow, laid an arrow on it, and shooting it into the sky, he called on Ahuramazda to grant him vengeance on the Athenians. Then he bade one of his servants say to him thrice each time he dined, "Master, remember the Athenians."

The assistance was in vain. The immense resources of the empire were mobilized to crush the rebels, and the Greeks suffered a devastating naval defeat in 494 B.C. Alerted by these storm warnings and foreseeing a long struggle with the Greek mainland ahead, the Persians proceeded to try to ensure the good will of the Ionian cities by reorganizing them as democracies. Then they went on to conquer the Aegean coast up to the Hellespont.

The Persian Wars broke on Greece in two waves from 490 to 479 B.C.

❖ *The Miracle of Marathon*   Eretria and Athens had dared to actively

The First Persian Invasion

encourage a revolt against Persia; they must be taught a lesson. In 490 B.C. the Persians struck, determined to mete out the proper punishment and to restore Pisistratus' son, Hippias, whom they had brought with them, as a quisling tyrant. The force of approximately 40,000 Persians[1] met with only scattered opposition and took Eretria with comparatively little effort. Then they partially disembarked at Marathon on the east coast of Attica, about 25 miles north of Athens.

Sparta had promised the Athenians aid. But when the famous distance runner Pheidippides covered the 140 miles to Sparta in 48 hours to solicit aid, tradition has it that the Spartans refused because they were in the midst of a religious festival. So 10,000 Athenians were left alone, except for 1000 Plataeans, to face a force of about 20,000 Persians at Marathon.

But a strange quirk of fate had removed one of the Greeks' most formidable obstacles. Thanks to some Ionians in the Persian camp, the Athenian general Miltiades received the priceless information that the Persians were in the habit of grazing and watering their horses at night by the springs at the far end of the Marathon plain. For the time being, then, the dreaded Persian cavalry was absent. The Greeks had to act

[1]Contemporary figures for the size of armies in ancient and medieval times are usually unreliable. While it is impossible to be certain, the figures given in the following pages are reasonable modern estimates.

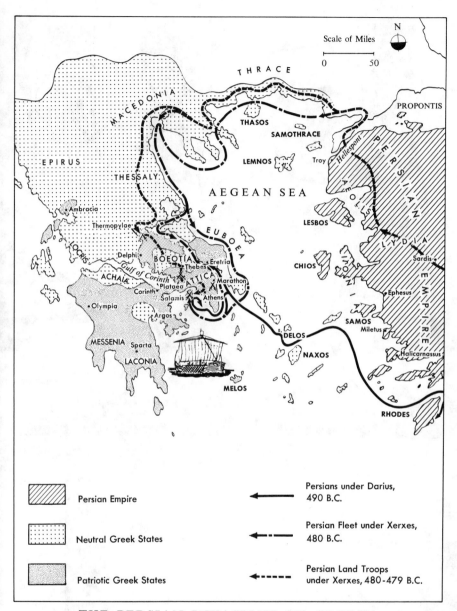

THE PERSIAN INVASIONS OF GREECE

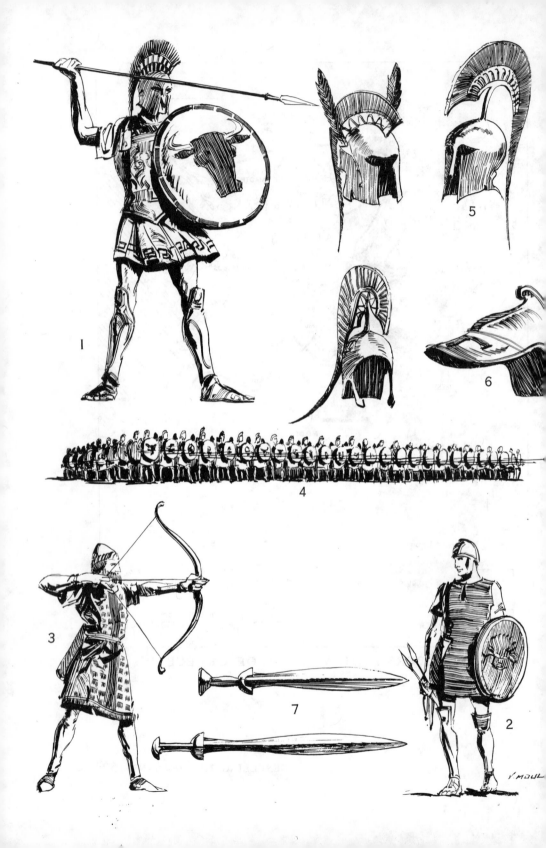

1

5

6

4

3

7

2

V.MOUL

quickly. At dawn the hoplites advanced across the plain, breaking into a run as they came within range of enemy arrows. Then, letting his centre ranks sag inwards to engage the bulk of the Persian host, Miltiades wheeled his heavily reinforced wings to envelop the enemy from the rear. The Persians were thrown into confusion. The superior defensive armour, longer spears, and better discipline of the Greek infantry had won the day.

The brilliant victory at Marathon is forever the glory of Athens. Leaving behind their 6400 dead (the Greeks lost 192), the Persians fled to their ships. The Spartans did not arrive until two days after the battle, and then brought only 2000 men, their tardy arrival with this comparatively small force having more to do with fear of a helot revolt at home than with a religious festival.

The Persian fleet sailed round the coast hoping to catch Athens undefended, but Miltiades marched his Athenians back to the city quickly enough to face the Persians again. The proud enemy retreated to Asia without giving battle.

The "miracle of Marathon," as it has been called, had a threefold significance. First, it keyed the Athenians up to a hitherto unimaginable patriotic pitch. "They were the first of the Greeks," wrote Herodotus, "who dared to look upon the Median [Persian] garb, and to face men clad in that fashion. Until this time the very name of the Medes had been a terror to the Greeks to hear." Second, Sparta had been shown that it was possible for Greeks to defeat Persians. Third, and most important, other Greek city-states were inspired and emboldened to resist the future Persian invasions that were bound to come.

❖ *A Fight to the Death* The Greeks were fortunate in having ten years to prepare for the next Persian onslaught. During this time the democrat

---

The Greek hoplite of about 500 B.C. (1) wore body armour called a *cuirass,* usually over a short skirt. *Greaves* (armour tailored to the legs) needed no straps to be held in place and extended high enough to protect the knees. The light-armed skirmishers (2) were equipped with slings as well as javelins and had smaller shields, leather instead of metal armour, and less elaborate helmets. Greek armour was generally made of bronze, although iron had been in use for some time.

It is more difficult to portray a typical Persian soldier (3) because of the great variations in the personnel of Persian armies. Scale armour, which was used in the East at this time, was sometimes worn, and the favoured weapon was a short bow, quite unlike the later long-bow of medieval times.

In the famous Greek phalanx (4) the hoplites stood in solid lines up to 16 ranks deep with shields close or overlapping, a formation virtually invincible when reinforced by cavalry. The Greeks wore a great variety of helmets, four examples of which are given in (5) and (6). Greek swords (7), like most Greek creations, were extremely beautiful in design, with both edges curved and usable. They were usually of bronze.

Themistocles (528-462 B.C.) rose to power. It was providential for Athens that she had such a leader at this stage of her history.

Themistocles' appearance was deceptive. This popular citizen was a broad-faced, thick-necked man whose drooping moustache undulated amiably on a jovial face. He was a family man, twice married, who knew everyone by name and never forgot a face. One can imagine this stocky politician being continually stopped in the market-place by petitioners who misjudged his approachableness for soft-heartedness.

They were mistaken. Themistocles was a man of strong and uncompromising opinions who did not hesitate to remove his rivals by ostracism. Above all, he had an extraordinary ability to analyze a complex situation and then to deal with it by rapid action. When a fellow democrat named Aristides proposed that a new rich vein of silver which had been discovered in the mines at Laurium be divided as spoil among the citizens, Themistocles insisted that instead it be used to build a strong fleet of at least two hundred ships. In the end the unfortunate Aristides was ostracized, and the Athenian fleet was made ready to give battle to the Persians. Henceforth it was to be the bulwark of the Athenian empire.

The Second Persian Invasion   The Persian expedition of 480 B.C. was organized on a vast scale by the new king, Xerxes (485-465 B.C.). Xerxes had 500 warships. Small wonder that the Peloponnesians, headed by Sparta, turned to Athens and her navy.

In order to prevent the Greek fleet from being cut off from its land bases it was decided to oppose the Persian army at the narrow pass of Thermopylae. A small force of about 7300 manned the pass, but they were betrayed when a traitor led the Persians by a secret mountain road to attack the Greeks from the rear. While the main Greek force managed to retreat in the hopes of gaining time for a decisive meeting of the fleets, a gallant force of only 1000—300 Spartans and 700 Thespians— stayed behind to hold the pass. They were slaughtered to a man.

Athens had to be evacuated, and when the Persians arrived they sacked and burned the stately acropolis. But though Xerxes had taken a city he had not won a war. There still remained the Greek navy, and once more Themistocles had his way. Let the Greek ships, he argued, be stationed in the bay of the island of Salamis, there to await the Persian fleet in a narrow strait four miles long and one mile wide. The trick was to make sure the Persians would come to them. Here again Themistocles left nothing to chance. He saw to it that false information reached the

Persians to the effect that the Greeks were about to slip out of Salamis bay. The Persians reacted precisely as Themistocles had intended. Determined to keep the Greek ships bottled up, the Persian fleet rowed all night to meet them.

At daybreak one September day in 480 B.C. the two fleets clashed. *Salamis* The confident Xerxes had his golden throne set up on a headland, from which vantage point he could watch in ease and elegance while his fleet destroyed these Greek upstarts once and for all. But here, in the words of Herodotus, is the scene that met his eyes:

Far the greater number of the Persian ships engaged in this battle were disabled. . . . For as the Greeks fought in order and kept their line, while the barbarians were in confusion and had no plan in anything that they did, the issue of the battle could scarce be other than it was. Yet the Persians fought far more bravely here than at Euboea, and indeed surpassed themselves; each did his utmost through fear of Xerxes, for each thought that the king's eye was upon himself.

There fell in this combat Ariabignes, one of the chief commanders of the fleet, who was son of Darius and brother of Xerxes, and with him perished a vast number of men of high repute, Persians, Medes, and allies. Of the Greeks there died only a few; for, as they were able to swim, all those that were not slain outright by the enemy escaped from the sinking vessels and swam across to Salamis. But on the side of the barbarians more perished by drowning than in any other way, since they did not know how to swim. The great destruction took place when the ships which had been first engaged began to fly; for they who were stationed in the rear, anxious to display their valour before the eyes of the king, made every effort to force their way to the front, and thus became entangled with such of their own vessels as were retreating.

The King of Kings had seen enough. His glorious armada, unable to manoeuvre in the narrow strait, had been fatally crippled. Its shattered remnants were ordered to sail to the Hellespont, where Xerxes met them with the larger part of his army, which had been evacuated after a gruelling forty-five day march from Thessaly.

But the Greeks dared not relax their vigilance. The best cavalry and infantry of Persia had been left in Greece for the winter, and all could yet be lost for the allies. The next August they took a solemn oath: "I shall fight to the death, I shall put freedom before life, I shall not desert colonel or captain alive or dead, I shall carry out the general's commands, and I shall bury my comrades-in-arms where they fall and leave none unburied." For three weeks the Persian cavalry harried the Greeks on the plain outside Plataea; but they were not to be provoked into fighting before they were ready. When at last the battle was joined in September of 479 B.C., 60,000 Greeks defeated 80,000 Persians, and the Spartan hoplites proved themselves to be the finest troops in the civilized world. According to tradition, it was on the same day that the Greek navy caught and burned the remainder of the Persian fleet.

By 479 B.C. the Greeks were supreme. A group of tiny city-states had defeated the mighty Persian Empire. Looking back some twenty-four centuries later it still seems miraculous—and the irony is that the Persians themselves indirectly contributed to their own downfall.

By making the Greeks fight for their very homes, the Persians had done for the Greeks what the Greeks could not do for themselves: they had temporarily wiped out city-state jealousies by immeasurably strengthening the sense of unity of all Greeks as opposed to all "barbarians" (a term which simply meant non-Greeks). Yet this was to be no union of equals. Athens came out of the wars the leading power in Greece, and her navy was henceforth her wall of defence and source of power. These two factors, combined with the increased political importance of the Athenian generals, were to make Athens the head of a large and unwilling empire.

CHAPTER 19

Athens Becomes Imperialistic

All who have taken it upon themselves to rule over others have incurred hatred and unpopularity for a time; but if one has a great aim to pursue, the burden of envy must be accepted, and it is wise to accept it.

PERICLES

Even after the Persians were gone from the mainland, it was only natural for the Greek confederacy to continue. There were good reasons for maintaining Greek unity: the danger of further Persian aggression, and the fact that Greek colonies in Asia Minor had still to be liberated. Yet it did not take long, once outside pressure was removed, for Athens and Sparta to fall out.

❖ *Athens Takes Over*   Sparta had long been the leader of Greece, a leadership which the Athenians acknowledged. But now that the enemy had been driven out Sparta made a disconcerting proposal. Athens, she said, should not rebuild her ruins; they should be left as a perpetual reminder of what Persia had done. Immediately Athens' suspicions were aroused. If she did not rebuild her city—and this included her walls—she would be at the mercy of any attacker, even of Sparta. There was only one thing to do.

Themistocles went to Sparta to discuss the whole matter. He assured the Spartans that Athens would not refortify; but even as he parleyed the walls of Athens were rising again. Spartan observers were sent to Athens, only to be detained there—on the instructions of Themistocles. Then, when the word came to the wily Athenian leader that the walls were high enough to be defensible, he admitted all to the Spartans. Sparta had been outfoxed. She could only accept what had already been done.

Next, trouble arose involving the commander of the allied expeditionary force in Asia Minor. Throughout the war, military leadership had been given almost as a matter of course to the Spartans. But the Spartan commander of the Greek force that captured Byzantium began to intrigue with the Persians to become despot there and was recalled by his home government. The Greek contingents had already been antagonized by the overbearing conduct of the Spartan generals, and now they jumped at the chance to change to Athenian command. Sparta withdrew her troops and commanders from Asia Minor and sulked in the Peloponnesus, while Athens accepted the bid for leadership with alacrity. After all she was the great sea power among the states, and only a sea power could command the coasts and islands of the Aegean.

Since Sparta had gone off in a corner by herself, the other city-states decided to let her stay there. Now, under Athenian leadership, they formed a new organization without her: the Confederacy of Delos (478 B.C.). In this League each member state was pledged to contribute men plus either ships or money, and most of the states contributed money, which the Athenians then used to build and man new naval squadrons in order to keep Mediterranean sea-lanes free from Persian interference. In other words, Athens was providing the teeth of the new organization. Moreover, the constitution of the League provided that no state might withdraw without the consent of all. Events were soon to prove that this really meant the consent of Athens—and that this consent would never be given.

The Confederacy of Delos

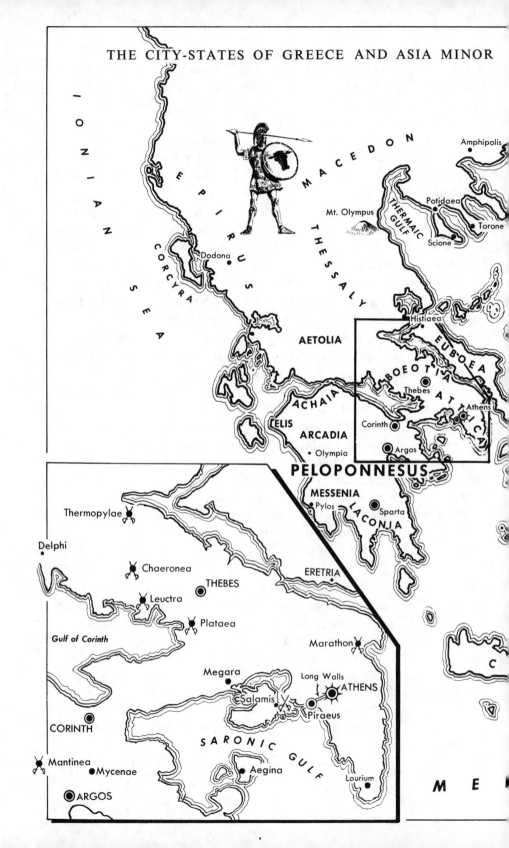

THE CITY-STATES OF GREECE AND ASIA MINOR

IONIAN SEA

CORCYRA

EPIRUS

MACEDON

Amphipolis

Potidaea

Torone

Mt. Olympus

THERMAIC GULF

Scione

Dodona

THESSALY

AETOLIA

Histiaea

EUBOEA

BOEOTIA

Thebes

ATTICA

Athens

ACHAIA

ELIS

ARCADIA

Corinth

Olympia

Argos

PELOPONNESUS

MESSENIA

Pylos

Sparta

LACONIA

Thermopylae

Delphi

Chaeronea

THEBES

ERETRIA

Leuctra

Plataea

Gulf of Corinth

Marathon

Megara

Long Walls

ATHENS

Salamis

Piraeus

CORINTH

SARONIC GULF

Mantinea

Mycenae

Aegina

Laurium

ARGOS

ME

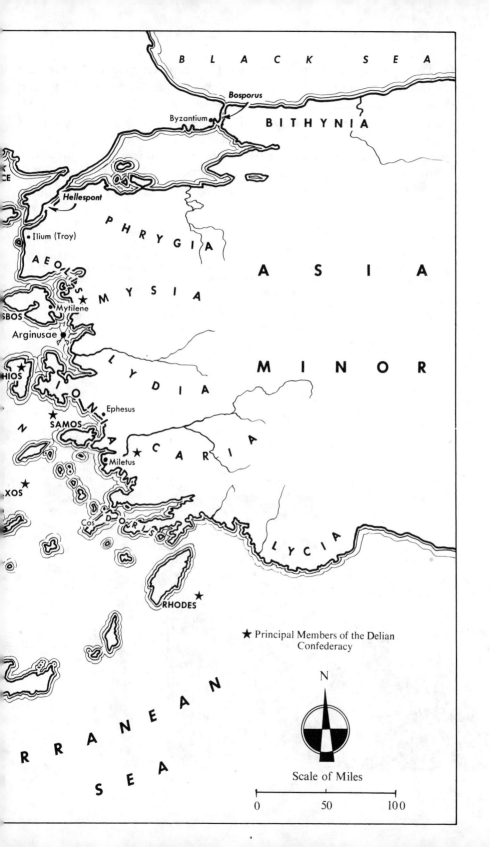

BLACK SEA

Bosporus

Byzantium

BITHYNIA

Hellespont

PHRYGIA

ASIA

Ilium (Troy)

AEOLIS

MYSIA

Mytilene

LESBOS

Arginusae

MINOR

LYDIA

CHIOS

I O N I A

Ephesus

SAMOS

CARIA

Miletus

NAXOS

Cos

D O R I S

LYCIA

RHODES

★ Principal Members of the Delian
Confederacy

MEDITERRANEAN

SEA

N

Scale of Miles

0   50   100

Trouble erupted when Naxos and Thasos proclaimed that, since the League had been formed to drive out Persians and since this had by then been accomplished, they should be allowed to withdraw. This was not agreeable to Athens. Why should non-members enjoy the benefits of membership while those who continued as members bore a higher proportion of the cost? Would not the Confederacy, in fact, break up? Then who would be safe from the Persians? So Naxos and Thasos were crushed, tribute was imposed on them, and they were pressed hard under

About 500 feet above the city of Athens rises the Acropolis, covering two modern city blocks. Originally the Acropolis was the city itself, but later it became the dwelling-place of the goddess Athena and the site of a magnificent group of buildings. The most famous of these—and the largest—is the *Parthenon.* Inside this magnificent temple once stood the great 40-foot gold and ivory figure of Athena by Phidias, while majestic sculptures of the gods graced the pediment over the columns. To the left of the Parthenon towered the great bronze statue of Athena, 70 feet high and visible far out to sea. The Parthenon remained intact until A.D. 1687, when a powder magazine located in the building blew up.

the Athenian thumb. Finally in 454 B.C. the common treasury, which had at first been kept on the island of Delos, was moved to Athens. With the treasury went the annual congress of members. It was the last step to complete control of the League by Athens. Henceforth the Athenian court became the court of appeal for disputes between states.

Thus within a generation Athens had built up a formidable maritime empire, and had gained an unenviable reputation as the "enslaver of Hellas." What had driven her to this extreme?

❖ *Greece Divided* Themistocles clearly saw that Athens' existence was dependent upon sea power. Because she could not produce enough food to support herself she must draw on Sicily or the Black Sea area for grain. She therefore had to compete with the great commercial city of Corinth for Sicilian grain, and to make sure that Persia did not cut off her grain supply from the Black Sea. Themistocles had already encouraged the Athenians to rebuild the walls of their ruined city. Now

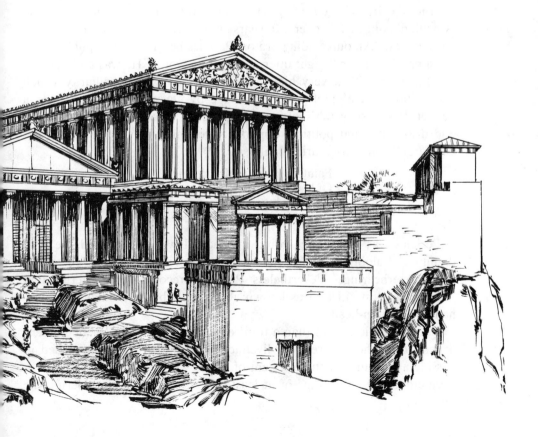

he determined that the Piraeus, the port of Athens, likewise should be fortified. He was determined that no one, at home (and here he was darkly suspicious of Sparta) or abroad (he had learned from the bitter war years to be wary of ambitious foreigners), should threaten Athens' naval bases.

Yet, great statesman that he was, Themistocles hopelessly divided Greece between Athens and Sparta, and his successor Pericles was to continue the same policy. Moreover, by making many enemies among the aristocrats of what may be called the conservative party, Themistocles split Athens itself up the middle between conservatives and democrats. The democrats, as the name indicates, usually moved in the direction of liberalizing the government, passing measures such as those which reduced the power of the Council of Elders or established regular pay for jurymen in the Athenian courts. Conservatives, on the other hand, were suspicious of the masses, or of anyone who made overtures to them. Such contrasting philosophies were to rend Athens for the rest of the century, long after Themistocles himself had been exiled.

Pericles

❖ *Athens' Greatest Citizen* The democrat who was to dominate Athenian politics for over 30 years was Pericles, a grand-nephew of Cleisthenes. An outstanding orator, Pericles never spoke in public without a prayer that he "might utter no unfitting word." He was an imposing looking man with a very high forehead—a physical peculiarity which his sculptors were careful to camouflage by always having him wear a helmet. But alas, even his lofty position did not protect him from ridicule, and dramatists and political opponents delighted in making fun of his overlarge head, caricaturing him as

> Fainting underneath the weight
> Of his own head; and now abroad
> From his huge gallery of a pate
> Dispenses trouble to the state.

Pericles was a thorough-going intellectual who maintained the cool dignity and aloofness appropriate to his office. Perhaps he even tended to be overbearing. Nevertheless Plutarch records for posterity that Athens' greatest citizen was known about town by the undignified nickname of "onion-head"!

Under Pericles, more than a third of the Athenian adult male citizens depended on the empire for a livelihood. In 450 B.C. he succeeded in passing a measure for the payment of jurors who, it has been calculated, were employed an average of at least 300 days a year. Considering the fact that all the lawsuits from the empire passed through Athenian courts, it is evident that the empire provided ample business for paid jurors. Then by 430 B.C. all the magistrates of the Boulê, too, were paid, as well as soldiers and sailors on active service. Pericles also extended Athenian fortifications by building the Long Walls to protect the Piraeus. No longer were there two separate cities to defend.

It is not surprising that many of these measures were unpopular with Pericles' enemies. Some people accused him of catering to the masses, and it is true that he had a genius for presenting arguments to them so as to win their support. Besides, whereas under Cleisthenes a third of the citizen body had been urban dwellers, under Pericles at least half lived in the city—a proportion well worth catering to. It was natural for the propertied classes of Athens to resent their loss of political influence to these masses. It was even more natural for the allied states to resent some of their money being used, not for League business, but for the beautification of the Athenian acropolis. And it was certainly natural for Sparta to look with increasing fear on the ever-growing power of Athens.

Yet Pericles was undoubtedly carrying out the policy which he was convinced would serve the best interests of his city-state. The tragedy is that through this policy of putting Athens first he led his state into a world war which destroyed the very democracy he sought to serve.

CHAPTER 20

The Greek World War

In times of peace and prosperity cities and individuals alike follow higher standards, because they are not forced into a situation where they have to do what they do not want to do. But war is a stern teacher; in depriving them of the power of easily satisfying their daily wants, it brings most people's minds down to the level of their actual circumstances.

THUCYDIDES

In the last third of the 5th century B.C. democratic Athens faced her most severe test. She faced it and she failed. Within the space of two generations Athens plunged from the heights to the depths. The city that had pioneered in political democracy had taken liberty from others, and ended by losing it herself.

It was a soul-stirring tragedy, and later generations have never ceased to be fascinated by how it happened and why.

❖ *A Cold War Mentality*   The Great Peloponnesian War broke out in 431 B.C., and continued, off and on, until 404 B.C. This twenty-seven years' war has been given a remarkable emphasis in history books because it so happened that one of the Athenian admirals was a man named Thucydides (460-400 B.C.). Thucydides was alleged to have cared more for the protection of his own property than for the city that he was supposed to be guarding. The charge produced his banishment—and the leisure necessary to compose his *History* of the Peloponnesian War, a book that made the war forever famous.

Thucydides

Although the book is unfinished (it goes only to 411 B.C.) it is a remarkable narrative, composed, according to its author, with a set purpose. "The absence of everything mythical from my work perhaps will make it less agreeable to those who hear it read. I shall be contented, however, if it appears useful to those who wish to have a clear idea of the past and hence of the conditions and events which, according to the course of human affairs, will be repeated." How modern this ancient historian sounds! His account of the breakdown of his world cannot help but remind the 20th century reader of the devastating effects of our own two World Wars.

We today are only too familiar with the term "cold war." This was the depth to which relations between Athens and Corinth had sunk in the face of their bitter trade rivalry. Alarmed by Athens' growing power, Corinth appealed to Sparta and her allies to join in an attack on this rich and domineering competitor. A series of incidents involving Corinthian colonies followed, and a complicated network of alliances and counter-alliances was formed. Pericles acted decisively by using blockades and trade embargoes—one more step in the Athenian domination of the Isthmus of Corinth. An angered Athens had shown the other states that she could close her fist on their trade if they did not please her.

It was almost inevitable that one of these states, fearing Athens' stranglehold on the isthmus, should inch to the brink of war. On a rainy spring night in 431 B.C. three hundred Thebans attacked Athens' ally, Plataea. The Greek world was plunged into a generation of war.

❖ *Might Becomes Right*   Land warfare for the Greeks, as for most ancients, often consisted of a series of summer raids. In the winter

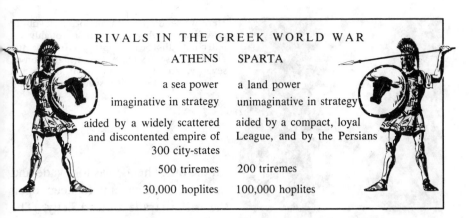

ATHENS	SPARTA
a sea power	a land power
imaginative in strategy	unimaginative in strategy
aided by a widely scattered and discontented empire of 300 city-states	aided by a compact, loyal League, and by the Persians
500 triremes	200 triremes
30,000 hoplites	100,000 hoplites

everyone went home until the next spring. When the Plataeans beat off the Theban attack of 431 B.C., the Spartans invaded Attica and the Athenians retired inside their walls to watch their crops and homes burn —not an easy thing to do.

Their land was being laid waste in front of their very eyes—a thing that the young men had never seen happen and that the old men had seen only at the time of the Persian invasion. Naturally enough, therefore, they felt outraged by this and wanted, especially the young, to march out and stop it. There were constant discussions with violent feelings on both sides, some demanding that they should be led out to battle, and a certain number resisting the demand. . . . Thus the city was in a thoroughly excited state: they were furious with Pericles and paid no attention at all to the advice which he had given them previously; instead they abused him for being a general and not leading them out to battle, and put on him the whole responsibility for what they were suffering themselves.

However, Pericles managed to hold the Athenians in check, and at the close of the campaigning in 430 B.C. inspired them to new military efforts by his famous *Funeral Oration* (selections from which may be read in the Source Reading on pages 216-217. The moving oration is a classic defence of Athenian democracy—though it must still be recognized as a wartime speech designed to whip up patriotic enthusiasm. This does not mean that it is untrue, but it may mean that it is a selection of facts designed to emphasize only the better side of Athenian life.

*Pericles'
Funeral
Oration*

The next year an epidemic of typhus ravaged the city and killed their great statesman; but the Athenian war strategy had already been determined. It was to stay inside the walls, while at the same time breaking down the Peloponnesian morale by coastal raids, and cutting off their food supplies by a naval blockade. The strategy of Sparta and her allies,

Here we see Pericles in one of his favourite poses—thoroughly dignified, thoroughly intellectual, thoroughly Greek. Indeed, the proud face shows more than a suggestion of severity, and the mouth might be on the verge of a sneer.

on the other hand, was to invade and devastate Attica and to keep open the western trade route to Sicily. The war soon turned into an endurance test, with neither side strong enough to deliver the knockout punch.

The conflict dragged on, until after four years all sense of right and wrong had been abandoned. Might was right. When the people of Mytilene, the chief city of the island of Lesbos (one of the charter members of the Confederacy of Delos) revolted, they asked for Spartan aid. But before the aid arrived, Athens blockaded the island and starved Mytilene into submission. The whole incident badly unnerved the Athenians. How, they debated, should they punish these Mytilenian upstarts? In the Assembly at Athens a rabble-rousing leather merchant named Cleon was among the candidates aspiring to fill the position left vacant by Pericles' death. Slapping his thigh, disarranging his clothing, running back and forth, Cleon delivered his harangue. With his shrill voice squealing like a "singed sow's," he exhorted Athens to execute all the men of Mytilene and enslave the women and children. His motion was carried in the Assembly, and a trireme bearing the order was dispatched to Mytilene.

Cleon

Fortunately sober second thoughts soon took over. The very next day the Assembly met and rescinded its brutal decree, despite Cleon's even blunter speech on this occasion. A second trireme sped across the Aegean, the crew eating as they rowed and sleeping in relays. The people of Mytilene were lucky: the trireme was in time. They were spared.

On the other side of Greece, at Corcyra in the Ionian Sea, the people were not so lucky. When a revolution broke out there in 427 B.C., the horrible massacre of oligarchs by democrats was given the moral support of an Athenian fleet standing by.

As the war stretched out, it became much more difficult for any Greek state to remain neutral. To Athens, those who were not for her were against her; and it was in this manner that she reasoned in 416 B.C. to the little state of Melos, a small island that had remained outside her empire. Thucydides, who was no democrat, puts the matter in its most cynical light when he reports the Athenians' callous statement to the Melians: "The powerful exact what they may, and the weak grant what they must." His desire to blacken the record of Athenian democracy prevents his also telling us that the Melians had previously subscribed to the Spartan war fund and had sheltered the Spartan fleet ten years earlier. But even so, even taking into account prior Melian sympathies, the awful Athenian punishment exacted still horrifies us. The men were executed, and the women and children sold into slavery.

❖ *Doomed to Disunity*   But the tide was about to turn. In 415 B.C. the Athenian fleet set sail to support weaker Greek states against Corinth's Sicilian colony, Syracuse. In the next two years another expedition came to relieve the first. Both were lost. Thucydides says simply, "Fleet and army perished from the face of the earth; nothing was saved, and of the many who went forth, few returned home."

Somehow, by a superhuman effort, Athens managed to construct a new fleet of triremes within a year. By now Persia had allied herself with Sparta and had returned to the Aegean, and the two proved more than Athens could cope with. When the Athenian fleet was trapped in the harbour of Mytilene the desperate citizens feverishly built and manned another, their fourth in less than ten years. A brilliant victory was won at Arginusae, but many crews were lost when the fleet was lashed by a storm, and the democratic generals who returned to Athens were executed for negligence—an insane act on the part of the Assembly. Still Athens refused to make peace with Sparta. Finally the last Athenian fleet was caught in the Hellespont and annihilated. When the news of this defeat reached Athens

a wail of lamentation arose from the Piraeus, sweeping up the space between the Long Walls to the city, as each passed the news on to his neighbour. That night not a soul slept, as they mourned not alone for the dead, but still more for themselves, imagining that they were about to suffer such ills as they had imposed on the Melians . . . or on the citizens of Histiaea or Scione or Torone or Aegina, and on many other Hellenes.

The end was not far off. After six months' blockade, with all food gone, Athens surrendered—twenty-seven years after the war had begun. The shortest-lived (478-404 B.C.) and the smallest of ancient empires had collapsed. The Athenian attempt to unify Greece had failed once and for all.

❖ *Death of the City-State*   The Spartans knew no means but force to rule men; hence it is not surprising that they had no long-range plans for Greece. The Long Walls were demolished—though Sparta resisted the demands of Corinth and Thebes to wipe out the great city itself—and in Athens, as in many other Greek cities, the Spartans backed the oligarchical parties with garrisons.   But so brutal was the reactionary regime of the "Thirty Tyrants" in Athens that within months they were overthrown and the democracy restored.

Only a generation later Thebes defeated the Spartan army at Leuctra (371 B.C.) under the brilliant military leader Epaminondas. The massed

Sparta loses the peace

The Greek *trireme* was propelled by a crew of 170 seated at three banks of oars, and could also be assisted by its square sail. In battle the mast was lowered or put on shore, and the oarsmen tried to manoeuvre the ship so as to sink their opponents by means of the bronze ram attached to the prow. The rowers of a trireme were seated as shown in the cross-section drawing below. By means of a projecting outrigger a third bank of oarsmen (whose rowing job was most wearing of all because of the sharp angle) could be added without the construction of a deeper, heavier hull. The result was a ship of great speed, manoeuvrability, and power. It is easy to understand why, in the 5th and 4th centuries B.C., triremes became "the unchallenged queens of the sea."

weight of Theban spears punched right through the Spartan phalanx to end the Peloponnesian League. But meanwhile Athens was resurrecting herself, and in 362 B.C. she reduced both Sparta and Thebes to the status of second-class powers.

Philip of Macedon
It has been said that in the 4th century B.C. "the Greeks devoted their activities to art, science, and mutual extermination, in all of which they were unprecedentedly successful." What was needed was a strong man to end all bickering. That man was Philip of Macedon, who came on the scene to bring order out of chaos.

Philip II had come to the throne of Macedon, a wild, hilly country in northern Greece, at the age of twenty-three. He was an able ruler— soldier, diplomat, and athlete all in one. He had been a hostage in Thebes in his youth and had learned well the lesson of Epaminondas: the Macedonian phalanx, armed with spears some 14 feet long, was invincible.

Philip soon succeeded in welding the unruly hill tribes together, and went on to pin down his conquests by building roads and fortresses. Even more important, he created the most magnificent professional army the world had yet seen. To the phalanx of "foot companions" were added archers, slingers, and light and heavy cavalry. His men were in constant training, and his system of rewards and promotions ensured their complete devotion to him.

Fully aware of the advantage he held because of the Greek cities' family squabbles, Philip managed to build a fleet and to replenish his treasury by seizing their northern gold mines. Athens, a prey alike to internal party strife and discontented allies, was in no condition to stand up to Philip while he consolidated his power. By 352 B.C. he was master of Thessaly. And still the Athenians lived on in a state of false security. Finally in 351 B.C. the Athenian orator Demosthenes sought in ringing words to open the eyes of his fellow citizens to the northern menace:

If any man supposes this to be peace, when Philip is conquering every one else and will ultimately attack you, he is mad. If we wait for him actually to declare war on us we are naïve indeed, for he would not do that even though he marched right into Attica, if we may judge from what he has done to others.

Athens made peace in 346 B.C., but Demosthenes regarded it as only a breathing spell. Philip was within a few hours' march of the city— protesting friendship, of course—and allied with Thebes. A few years more and Demosthenes' storm warnings were heeded. A hasty alliance was plastered together with Thebes, and in 338 B.C. an allied army faced Philip at Chaeronea. But the Greeks had sought strength in unity too late. Though the armies were nearly evenly matched, Philip's superior tactical skill won the day.

The Greek city-state was dead. It had died, really, of suicide, of self-strangulation because the Greeks could not understand how any political unit larger than the city would work. The historian cannot help wondering what is the modern moral of ancient Greece. Perhaps it is simply this: Unless we solve the political problems of our own nation states we may not have any other problems to solve. We may tear each other apart as surely as (and more quickly than) the Greek city-states of 2400 years ago.

CHAPTER 21

Greek Civilization

The unexamined life is not worth living.

SOCRATES

If you have ever wondered what the universe is made of, what causes disease, what makes one action good and another bad, or what a building ought to look like, then you have been thinking like the Greeks. They too puzzled over such problems, and the answers they gave went far beyond the confines of their little city-states.

In fact so inquisitive a people were the Greeks that they seem to have blazed almost all our intellectual trails. The chances are that if you think you have had an original idea you will find a Greek thought of it first. What problems did the Greeks try to solve, and how did we inherit their learning?

❖ *The Love of Wisdom* "Philosophy" is a difficult word. It means, literally, "the love of wisdom." Perhaps no other people have believed so completely in plain living and high thinking as did the Greeks. They seemed almost to scorn physical comforts in their homes, and believed that the pursuit of wisdom was the highest function of man. This wisdom, they were convinced, could be attained only through the exercise of reason. Such a strong belief in reason first showed itself in speculations about the universe.

Thus early Greek philosophy dealt with problems that we today would say belonged to science rather than to philosophy. The early Greek philosophers began by attempting to answer two basic questions:

(1) What exists?

(2) How does change occur?

Many different philosophers tried to answer such questions, and because these men were attempting to explain the nature of the universe they are called "Nature Philosophers."

Thales   The first Greek philosopher of note was Thales. He decided that originally everything was water, which may exist as a vapour, or as a fluid, or even as a solid. Another philosopher thought rather that air was the original substance. Still another held that the fundamental fact was the changeability of all matter. "You cannot," said this philosopher, "step into the same river twice." He meant, of course, that by the second step it will have flowed on and not be the same. If, then, any one thing is always changing into something else, what at any instant does exist?

If you think the ancient Greeks were merely shadow-boxing with fine shades of meaning, try defining such a simple thing as a tree. What is a tree? It may be waving its branches of red and gold leaves outside your window now. But in a few months it will be bare. Then in the spring it may have blossoms, and later green leaves. Or in the science laboratory in your school you may examine the seed of a tree. Explain how the oak is *in* the acorn. You see, it is much easier to talk about something, even a tree, than it is to define it. The early Greek philosophers were asking fundamental questions to which many of us would be hard put to give answers.

❖ *The Quibblers and the Questioner*   In the 5th century B.C., after the victory over the Persians, the trend in Greek philosophy changed. The questions now centred not on nature but on man:

(1) How can man be certain about any knowledge?

(2) What is knowledge?

(3) What are the uses of knowledge?

(4) What, for man, is the good or the just life?

The Greeks believed that all these problems could be solved by clear, logical thinking. One group of teachers called the *Sophists* (*sophia* means wisdom) taught that all knowledge is relative to man. "Man," they said, "is the measure of all things." Clever sophists, however, could easily confuse common men by their involved arguments. For example, was man's action wicked or did it merely *appear* wicked? If all was relative, that is, if there was no absolute truth but truth differed with each person's interpretation, then what was wrong—or right, for that matter? It is easy to see how the word sophist came to mean "quibbler."

One man was dissatisfied with the misleading arguments of the Sophists. He was a squat, grotesque looking little individual who demonstrated a fine indifference to comfort by going barefoot summer and winter, and was much ridiculed by the populace (who put great store on a dignified gait) because he swung his arms vigorously as he walked. But the looks belied the man. This insignificant appearing fellow with the pug-nosed face had a razor sharp intellect and a magnetic charm that made him the idol of the aristocratic youth of Athens. He was one of the greatest teachers of all time, Socrates (469-399 B.C.). *Socrates*

Perhaps the fact that this stone-mason had served in the army as a hoplite and took pride in his strong physique attracted youth to him; certainly his keen sense of humour did. At any rate he was a colourful character, and he made a revolutionary discovery: the "soul"—that quality in any person which makes him an individual. To Socrates the soul was as real as anything that could be touched, drawn, or measured. It existed independently of physical matter, and was created for the purpose of reasoning.

Socrates' method of teaching was simple: he just asked questions. Yet this method was so effective that it has been copied ever since and has been given his name, "Socratic." When his followers answered his questions Socrates would point out the logical fallacies in their answers and then probe them further, until gradually he made his disciples clarify their thinking and sharpen their own definitions of such abstract ideas as temperance, justice, or courage. In this way Socrates painstakingly examined human motives and set extremely high standards of conduct.

But Socrates made one naïve assumption. He assumed that if men only knew what was the right thing to do they would proceed to do it. Unfortunately not all men had Socrates' will-power.

Socrates proclaimed no dogmas; he wrote no books; he collected no fees. Yet this great teacher was executed by his fellow Athenians in 399

B.C. Why? Part of the reason was guilt by association. Athens had just lost her Great War, and some of those who had helped Sparta to win had been pupils of Socrates. What was more natural than to blame the pupils' acts on the teacher? Moreover, Socrates' interminable questions ruthlessly exposed the ignorance of those who thought they were wise—something that never makes a man popular. Why did Socrates deliberately antagonize people in his strange quest for wisdom? He gives some of his reasons in the Source Reading on pages 218-220.

We still study Socrates because of his unshakable conviction that man can know what is true and good. The words that he spoke at his trial are a fair measure of the man:

I spend all my time going about among you persuading you, old and young alike, not to be so solicitous about your bodies or your possessions, but first of all and most earnestly, to consider how to make your souls as perfect as possible; and telling you that wealth does not bring virtue but that rather virtue brings wealth and every other human good, private or public.

❖ *Reflections of Reality* One of the young aristocrats who succumbed to Socrates' charm was Plato (429-347 B.C.), a youth who seemed to have

Yes, Socrates was really this homely—so homely that one of his pupils compared him to the Greek model of ugliness, a satyr. Yet this statue of Socrates also shows the powerful dignity and stalwart defiance that sustained this wisest man in Greece through the ordeal of his execution, and made it his finest hour.

been given everything. He came from one of Athens' distinguished families, had the frame of a football player ("Plato" is only a nickname; it means "broad"), and appeared to excel at everything he turned his hand to, whether it be music, mathematics, rhetoric, or poetry. He was attempting to decide between poetry and politics as a career when, at the age of twenty, he met Socrates. It was a meeting that changed his life. Not only did the pupil set himself to write down his master's work in the form of dialogues (in which Socrates is often represented as the chief questioner), but he went beyond this work to form a philosophical system of his own.

Perhaps because Plato, who was twenty-four at the time, lived through the tremendous political upheaval which followed the fall of Athens, he adopted a more constructive approach than Socrates. Whereas Socrates had concentrated on wiping out man's preconceived notions, Plato sought to replace them with positive conclusions. He taught that all physical objects were illusions, that is, they were not real. In fact if he were alive today he might say that the things of this world bear somewhat the same relationship to reality as the images on a television screen bear to what is going on in the studio miles away. The only real things are the "Ideas" or "Forms" of which the material world provides only approximate copies.

Plato also wrote a book called the *Republic* in which he planned an ideal state. Since reason, he believed, is man's one true guide, the ideal state should be run by philosophers. "Unless either philosophers become rulers," reasoned Plato, "or those who rule become lovers of wisdom, and so political power and philosophy are united, there can be no respite from calamity for states or for mankind." It is easy to see why the *Republic* has always been popular with those who distrust democracy and advocate government by the chosen few.

❖ *Plato Diluted*   Plato and his student for twenty years, Aristotle (384-322 B.C), must have made an odd-looking pair. Beside the comely teacher the thin-legged, balding, small-eyed student with the pronounced lisp must have presented anything but a prepossessing appearance. Nevertheless the young man was nothing short of a genius.

Aristotle

Like Plato, Aristotle came from a good family. He was a well dressed, well educated young man who, we are told, was the first philosopher "to write like a professor." Aristotle's theories have been described as "Plato diluted by common sense"—a description which does not necessarily mean they are easy to understand. Nor does it mean that he shared his master's view of the universe. Aristotle thought reality *did* exist in particular objects in nature: every individual object had *both* Form and Matter.

Such a philosophy explains why Aristotle's interests are very different from those of Socrates and Plato. In his *Ethics,* for instance, Aristotle recognized (as Socrates and Plato had not) man as he really is—a creature who may know what is the right thing to do but may be too lacking in will-power to do it. The common man, says Aristotle, may have to work at being good.

We acquire virtues by exercising them, as is true of any art. We learn by doing. As men become carpenters by building houses and lyre players by playing the lyre, we become just by acting justly, moderate by doing things in moderation, courageous by showing courage.

And because man lived in a *real* political state Aristotle could describe no abstract ideal state, as Plato had done. Instead, his *Politics* examined the constitutions of 158 Greek city-states in order to find out what made a government good or bad. Yet both Plato and Aristotle were aristocrats at heart. They condemned the lower classes, who were blinded by their selfishness, as unfit to rule. Government by the masses, said Aristotle, "will have many supporters, for most people prefer to live in a disorderly rather than a sober way. . . . In the best governed state the citizens must not be businessmen or manual workers, for such a life is lacking in nobility and is hostile to virtue; and they must not be farmers, since farmers lack the leisure which is necessary for the cultivation of virtue and political activity."

Aristotle was concerned with the real world of nature, with finding out all he could about the workings of the universe. Indeed, some historians have contended that he was a scientist first and a philosopher second. He was the founder of biology, gathering information for his *History of Animals* by studying anatomy, collecting specimens, and interviewing farmers and fishermen. But he also wrote on physics, astronomy, biology, psychology, metaphysics—the range of his work was encyclopaedic. He applied his deductive reasoning to what he observed, and often gave such reasonable explanations for his scientific theories that men accepted many of them for two thousand years even when they were totally wrong. Over the centuries, men were to revere him almost blindly as "the master of those who know."

❖ *The Spirit of Modern Science* The inquisitive Greek mind did not, however, stop at scientific speculation. In their travels the Greeks learned a primitive mathematics and astronomy from the Egyptians, and Thales is said to have calculated the distance from ship to shore by the geometry he introduced from Egypt. Pythagoras will ever have his name associated *Pythagoras* with the theorem that in a right-angled triangle the square on the hypotenuse is equal to the sum of the squares on the other two sides. And Anaxagoras even went so far as to describe the sun as a mass of burning rock *larger than the whole Peloponnesus*! He also explained variations in climate as the result of the earth's tilt on its axis.

The Greeks made their nearest approach to the spirit of modern Western science in medicine. Greek doctors kept careful case histories of the symptoms and progress of diseases, and some of our Western medical terms such as "chronic," "dose," "crisis," and "physician" are of Greek origin. The most famous school of medicine was founded by *Hippocrates* Hippocrates in the 5th century B.C. He bluntly rejected the earlier Greek theory that disease was caused by evil spirits entering the body through the mouth:

The fact is that invoking the gods to explain diseases and other natural events is all nonsense. It doesn't really matter whether you can call things divine or not. In nature all things are alike in this, that they all can be traced to preceding causes.

The name of Hippocrates is forever immortal in the medical world. On graduation from medical school, doctors still take the Hippocratic Oath as their promise to observe the proper code of conduct for the medical profession.

❖ *In Search of Beauty* "When you copy types of beauty," said Socrates, "it is so difficult to find a perfect model that you combine the most beautiful details of several, and thus contrive to make the whole figure look beautiful." The Greeks tried to make their sculpture represent, not reality, but ideal beauty. They also wanted their architecture to show a harmonious unity, "a sense of the wholeness of things," with the result that both gracefulness and proportion marked their buildings.

The first Greek art appeared in the 10th century B.C., and consisted of simple bands and geometrical designs on clay pots. Animal and human figures later came to replace these designs, but the figures were simply done.

Much of Greek art and architecture centred around the temples. In *Architec-* the early days the Greeks had sought their gods in groves and caves in *ture* the country; but with the development of cities, temples were built to house the state gods. At first these were merely rooms with porches in front of them, but even in the beginning the porches were supported by a row of columns. As time went on three styles of columns developed: Doric, Ionic, and Corinthian. The Doric column was the simplest, and the Corinthian the most ornate.

About the middle of the 5th century B.C. the Athenians began to build a magnificent temple to their goddess Athena. They placed the Parthenon, as the temple is called, high on their acropolis so that it would dominate the whole countryside. The Parthenon has been described as "the most thrilling building there is"; but many an ally must have regarded it with anything but pleasure, since it was financed by tribute from the Confederacy of Delos. When it was built, thousands of separate contracts were let—one citizen contracted to deliver ten cart-loads of marble, another to flute one column—and the wonder is that the entire building was completed in only ten years.

The simple appearance of the Parthenon is deceptive. The columns lean imperceptibly inward and taper toward the top, and all the prominent lines of the building have a slightly convex curve to correct the optical illusion of sag. Every part of the building blends into a single architectural concept—again the Greek sense of wholeness. Nor was the temple as starkly white and solitary as it appears in photographs today. The glare of the chalky marble would shock its builders, who originally painted the gables blue and tinted the frieze of mythological figures in varied hues. We have lost, too, the huge gilded statues of gods with which Greeks liked to crowd their temples.

Sculpture   The first Greek statues were stiff, awkward looking creations carved from wooden posts. Stone followed, and then bronze. By the Age of Pericles sculptors excelled in portraying the human body. Myron, an Athenian, is most famous for his *Discus Thrower,* which shows the athlete at the moment of extreme strain just before releasing the discus. The statue is usually regarded as one of the greatest of all time, and although we no longer have Myron's original creation we are fortunate in having good Roman copies of it. Myron is also reputed to have created a bronze cow so lifelike that living cattle mistook it for one of themselves and surrounded it in the field.

Looking serenely over Athens stood a great figure about 40 feet high, the celebrated statue of *Athena* by Phidias. But his enthroned *Zeus,* conceived on an even larger scale for the Temple of Zeus at Olympia,

This photograph shows a 1962 production of the *Bacchae* of Euripides being presented at Epidaurus in southern Greece. At the centre of the theatre's *orchestra* or circular dancing floor can be seen a small round altar. Note the absence of scenery, and the members of the *chorus* ranged in a formal circle about the three actors. The function of the chorus is to express the emotions aroused by the tragedy.

was even more famous in its day. "Fare ye to Olympia," wrote an ancient author, "that ye may see the work of Phidias, and account it a misfortune, each of you, if you die with this still unknown." So divinely beautiful was the statue that on its completion, men said, Zeus hurled a thunderbolt to the ground to signify his approval. It is unfortunate that neither of Phidias's mighty statues survived for posterity.

Like the *Discus Thrower,* both the *Athena* and the *Zeus* were statues of types rather than individuals, formal figures with idealized, almost expressionless, faces. It is only with the 4th century B.C. sculptor Praxiteles that the body became relaxed and the expression lifelike. Praxiteles' *Hermes,* with the infant god Dionysus (an appealing baby) on his arm, is the only renowned classical Greek statue that has come down to us from the hands of its creator; of the other famous originals only Roman or later Greek copies remain. But even in the original we probably do not see the *Hermes* as it was conceived, for the Greeks usually tinted their statues—sun-tan for the body, red for the hair, lips, eyebrows, and eyes.

There is an anecdote that illustrates the increasing realism of the 4th century B.C. Two of the greatest artists were Zeuxis, who is said to have died laughing at one of his own paintings, and Parrhasius.

The story runs that Parrhasius and Zeuxis entered into competition, Zeuxis exhibiting a picture of some grapes so true to nature that the birds flew up to the wall of the stage. Parrhasius then displayed a picture of a linen curtain realistic to such a degree that Zeuxis, elated by the verdict of the birds, cried out that now at last his rival must draw the curtain and show his picture. On discovering the mistake he surrendered the prize to Parrhasius, admitting candidly that he had deceived the birds, while Parrhasius had deluded himself, a painter.

❖ *Tragedy and Comedy* When we think of Greek literature we think, of course, of that rich fountainhead of embroidered history, the *Iliad* and the *Odyssey*. Homer was the Greeks' Shakespeare. His delight in life is blended with a shrewd understanding of human character, and he was keenly aware of the final call of death which even a being as unique as a Greek must obey. These brooding lines are from the *Iliad*:

As is the life of the leaves, so is that of men. The wind scatters the leaves to the ground: the vigorous forest puts forth others, and they grow in the spring-season. Soon one generation of men comes and another ceases.

In the 7th and 6th centuries B.C. Greek lyric poetry flourished, and it was an accepted part of after-dinner entertainment for each guest to sing something—often a lyric poem—while accompanying himself on the lyre. The Greeks also enjoyed drama, and built large amphitheatres (the Athenian theatre could seat 14,000) in which to present their plays. Their actors, who were professionals hired by the state, would have appeared most strange to you because they wore heavy masks, whose wide mouths served as amplifiers, and walked on club-soled shoes to increase their stature (and hence, they hoped, their dignity). Each actor played several characters, and a change of mask indicated a change of role. Since there was no curtain and no change of scenery, a group called the chorus marked the ends of acts by singing a choric ode.

Aeschylus   Aeschylus (525-456 B.C.) was a profoundly religious dramatist who centred his tragedies around the relationship of man to the gods. Only seven of his ninety plays survive, but they prove him to be a giant among dramatists. His poetry is the most majestic in Greek literature, his characters are heroic men and women trapped, not by their own foibles, but by a terrible and relentless Fate. Aeschylus' *Agamemnon* is considered by many to be the greatest tragedy produced in Attica.

Sophocles   Canadians, however, will be more familiar with Sophocles (496-406

B.C.), since one of his most famous plays, *Oedipus Rex,* was performed at the Stratford Festival in 1954 and 1955. In this tragedy it is prophesied even before Oedipus is born that he will kill his father and marry his mother, and he unwittingly fulfils these prophecies through ignorance of his parents' identities. Sophocles, unlike Aeschylus, was more of an artist than a thinker—a genius of a playwright whose characters, like the statues of the time, are types rather than individuals.

Euripides (480-406 B.C.) was also a tragedian. His plays were com-   *Euripides* posed during the Peloponnesian War, and their speeches reflect the Sophists' ideas. It is little wonder that Euripides was unpopular and that he seldom won the festival prize. Whereas Sophocles had been careful never to introduce his own views into his plays, Euripides' characters reflect his own doubt in the gods and the value of human suffering without substituting any answers to man's problems. Nevertheless Euripides had a profound understanding of human nature. He was a sensitive person who became so embittered that finally, disillusioned with democracy, he left Athens to live in Macedon.

The fourth dramatist, Aristophanes (450-385 B.C.), was a writer of   *Aristoph-* outrageous comedies. He ridiculed war, democracy, education, and, of   *anes*

A 5th century B.C. sculptor created this striking portrayal of Heracles, the most popular and widely worshipped hero of Greek legend. The statue is impressive even today; but can you picture how resplendent Heracles must have looked in his original state when he formed part of a temple's pediment, the sun glinting on his lead hair, brightly painted form, and taut bow? This sculpture provides a good example of the perfection to which Greek artists aspired: the bowman's back, which was never intended to be seen, is as perfectly carved as the rest of the figure.

course, Socrates. Actually Aristophanes was a serious political thinker who longed for the good old days before Pericles and his imperialist democracy, and he satirized the politicians of his day mercilessly. In the *Knights,* produced in 424 B.C. after the war had gone well, there are two generals, Demosthenes and Nicias, who want to get rid of Pericles' successor, the democratic leader Cleon. Realizing that the only way to do this is to put up a rival whom the people will prefer to Cleon, they select as their perfect democratic leader a sausage-seller, a simple soul who stands in the market-place selling his wares. Naturally the fellow protests to Demosthenes his unworthiness for the job.

S.S. Tell me this, how can I, just a sausage-seller, be a big man like that?

D.   It's the easiest thing in the world. You've got all the qualifications: low birth, market-place training, impudence.

S.S. I don't think I deserve it.

D.   Not deserve it? It looks to me as if you've got too good a conscience. Was your father a gentleman?

S.S. By the gods, no! My folks were blackguards.

D.   Lucky man! What a good start you've got for public life!

S.S. But I don't know a thing except how to read, and hardly that.

D.   The only trouble is that you know anything. To be a leader of the people isn't for learned men or honest men, but for the ignorant and vile. Don't miss this wonderful opportunity!

This is pretty bitter satire.

❖ *Gods and Games*   Most Greek literature drew its themes from stories of the gods—not as awe-inspiring subject matter as you might think. For the gods were anything but divine in their conduct. They quarrelled and deceived each other, and Homer shows them as being able to come down from their lofty home on Mount Olympus to interfere with the fate of mere mortals or simply to enjoy themselves. Countless local gods and goddesses were worshipped at rustic shrines, and most Greeks, in their eagerness to know the future, consulted oracles such as the famous ones at Delphi and Dodona. At Delphi a priestess wildly proclaimed the will of Apollo; at Dodona, Zeus spoke to men in the rustling of the oak leaves.

Greek religion   Greek religion was both confusing and reassuring. There was no priesthood, no organized church, no single sacred book. Religion for the Greeks was not so much a matter of beliefs as of carrying out a service of worship. The city god's statue was kept in his temple, and a bull, sheep, or pig was sacrificed on the altar outside. But the proud Greek did not choose to kneel even before his god. He prayed standing, looking upward, his voice loud and clear, his palms open to receive the blessing that he did not doubt would come.

The Greeks were very superstitious. They prayed before any undertaking, were continually pouring libations to various gods, and offered special sacrifices in time of trouble and joy. The bride took sacred fire from the altar of Apollo outside the door of her home to offer to Apollo in her new abode. Dreams were implicitly believed in as being significant, and nature was full of omens: the flight of birds, a burst of thunder, an eclipse, an earthquake, any unnatural occurrence, all these were signs of good or of ill. If a misfortune occurred the Greek immediately inquired, "What god have I offended?" Greek religion seems to have been a collection of superstitions with very little moral instruction or influence.

Eventually sixty or seventy festivals a year came to be celebrated to honour the gods through athletic games and contests in the arts. Each city had its local festival with sports, music, poetry, even beauty contests. But every four years all the Greek world gathered for the five-day festival at Olympia. So important did the Greeks consider the athletic competitions there that for a whole month (as you will be reading later on) they suspended warfare for them. We still preserve these games—and even some ancient Greek sports—in our vast international Olympic contests.

Thus, although much of Greek religious lore seems superstitious to us if not crude, it was the Greek gift to transform these myths into an enduring legacy. They took their earthy legends and turned them into great dramas, or they celebrated in honour of their gods at national festivals—festivals which to some extent counteracted the narrow loyalty of the city-state.

❖ *The Minority Transforms the Majority*   It would, of course, be quite wrong to think that *all* Greeks spent their days in philosophical discussions, breaking off only to create a beautiful statue or attend a tragedy in the theatre. Most Greeks had to work for their living at least 300 days a year, or considerably more than the average five-day-a-week Canadian. Life had few comforts for the farmers who made up the majority of the population; but neither did the townsmen enjoy many luxuries. Indeed, the Greeks seemed almost to go out of their way to be uncomfortable, many of them, for example, allowing themselves no extra garments to make up for the decided rawness of rainy winter days.

Elegance in Greece seemed to be reserved for public buildings. Because the climate was dry and sunny three-quarters of the year, the average male citizen spent most of his time outdoors, often at the marketplace. Perhaps this accounts for the fact that the ordinary town house was a dreary place, a humble structure of plain stucco or sun-dried brick with a dark, comfortless interior. The streets, too, were inelegant. Even in a noble city like Athens they were crooked and dirty, with little paving and no sidewalks. Slops were thrown into the streets (with a cry "Existo!" —"Look out!"), and sanitary conditions left much to be desired. Such inns as existed were popular with robbers and vermin; Aristophanes even has the god Dionysus inquiring for "the eating-houses and hostels where there are the fewest bugs"!

Yet some of the culture of the minority did reach the majority, perhaps because the Greek state was so small. In his great *Funeral Oration* Pericles addressed not just the intellectual élite but all Athenians. And thousands of ordinary Greeks sat on wooden or stone seats for a whole spring day, the sun blazing down on their bare heads, in the Athenian theatre. Our 20th century cannot help but be impressed by such an appetite for culture. The minority did indeed transform the majority: Greek culture was more than an upper class veneer.

CHAPTER 22

Alexander the Great and the Hellenistic Age

For my part, I assure you, I had rather excel others in knowledge of what is excellent, than in the extent of my power and dominion.

ALEXANDER THE GREAT WRITING TO ARISTOTLE

After that black day in 338 B.C. when Philip defeated the Greek allies, the conqueror had marched on into the Peloponnesus and called a congress of Greek states at Corinth. Each state was granted autonomy, but was also enrolled in a Hellenic League which soon pledged itself to assist Philip in an expedition into Asia Minor against the Persians. Within a year and a half, however, Philip was dead—cut down, like many a

Macedonian before him, by the assassin's hand. His son Alexander, a youth of twenty, found himself king.

❖ *"Look Thee Out A Kingdom"*   Alexander is one of the most romantic figures in all history. He was, apparently, fair-skinned and clean-shaven (Plutarch tells us that he believed whiskers offered the enemy too ready a handle to grasp), of average height and athletic build. His father had been anxious that his boy should study philosophy, "so that," he said, "you may not do a great many things of the sort that I am sorry to have done." To this end Philip engaged as Alexander's tutor the incomparable Aristotle, and the three years that the young prince spent with the philosopher undoubtedly whetted his passion for knowledge.

One of the most engaging pictures of the youthful Alexander tells of the day that a certain Thessalian offered to sell Philip a horse named Bucephalus.

When they went into the field to try him, they found him so very vicious and unmanageable, that he reared up when they endeavoured to mount him, and would not so much as endure the voice of any of Philip's attendants. Upon which, as they were leading him away as wholly useless and untractable, Alexander, who stood by, said, "What an excellent horse do they lose for want of address and boldness to manage him!" Philip at first took no notice of what he said; but when he heard him repeat the same thing several times, and saw he was much vexed to see the horse sent away, "Do you reproach," said he to him, "those who are older than yourself, as if you knew more, and were better able to manage him than they?" "I could manage this horse," replied he, "better than others do." "And if you do not," said Philip, "what will you forfeit for your rashness?" "I will pay," answered Alexander, "the whole price of the horse." At this the whole company fell a-laughing; and as soon as the wager was settled amongst them, he immediately ran to the horse, and taking hold of the bridle, turned him directly toward the sun, having, it seems, observed that he was disturbed at and afraid of the motion of his own shadow; then letting him go forward a little, still keeping the reins in his hands, and stroking him gently when he found him begin to grow eager and fiery, he let fall his upper garment softly, and with one nimble leap securely mounted him, and when he was seated, by little and little drew in the bridle, and curbed him without either striking or spurring him. Presently, when he found him free from all rebelliousness, and only impatient for the course, he let him go at full speed, inciting him now with a commanding voice, and urging him also with his heel. Philip and his friends looked on at first in silence and anxiety for the result, till seeing him turn at the end of his career, and come back rejoicing and triumphing for what he had performed, they all burst out into acclamations of applause; and his father shedding tears, it is said, for joy, kissed him as he came down from his horse, and in his transport said, "O my son, look thee out a kingdom equal to and worthy of thyself, for Macedonia is too little for thee."

This was the lad who at twenty won the allegiance of his father's army and was soon elected by the Hellenic League as commander-in-chief of the war against Persia. By the spring of 334 B.C. he was ready to set forth into Asia—undoubtedly with no idea at this stage of trying to conquer the whole Persian Empire, but rather because his father had, in the last few years of his life, planned a war of revenge against these long-time foes. Accordingly, Alexander crossed the Dardanelles to attack Darius III (336-330 B.C.).

Alexander's army

Alexander made the Macedonian cavalry his striking arm. Small mobile units, each of 250 men, were capable of delivering, collectively, a series of terrific punches against enemy lines. Their success, however, depended upon the effectiveness of the phalanx, a formation up to 16 men deep, that "bristling rampart of outstretched pikes" which struck

Here we have a portion of a Greek mosaic floor—an intricate creation consisting of an estimated million and a half tiny stones, each the size of a grain of rice. The floor was originally laid at Alexandria, and was damaged when it was taken up and removed to the House of the Faun at Pompeii, Italy. The mosaic portrays the battle of Issus (333 B.C.) at the moment when Alexander the Great, riding his magnificent charger Bucephalus, presses the attack against Darius, who looks back in anguish from his chariot. The highlights on Alexander's face make it glisten with the exertion and tension of the struggle, while his burning gaze seems to pass beyond the battle scene to his vision of world dominion.

dumb terror into the hearts of the Persians. Along with the army travelled a series of movable towers covered with hides to protect them from fire. These immense platforms, some of which were 150 feet high, could be pushed up to the walls of a besieged city. Meanwhile the Cretan archers rained arrows with deadly accuracy, and the torsion catapults fired huge arrows and fifty-pound stones to a range of 200 yards. Alexander's formidable war machines were not rendered obsolete until the advent of cannon and gunpowder—1600 years later.

❖ *Conquering a Continent* Among the countless sieges and minor skirmishes fought by Alexander, four great battles stand out: Granicus (334 B.C.), Issus (333 B.C.), Gaugamela (331 B.C.), and Hydaspes (326 B.C.).

The Persians made their initial stand at the River Granicus in western Asia Minor. Here Alexander's 35,000 men charged across the river, and his heavy cavalry shattered the smaller Persian army. The victory almost cost Alexander his life: a Persian had raised his sword to strike him from behind when, in the nick of time, one of Alexander's Macedonian

Granicus

generals saw his leader's predicament and cut off the assailant's arm. But the conqueror was saved, and Granicus opened the route to the south where Alexander could march along the Asia Minor coast liberating Greek cities.

Alexander spent the winter consolidating his position in Asia Minor. Then he decided to push on into Syria. But Darius's forces were threatening the ever-lengthening Macedonian lines of communication and supply, and he must be dealt with. Accordingly in late October 333 B.C. Alexander and Darius faced each other for the first time, at Issus. Although their armies seem to have been about equally matched (at approximately 30,000 men each) the Greek cavalry again caused things to go badly with the Persians, and when their king saw his left wing take to its heels he wheeled his chariot and fled. Perhaps it was that night, as he sat down to dinner in Darius's elegantly appointed tent, that Alexander resolved to conquer the entire Persian Empire.

Any conqueror of the Persians, Alexander realized, would have, first of all, to deal with the Persian fleet. So instead of turning eastward into Mesopotamia in pursuit of Darius, Alexander moved south against Phoenicia, the source of Darius's ships and sailors. Again fortune was with the Greeks. One Phoenician city after another fell, men deserted wholesale, and the fleet simply melted away. The next conquest was Damascus—with the added bonus of the Persian war treasury, which had been transferred there. Then came a seven-months' siege of Tyre. Before it capitulated, Darius tried to bribe Alexander into going home by offering him a ransom of 10,000 talents for the Persian royal family (captured at Issus), all the land west of the Euphrates, and his daughter's hand in marriage. But Alexander refused. He had drunk too deeply of the heady wine of conquest. Why stop at the Euphrates? On he went to Egypt, where he was crowned Pharaoh and where he drew up the plans for the most famous of the many cities named, after him, Alexandria.

At length, in 331 B.C., having retraced his steps, he was ready for the final reckoning with Darius. It came after he had crossed the Tigris, at Gaugamela. Backed by the largest army he had ever commanded, some 47,000 men, Alexander faced an even greater Persian force. Once again the Greek cavalry triumphed; once again Darius fled at a critical moment. It was the last time the Persian was to face the Macedonian. In 330 B.C. Darius was murdered by one of his own satraps in far-off

Bactria (modern northern Afghanistan), just a little while before Alexander caught up with him.

The whole east had opened to Alexander with Gaugamela, and by 327 B.C. a Greek army of 30,000 was labouring with superhuman tenacity across the Hindu Kush mountains and through the Khyber Pass into India. The next year the conqueror fought one of his hardest battles when he met Porus, king of the Pauravas, at the River Hydaspes, a tributary of the Indus. The Greeks might well have taken to their heels at the fearsome adversary that faced them, for besides outnumbering them the Indian army boasted a mighty advantage: 200 elephants. *Hydaspes*

Since Alexander's horses would not approach these immense beasts, his cavalry was badly handicapped. All he could do was try by a concentrated attack on the enemy's left wing to draw Porus's cavalry there away from the elephants, and eventually to draw the right wing cavalry away too. Confusion reigned, and in the end the Indian infantry were forced to flee to the shelter of their elephants "as to a friendly wall of refuge." Now the Macedonian phalanx advanced, and the battle of men and beasts began. The elephants attacked and the struggle was a desperate one; but the Greeks persisted. One by one the mahouts (elephant-drivers) were cut down, and "when the beasts were tired out . . . they began to retire slowly, facing the foe like ships backing water, merely uttering a shrill piping sound."

Eight hours later the battle was over. The wounded Porus, who had valiantly fought to the last and been bereft of his son, made a leisurely exit on his enormous elephant, and the Greeks were left to lick their wounds. What their casualties were Alexander carefully concealed. The elephants had taken a terrible toll. Most of all the great commander mourned the loss of Bucephalus, who had died on the field. A city named Alexandria Bucephala was founded by Alexander on the site of the battlefield in honour of his beloved steed.

When the regal Indian adversary finally surrendered, Alexander asked him how he wished to be treated. "Like a king," answered Porus. Alexander admired the rajah's proud spirit. Porus was left free to govern his kingdom under Macedonian overlordship.

Alexander was still not satisfied: he had ambitions to push even deeper into the east. But his soldiers at last mutinied. For eight years they had followed him over 11,000 miles to the very ends of the earth. Now they would go no farther. There was nothing for Alexander to do but go

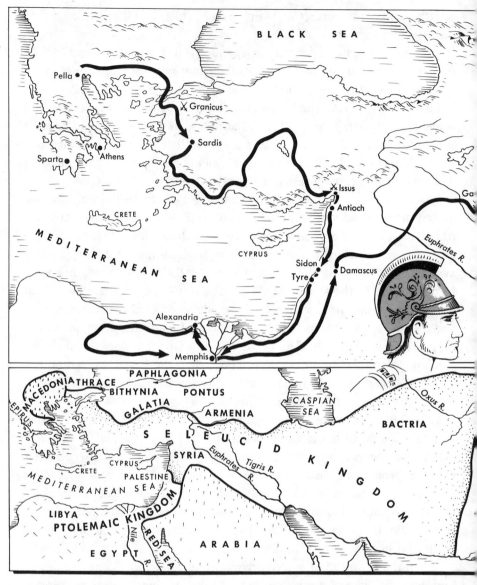

home.   By 323 B.C. he was back at Babylon, his restless mind still full of the problems of governing his immense empire.

The death of Alexander

But he had driven himself too hard for too long.   He had exhausted himself both mentally and physically, and when he caught malaria he was unable to throw it off.

On the sixth day of his fever, he was very seriously ill and was carried into the palace; he could still recognize his officers, but he could not speak.   That

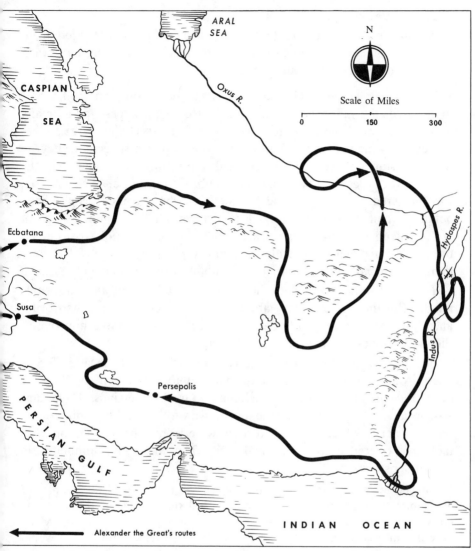

THE HELLENISTIC WORLD AND ITS KINGDOMS

night he was in high fever, and the day following and the next night, and the next day. His soldiers longed to see him; some that they might behold him while he was yet alive; others because it was announced that he was already dead, and they thought that his death was being hushed up by the bodyguard; most of them, because of their grief and longing for him, forced their way into his presence. They saw that he was speechless, but, as they filed past, he greeted them one by one by just raising his head and signing to them with his eyes.

The next evening he died. He was only thirty-two.

Alexander never lost a battle, and Napoleon, whose military judgment was worth something, thought him a genius. Was he anything more than an incredibly successful young general?

❖ *The Greatest Dream* Undoubtedly Alexander's conquests had a profound civilizing influence on the world. He founded perhaps as many as 70 cities, and these played a crucial role in spreading Greek ideas and customs far and wide. Throughout the empire a silver currency on the Attic standard was introduced, with the result that Athens and the Aegean world became the commercial hub of the empire. Science, too, was furthered. Along with the conquering army travelled geographers, botanists, and zoologists, and Alexander set aside an immense grant of 800 talents to be used for research under the direction of Aristotle. At the time of his death Alexander was busily planning two naval expeditions, one to explore the Caspian Sea, another to circumnavigate Arabia.

There is no doubt that Alexander possessed a brilliant and inquisitive mind. But there is one story about him that suggests more than brilliance. It reveals a profound depth in him that would make him one of the most remarkable men in world history.

In 324 B.C. at Opis on the Tigris River, after a full decade of conquest, Alexander gave an immense banquet to 9000 men representing every race in his empire. Macedonians, Greeks, Persians, Egyptians, Asians all ate together. The banquet was followed by a libation, a religious act in which all present drew wine from a great bowl on each table and offered it to a universal God. The ceremony culminated in Alexander's prayer.

He prayed for peace, and for partnership in the realm of all the peoples of his empire there assembled, and lastly that all the peoples of the world he knew might be of one mind together and live in unity and concord. Many have dreamt that dream since; but he was the first. Had he lived, he would have tried to make it a reality, and would have failed as men have failed ever since; but that dream was probably the greatest thing about one of the greatest of mankind. . . . He had set out with Aristotle's belief that Asiatics were only fit for slaves. He soon saw that that was wrong . . . to him the distinction of Greek and barbarian lost all meaning—a revolution in itself. . . . But his active mind soon went farther: he declared that all men were sons of one Father, the earliest expression known of the brotherhood of man.[2]

It is Alexander's prayer at Opis that should be his lasting memorial.

[2]W. W. Tarn in E. Barker, G. Clark, and P. Vaucher, editors, *The European Inheritance* (Clarendon Press, 1954), I, 184.

❖ *A Brilliant Experiment*   It is not surprising that the mighty empire of Alexander should soon disintegrate, for it had never been closely knit. Rather it was his own peculiar creation, all of its parts bound solidly together by personal ties to the conqueror. Alexander's only heirs were a half-witted half-brother, Philip, and a son born posthumously. The half-brother was soon assassinated, and the son imprisoned and murdered. Eventually three of Alexander's generals cut the empire up for themselves: Egypt and some fringe lands went to Ptolemy, Asia Minor and the old Persian Empire to Seleucus, Macedon and Greece to Antigonus and his son Demetrius.

It is impossible to trace here the extremely involved political history of these three Hellenistic kingdoms. There is one area, however, that is worth singling out: India.

In the 6th century B.C. Darius I of Persia had set up the satrapy of Bactria, and thence Alexander the Great journeyed in 329 B.C. When Alexander invaded India he found only a number of disconnected states; but soon after his death an Indian adventurer, Chandragupta Maurya (322-298 B.C.), unified all the northern section of the land. His grandson, Asoka (269-232 B.C.), became a convert to Buddhism, renouncing war—but only, it must be noted, after he had consolidated his empire and no further conquests tempted him—and teaching that there was a universal moral law for all men.

The Mauryan Empire

After Asoka died, the Mauryan Empire broke up, and a Greek kingdom was established in the north-west. This kingdom of Bactria and India reached its height under Demetrius (189-167 B.C.), a Greek who modelled himself after the great Alexander. Demetrius proclaimed that Greeks and Indians were to be partners, and issued a bilingual coinage. Indians were admitted to Greek citizenship, the provincial administration became Graeco-Indian under Greek generals, and the two peoples lived harmoniously together.

The Greeks of Bactria and India finally fell prey to civil wars and foreign attacks, and by the middle of the 1st century A.D. their influence in India was ended. All trace of it vanished. Indeed, it has been said that India would be exactly the same today had the Greeks never existed. Demetrius had tried to turn Alexander's dream into a reality and had failed because he, like Alexander, could not subdue nationalism. Nevertheless it is interesting to look back over 2000 years to a time when, in far-off India, a Greek general tried a brilliant experiment in civilized living.

❖ *The Hellenistic Age*   It is the cultural consequences of Alexander's conquests that are finally most important. Because of him, foreign philosophy, art, science, literature, and religions flowed into Greeks moulds, and a Greek attitude to life became world-wide. In other words the known world became *Hellenized.* For this reason the three centuries following Alexander's death are known as the Hellenistic (Greek-like) Age. In his brief career he had forever diverted the stream of civilization.

Few men have so changed the world; nothing after him could be as it was before. He did more than enlarge the field of human endeavour; the Hellenistic world was in effect his creation, and it was that world, and not classical Greece, which taught Rome and through Rome has influenced the modern world. And it was due to the impulse he gave to the Hellenization of western Asia that Christianity, when it came, had an easy medium at the start in which to spread.[3]

❖ *New Philosophies and New Gods*   During the 4th century B.C. conditions of chronic unemployment arose, and a great gap between rich and poor developed. Human happiness became the supreme preoccupation of Hellenistic philosophers. Epicurus (342-270 B.C.) emphasized tranquillity as the solution to human woes. "Be happy with little, for being interested in and needing much brings unhappiness." Happiness, that is, freedom from pain, ought to be man's goal. Epicurus prescribed a code of social conduct that included honesty, prudence, and justice in dealing with others; but while the code was commendable the motive for maintaining it was not. The individual should adopt these virtues, not because they were good in themselves, but because he would thereby save himself from being punished by society. Social approval is a fickle master, and with such unstable roots one can see how in later ages a sort of wine, women, and song Epicureanism (a far cry from the original ideas of Epicurus) could develop.

Epicureanism

Stoicism

The greatest philosophy of Hellenistic times was Stoicism, named after the *stoa* (porch) where Zeno (336-264 B.C.), the founder of this philosophy, taught his followers to repress all physical desires, to live in equality with all other men, and not to complain but to do their duty resolutely. Stoicism was an ennobling philosophy followed mainly by

[3]*European Inheritance,* I, 184.

members of the upper class. Its ideals are well illustrated in this short prayer.

> Lead me, O Zeus, and thou, O Destiny,
> Lead thou me on.
> To whatsoever task thou sendest me,
> Lead thou me on.
> I follow fearless, or, if in mistrust
> I lag and will not, follow still I must.

Religion

Alexander brought together the East and the West, and it is particularly in religion that the Hellenistic fusion of Greek and Oriental can be seen. Now the Greek world was invaded by countless Oriental cults in which immortality was promised to converts, and an elaborate ritual assured communion with a god who had risen from the dead. Superstition, too, flourished. Cities adopted stars as their guardians, and many a horoscope was cast. But it is the appearance of ruler-worship that is especially Oriental. It was encouraged by Alexander the Great, and soon states were deifying their Hellenistic kings. Even the once proud Athenians glorified their ruler in this way: "Thou alone art a true god; the others are asleep or away, or are not."

❖ *Everything in Excess* Greek art had always prided itself on the motto, "Nothing in excess," and classic simplicity and cold realism had been the keynotes. The Hellenistic Age saw a reversal of this attitude. Now more palaces, theatres, and libraries were built than temples. Art was created for the money it would bring, and became the preserve of rich patrons rather than the possession of ordinary citizens.

Sculpture

One of the finest Hellenistic sculptures is the *Winged Victory* of Samothrace. This majestic portrayal of a winged goddess riding the prow of a ship now stands at the head of a staircase in the Louvre in Paris, where it seems literally to surge forward toward the onlooker. But magnificent as the finest Hellenistic sculptures are, expert opinion rates them below the classical Greek art of centuries earlier. Often the striving after realism turns into a striving after effect, so that the figures look restless and tense. The Hellenistic passion to provide a thrill, even in stone, too often led to contortion and strain. This is nowhere better illustrated than in the churning *Laocoön*, a frighteningly realistic portrayal of a priest and his two sons being strangled by serpents—hardly the Greek ideal of "nothing in excess"!

Science

In science, more progress was made during the Hellenistic Age than in any other comparable period of time before the 15th century A.D. A so-called "Museum" was established at Alexandria in Egypt as a home for scholars whom the government subsidized. Far from being a museum in our sense of the word, this institution was a combined library, research institute, and university where literature, mathematics, astronomy, and medicine were all studied. It made Alexandria the scientific capital of the world.

Hellenistic scientists specialized in theories rather than in practical inventions. Nevertheless, Hero of Alexandria invented an automatic device to open and shut temple doors by steam-power (though in an age of abundant slave labour the steam-engine could not be expected to *Archimedes* flourish), and Archimedes of Syracuse, who established the principle of the lever, constructed a spiral pump of a type which is still used for drawing water up out of the Nile. However, he is best remembered for his law of floating bodies. It is said to have been based on his observation of the water displaced in a tub by his own floating body, a discovery you can read about on pages 220-221.

Less spectacular was the post-mortem dissection of the human body performed by Hellenistic doctors. Such a thing had been impossible in classical Greece, because the dead were cremated. Of the many consequences of dissection, one was a correction of the earlier notion that the arteries were filled with air.

Euclid You have all heard of the famous mathematician, Euclid, and of his mathematical treatise entitled *Elements of Geometry*. In these 13 books Euclid wrote down 465 propositions, many of which you will be studying in geometry.

The astronomers and geographers of this great age of science came to some startling conclusions, such as that the earth rotated on its axis every 24 hours, and that the sun was fixed and the earth and planets revolved around it. Eratosthenes stated that the oceans were all one body of water and calculated the earth's circumference at 24,662 miles (it is actually 24,857). This estimate was reduced by a later Hellenistic scientist who also suggested that India might be reached by sailing westward from Cadiz—a theory that fired the imagination of a man named Columbus some fifteen centuries later.

Literature Every kind of literary creation abounded in Hellenistic times, but of the 1100 writers whose names are known we will mention but two. Menander was the most gifted writer of a new type of drama called the "New Comedy" ("new" as contrasted with the "Old Comedy" of Ari-

DISCOBOLO
DI MIRONE

In this marble Roman copy of Myron's *Discus Thrower* there are
two deviations from the bronze original. A tree stump has been
added to reinforce the legs, and the head is wrongly attached so
that the athlete looks away from the discus instead of towards it
as in Myron's original. Yet the copy retains that sinewy grace
and supple perfection which make it—even after 2400 years of
further experiment in moulding the human figure—one of the
greatest statues of all time.

stophanes), a comedy of manners which centred around the life of the newly-rich of Athens. Almost without exception the plot revolved around a love story, with elaborate complications and invariably happy endings. Menander's plays were outstanding because of his delicate characterization and astute insight into motives and ideas, and some of the lines, such as "Whom the gods love die young," have become proverbial. A contrast to Menander's sophisticated writing was provided by Theocritus. Theocritus was the originator of pastoral poetry, verse that deals with happy scenes of rustic life peopled by love-sick shepherds. It was Theocritus who provided inspiration for the Roman Virgil and the English Milton, as well as for hosts of "pastoral" poets smitten by love.

There was also a great deal of pessimism in literature. The civilization seemed tired; life appeared futile and meaningless. Yet among many sour epigrams survives this gentle story.

Along with five others Charmus ran the distance race, and, strange to relate, came in seventh. When there were only six, you will say, how did he come in seventh? Well, a friend of his wearing a heavy mantle ran alongside yelling, "Come on, Charmus!" So Charmus came in seventh. If he had had five more such friends he would have come in twelfth.

Poor Charmus! How the mighty Greeks had fallen by the end of the Hellenistic Age.

CHAPTER 23

A Day in the Life of a Greek Athlete

. . . many a wondrous sight may be seen, and not a few tales of wonder may be heard in Greece; but there is nothing on which the blessing of Zeus rests in so full a measure as the rites of . . . the Olympic Games. . . .

PAUSANIAS

The great moment had come. The athletes, brown-skinned from the last thirty days of intensive training under the constant Greek sun, stood gracefully at attention, their naked bodies glistening with oil. Nearby were gathered their coaches, friends, and sponsors, craning their necks to get a good look at the official who intoned the injunction to the competitors:

If you have exercised yourself in a manner worthy of the Olympic Festival, if you have been guilty of no slothful or ignoble act, go on with a good courage. You who have not so practised, go whither you will.

Tromes glanced sideways at a dark, intent young man standing at the edge of the crowd. How *could* he be so bold? Surely everyone knew who he was. Let him enter his chariot in the race in the name of the Boeotian State if he would, his accent was unmistakable. Lichas, the *Spartan*. Yes, a Spartan, despite the fact that the Spartans had violated the Olympic Truce and had therefore been barred from participating in (though not from attending) the games for this year of 420 B.C. And well they might be, for had not the heralds gone to Sparta, as to all the Greek states, to proclaim in the name of the most holy Zeus a Sacred Truce of a month, so that not only the five days which constituted the festival proper but also the journeys made to Olympia by pilgrims from every part of the Greek world would be free from danger? Yet Sparta had violated the truce—and here, Tromes was sure, was a Spartan.

Still, he dared not voice his suspicions to more than one close friend. After all, Lichas, like the others, had had to satisfy the judges that he was of Greek birth. Like the others he had arrived a month or more ago to watch his charioteer receive his special training by professionals under the rules of the games, and had been given special quarters in the section reserved for game personnel. Each candidate had been obliged to prove that he had passed his local and municipal elimination trials, that he had undergone the required athletic training of Greeks plus the special ten-month training period before coming to Olympia, and that he had not been convicted of any crime, nor been guilty of any impiety or disrespect to the gods. Now the contestants had practised for the last time, and their names were to be entered on a white board. Thereafter, should any man withdraw he was branded as a coward.

The official had ceased speaking, and there was a moment of silence before the athletes moved to be officially enrolled. *Should he speak out against Lichas now?* He cleared his throat, but the words would not come. If he were wrong, if this Lichas really was a Boeotian as he vowed, then he, Tromes, would undoubtedly be disqualified himself for defamation of character. The risk was too great. Surely Lichas would have enough fear of the gods to withdraw his chariot entry if he was deceiving the officials. Surely no one would be brash enough to go through the sacrifice to Zeus and the ensuing oaths if he were an outright liar.

Now the dignified and colourful procession to the temple of Zeus began. The boar had been prepared for sacrifice, and the priests were ready. The sacred spot where the temple and altars of Zeus stood looked strangely bare amidst the great conglomeration of men, tents, and stalls which surrounded it. All around swarmed the visitors to the games, visitors from each of the Peloponnesian states and from the whole Greek world—prosperous citizens from Corinth, Athens, and Thebes, semi-nomads from the shores of the Black Sea, the richly-robed Ionians who had adopted so many habits from their Oriental neighbours, merchants from the western colonies from Italy to Southern Gaul, even the handsome, dark-skinned foreigners from distant Egypt. All were different, yet here all were one in their performance of the rites of this the true religion of the Greeks: the worship of health, beauty, and strength. "There is no greater glory for man as long as he lives," says the *Odyssey*, "than that which he wins by his own hands and feet."

"And this," thought Tromes as he moved along with the procession, "is what my whole life has been preparing for." Like all Athenian boys he had been under the care of his mother until he was seven, playing in the women's quarters (for the women's quarters in the Athenian dwelling were separate from the men's) with his hoops and tops and toy carts, and running with his pet dogs, tortoises, and ducks. He had loved to watch for the snakes and weasels (the Athenian mouse-catchers), and, like the slaves, to blame the weasels for the breakage of pottery jars which had a habit of disintegrating at the most embarrassing moments.

Despite the fact that his mother, like all Athenian women, was expected, as Xenophon said, "to see as little as possible, to hear as little as possible, to ask as few questions as possible," he noticed that his father paid considerable attention to any advice she might give. Of course his father was much older—the marriage had been arranged when his mother was 15 and his father was 34—and his mother's life was limited to running the household and the slaves. No pilgrimages to Olympia for her: women were not allowed at the games. Her outdoor excursions consisted of attendance at funerals, weddings, and certain festivals. She had even been known to attend an occasional "hen party." But she could not go out on the street unattended, and had been given no book learning as all Athenian boys were. Even her birth had not been welcomed.

"At sixteen he . . . betook himself to the best athletic coach in the most expensive school in Athens for special training in wrestling . . ."

A GREEK ATHLETE/209

Some mothers had been known to exchange their baby girls for poorer women's infant sons! Nevertheless Tromes' mother seemed to accept her fate philosophically. The Athenian man was expected to give his service wholly to the state; the Athenian woman was expected to give hers wholly to the home.

Yet even if she did not have as much freedom as her sisters from other Greek states, it was true in Athens, as in the world ever since man was created, that the hand that rocks the cradle rules the world. Many a time Tromes had seen his mother pretty herself up specially when she knew his father would come home for lunch instead of taking it at the Agora (market-place), or when he had been away for some time because it was his turn to be "commander" of a ship, that is, to outfit it and keep it in good repair for a year in place of paying his direct tax. On these occasions she would don her most becoming saffron-coloured tunic. Then she would carefully dress her blue-black hair (sometimes much blacker than others, Tromes noted), and make up her face by applying white-lead, vegetable dyes, and rouge, and rubbing lamp-black under her eyes and on her eyebrows. And so, beautified and perfumed, she would seat herself gracefully in a chair beside her husband's couch, and as the meal progressed would adroitly steer the conversation towards some particular objective which she intended to win that day!

In his eighth year a Greek boy, "the most unmanageable of animals," according to Plato, left the pleasant associations of the women's quarters in that most austere and draughty of domiciles, the Athenian house, and began his formal schooling. His father paid for this. All fathers did, and, no matter how poor they were, there was probably some hapless schoolmaster who would be so indigent that he would accept another student for very little pay. Teaching in Athens was the most miserable of occupations, as is demonstrated by the proverb, "He is either dead or teaching A B C"! Tromes' constant companion was now his "pedagogue," Nausinicus, an elderly male slave who looked after his comings and goings from school, made sure he regarded the pavement modestly and avoided a bustling gait as he walked, that he did not sit with his legs crossed, that he rose when elders entered the room, and that he kept quiet in their presence. Nausinicus also made sure he did his homework, for the schoolmaster carried a forked stick and applied it with a will to naughty students.

And so Nausinicus and Tromes trudged off to school at dawn and did not return until dusk in order that the boy should, as public opinion insisted in this democratic state, receive an adequate education. True, there was no law to insist that he do so; but it was a kind of old age insurance for his father. A son who had not been given a proper education was not obliged to support his aging parent, as those who had were bound to do. Accordingly the Greek boy was educated, first in reading and in memorizing the poets, particularly Homer, then, at about thirteen, in music, probably in playing the lyre (the Greeks believed that music moulded character, and Plato stressed this theory), and all the while in dancing, swimming, and physical culture. For his athletic training Tromes had special teachers in what were known as wrestling schools, and here, despite the fact that the master used the whip and the cane unstintingly, Tromes gloried most to be.

Tromes could not remember a time when he had not daydreamed of this moment when he would represent Athens in the Olympic games. As a small boy he had practised jumping and wrestling with his little brother. At school he had idolized his master of physical culture and spent all the extra hours he could in perfecting the chief exercises of wrestling, running, and leaping. At sixteen he bade goodbye to the services of his old watchdog Nausinicus and, being of an affluent family who did not require him to go right to work, betook himself to the best athletic coach in the most expensive school in Athens for special training in wrestling, boxing, spear-throwing, and riding. How well this training was soon to serve him! At eighteen he underwent his two years of compulsory military training, being, like other trainees, considerably knocked about before he was presented with a spear and shield and sent to patrol the frontiers and dig trenches. This rigorous period was not a pleasant experience, but it was an accepted part of a Greek youth's life. So, too, were the years when, later, he read the mobilization orders in the Agora and had to take down his shield and spear from the rafters, gather up his three-day rations of salt fish, onions, and garlic, and go off with the other members of the citizen army—who might range from svelte 18 to puffing 60—to fight the Spartans.

The Spartans! There was Lichas, along with the other trainers, judges, and athletes, taking his sacred oath that he was a full Greek citizen, that he had fulfilled all the conditions necessary for the games, and that he would abide by the rules of the contest. How solemn were these promises! In more than a thousand years only six or seven competitors were recorded as having broken their oaths. How solemn—and how binding. For they were spoken before the mighty statue of Zeus seated on a throne carved of ivory and ebony, a masterpiece so majestic that "those who enter the temple there no longer think that they are beholding the ivory of India and the gold from Thrace, but the very deity translated to earth by Phidias." Some said that Phidias must either have been visited by the great god himself or else have ascended to heaven and beheld him there in order to work such a miracle of beauty and life-likeness. Dared anyone—even a Spartan—take an oath before the great Zeus and then break it?

The Olympic games usually took place some time in August or September. The first day was taken up with sacrifices and the splendid processions of state representatives in their chariots bearing rich gifts to the treasury of the temple. This was the time when tension became almost unbearable among the contestants, and that night Tromes prayed earnestly to Zeus that he might be granted the coveted olive and so take glory back to Athens, and that in all of this he might honour the mighty king of the gods.

The day dawned bright and clear. Long before the first rays of sun had warmed the stadium every available space was occupied, and no spectator dared leave his seat thereafter for an instant or he would find it taken. There he would sit the livelong day, hatless (hats were forbidden), bitten (despite frequent sacrifices to Zeus Averter of Flies) by flies and mosquitoes, and thirsty (the water was bad). Now the grounds around the stadium, so noisy and gay the day before, lay almost deserted. The merchants with their rare goods, the poets reciting their poems, the hucksters drumming up business for their booths, the heralds announcing the terms of treaties between different states, the gymastic trainers hoping to learn new methods for their pupils, the jugglers who ate fire and swallowed swords, the sculptors, musicians, philosophers, politicians, conjurors, acrobats, pickpockets, beggars, and thieves—all had crowded into the stadium for the first contests.

The herald proclaimed the names of the competitors—including Lichas of Boeotia—and the first event, the chariot race, began. Round and round the hippodrome flashed the chariots, the crowd roaring, the dust from the dry earth enveloping the contestants so that it was impossible to see who crossed the finish line first. The judges in their purple robes announced the victor, and a herald proclaimed in a loud voice, "The winner of the race is the chariot and pair owned by Lichas, of the Boeotian State!" The charioteer, dust-grimed but triumphant, descended from his chariot to be acclaimed the winner.

But he never quite made it. At that moment someone cried "Spartan! Traitor! Spartan!" Another voice, then another, took up the chant, while Lichas dashed out onto the course and attempted to ensure his victory by crowning the charioteer himself. In short order a free-for-all began which promptly grew into a riot, in the middle of which the judges, who were being pushed and shoved about, attempted to retain their dignity and their decision. In no time their hair-dos, which they, like all Greeks, had lavished such care on that morning, were disarrayed, and their robes pulled until they dragged—oh woeful transgression on good taste and decorum!—on the ground. The umpires who carried not a whistle but a good strong rod (and with good reason: Greek athletes, notwithstanding their oath, were not averse to "jumping the gun"), were now using these rods with admirable dispatch and efficiency, particularly on the hapless Lichas, while the rest of the athletes jumped with great joy into the fray, delighted to be able to give a practical demonstration of their skill in boxing and wrestling.

When at length order was restored, Lichas had a great lump on his head and a very black eye, and deemed it the better part of wisdom to lose the right to participate in the Olympics and remain alive rather than collect his prize and have it recorded on his tombstone. The affair thus terminated, the rest of the day went according to plan—although there were those who actually feared that the Spartans would use force in order to take part in the sacrifices. However they did not, and allowed the rest of the festival to pass off quietly, even to the final banquets and feasting that followed the end of the games. These went far into the night, and some of the grosser feeders from Boeotia and epicures from Corinth became pretty boisterous and offensive; but the more abstemious Athenians considered a banquet an occasion for good conversation rather than debauchery, and behaved themselves.

And so the competition continued. The horse race without saddle or stirrup was accomplished, and then, for Tromes, came the most crucial contest in the whole Festival—the one for all-round athletes, the *pentathlon*. It consisted of five events: the broad jump, in which the contestant carried weights in his hands to propel him forward as he leaped from a standing start; the throwing of the discus, a circular plate of metal or stone weighing about twelve pounds; the hurling of the javelin or spear; the stadium sprint; and wrestling. In none of these save the last was winning more important than grace of execution, so much so that they were accompanied by the music of the flute. The man who won three out of five events was counted the winner.

". . . and the winner," bellowed the herald, "is Tromes of Athens!"

Tromes heard the words almost numbly. Then jubilation filled his being. He had done it! He was an Olympic hero!

The third day Tromes enjoyed to the full, for it was the boys' events of a foot race, wrestling, and boxing, and he not only had the pleasure of being a spectator but of seeing a young protégé of his carry off two prizes. On the fourth day came the men's foot races, wrestling, and some extremely vigorous boxing in which there were no rules against hitting a man when he was down, and there were no rests or rounds. Since boxers were not classified by weight the sport, as might be expected, in time degenerated into a battle of brawn. Even so it was tame as compared to the *pankration*, a brutal rough-and-tumble fight in which anything—even a kick in the stomach or the breaking of fingers—was acceptable except biting or gouging out eyes. One man is said to have been strangled to death rather than admit defeat. The final event of the Olympics, the race of men in full armour, must have been a sort of anti-climax to this electrifying sport. Nevertheless it undoubtedly reminded spectators of an important reason for their worship of athletics: all the Greeks must be physically fit in order to be, at any time, ready and able to bear arms in the service of their city-state.

The last day was for Tromes a day to be remembered all his life, to recount to his sons and to his grandsons, and to be recorded in the proud annals of his city. For on this day he received the simple but cherished symbol of victory, a crown of wild olive. This would be, for the rest of his mortal days, his most prized possession. At home great glory awaited him. Some cities tore a hole in their walls to make a special entry for their hero where no man before had trod; some provided free meals for life; some made their victors generals; some gave them substantial money prizes. Poets wrote odes about them. Sculptors made statues of them. The crowd idolized them. All of these marks of respect were welcome, but for Tromes there was a more important reward.

In proving himself a superior athlete, Tromes felt he had fulfilled the conditions for the ideal of Greek manhood. He had striven for grace of movement, strength of limb, and intelligence of discourse; and he had excelled. It was a good feeling. Pindar, the Greek poet who most often sang of the Olympic games, understood it exactly: "He that overcometh hath, because of the games, a sweet tranquillity throughout his life for evermore."

SOURCE READINGS

(a)

PLUTARCH (A.D. 46-127) was a Greek biographer and essayist. He is best known for the fifty biographies of Greek and Roman statesmen in his *Parallel Lives,* a book which appeared in the years A.D. 105-115 and has been one of the most widely read in the world. Shakespeare drew heavily on it for several of his plays. The following selection from the life of Lycurgus describes the education of young Spartans.

[The] offspring was not reared at the will of the father, but taken and carried by him to a place . . . where the elders of the tribes officially examined the infant, and if it was well-built and sturdy, they ordered the father to rear it . . .; but if it was ill-born and deformed, they sent it to . . . a chasm-like place at the foot of Mount Taÿgetus, in the conviction that the life of that which nature had not well equipped at the very beginning for health and strength, was of no advantage either to itself or the state. On the same principle, the women used to bathe their new-born babes not with water, but with wine, thus making a sort of test of their constitutions. For it is said that epileptic and sickly infants are thrown into convulsions by the strong wine and lose their senses, while the healthy ones are rather tempered by it, like steel, and given a firm habit of body. Their nurses, too, exercised great care and skill; they reared infants without swaddling-bands, and thus left their limbs and figures free to develop; besides, they taught them to be contented and happy, not dainty about their food, nor fearful of the dark, nor afraid to be left alone, nor given to contemptible peevishness and whimpering. . . .

. . . But Lycurgus would not put the sons of Spartans in charge of purchased or hired tutors, nor was it lawful for every father to rear or train his son as he pleased, but as soon as they were seven years old, Lycurgus ordered them all to be taken by the state and enrolled in companies, where they were put under the same discipline and nurture, and so became accustomed to share one another's sports and studies. . . .

Of reading and writing, they learned only enough to serve their turn; all the rest of their training was calculated to make them obey commands well, endure hardships, and conquer in battle. Therefore, as they grew in age, their bodily exercise was increased; their heads were close-clipped, and they were accustomed to going bare-foot, and to playing for the most part without clothes. When they were twelve years old, they no longer had tunics to wear, received one cloak a year, had hard dry flesh, and knew little of baths and ointments; only on certain days of the year, and few at that, did they indulge in such amenities. They slept together, in troops and companies, on pallet-beds which they collected for themselves, breaking off with their hands—no knives allowed—the tops of the rushes which grew along the river Eurotas. . . .

. . . one of the noblest and best men of the city was appointed . . . inspector of the boys, and under his directions the boys, in their several companies, put themselves under the command of the most prudent and warlike . . .

[youths of twenty years of age. Each such youth] commands his subordinates in their mimic battles, and in doors makes them serve him at his meals. He commissions the larger ones to fetch wood, and the smaller ones potherbs. And they steal what they fetch, some of them entering the gardens, and others creeping right slyly and cautiously into the public messes of the men; but if a boy is caught stealing, he is soundly flogged, as a careless and unskilful thief. They steal, too, whatever food they can, and learn to be adept in setting upon people when asleep or off their guard. But the boy who is caught gets a flogging and must go hungry. For the meals allowed them are scanty, in order that they may take into their own hands the fight against hunger, and so be forced into boldness and cunning.

. . . The boys make such a serious matter of their stealing, that one of them, as the story goes, who was carrying concealed under his cloak a young fox which he had stolen, suffered the animal to tear out his bowels with its teeth and claws, and died rather than have his theft detected.

Plutarch's Lives, translated by B. Perrin, Loeb Classical Library (William Heinemann, 1914), I, 255-263.

(b)

THUCYDIDES (460-400 B.C.), it has been said, "saw more truly, inquired more responsibly, and reported more faithfully than any other ancient historian." The extract below is from Pericles' *Funeral Oration,* the address delivered by the general at the state funeral held in 430 B.C. for the Athenian soldiers who had been killed in the first year of the Peloponnesian War. Thucydides explains that he and his informants found it difficult to recall the precise words of the speeches that he later recorded in his *History,* and that therefore they "are given here in the form in which I thought the persons concerned would most likely have said what was called for under the circumstances, while keeping as close as possible to the general gist of what was actually said."

Our constitution is named a democracy, because it is in the hands not of the few but of the many. But our laws secure equal justice for all in their private disputes, and our public opinion welcomes and honours talent in every branch of achievement, not for any sectional reason but on grounds of excellence alone. And as we give free play to all in our public life, so we carry the same spirit into our daily relations with one another. . . .

Yet ours is no work-a-day city only. No other provides so many recreations for the spirit—contests and sacrifices all the year round, and beauty in our public buildings to cheer the heart and delight the eye day by day. Moreover, the city is so large and powerful that all the wealth of all the world flows in to her, so that our own Attic products seem no more homelike to us than the fruits of the labours of other nations.

Our military training too is different from our opponents'. The gates of our city are flung open to the world. We practise no periodical deportations, nor do we prevent our visitors from observing or discovering what an enemy might usefully apply to his own purposes. For our trust is not in the devices of material equipment, but in our own good spirits for battle.

So too with education. They toil from early boyhood in a laborious pursuit after courage, while we, free to live and wander as we please, march out none the less to face the self-same dangers. . . . Indeed, if we choose to face danger with an easy mind rather than after a rigorous training, and to trust rather in native manliness than in state-made courage, the advantage lies with us; for we are spared all the weariness of practising for future hardships, and when we find ourselves amongst them we are as brave as our plodding rivals. Here as elsewhere, then, the city sets an example which is deserving of admiration.

We are lovers of beauty without extravagance, and lovers of wisdom without unmanliness. . . . Our citizens attend both to public and private duties, and do not allow absorption in their own various affairs to interfere with their knowledge of the city's. We differ from other states in regarding the man who holds aloof from public life not as "quiet" but as useless; we decide or debate, carefully and in person, all matters of policy, holding, not that words and deeds go ill together, but that acts are foredoomed to failure when undertaken undiscussed. . . .

In a word I claim that our city as a whole is an education to Greece, and that her members yield to none, man by man, for independence of spirit, many-sidedness of attainment, and complete self-reliance in limbs and brain.

Such then is the city, for whom, lest they should lose her, the men whom we celebrate died a soldier's death: and it is but natural that all of us, who survive them, should wish to spend ourselves in her service.

A. Zimmern, *The Greek Commonwealth* (Clarendon Press, 5th edition, revised, 1931), pp. 203-206, slightly adapted.

(c)

The "OLD OLIGARCH" is the anonymous author of a pamphlet entitled *On the Constitution of Athens*. We know nothing more about him, though scholars think that he may have been an Athenian who wrote some time between 431 and 415 B.C. At any rate the Old Oligarch, whoever he was, will always be remembered for his tirade against the ill effects of Athenian democracy.

. . . Everywhere the best people are opposed to democracy, because among the best element there is least excess and injustice, and most self-discipline to useful ends. Among the people, on the other hand, ignorance is at its height, as well as disorder and vulgarity. For poverty, lack of education, and in some cases the ignorance which arises from lack of money lead them more to unseemly conduct. . . .

. . . if the decent people were to do the speaking and the deliberating, for those who were like themselves it would be advantageous, but not so for the popular party. But as it is, any scoundrel who pleases can get up, say his say, and get what is good for him and his like. It might well be asked, "What that is good for himself or for the state would such a man know?" But the people know that this man's ignorance, commonness, and good will profit them more than the virtue, wisdom, and disaffection of the conservative. Perhaps it is not as a result of such practices that a state becomes perfect, but this is the way democracy would be best preserved. For what the people want is not that they should be enslaved in a well-ordered city, but that they should be free and that they should rule; and bad government concerns them but little. . . .

Speaking of slavery, at Athens the effrontery of slaves and resident aliens is at its height; to strike them is not allowed there, and yet a slave will not stand out of the road to let you pass. And this is why that is the custom there: if it were lawful for a slave to be struck by a free man, or for an alien or a freedman to be beaten, you would often think an Athenian a slave and beat *him*. For in dress the people there are no better than slaves or aliens, and in appearance they are no better either. . . . they allow the privately owned slaves there to put on airs, and some of them to live downright magnificently. . . . So we have allowed even slaves free speech in their relations with free men, and resident aliens free speech in their relations with citizens, because the city needs resident aliens on account of the number of trades and on account of sea-faring. This is the reason then why we grant free speech also, reasonably enough, to resident aliens.

The people have driven the practice of gymnastics and music out of fashion in Athens, ostensibly on moral grounds, but really because they know they have not the ability to practise these arts themselves. Moreover, in having the rich pay for choruses, direct gymnasia, and outfit triremes, the people know that they dance while the rich pay the piper, and that in directing the gymnasia and outfitting the triremes the rich have the expense, the poor the entertainment. At any rate, the people take it for granted that they should be paid for singing, running, dancing, and going sailing in the ships, so that they can have money and the rich get poorer. And in the courts they care not so much about justice as about their own advantage.

As for the allies, because the Athenians sail out seemingly to persecute and blackmail those they govern, and hate decent citizens (knowing that the ruler must be hated by the ruled, and that if the rich and the decent gain power in the allied cities short-lived indeed will be the power of the people of Athens), for this reason they disfranchise decent people, confiscate their money, exile them, and execute them, but scoundrels they exalt.

P. MacKendrick and H. M. Howe, editors, *Classics in Translation,* Vol. I, *Greek Literature* (University of Wisconsin Press, 1952), pp. 224-226.

(d)

SOCRATES (469-399 B.C.) was tried and condemned to death on a charge of not believing in the state gods and of teaching his disbelief.

Since Socrates himself wrote nothing, our best source of information about him is in the writings of his pupil Plato. Plato's *Apology,* from which the following extract is taken, presents the speech that Socrates gave in his own defence at his trial. Far from admitting that he ought to be punished, Socrates said that he should be treated as a public benefactor and rewarded with free meals for life!

Your witness to my wisdom, if I have any, and to its nature, is the god at Delphi. You certainly knew Chaerephon. He was a friend of mine from our youth, and a friend of your popular party as well; he shared in your late exile, and accompanied you on your return. Now you know the temper of Chaerephon, how impulsive he was in everything he undertook. Well so it was when once he went to Delphi, and made bold to ask the oracle this question—and, Gentlemen, please do not make an uproar over what I say; he asked if there was any one more wise than I. Then the Pythian oracle made response that there was no one who was wiser. To this response his brother here will bear you witness, since Chaerephon himself is dead.

Now bear in mind the reason why I tell you this. It is because I am going on to show you whence this calumny of me has sprung; for when I heard about the oracle, I communed within myself: "What can the god be saying, and what does the riddle mean? Well I know in my own heart that I am without wisdom great or small. What is it that he means, then, in declaring me to be most wise? It cannot be that he is lying; it is not in his nature." For a long time I continued at a loss as to his meaning, then finally decided, much against my will, to seek it in the following way.

I went to one of those who pass for wise men, feeling sure that there if anywhere I could refute the answer, and explain to the oracle: "Here is a man that is wiser than I, but you said I was the wisest." The man I went to was one of our statesmen; his name I need not mention. Him I thoroughly examined, and from him, as I studied him and conversed with him, I gathered, fellow citizens, this impression. This man appeared to me to seem to be wise to others, and above all to himself, but not to be so. And then I tried to show him that he thought that he was wise, but was not. The result was that I gained his enmity and the enmity as well of many of those who were present. So, as I went away, I reasoned with myself: "At all events I am wiser than this man is. It is quite possible that neither one of us knows anything fine and good. But this man fancies that he knows when he does not, while I, whereas I do not know, just so I do not fancy that I know. In this small item, then, at least, I seem to be wiser than he, in that I do not fancy that I know what I do not." Thereafter I went to another man, one of those who passed for wiser than the first, and I got the same impression. Whereupon I gained his enmity as well as that of many more. . . .

Such, fellow citizens, was the quest which brought me so much enmity, hatreds so utterly harsh and hard to bear, whence sprang so many calumnies, and this name that is given me of being "wise"; for every time I caught another person in his ignorance, those present fancied that I knew what he did not. . . . So even now I still go about in my search, and, in keeping with the god's intent, question anybody, citizen or stranger, whom I fancy to be wise. . . .

Plato, On the Trial and Death of Socrates, translated by L. Cooper (Cornell University Press, 1941), pp. 53-56.

(e)

ARCHIMEDES (287-212 B.C.) of Syracuse was the ancient world's greatest mathematician. He was killed when the Romans captured Syracuse in the First Punic War (see pages 241-243). Two of his sayings have become particularly famous: first, his boast that he could move a great weight by a small force—"Give me a place to stand on and I will move the earth"; and second, his exclamation when he discovered a method for measuring specific gravity — "Eureka!" This account, composed in 25 B.C. by the Roman architect and military engineer, VITRUVIUS POLLIO, records the circumstances of this discovery.

The discoveries of Archimedes were many and ingenious, in widely different fields, but of them all that which I am now going to describe seems to me best to display his unlimited cleverness.

Since the affairs of King Hiero of Syracuse had prospered and his power had been much increased, he decided to offer a golden crown in a certain temple in thanks to the immortal gods. He therefore let out a contract to a goldsmith, to whom he paid a fee for making the crown and enough beside for the exact weight of the gold that would be necessary. At the proper time the goldsmith presented a beautifully made crown to the king, having, to judge by the weight of the crown, used all the gold that had been issued to him. But a little later the king got wind of a story that the goldsmith had abstracted some of the gold and replaced it with an equal weight of silver. Hiero was furious at having been tricked, but he saw no way to prove the theft; he therefore asked Archimedes to think over his problem.

While Archimedes was considering the matter, he went one day to the city baths. There he went into a small pool (with an overflow pipe), and while in it he reflected that the submerged part of his body made its own volume of water overflow. Realization of this showed him the principle on which his whole problem hinged, and in his delight he leaped from the pool and ran home without bothering about his clothes, announcing in a loud voice that he had found what he was looking for. For as he hurried along he kept shouting in Greek, "I've got it! I've got it!" (Eureka! Eureka!)

The story goes on that after he had made this start he took a slab of silver and another of gold, each weighing the same as the crown. He then filled a large pot to the brim with water and dropped in the silver. Water equal in bulk to the silver ran over the edge of the pot; after removing the slab he measured the amount of water it took to refill the pot. Thus he found what weight of silver equalled that of a known bulk of water.

Next he dropped in his slab of gold, removed it, and measured the amount of water needed to replace the overflow; it was much less than had been the case with the silver—a difference corresponding to the smaller bulk of the gold, compared with the same weight of silver. Finally, he lowered in the crown, and found that more water ran over than had done for the pure gold, although their weights were the same. From the difference in overflows of the crown and the pure gold Archimedes calculated the amount of silver alloyed with the gold in the crown, and thus proved the guilt of the goldsmith.

W. R. Agard, *The Greek Mind* (Anvil Books, Van Nostrand, 1957), pp. 166-168.

Reprinted with permission of the Regents of the University of Wisconsin, from Paul MacKendrick and Herbert M. Howe, *Classics in Translation*, Vol. 1, 1963, University of Wisconsin Press.

BOOKS TO READ

1. GENERAL

Grant, M. and Pottinger, D., *Greeks* (Nelson)
Green, R. L., *Ancient Greece* (Weidenfeld and Nicolson)
Milliken, E. K., *The Greek People* (Harrap)
Mills, D., *The Book of the Ancient Greeks* (Putnam)
Quennell, M. and C. H. B., *Everyday Life in Ancient Greece* (Batsford)
Taylor, D., *Ancient Greece* (Methuen)

2. MINOANS AND MYCENAEANS

Cottrell, L., *The Bull of Minos* (Pan paperback)
Mireaux, E., *Daily Life in the Time of Homer* (Allen and Unwin)
Vaughan, A. C., *The House of the Double Axe* (Doubleday)

3. FROM CITY-STATES TO THE HELLENISTIC AGE

Anderson, P., *Finding Out About the Athenians* (Muller)
Davis, W. S., *A Day in Old Athens* (Allyn and Bacon)
Lamb, H., *Alexander of Macedon* (Bantam paperback)
Renault, M., *The Lion in the Gateway* (Harper and Row)

4. HISTORICAL FICTION

Coolidge, O., *Trojan War* (Houghton) [the Iliad and Odyssey retold]
Coolidge, O., *Men of Athens* (Houghton) [fictional biographies of great Athenians]
Davis, W. S., *A Victor of Salamis* (Macmillan) [an Athenian at the battle of Salamis]
Milton, R., *Tell Them in Sparta* (Four Square paperback) [the second Persian invasion]
Snedeker, C. D., *Theras and His Town* (Doubleday) [Athens and Sparta in the age of Pericles]

PART V

THE GRANDEUR OF ROME

INIS SERVATAM IVL CAR SIX EI IIII PONT NEPOS HI

CHAPTER 24

A City Conquers Italy

Senators, a victory which neither god nor man could begrudge, you and your general have won over us. We surrender to you because we believe (and what could be handsomer for a victor?) that life will be better under your administration than under our own laws.

THE CITIZENS OF FALERII IN THE SENATE AT ROME, 395 B.C.

Jutting more than 600 miles into the Mediterranean is a long, slender peninsula shaped amazingly like a boot. This peninsula, as you know, is Italy—the home of the Romans, that ancient people whose empire once stretched from Scotland to India. Many of our roots go back to Rome, and the successes and failures of the Romans have always had a special fascination for modern students. How they acquired their empire, why they lost democracy in governing it, how their military strength kept the peace of the world and, finally, why the whole system collapsed, all are questions which we ponder when we consider the grandeur that was Rome.

❖ *The Homeland* Italy's peninsula averages about 100 miles in width, and the whole country covers an area a little smaller than Newfoundland —about three times that of ancient Greece. The Apennines run the length of the peninsula like a rugged backbone. This barrier of mountains has made communication between various parts of Italy difficult, a fact of which the world was reminded during the Italian campaigns of 1943 and 1944 in World War II. The mountainous character of much of Italy has another effect: it robs her of any great rivers. With the exception of the Po in the northern plain, the rivers have too swift a current and too variable a volume of water to be navigable.

Throughout the long span of history the stately and powerful eagle has been the cherished emblem of peoples as widely separated as the Persians and the North American Indians. The Roman armies bore it on their standards during the early Republic, but only as the chief of several symbols carried into battle in a set order: eagles first, then wolves, minotaurs, horses, and bears. It was the famous Roman general Marius who decreed that the eagle alone should become the special standard of the legions, and in this way it came to be the proud symbol of the Roman Empire's supremacy over land and sea. Here it is framed by the corona civica, *the wreath of oak leaves and acorns bestowed on the soldier who saved the life of a Roman citizen in battle.*

Canadians do not often think of Italian geography in relation to their own, but if we superimpose Italy at its correct latitude on a map of North America, we will find that the northern end will be located over Montreal while the "toe" of the boot is in the vicinity of Washington, D.C. Nevertheless the Mediterranean Sea so moderates the Italian climate that the Po valley has the wide temperature variation of a continental climate (summer rain, moderate winter snow, wet spring and fall), and much of the peninsula enjoys the rainy winters and hot, dry summers of a Mediterranean climate.

Italy's one great geographical advantage is her central position in the Mediterranean basin. Despite 2000 miles of peninsular coastline her harbours are few: the coast is too regular to have the countless sheltered inlets of Greece. Moreover, the Mediterranean has no strong tides to scour out the river mouths and they soon silt up. Such good harbours as Italy does possess are found along the west coast. Hence in ancient days Italy faced west, whereas Greece faced east.

Although Italy's topography hampered her communications, her great economic potentialities contrasted sharply with Greece's poverty. True, there was not a rich supply of minerals, but there was plenty of good building stone and marble, and the wooded Apennine slopes provided ample timber for shipbuilding. The plains, enriched by lava dust from numerous volcanoes and silt washed down by the rivers, yielded profuse harvests of wheat and barley, apples and pears, peas and beans. And, as in all Mediterranean countries, the cultivation of grapes and olives was important, while sheep, goats, and cattle grew fat on the luxuriant highland pastures.

❖ *From Stone to Iron* How far does the history of man go back in Italy? Here, too, the Old and New Stone Ages ran their course, and sometime after 1600 B.C. a Bronze Age Indo-European culture appeared in the Po valley. It was brought there from the Danube region by a people who were superior farmers and livestock breeders, and who lived in huts of wattle and daub. Many were hunters and fishermen, and some were craftsmen as well, spreading their products—in particular gray and black vases—into central and southern Italy.

The Villanovans Slowly northern Italy passed from the Bronze to the Iron Age, and after 1000 B.C. another people appeared. These Villanovans, as the archaeologists call them, were probably caught up in the general dislocation forced by the Dorian invasions, and migrated across the Adriatic Sea. They became expert metalworkers, and by the 8th century B.C.

Bologna was the "Hamilton" of early Italy, the centre of a flourishing export trade in bronze and iron work.

Gradually the Villanovans spread down the east coast of Italy, building their villages of round huts as they went. But the mineral wealth of Italy, in particular the rich copper of Etruria, drew new marauding bands to Italian shores. The Villanovans were eventually to become fused with these latest invaders, the mysterious Etruscans, one of the two peoples who were destined to affect the Romans most deeply.

❖ *Bearers of Civilization*   The Etruscans probably came into Italy between 1000 and 800 B.C. from some point on the shores of Asia Minor. They settled first in Etruria (modern Tuscany), and then expanded across the Tiber to the south. Nevertheless the various Etruscan cities remained politically independent of each other, so that a unified state was never established.

The Etruscans

At least 10,000 Etruscan inscriptions have survived, and while their language has not been completely deciphered, scholars have been able to partially translate the twenty-seven letter alphabet adapted from the Greeks. Unfortunately these inscriptions do not tell us much because they consist mostly of proper names used for religious dedications or epitaphs.

The Etruscan language reveals little beyond a people whose religion was preoccupied with gloomy thoughts of death. But this would indeed be a misleading impression of their civilization. For the Etruscans loved to bedeck themselves with jewels and live a life of pleasure; they took delight in a good feast, a sprightly dance, and such exciting sports as horse-racing. More surprising is the knowledge that even at this early date women played a prominent role in society, as is known from the fact that often a man's epitaph records the name of his mother.

Etruscan men were first of all warriors: it was Etruscan nobles who introduced the chariot into Italy. They were also pirates and traders: their merchants traded widely with the Phoenicians, Greeks, and even the Egyptians. And they were farmers, who cleared forests, drained land, and began to cultivate grapes and olives. But above all—and here lies their main significance—the Etruscans were great engineers, masters of the arts of building, a skill which they passed on to the Romans. Even today their genius in constructing walled cities, in mining, and in building aqueducts, harbours, and drainage systems is abundantly evident in Roman ruins. For these and other reasons the Etruscans have been called the civilizers of Italy.

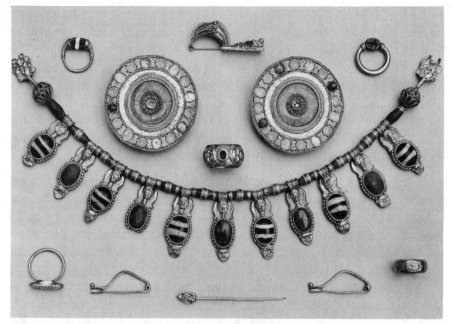

The Etruscan upper classes enjoyed lives of elegance and splendour, as may be seen by these examples of gold, glass, and carnelian jewellery from about 500 B.C. The Greeks probably would have disapproved of the Etruscan women's immodest display of elaborate necklaces, brooches, pins, and rings—although they, like the Etruscans, were not above using make-up and hair bleach!

The other bearers of civilization to Italy were the Greeks, who as early as the 8th century B.C. had founded colonies in the western Mediterranean. They settled in Sicily and along the southern coasts of Italy as far north as modern Naples. It was in these early days that the Romans coined the name *Graeci,* or Greeks, for their Hellenic neighbours. The Greeks had faithfully exported their superior culture to their colonies, and it so stimulated the Romans that it eventually supplanted Etruscan influence in Rome.

Who were these Romans who were caught midway between the Etruscans and the Greeks?

❖ *The People of the Plain* The Romans had a simple solution for history's gaps: what they did not know they made up. Hence the Romans, anxious to rival the Greeks' glorious history, invented their own version of the founding of their city.

The Latins Rome was founded, they said, by twin boys called Romulus and Remus. These boys were descended from the Trojan hero Aeneas, who had escaped from Troy to Italy. Just after they were born a palace revolution overthrew their grandfather, the king of Alba, and orders were given that the babies should be placed in a basket and left to drown in the floodwaters of the Tiber. But a she-wolf, hearing their cries, mothered them until eventually the wild boys were discovered and raised by a shepherd.

Romulus and Remus restored their grandfather to his throne. Then they decided to build a city on a hill overlooking the spot where they had been exposed as babies, and it was thus, says the legend, that Rome was founded (in 753 B.C.) on the borderland of Etruria and Latium, about fifteen miles up the Tiber.

None of this story, of course, is historical. The truth is that as early as 1000 B.C. the Latins, who lived south of the Tiber in Latium, had settled themselves on a site which was a good choice for two reasons: it was surrounded by a ring of hills which made defence easy, and there was an island which facilitated the fording of the river Tiber.

Early government of Rome

Before long the Latins found themselves dominated by foreigners, the Etruscans. These first rulers of early Rome, like those of most Middle Eastern countries, were kings who exercised the functions of commander-in-chief of the army, high priest, and supreme judge. The king was assisted by a council of aristocrats called the Senate, and a general assembly of the people called the Curiate Assembly. The job of the Curiate Assembly was mainly to approve what had already been decided by the aristocrats: it sanctioned a new king or a declaration of war.

About 509 B.C. the aristocrats expelled their despotic kings, thereby abolishing the monarchy. The Etruscan overlordship had been ended.

❖ *The Reluctant Imperialist*   In the confusion of the 6th century B.C. Rome was just one of many fortified towns in the peninsula, albeit the chief town of Latium controlling about 300 square miles. Yet even at such an early period in her history she was beginning to stand out from her allies. This was evident when she joined in a defensive league with the other Latin towns; for although each ally gave the other equal rights of citizenship, Rome's vote equalled that of all the other members of the League combined.

The Latin League

Rome was never left at peace for long. The valley of the Tiber was a prey to mountain tribes who raided Roman territory year after year. Her most dangerous enemy in the 5th century B.C., however, was the Etruscan city of Veii, which lay only a few miles away north of the

A CITY CONQUERS ITALY/227

Tiber. By the end of this century Veii was conquered. Thus Rome had become supreme in central Italy, not because she was blatantly imperialistic and coveted more territory, but simply because she continually had to capture the bases of enemies who were making sorties into her domains.

The Gauls   Rome had barely conquered Veii when a new invader appeared. Down from what is now modern France swept an undisciplined horde of fair-haired, blue-eyed giants—the Gauls. They sacked and burned Rome; but fortunately for the Romans the invaders wanted plunder more than territory, and eventually marched away after extorting a ransom for the city. The people quickly rallied to rebuild their ruined homes—and later manufactured stories of how they had beaten off a stubborn foe. Here is one of the most famous of these legends.

The citadel of Rome and the Capitol were in very great danger. For the Gauls had noticed the tracks of a man, where the messenger from Veii had got through, or perhaps had observed for themselves that the cliff near the shrine of Carmentis afforded an easy ascent. So on a starlit night they first sent forward an unarmed man to try the way; then, handing up their weapons where there was a steep place and supporting themselves by their fellows or affording support in their turn, they pulled one another up, as the ground required, and reached the summit, in such silence that not only the sentries but even the dogs . . . were not aroused. But they could not elude the vigilance of the geese, which being sacred to Juno had, notwithstanding the dearth of provisions, not been killed. This was the salvation of them all; for the geese with their cackling and the flapping of their wings woke Marcus Manlius . . . who, catching up his weapons and at the same time calling the rest to arms, strode past his bewildered comrades to a Gaul who had already got a foothold on the crest and dislodged him with a blow from the boss of his shield. . . . And by now the rest had come together and were assailing the invaders with javelins and stones, and presently the whole company lost their footing and were flung down headlong to destruction. Then after the din was hushed, the rest of the night . . . was given up to sleep.

The Gauls came back on several other occasions, but the second time (in 349 B.C.) the Romans were ready for them and the attackers retreated without a battle. By now Rome was clearly the champion of the central Italian peoples.

❖ *The Lengthening Shadow*   Rome's leadership in Latium did not, however, go unchallenged, and eventually the Latin League revolted. Rome defeated the League and dissolved it, incorporating most of the Latin cities into the Roman state.

ROME'S CONQUEST OF ITALY TO 218 B.C.

Naturally there were those who feared the lengthening shadow of *The* Rome. These now took their lead from Samnium, the most powerful *Samnites* state in the interior of the peninsula. The Samnites were a brave, hardy people whose life in the southern Apennines had accustomed them to mountain fighting, whereas the Romans were supreme fighters in the open country. For this reason the Romans thought it prudent to defeat the Samnites by hemming them in with encircling alliances.

It took a long time. Off and on during the next generation the Romans warred with the Samnites, who were aided and abetted by Rome's old foes, the Etruscans and the Gauls. By 290 B.C. Italy from Etruria in the north to Lucania at the "instep" of the Italian boot was dominated by Rome. But strange to tell, Rome's many wars did not exhaust her; rather with each victory she seemed to gather strength.

Rome now came face to face with the Greeks of southern Italy. When some Greek cities became Roman allies, Tarentum began to fear that she, too, would come under Roman domination. So the Tarentines provoked a war, and then appealed to Pyrrhus, the king of Epirus in north-west Greece. Pyrrhus sent an army of 25,000 men and 20 elephants, and although he defeated the Romans the struggle cost him so dearly that the term "Pyrrhic victory" has been coined for one in which the victor's losses are excessively high. After a second success, also bought at great cost, Pyrrhus is said to have remarked, "Another such victory will ruin us." Pyrrhus was a brilliant general but an unstable one, and finally he returned to Greece with the survivors—only a third —of his original force. By 265 B.C. Rome had overcome the last Samnite and Etruscan opposition and become mistress of the entire Italian peninsula south of the Po.

❖ *The Secret of Success*　What was the secret of Rome's success? It was that above all else the Romans were willing to submit to organization and discipline. This discipline, of course, showed itself first and foremost in the tough Roman soldier.

The Roman army
Because every soldier had to provide his own equipment, the landless poor were automatically excluded from the army. The richest, those able to afford a horse, composed the cavalry. The ordinary foot-soldier provided his own helmet, shield, armour, and weapons. Also, he had to bring his own pack of auxiliary equipment consisting of a spade, hatchet, saw, bucket, cooking-pot, and half a month's ration of wheat meal. Armour and weapons weighed about 45 pounds, and the auxiliary equipment as much again.

From the Etruscans and Greeks the Romans had learned to use the phalanx, the disciplined mass of foot-soldiers armed with lances and protected by shields and leather or bronze body armour. Then, some time before the beginning of the Carthaginian Wars in 264 B.C., the Romans broke the phalanx up into sections called *maniples,* each of which consisted of two *centuries.* The maniples were organized into divisions called *legions,* which were reinforced by bodies of cavalry and light-armed skirmishing troops.

By the 3rd century B.C. the arrangement of the heavy-armed legionary foot-soldiers was as follows:

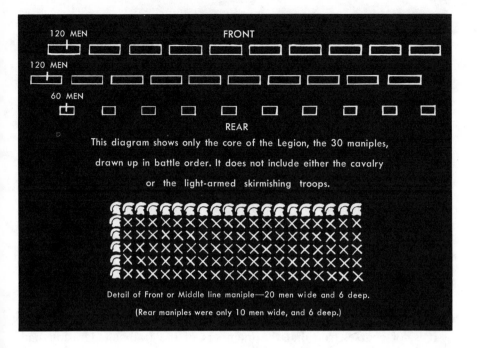

120 MEN

FRONT

120 MEN

60 MEN

REAR

This diagram shows only the core of the Legion, the 30 maniples,

drawn up in battle order. It does not include either the cavalry

or the light-armed skirmishing troops.

Detail of Front or Middle line maniple—20 men wide and 6 deep.

(Rear maniples were only 10 men wide, and 6 deep.)

The front line was made up of younger men armed with a short sword and one or two heavy throwing spears. In the second line, similarly armed, were the middle-aged legionaries. The seasoned veterans, armed with a sword and a light thrusting spear, formed the rear line. Thus the usual legion consisted of:

$$
\begin{array}{ll}
\text{10 maniples of } 120 = 1200 & \text{(front line)} \\
\text{10 maniples of } 120 = 1200 & \text{(middle line)} \\
\text{10 maniples of } 60 = 600 & \text{(rear line)} \\
\text{light-armed troops} = 1200 & \\
\text{cavalry} = 300 & \\
\hline
\text{LEGION} = 4500 \text{ men} &
\end{array}
$$

Rome's 3rd century B.C. armies consisted of eight legions.

The discipline was magnificent. The best example of the legendary iron will of the Roman legions may be found in their camps. At nightfall, no matter what the day had included, no matter how much marching or fighting had been done, the legionaries would build a fortified camp with a moat, earthen ramparts, and palisades. There was a set plan for the camp, and every soldier was assigned his specific place and task.

With such an army, in less than two and a half centuries Rome had achieved the status of a world power.

❖ *A Sensible Solution* It has been said of the British Empire that it was acquired in a fit of absent-mindedness. What is meant by this statement is that there was no long-range plan of conquest, often no desire for foreign territory other than that required to ensure safety at home—an argument always more convincing to the victor than to the vanquished. At least in the beginning, the foregoing was also true of Rome. She did not seek quarrels with her neighbours. But when they would not leave her alone she absorbed them one by one, thus being led on from one frontier to another. The logical conclusion had to be control of all Italy.

But could Rome stop there? Perhaps she could—if no other power interfered with her plans for Italy. So far, then, a jury pronouncing on the evidence of Rome's imperialism might declare her comparatively innocent. Before we pass final judgment, however, let us examine the way in which Rome had organized her Italian empire.

It is, of course, true that the members of the Italian federation had now lost their independence to Rome. Yet it is also true that Rome gave them peace at home and protection from any foreign invader. Nor was any one overall unified system forced upon them. The Romans were clever and practical enough to adapt themselves to varied conditions.

There were two classes of Roman citizens and two classes of allies, as shown below:

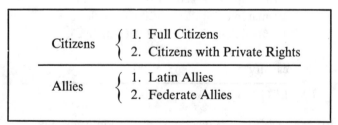

Only the full citizens, who lived in the city of Rome, in adjacent towns, or in Roman colonies, could hold office at Rome and vote in the Roman Assemblies. (These Assemblies, it must be noted, met only in the city of Rome itself.) The citizens with private rights, on the other hand, were really only half-way along the road to full citizenship, and were denied a vote or office at Rome.

A E K T

λ E ∤ T

The Romans borrowed their letter forms from the Greeks, probably through the Etruscans, and we in turn have retained many of them unchanged in our modern printing. Letters from the inscription on Trajan's Column in Rome of about A.D. 114 (upper line) are typically Roman in design, combining beauty and simplicity. The lower line shows Roman hand-writing of about 50 B.C.

The Latin allies had full rights of local self-government and a constitution modelled on that of Rome. But the extent of privileges granted to Federate allies depended on whether they had entered the alliance voluntarily or by conquest. No ally had any control over its own external affairs, but neither did it have to pay taxes or tribute to Rome, although it was obliged to furnish troops, which served alongside the Roman legions.

In this way "Rome became the mother of Italy," writes an eminent historian, "training her children by carefully graded stages up to the privilege of full family life. This was an immense stride forward in Rome's history and indeed in the history of mankind. The conquered people were not to be dragged along at Rome's chariot wheels as slaves; they were asked to share in the privileges and responsibilities of their conqueror." The Roman grant of citizenship to subject states was something of which the Greeks could not conceive, but given this sensible Roman solution to a difficult problem, Rome's rule was firmly established in Italy by the 3rd century B.C.

❖ *The Men Who Ruled Rome*   The Roman ability to make practical adjustments according to the demands of circumstances, to learn by experience rather than to act according to theory, is once again shown in the development of their government. "Our Republic," a stern Roman once said, "was not made by the services of one man, but of many, not in a single lifetime, but through many centuries and generations." The evolution of the Roman constitution was a slow process, stretching from the 6th to the 3rd century B.C.

When the Etruscan kings were expelled from Rome they were replaced by two chief magistrates called *consuls*. Each consul could veto any public act of the other. This check, it was felt, would prevent the office from growing too strong for the good of the state. In peacetime the consuls alternated their rule within Rome monthly, but on the battlefield their command of the army, incredible as it may sound, alternated daily.

Consuls

The consuls also presided over the Senate, although they were there as much to listen as to give advice.

Other magistrates If the two consuls reached an impasse or if a crisis overtook the state, the Senate could endorse one man as *dictator* for a term of six months, a step that amounted to a temporary decree of martial law.

The magistrates ranking next to the consuls were the eight *praetors,* one of whom presided over the Senate if the consuls were away from Rome. Only the consuls, dictator, and praetors had the right to command an army, preside over an assembly, and try important cases.

Next in importance were eight *aediles,* who were responsible for the administration of public works, roads, and the control of weights and measures in Roman markets. Last came the four *quaestors*; two were in charge of the public treasury, and two were special assistants to the consuls.

All the magistrates so far described were elected yearly, although under unusual circumstances (for example, a consular military campaign) the Senate could prolong the term of office. Two special magistrates, however, were elected only once in five years. These were the *censors* (usually ex-consuls), whose job was to register all Roman citizens and their property, and to revise the list of senators. So honoured were these magistrates that they were buried in the rich purple toga of royalty.

Tribunes of the People As the power of the lower classes (*plebeians*) increased they acquired officers of their own to protect them from exploitation at the hands of the aristocrats (*patricians*). These ten *tribunes of the people* (who were not allowed to be absent from the city overnight nor to lock their own doors) attended meetings of the Senate and proposed legislation for the Tribal Assembly. They were so powerful that they could arbitrarily veto any act of the magistrates, or any laws. Indeed a single tribune could even veto the acts of the other nine!

The diagram opposite shows the established order of progression up the stairway of civic and political fame, from quaestor to consul. The dictator, of course, would appear only in time of crisis, while the special role played by the tribunes has already been explained.

❖ *A Far Cry from Democracy* Sharing the conduct of the day-to-day business of the state with the elected magistrates was the *Senate,* whose origins went back to the traditional council of aristocrats who had advised the king. The 300 senators were chosen for life by the consuls. They provided the state with both experience and knowledge, and at first

The Senate

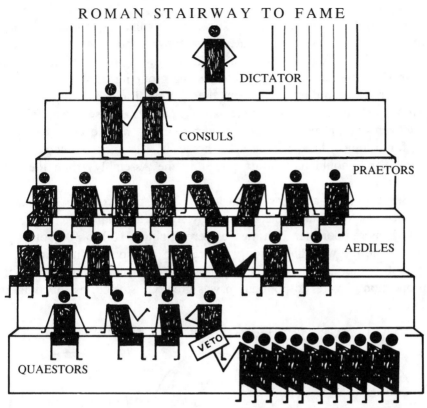

ROMAN STAIRWAY TO FAME

DICTATOR

CONSULS

PRAETORS

AEDILES

VETO

QUAESTORS

TRIBUNES OF THE PEOPLE

their sanction was necessary before assembly measures could become law. Even when this sanction was no longer required (after 287 B.C.) the Senate still exercised considerable influence. Its members not only advised magistrates and assigned them their duties, but they also drew up the state budget and supervised foreign affairs. Above all, in times of emergency the Senate could suspend constitutional liberties and declare martial law.

It is no accident that in those four famous initials which the Romans were to carve on thousands of their monuments — *S.P.Q.R.* (*Senatus Populusque Romanus,* the Senate and People of Rome)—the Senate precedes the people.

The people of Rome were represented by two Assemblies, the Centuriate Assembly and the Tribal Assembly. Both had been developed in the 5th century B.C., and their membership overlapped.

The Centuriate Assembly gradually replaced the older Curiate Assembly (see page 227). It voted on laws submitted to it, and declared

The Centuriate Assembly

war and ratified peace treaties. However, it came to be mainly a body for electing the senior magistrates—the consuls and praetors. It derived its name from the fact that it was organized into groups of voters called *centuries*. The centuries originated in the grouping of citizens for military service according to the arms they could afford. This army classification was adapted to the Centuriate Assembly because it was felt that a citizen's voting power ought to correspond to his worth as a soldier. If, for instance, he could afford a horse, he was more valuable to the army (and should have more power in the Assembly) than the foot-soldier.

Because the particular century to which any voter belonged depended on his wealth, the centuries were of unequal size. There are always more poor than rich; hence there might be 100 to 300 voters per century in the wealthiest group, whereas in the poorest there might be 25,000 or more. Yet each century had only one vote. Consequently, the proportion of votes to population was greatly distorted, as this diagram shows.

VOTING IN THE CENTURIATE ASSEMBLY

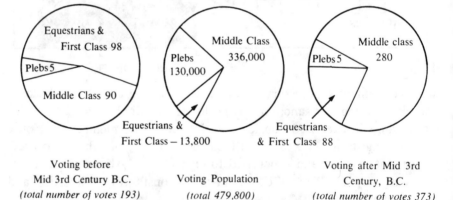

| Voting before Mid 3rd Century B.C. *(total number of votes 193)* | Voting Population *(total 479,800)* | Voting after Mid 3rd Century, B.C. *(total number of votes 373)* |

In actual practice, the mass of the people of Rome had virtually no influence in the Centuriate Assembly.

The Tribal Assembly   Where the people *did* have some influence was in the Tribal Assembly, so called because of the 35 "tribes" or electoral districts of which it consisted. The Tribal Assembly elected the junior magistrates (aediles and quaestors) and the tribunes, and was also a court for trying magistrates accused of breaking the laws. Gradually this Assembly became the chief legislative body at Rome. The people had some influence in the Tribal Assembly because they could register their vote in their particular

236/ROME

"tribe," regardless of wealth. Nevertheless, even though it was more democratic than the Centuriate Assembly, its votes were not apportioned by population either. The number of voters in any one tribe varied greatly, yet each district had a single vote regardless of size. Moreover, the 31 tribes scattered over Italy found it difficult to journey into Rome to cast their votes, so that they were apt to have little voice in their Assembly's deliberations as compared to the 4 tribes in Rome itself. It is obvious, then, that the Tribal Assembly, too, was still a far cry from democracy.

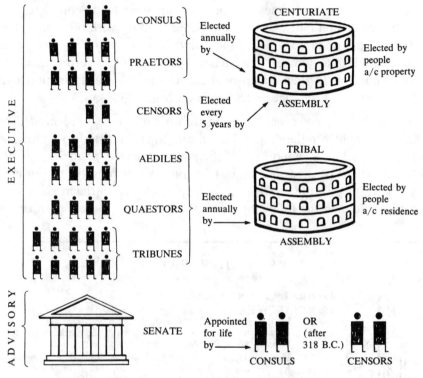

CHOOSING THE ROMAN GOVERNMENT

❖ *The Haves and the Have-Nots* At about the time of the abolition of the monarchy, the people of Rome (excluding slaves) were divided into two distinct social classes: the patricians and the plebeians. The patricians were the aristocrats, the great landowners who had the right to sit in the Senate, to hold the consulship and other magistracies or to assume important religious offices. The plebeians or plebs, on the other

Patricians and plebeians

hand, were made up of a number of smaller groups (city artisans, traders, and peasant farmers).

It was very hard on the poorer plebeians when money replaced barter. The aristocrats were able to buy the new lands that Rome was acquiring and thereby increase their estates, but the peasant farmer could not. Moreover, the peasant was not permitted to mortgage his land. The only security he was allowed to put up was his person, whereas the owners of large estates could pay for improvements and afford to tide themselves over bad years. Many plebeians were simply sucked under by hard times. Some gave up their lands completely to become tenants on patrician estates. Some tried to work off their debts, and were punished for their failure by imprisonment, slavery, even execution. But a number managed to stick it out, determined at all odds to hold on to their independence. It was this determination that led them to adopt the tactics described on pages 335-336.

The plebs did, however, hold one trump card: they were needed as soldiers to fight for the state. This meant that from time to time the patricians had to surrender to plebian demands for political equality if Rome was to be defended against foreign foes or preserved from civil war. The story of the concessions wrung from the patricians is a very complex one, and the following table presents it in a simplified form.

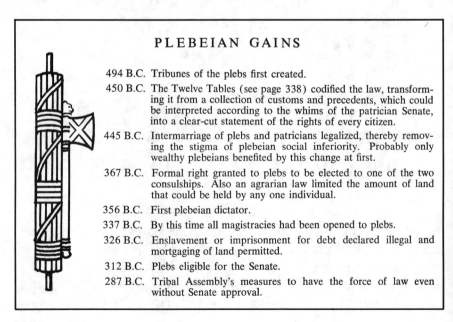

PLEBEIAN GAINS

494 B.C. Tribunes of the plebs first created.

450 B.C. The Twelve Tables (see page 338) codified the law, transforming it from a collection of customs and precedents, which could be interpreted according to the whims of the patrician Senate, into a clear-cut statement of the rights of every citizen.

445 B.C. Intermarriage of plebs and patricians legalized, thereby removing the stigma of plebeian social inferiority. Probably only wealthy plebeians benefited by this change at first.

367 B.C. Formal right granted to plebs to be elected to one of the two consulships. Also an agrarian law limited the amount of land that could be held by any one individual.

356 B.C. First plebeian dictator.

337 B.C. By this time all magistracies had been opened to plebs.

326 B.C. Enslavement or imprisonment for debt declared illegal and mortgaging of land permitted.

312 B.C. Plebs eligible for the Senate.

287 B.C. Tribal Assembly's measures to have the force of law even without Senate approval.

Thus in two centuries the plebs had won all their political objectives. The magistracies and the Senate had been opened to them, and measures passed by the Tribal Assembly had become law. In theory at least, Rome was a democracy. Nevertheless, like the Athenian democracy it did not by any means give the vote to everyone.

DUTIES AND POWERS OF ROMAN OFFICIALS

OFFICE	DUTIES	SPECIAL POWERS
CONSULS	– presided over Senate – selected senators – commanded army	could veto each other
PRAETORS	– presided over Centuriate Assembly – tried important legal cases – substituted for consuls in Senate and army in their absence from Rome – could be provincial governors	
AEDILES	– administered public works – controlled weights and measures	
QUAESTORS	– 2 in charge of treasury – 2 consular assistants	
CENSORS	– took census – revised lists of Senators	
TRIBUNES	– protected rights of plebeians – attended meetings of Senate – proposed legislation for Tribal Assembly	could apply veto against legislative power of State
SENATE	– advised magistrates – assigned magistrates' duties – drew up budget – supervised foreign policy	could declare martial law in crisis
CENTURIATE ASSEMBLY	– elected senior magistrates – voted on laws submitted to it – ratified peace treaties	
TRIBAL ASSEMBLY	– elected junior magistrates – elected tribunes – tried erring magistrates – made laws after 287 B.C.	

❖ *A System of Checks and Balances*   Perhaps the machinery of Roman government will become clearer to you if we compare it with our own.

The Canadian system is based on a British model which, like the Roman, evolved in an unplanned way over the centuries. Our government is in the hands of an executive committee, the Cabinet, responsible to the House of Commons, which is in turn elected by the people. The "people" comprise all Canadian citizens 21 years of age and over.

Roman voters did not include women, and only those citizens who could be in Rome when the 35 tribes of the Tribal Assembly were called together could vote on new laws or the election of junior magistrates. Imagine how undemocratic our system would be if every Canadian had to travel to Ottawa to register his vote! Then, too, the Centuriate Assembly had, as we have seen, a system of voting weighted in favour of wealth. Thus in neither Roman assembly was the procedure truly democratic.

The Romans had no fully representative assembly such as our House of Commons. Indeed, action was often blocked by the arbitrary veto of the tribunes. And because the Senate had very little real power of its own it resorted to various political deals in an attempt to control the Assemblies. The Roman system had been carefully provided with checks and balances in order to prevent any one group from exercising too much power. But it had to *keep* in balance to get anything done. Unfortunately, such balance was very rarely attained.

CHAPTER 25

Italy Conquers the Mediterranean

What man is so indifferent or so idle that he would not wish to know how and under what form of government almost all the inhabited world came under the single rule of the Romans in less than fifty-three years?

POLYBIUS, *Histories*

Now that Rome was a world power she had to watch carefully the moves of the other four world powers of the time: the great empire of Carthage in the west, and the three Hellenistic monarchies of Egypt, Syria, and Macedon in the east. All too soon she was to realize how right she had been to watch Carthage. That North African city proved to be one of Rome's most dangerous and stubborn foes.

❖ *A Hard and Gloomy People*   All that we know of early Carthaginian society does not add up to a very attractive picture. Archaeological excavation has, for example, confirmed the gruesome tales of human sacrifice, particularly the death by burning of young children. Carthage's vast armies were made up of conscripted subjects from Libya, Sardinia, and Spain, as well as of troops hired from Algeria and Morocco, and to command these armies meant very uncertain glory. The reward for the general who succeeded in whipping his unruly mass into an efficient fighting machine could be fame and riches; for the one who failed, crucifixion. Plutarch's estimate of the Carthaginians is probably not far wrong:

. . . a hard and gloomy people, submissive to their rulers and harsh to their subjects, running to extremes of cowardice in times of fear and of cruelty in times of anger; they keep obstinately to their decisions, are austere and care little for amusement or the graces of life.

In time Carthage came to dominate the western end of the Mediterranean and part of Sicily. She was ruled by an oligarchy of rich merchants and, as befitted a mighty commercial power, maintained an imposing fleet—a fleet which was in the habit of sinking at sight any foreign vessel that crossed Carthaginian sea lanes.

When brigands on the northern tip of Sicily accepted protection from Carthage they soon found themselves under the iron heels of a Carthaginian garrison. An appeal was sent to Rome. Determined not to be shut out of the Straits of Messana, Rome answered the call. The result: war with Carthage.

❖ *The Raven*   The war that broke out lasted twenty-three years (264-241 B.C.), and was only the first of a series which were to follow before either state could finally declare itself victor. These were called the *Punic* Wars because the Carthaginians' ancestors had come from the ancient Phoenician city of Tyre, and the Roman name for Phoenician was "Punic."

The First Punic War

Now it was clear from the beginning that if Rome were to push the Carthaginians out of Sicily she would sooner or later have to create a navy. Accordingly in 260 B.C. the Senate called for the construction of 100 quinqueremes. Why quinqueremes? The quinquereme was the

The Roman navy

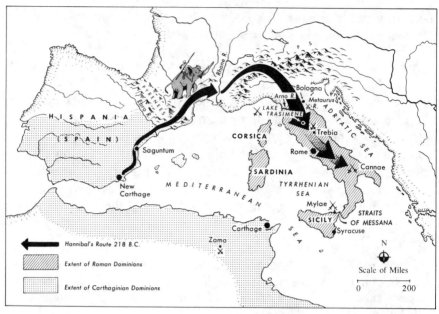

THE PUNIC WARS

pride of the Carthaginian navy, a one-deck vessel with from 20 to 60 oars, five men to an oar. It was, it is true, heavier and slower than the trireme, but it was better suited for ramming and sinking an enemy. And it had another important advantage. In a trireme every rower had to be a skilled oarsman; in a quinquereme one man directed the sweep and the other four had only to supply muscle power. Rome had no time left to waste in training multitudes of skilled oarsmen—and even at that it was said she trained her rowers sitting on benches on the dry land.

The Romans now added an ingenious device to their quinqueremes. It was known as the *corvus* ("raven"), and was simply a gangplank thirty-six feet long and four feet wide with a heavy spike (the raven's "beak") on the end. The corvus could be raised upright by means of ropes running through pulleys fastened to the mast. A quinquereme could close with an enemy vessel, drop the raven, which, with its spike, would hold fast to the enemy deck, and then send a boarding force rushing across the gangplank. The boarding force consisted of no fewer than 120 legionaries. In this way the Romans managed to convert sea battles into land battles and so make use of their prime resource, their magnificently disciplined army.

The untried Roman fleet met the mighty Carthaginian armada in 260 B.C. off Mylae, not far from Messana, and the Carthaginian admiral recklessly pressed forward, intending to ram the Roman ships. But he was in for a surprise. The Roman gangplanks thudded down and the legionaries streamed across. Doubtless the admiral was even more stunned at the final outcome of the encounter: Carthage lost 44 ships and 10,000 men in the engagement. The Senate, scenting victory and determined to win Mediterranean naval supremacy, pushed ahead with its ship-building programme. It was rewarded by three more naval victories. Finally a Roman expeditionary force was put ashore in North Africa.

But the Carthaginians were not going to let an invader molest their home land with impunity. The Romans suffered a crushing defeat at the hands of stubborn Carthaginian troops bolstered by a hundred elephants. Nor were the Carthaginians idle on the seas. After further naval defeats they crucified some of their admirals, and began to construct lighter ships, swifter and more seaworthy than the lumbering Roman quinqueremes with their clumsy gangplanks. By these means the Carthaginians retrieved their mastery of the seas and were at length able to establish their most brilliant general, Hamilcar Barca (Barca = "Blitz" or "Lightning") in Sicily. This young commander's lightning raids on the Italian coast convinced the Romans that their only hope of victory lay on the sea.

And so again Rome constructed a fleet, this time by calling on the wealthiest citizens to advance loans—repayable only in the event of victory! Meanwhile Carthage became so engrossed in the conquest of further lands in Africa that the Sicilian operation took second place. The final battle was fought off the western tip of Sicily in 241 B.C. The Romans sank 50 ships and captured another 70. Carthage was beaten.

Rome came out of the war having won her first province, Sicily. She had also gained complete control of the western Mediterranean. The war had been costly enough—500 ships and 200,000 men. But the gains were also great. Sicily brought to Rome an annual tribute of half a million bushels of wheat, and Romans came into even closer contact with the Greek culture of the Sicilian colonies. More important, still, Rome had developed an excellent fighting machine, and her allies had stuck by her through all twenty-three years of the war. It was a good omen.

❖ *The Aggressor Unmasked* Rome had won the first round, but soon there was a new worry. Carthage was beginning to expand in Spain, an expansion which was directed by that same Hamilcar who had been forced to capitulate to Rome in Sicily only a few years earlier. Hamilcar extended Carthaginian territory in Spain, and then set about training the conquered Spaniards in warfare.

Rome watched all these goings-on warily, hopeful that Carthage was not as aggressive as she appeared. Then in 226 B.C. both sides agreed to partition Spain along the line of the River Ebro. Still suspicious of Carthaginian intentions, Rome was deliberately provocative. She technically violated the treaty by allying herself with Saguntum, a city south of the Ebro in the Carthaginian section of Spain.

Hannibal   Now if Carthage had no aggressive intentions she could ignore the challenge, refuse to call Rome's bluff, and leave Saguntum alone. If, on the other hand, she was planning to use Spain as a springboard for an attack on Italy, she would not allow this alliance to continue. We can imagine with what apprehension Rome watched her small Spanish ally, and in 219 B.C. she got her answer. In that year Hamilcar's son, Hannibal, who at twenty-five had succeeded to the Carthaginian command, advanced against Saguntum, and the city fell after a long siege. Rome, busy elsewhere, did not send aid, but after Saguntum was captured dispatched an embassy to Carthage demanding the evacuation of Saguntum and the surrender of Hannibal as a war criminal. "Here I bring peace and war," said the chief Roman envoy holding up two folds of his toga. "Choose which you will." When he was told to make the choice himself, he dropped the folds and said simply, "Then I give you war."

By 218 B.C. the two great powers were locked in a life and death struggle. Peace was not to be finally made until 201 B.C.

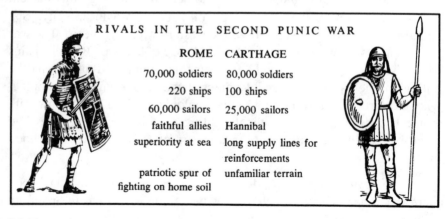

RIVALS IN THE SECOND PUNIC WAR

ROME	CARTHAGE
70,000 soldiers	80,000 soldiers
220 ships	100 ships
60,000 sailors	25,000 sailors
faithful allies	Hannibal
superiority at sea	long supply lines for reinforcements
patriotic spur of fighting on home soil	unfamiliar terrain

❖ *Men against Mountains*   Rome thought that hers would be the choice of battlegrounds; so she sent one army to southern Gaul and rushed another to Sicily, on its way to Africa. But she reckoned without the genius of Hannibal, a superb leader whose men would follow him anywhere. The Roman historian Livy draws a brilliantly-hued picture of the young commander.

Upon his first arrival in Spain Hannibal became the centre of attention in the whole army. The old soldiers thought that a younger Hamilcar had come back to them. They saw in him the same features, the same liveliness of expression, the same fire in the eyes. But shortly his resemblance to his father was only the least among their reasons for devotion to him. . . . There was no leader under whom the army fought with greater confidence and daring. When danger was to be faced it was Hannibal whose spirit was the boldest, and in a crisis his strategy was the shrewdest. Under no hardship did his energy wane or his spirits flag. He could face heat or cold with equal endurance. His appetite for food and drink were controlled by hunger and not by pleasure. His waking and sleeping were not fixed by day and night.What time remained after the task in hand was done he gave to sleep, and this without any need of soft bed or quiet. Many a time he could be seen lying on the ground among the sentries and pickets off duty, covered only with a soldier's cloak. His dress was no different from that of his fellow-soldiers, but his weapons and his horses were of the finest. He was the best among cavalry and infantry alike, always the first to go into battle and the last to leave any clash of arms.

Never did Rome have a more dangerous foe.

Hannibal was convinced that if Rome were ever to be beaten it must be in Italy where, so he believed, the Roman allies were just waiting for the chance to be liberated. By freeing these allies he could smash Rome's power once and for all. His goal, then, was clear: he must isolate Rome from the rest of Italy. To this end he moved swiftly. Commanding 40,000 infantry, 6000 cavalry, and 37 elephants, he left New Carthage in southern Spain in April, 218 B.C., was north of the Ebro in June, and to the Rhone by mid-August. Just three days before the Roman army arrived to intercept him, he slipped across the Rhone and got clean away on his march to the Alps.

It was autumn when Hannibal reached the mountains, and the treacherous passes, inhabited by hostile tribes, were already deep with snow. Yet grimly he pushed on. Nothing else he ever did has so caught the imagination of the world.   *Crossing the Alps*

On the ninth day they arrived at the summit of the Alps. . . . Exhausted and discouraged as the soldiers were by many hardships, a snow-storm . . . threw them into great fear. The ground was everywhere covered deep with snow

Perhaps no more striking procession ever wended its way than this—the thin line of Hannibal's troops silhouetted against the white-mantled Alps with the gigantic beasts lumbering in the lead, their fierce trumpeting echoing and re-echoing in the icy gorges as the sharp cries of commanders ring out above the muffled tramp of thousands of feet. How strange these 3rd century B.C. "tanks" must have looked in battle! African elephants are much more savage than the Indian species, and only the Carthaginians ever succeeded in breaking them in. Little wonder they were a terror to the Romans at the River Trebia. The Carthaginians' fearsome advantage was, however, short-lived. All but one of the elephants was dead by the next spring, Hannibal's mount alone surviving the war.

when at dawn they began to march, and as the column moved slowly on, dejection and despair were to be read in every countenance. Then Hannibal, who had gone on before the standards, made the army halt on a certain promontory which commanded an extensive prospect, and pointing out Italy to them . . . he told them that they were now scaling the ramparts not only of Italy, but of Rome itself; the rest of the way would be level or downhill; and

after one or at the most two battles, they would have in their hands and in their power the citadel and capital of Italy. . . .

But . . . above the old, untouched snow lay a fresh deposit of moderate depth, through which, as it was soft and not very deep, the men in front found it easy to advance; but when it had been trampled down by the feet of so many men and beasts, the rest had to make their way over the bare ice beneath and the slush of the melting snow. Then came a terrible struggle on the slippery surface, for it afforded them no foothold, while the downward slope made their feet the more quickly slide from under them. . . . But the baggage animals . . . would sometimes even cut into the lowest crust, and, pitching forward and striking out with their hoofs, as they struggled to rise, would break clean through it, so that numbers of them were caught fast, as if entrapped, in the hard, deep-frozen snow.

At last, when men and beasts had been worn out to no avail, they encamped upon the ridge, after having, with the utmost difficulty, cleared enough ground even for this purpose. . . . The soldiers were then set to work to construct a road across the cliff—their only possible way. Since they had to cut through the rock, they felled some huge trees that grew near at hand, and lopping off their branches, made an enormous pile of logs. This they set on fire, as soon as the wind blew fresh enough to make it burn, and pouring vinegar over the glowing rocks, caused them to crumble. After thus heating the crag with fire, they opened a way in it with iron tools, and relieved the steepness of the slope with zigzags of an easy gradient, so that not only the baggage animals but even the elephants could be led down. Four days were consumed at the cliff, and the animals nearly perished of starvation; for the mountain tops are all practically bare, and such grass as does grow is buried under snow.

At long last, after fifteen days, the tortuous crossing was accomplished. The great army had won a strange battle—but at what a cost! When Hannibal assembled his force on the sunny plains of northern Italy, there were left 26,000 infantry, 4000 cavalry, and 25 elephants.

Even if they had tried, it would have been impossible for the Romans to guard all the passes in the western Alps. Now that the crafty Carthaginian had slipped through they hoped to catch him at one of the river crossings in northern Italy. But they were stalking very wary game. Despite the fact that they were fighting on their own home soil the Romans were destined to suffer only defeats. Three major ones followed in quick succession: Trebia (218 B.C.), Lake Trasimene (217 B.C.), and Cannae (216 B.C.).

❖ *The Master Strategist*   When it became clear to the Romans that Hannibal, not they, had chosen the battleground, and that the battleground was Italy, the African expedition was cancelled and the combined Roman armies totalling 40,000 men assembled at the River Trebia one bitterly cold December morning. Before the Romans had even had their breakfast Hannibal sent a weak cavalry detachment across the river against them. It was easily defeated, and the Romans exultantly charged through the ice-cold river after it. They had fallen into Hannibal's trap. A strong Carthaginian force was lying in wait for them, and they were ambushed.

River Trebia

Winter came and Hannibal rested at Bologna. Rome—who had lost 30,000 men at Trebia—licked her wounds and feverishly raised new armies. It was obvious that north Italy would have to be abandoned to Hannibal.

Lake Trasimene

The next May Hannibal crossed the Apennines. Then misfortune struck him. In the marshes flooded by the River Arno he contracted ophthalmia and lost the sight of one eye—yet still, riding high on his elephant, got his army through in four days. He proceeded to march south towards Rome, ravaging the land as he went, while an outnumbered Roman army of 25,000 trailed along in his wake declining battle. But once again Hannibal outwitted them. In the hills surrounding Lake Trasimene, the Carthaginians waited in the early mists of morning until the unsuspecting Roman army marched into a narrow defile. Two hours later 15,000 Romans lay dead and most of the rest were captured.

Panic swept Rome. In their desperation the people elected a dictator, Quintus Fabius Maximus.

Fabius soon earned the nickname "Delayer." His strategy was to avoid a pitched battle with the wily Hannibal until the Carthaginian could be forced to fight under conditions in which he could not use his cavalry. It was with this purpose that the patient Fabius dogged Hannibal's footsteps, always waiting for his chance, steadfastly refusing to aid Rome's allies whose lands the Carthaginians were laying waste. At last Fabius saw his opportunity. In the unfamiliar mountain country of Campania Hannibal found himself facing a pass commanded by Fabius —but what happened you will have to read in the Source Reading.

It was inevitable that these delaying tactics of Fabius would be criticized at Rome. Hannibal was wandering through Italy almost at will, and the wonder was that the allies still stood by Rome. Impatient Romans rejoiced to see Fabius out of office in 216 B.C., and readily granted permission to the eager consuls to force a battle.

Late in the summer the consuls found Hannibal near Cannae. Here in the plains by the Adriatic, a perfect place for a cavalry engagement, the 50,000 Romans faced even odds: 40,000 Carthaginian infantry and 10,000 cavalry. Although the Romans were greatly outnumbered in their cavalry, they had their legions; and Hannibal well knew how strong these were. Accordingly he drew up his line in a crescent-shaped formation bulging out in the centre towards the Romans, while on the wings he stationed his cavalry. The Roman infantry drove inexorably forward, forcing Hannibal's centre backwards until the crescent sagged into a hollow. On into this hollow they pushed, unaware that the Carthaginian cavalry, having routed the Roman wings, was about to strike again. With a wide sweep to the rear of the legionaries the Carthaginians completely surrounded the Romans, crushing them, vice-like, so closely together that they could scarcely move.

Cannae was a Roman slaughter-pen. 35,000 Romans perished; only 5700 Carthaginians were lost. It was a shattering blow to Rome's prestige,

Cannae

and with it many towns in the south went over to Hannibal. Nevertheless central and northern Italy remained loyal to her. And Rome herself was safe. Hannibal did not have and could not get the siege engines necessary to storm her walls.

The Romans had been taught a lesson at a terrible price: they had learned that they must revert to Fabian tactics to wear down their enemy. Hannibal, on the other hand, now tried to surround Italy with a circle of foes. He encouraged the Gauls to the north and the Greeks to the south (in Sicily) to be hostile; he advised his home government to prosecute the war in the west, in Spain and Sardinia; and he achieved an alliance with Macedon in the east. These various operations meant, of course, that he must continue in Italy without reinforcements, completely on his own. He found himself free to roam in southern Italy, but whenever he ventured very far to the north he had difficulty feeding his troops because the Romans either burned their crops or carried them inside the walls of their fortified cities.

Scipio

And so the see-saw contest continued, with neither side strong enough to knock out the other—the story of the Peloponnesian War all over again. One factor could tip the balance: a Roman general the equal of Hannibal. He appeared in the person of Publius Cornelius Scipio, whose father had been killed fighting the Carthaginians in Spain.

❖ *The Balance Shifts*   At his own request, Scipio was appointed commander in Spain in 210 B.C., when he was twenty-four. Here he faced the task of ousting the Carthaginian commander in Spain, Hannibal's younger brother Hasdrubal. The enterprising young Scipio proceeded to arm his troops more heavily, as well as to adopt a new troop formation similar to the one which Hannibal had used at Cannae. By 207 B.C. he had ended the Carthaginian empire in Spain.

But there was a grave omission. Scipio had not been able to prevent Hasdrubal from getting his troops out of Spain, and by the spring they had reached the Po valley, all 30,000 of them, bent on joining Hannibal in central Italy. The Romans now detailed one army to watch Hannibal and a second to try to intercept Hasdrubal. They had a single aim: to keep the brothers apart. For once fate favoured the Romans. They captured the dispatch-riders Hasdrubal was sending to Hannibal with a message arranging a meeting-place. Now they knew exactly where Hasdrubal planned to march, and they acted immediately. Leaving only a skeleton force in the south, the Roman commander there managed by forced marches to cover 240 miles in six days and link up with the

Although no one knows exactly what Hannibal looked like, he may have resembled this idealized portrait bust of him found at Capua. His eyes have the steely glint of the determined commander, but are rimmed with the weariness of a thousand marches; his mouth shows the sensitivity which made him beloved by his men, yet bears the marks of some deep disappointment. We can imagine that the profound sadness on this noble face has been etched there by the bitter knowledge of his failure as he looks back on the land of the enemy—the Italy he has come to love so well—after his recall to Africa.

northern army. Hasdrubal found himself with not one, but two Roman armies at the Metaurus River. At last, after eleven years, Rome savoured the taste of a major victory.

Metaurus River

A week later Hannibal received a grisly announcement of the disastrous defeat. Some Roman horsemen, riding hard past his camp, threw an object over the walls. It was his brother's head.

When Scipio returned from mopping up Spain he was elected consul for the next year. Fired by his conquests, he set about convincing the Senate that the war must be carried to Africa. Even though the Carthaginian government's desperate efforts to reinforce Hannibal were failing miserably, Scipio still argued that nothing short of crushing Carthage itself would leave Rome secure. He got his way. In 204 B.C. a Roman expeditionary force of 30,000 sailed for North Africa, with Hannibal still in Italy.

Carthage was hard to break, and Scipio campaigned for over a year before the Carthaginians sued for peace. But while the terms were under discussion a hero returned: Hannibal landed in Africa. Livy says that the great commander left Italy with as much grief as most men feel on going into exile, and it was probably true. He had entered Italy in 218

B.C. when he was twenty-nine. Now it was 202 B.C. and he was forty-five. He had never been defeated in Italy; yet the war was over—or so it seemed.

Zama   Hannibal's arrival in North Africa gave the war party enough courage to make a last-ditch stand. It came at Zama. Hannibal faced Scipio, his 40,000 men equalling the Roman force although his cavalry was slightly weaker. Before the battle the two generals met and Hannibal proffered peace terms, which Scipio promptly rejected.

Scipio came near regretting his action. It was never safe to under-estimate the skill of this master strategist, and the tactics Hannibal used at Zama were destined to be copied in tank battles in World War II. The great general ordered his weaker cavalry to pretend flight, in the hope that the Roman cavalry would be drawn away after it. Then he planned to throw all his infantry against Scipio, at the same time holding back a reserve force of veterans. For a time it seemed that he had manipulated the Roman cavalry into his scheme. They did pursue the retreating Carthaginians, but before Hannibal could get in a decisive blow with his reserves the Roman horsemen returned to decide the battle. It was Cannae in reverse. Hannibal escaped, but his army was cut to pieces. The long war was over.

The terms of peace were harsh. Carthage retained control over Tunisia, but in future had to have Rome's permission to make war; her elephants and her navy were surrendered; and 10,000 talents were to be paid to Rome in fifty annual instalments as reparations for the war. She had been reduced to utter dependence on Rome.

❖ *Epilogue for Two Heroes* Later ages have allowed the nobility of Hannibal to overshadow the greatness of his opponent; but it was not so in Scipio's day. After Zama, he returned to Rome almost a living legend. "Africanus" was added to his name to perpetuate the memory of his greatest victory (just as after World War II General Alexander took the title "Alexander of Tunis" and General Montgomery, "Montgomery of Alamein")—an honour richly deserved, for in a very real sense Scipio was the founder of the Roman Empire. Back in Rome, however, he did not turn out to be a conspicuous success as a politician and statesman, and eventually the rivalries of the Senate forced him back into private life. The time was not yet ripe for an uncrowned king of Rome.

And what of Hannibal? In the years following he did his best to re-build his shattered city's fortunes. But Rome could not forget or forgive, and ultimately he fled to Syria. Still the long arm of Rome reached out after him. Finally in 183 B.C. he committed suicide, "the noblest failure in antiquity."

Hannibal lost no major battle in Italy; he slaughtered at least 100,000 Roman soldiers in fifteen years; and he devastated the Italian country-side, destroying 400 towns in southern Italy alone. Yet he failed to win the war. Why?

For one thing, although Hannibal marched to within sight of Rome, he could not capture the city because of his lack of siege equipment. For another, Rome's Italian allies refused to join him in sufficient numbers to tip the balance against her. Moreover the home government was unable or unwilling to provide Hannibal with sufficient reinforcements to give him numerical superiority. And finally, the Romans never gave up, even when the outlook was blackest. When Hannibal reached the very gates of Rome in 211 B.C., the Romans were so confident of regaining the site of his camp that it was auctioned off—and sold at its normal price!

The Battle of Zama was a turning-point in the history of the ancient world. Henceforth Rome was all-powerful in the western Mediterranean. It was a significant beginning. If luck should be with her in the eastern Mediterranean, she might have a chance to impose on the world a unity unknown since the days of Alexander the Great.

❖ *The New Imperialism* Rome might be the strongest power in the Mediterranean, but she was still beset with problems. She became involved in a complex series of wars in the Middle East, and her new mastery brought her many involved issues and diplomatic problems to deal with. Every year envoys arrived from foreign kings, states and cities, bearing tales and asking for aid.

Finally, weary of sorting out the infinitely complicated claims and counter-claims, Rome lost both patience and restraint. In the west Carthage was destroyed in a third Punic War (149-146 B.C.) waged on a flimsy excuse, the inhabitants massacred or enslaved, and the very land on which the city had stood sowed with salt. In the east Corinth was sacked and burned, its treasures carried off and its inhabitants sold into slavery. Rome had become thoroughly imperialistic. There could be no doubt now about the mastery of the Mediterranean from one end to the other—especially when, in 133 B.C., the king of Pergamum died, leaving his kingdom to Rome. A few years later Pergamum became the Roman province of Asia. It was the seventh province Rome had formally organized within a century.

The Third Punic War

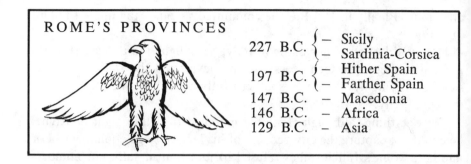

ROME'S PROVINCES

227 B.C.	{	– Sicily
		– Sardinia-Corsica
197 B.C.	{	– Hither Spain
		– Farther Spain
147 B.C.		– Macedonia
146 B.C.		– Africa
129 B.C.		– Asia

Some ancients saw Roman imperialism as an undeniable blessing, and advised against any further resistance to it. But others criticized it sharply. Something, they said, had gone wrong with Rome. Was this true? We must now consider the effects that her conquest of the Mediterranean world had on Rome herself.

❖ *Changes in the Wrong Direction* Rome was never the same again once she had sallied forth on the conquest of the Mediterranean. Her victories from 264 to 133 B.C. affected her politically, economically, socially, and culturally.

Political consequences of empire

In the first place, the Roman system of government was not equal to the strains of empire; the changes were in the wrong direction. Roman government officials received no salary. This fact, plus the expense involved in winning elections, meant that the middle class was automatically ruled out from the magistracies. Consequently there arose a new aristocracy, an aristocracy of wealth and office. The senators regarded these newly rich as vulgar amateurs. The senatorial aristocracy considered itself a race apart and was not willing to admit more families to its ranks, with the result that it became more and more exclusive and inbred. From 200 to 146 B.C. twenty-five senatorial families dominated the government to such an extent that only five men whose ancestors had not held office became consuls!

Governors of provinces (appointed yearly) were also unsalaried, and if they decided to enrich themselves at the expense of the provincials not a great deal could be done about it. True, a Senate jury was set up to try cases of extortion, but senators were somewhat reluctant to condemn men of their own social standing. The fact was that the system of tax collection lent itself to great abuses (as you can see from the Source Reading on page 339). In many provinces the collection of taxes was undertaken not by a group of imperial civil servants but by a private company of professional tax-collectors (*publicani*) who bid for the privilege. The highest bidder won the tax contract, and any taxes collected over and above the bid made up his income. Is it any wonder that the New Testament hardly ever mentions publicans without the accompanying phrase "and sinners"?

The great wealth that now poured into Rome also changed Roman agriculture. During the Second Punic War Hannibal had devastated southern Italy, and the small independent farmer had been called away from his farm to serve for long periods in the army. When he returned his land might have been seized for debt, or he might find it hopeless to compete with the slave labour and tribute grain which the conquests brought to Italy from the provinces. Under such circumstances great Roman ranches—financed by wealthy owners and manned by slaves— mushroomed, while earlier laws limiting the size of estates (see page 238) came to be openly disregarded. *Economic conse- quences*

Where could the landless peasants go? Even in the 2nd century B.C. all roads led to Rome. The city became a vast capital with a population of half a million, the landless who flocked there merging into a drifting unemployed mob which became the plaything of politicians. As the gap between rich and poor widened, certain Roman observers detected a moral degeneration as well.

❖ *A Greek Veneer* One class profited richly from Rome's conquest of the Mediterranean world: the Equestrians. Originally the Equestrians, as members of the cavalry, had been the richest and most powerful citizens in the Centuriate Assembly. In the 3rd century B.C. a new list of those who could afford cavalry service had been drawn up, and these men came to be known as the Equestrian Order, a group midway between the Senate and the people. *Social con- sequences*

In this age of expanding commerce the Equestrians became Rome's big businessmen. Singly or in companies they contracted to collect taxes, to supply the armies with equipment and stores, or to build roads, bridges, aqueducts, and temples. Many of them became well-to-do bankers and money-lenders. But the Roman aristocrat had a deep-seated contempt for tradesmen of any kind, and senators were forbidden to take public contracts or to engage in overseas trade. Hence the Equestrians were blocked from membership in the Senate. For political influence they would have to bide their time—and it was not long in coming. In the meantime these wealthy men could always build great

houses filled with costly works of art, and be waited on hand and foot by retinues of slaves who served elaborate banquets on silver plate while the guests reclined, Greek-fashion, on couches.

Cultural conse-quences

Many of the trappings of these ornate Equestrian homes were Hellenistic imports, a veneer of Greek culture on a Roman base. As one of the Roman poets was to put it later, "Captive Greece took captive her

BLACK SEA

Danube R.

BITHYNIA
75 B.C.

MACEDONIA
147 B.C.

EPIRUS
165 B.C.
Pharsalus X X

•Pergamum

ASIA
129 B.C.

CILICIA
102 B.C. •Antioch

SYRIA
64 B.C.

Athens
Corinth

AEGEAN SEA

ACHAEA
146 B.C.

RHODES

CYPRUS
58 B.C.

PHOENICIA

CRETE
67 B.C.

Tyre

N

S E A

Alexandria

CYRENAICA
74 B.C.

Nile R.

E G Y P T

rude conqueror." Yet the Romans both admired and despised the
Greeks. The upper classes admired Greek education, and in the early
days when schooling was a private affair tried to give Hellenistic culture
to their children through educated Greek slave-tutors in their households. Later the masters in the schools, too, were Greek. But Roman
children for the most part heartily despised their Greek slave-teachers,

an unhealthy situation which meant that the schoolmaster could have recourse to only one method of discipline: the rod.

Roman playwrights were strongly influenced by Greek plays, and noble Romans, always envious of Greece's illustrious origins, commissioned poets to produce epics which would heighten the glories of Rome's past. But not all Romans welcomed this Hellenistic influence. Some connected the new luxury and moral lapses with Greek ideas. One such was Cato the Elder (234-149 B.C.) who, as censor, tried to reduce luxury in Rome—even to the extent of ripping out water-mains leading into private houses—in an effort to bring back the virtues of former times. The following paragraph comes from a Roman history that Cato wrote for his son.

I shall speak in the proper place of those accursed Greeks; I shall say what I saw in Athens, and how it may be good to glance at their literature, but not to go into it deeply. I shall prove how detestable and worthless is their race. Believe me, Marcus my son, this is an oracular saying: "if ever that race comes to pass its literature to us, all is lost."

Thus by 133 B.C. Rome possessed a great empire whose political, economic, social, and cultural repercussions had begun to create grave problems for her. Economically the state was badly out of balance. While great landowners grew wealthier, a landless city mob swelled the ranks of the discontented in Rome. Rome's military problems became

This famous Portland Vase, one of the treasures of the British Museum in London, was recovered in the 16th century in a tomb beside the Appian Way. It had been made in the 1st century A.D., doubtless by a Greek craftsman. After the blue vase had been blown it was dipped in opaque white glass, which, once it had hardened into a firm layer, was cut away to reveal a pattern. The result was the ancestor of our modern Wedgewood pottery — a cameo-like effect against a deep blue background. In 1845 a fanatic smashed the vase to bits, but it has been skilfully restored.

critical because the system for recruitment worked against itself. Armies were recruited from freemen with land, freemen who supplied their own equipment for long campaigns. Yet these very freemen often lost their land either because of the length of the campaigns or the influx of grain and slaves that came from new conquests.

In the century following 133 B.C. these related problems of agriculture and army became increasingly pressing. Could Rome solve them? Could she afford *not* to solve them?

CHAPTER 26

The Fall of the Republic

It is due to our own moral failure and not to any accident or chance that, while retaining the name, we have lost the reality of a republic.

CICERO

Two brothers, Tiberius and Gaius Gracchus, thought they had the answer to Rome's problems. But instead they ushered in a series of revolutions, which ended only with the fall of the Republic. What were the plans of the Gracchi that went so far wrong?

❖ *Unprecedented Actions* Tiberius Sempronius Gracchus (162-133 B.C.) came from one of the noblest families in Rome. His grandfather, Scipio Africanus, had been the conqueror of Hannibal; his father had been a widely respected soldier in Spain and elsewhere; and his mother, Scipio's daughter Cornelia, was a woman of culture who employed Greek tutors for her children.

Tiberius Gracchus

It was while Tiberius was on his way to serve as quaestor in Spain that the dearth of free peasants was impressed upon him when he saw estate after estate being worked by gangs of slaves. Being a soldier, he must also have known how the system of recruitment for the army affected the small landowner. When he was elected tribune in 133 B.C. he determined to strengthen the state and the army by reviving the small farming class, and in forthright speeches he struck hard at the military system that exploited men who had nothing to fight for:

The wild beasts that roam Italy have their dens and lairs to shelter them, but the men who fight and die for Italy have nothing but air and light. Homeless and footless they wander about with their wives and children. In battle their generals exhort them to defend their sepulchres and shrines from the enemy: they lie. Not one among the host of Romans had his ancestral altar or the tomb of his fathers: it is for the wealth and luxury of others that they fight and die. They are called masters of the world, they have no clod of earth to call their own.

Perhaps, Tiberius thought, one way to remedy the agricultural and military problem was to revive the ancient agrarian legislation of 367 B.C. which limited the amount of public land that any tenant could rent. As a concession to present landholders Tiberius decided to double the limit, but land over and above this amount was to be surrendered—for due compensation—to the state, and reallocated to landless Romans and Italians.

At this point, however, Tiberius made a serious error in judgment. Instead of following the correct constitutional procedure and first submitting his proposals to the Senate he took them directly to the Tribal Assembly. A constitutional crisis resulted, and the Senate countered by influencing one of the tribunes to veto the legislation. Tiberius then took an unprecedented step: he persuaded the Assembly to depose the offending tribune on the ground that he was thwarting the will of the people. This was done and the new land law passed. The law was now binding on the Senate, but the senators tried to hold back the land commission by keeping operating expenses from them. Exasperated,

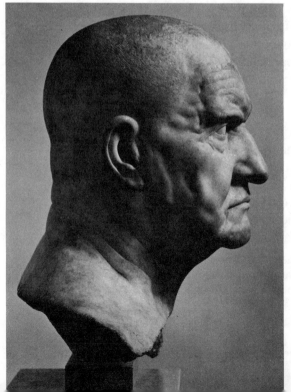

This unknown Roman by an anonymous sculptor of the 1st century B.C. is an excellent illustration of the Romans' skill at portraiture, a skill learned from the Etruscans. The hard-headed, practical citizen of the Republic whom we see here is no mere type, but an individual in his own right.

Tiberius took yet another unprecedented action. Tribunes, by established custom, held office only once; but Tiberius stood for re-election. It was the last straw. The Senate lost all restraint and started a riot in which Tiberius and three hundred of his supporters were murdered.

❖ *Champion of the People* Gaius Gracchus (153-121 B.C.) was even more emotional and intense than his older brother had been, and was an *Gaius* electrifying and fearless orator. "Those worst of men have murdered *Gracchus* the best of men, my brother!" he thundered. Gaius had been quaestor in Sardinia in 126 B.C., but instead of staying there for his full term of office had returned suddenly to Rome in 124 B.C. to deliver a stinging indictment of those who milked the provinces. "Alone of all who went on the expedition," says Plutarch, "he had carried out a full purse and had brought home an empty one, while others, after drinking up the wine they had carried out with them, brought back the wine jars filled again with gold and silver from the war."

The country folk well knew that Gaius Gracchus was their friend, and when he presented himself for the tribunate they flooded into Rome. "There came such infinite numbers of people from all parts of Italy to vote for Gaius, that lodgings for them could not be supplied in the city; and the Field not being large enough to contain the assembly, there were numbers who climbed upon the roofs and the tilings of the houses to use their voices in his favour."

Gaius was elected, and in 123 B.C. was re-elected tribune for the next year. (Re-election to the tribunate had been legalized five years after the death of Tiberius.) It was soon evident that his programme for economic reform was even more ambitious than Tiberius's had been and he proceeded to push hard for his reforms. His brother's land law was revived and amplified, but since much of the available land was by this time distributed Gaius also proposed to establish some new colonies in Italy and overseas in North Africa. Another law was enacted allowing the state to buy grain in bulk and sell it cheaply to the poor of Rome. Roads were improved throughout the peninsula to facilitate the transport of agricultural produce from farm to market. The state now furnished its soldiers with clothing and equipment free of charge. The Equestrians (who would not be slow to prosecute senators) were given the conduct of the extortion courts, hitherto the preserve of the Senate. Other reforms were carried out, but when Gaius proposed his most revolutionary measure—to give the citizenship to the Latin allies—both the Senate and the mob opposed it for fear of having their influence swamped in Rome. Gaius was beginning to lose his support.

Determined to exploit the rift in Gaius's supporters, the Senate put up a rival tribune who promised the mob more of everything Gaius had proposed. The unscrupulous tactic worked. Gaius was not re-elected tribune in 122 B.C., and sometime later he and 3000 of his followers were murdered by a gang of senatorial thugs in another outbreak of rioting.

❖ *The Real Tragedy*   It is hard to be moderate in judging the Gracchi. The tragic circumstances of their deaths and their essential nobility of character have remained a poignant chapter in Roman history. Why did they fail?

Perhaps history's final verdict on the two brothers must be that they were reformers in too much of a hurry. Instead of patiently trying to win over the Senate, they were prepared to take a short cut by attempting to make the Assembly the dominant force in politics. They tried to drive a wedge between the Equestrians and the Senate, and in so doing intensified class and political divisions. By thus splitting Rome up the centre, by creating conditions in which Romans slaughtered Romans, it may well have been that the Gracchi did more than most to hasten the fall of the Republic.

This, then, was their real tragedy: they destroyed once and for all any chance for a government in which a conservative Senate might exercise a moderating influence.

❖ *A Cure or A Disease?*   For the time being the triumphant Senate controlled events. But the bitterness ate deep into Roman life. In 119

Marius   B.C. Gaius Marius (157-86 B.C.), a member of an equestrian family, was elected tribune. He had proved himself a courageous fighter in Spain and had become noteworthy as an officer fighting in North Africa against Jugurtha, king of Numidia. Marius had political ambitions as well, but since none of his ancestors had held high office he was looked upon by the senatorial class as an upstart. Rough soldier that he was, when he came to Rome in 107 B.C. to campaign for the consulship he bluntly poured scorn on the nobles.

Compare me, the "new man," my fellow citizens, with those proud nobles. . . . What they learn from handbooks I know from service. . . . My own belief is that men are born equal and alike: nobility is achieved by bravery. . . .

My expressions are not elegant; I don't care. Merit itself makes a sufficient show. It is they who need art to gloze baseness with rhetoric. I never learned

Greek; I never wanted to, for Greek did little for the character of its professors. I did learn things far more useful to the state—to strike the enemy, to be vigilant on guard, to fear nothing except disgrace, to endure heat and cold alike, to sleep on the ground, to bear privation and fatigue at the same time. . . . They say I am vulgar and unmannerly because I cannot give a dainty dinner, that I have no entertainer or cook that costs more than a farm steward. I am happy to admit the charge, fellow citizens. From my father and other righteous men I learned that daintiness is appropriate to women, strenuousness to men, that good men ought to have more glory than riches, that weapons, not furniture, is the true ornament.

Not only did Marius manage to get himself elected consul by the Centuriate Assembly, but he persuaded the Tribal Assembly to go over the head of the Senate and give him the North African command as well. Here again Marius broke all precedent by recruiting a volunteer army in which there was no land-ownership qualification for service. With the successful conclusion of the war he returned to Rome in triumph and was re-elected consul.

Although the Jugurthine War had no great strategic significance, it was important in another way. The new army of volunteers was a far different one from the traditional conscript citizen army with its property qualifications for service. Marius's army was a professional one composed of soldiers whose trade was fighting and whose remuneration depended on the success and rewards of their commander. These men served for terms as long as 16 years. The organization of the legion was also changed. The 30 maniples were regrouped into 10 cohorts, each 600 strong, so that the legion itself was increased in strength to 6000. Thus the entire army was revitalized by the reforms of Marius, and its standards, the silver eagles of Rome, winged proudly everywhere.

It would seem that by no longer drawing on the smaller farmers for recruits, Marius had at one stroke solved those twin problems of agriculture and the army. But the solution was not as complete as it seemed. The Senate was beginning to lose control of the military forces of the state, and with that control gone the door to armed dictatorship was opened. As it turned out, the cure was worse than the disease.

Marius had saved Rome by preventing a new German invasion of Italy, and was so popular that he was repeatedly re-elected consul. But unfortunately for Rome he was not as good a politician as he was a soldier. When the ruling faction persisted in catering to the rabble, the Senate resorted to force and called in Marius to suppress the regime.

1

3

2

4

5

6

7

T.MOULD

That done, the tough old man, founder of the new Roman army and six times consul, suffered a political eclipse and withdrew to Asia.

The alarming thing about these troubled years was the increasing influence of the army in politics. The new army found itself dependent for rewards on its general. And if the state would not provide the necessary land and pensions, what might happen when a successful general came to Rome with an army at his back? This had not happened yet, but time was passing and the Senate's control was shaky.

❖ *A Horrible Revenge* If the early tendencies of Rome (or the suggestion of Gaius Gracchus) to grant eventual citizenship to the allies had only been followed, the war that finally erupted in Italy in 90 B.C. might never have been fought. As it was, the Federate allies, encouraged by the holocaust of political murder and degenerate politics in Rome, finally made a last desperate bid for the citizenship so long denied them. Rome weakened the hard core of the rebellion by at last granting citizenship to certain of the rebels, and finally, with the end of the war in 88 B.C., assured all Italy south of the Po—Latin and Federate allies alike—of a uniform Roman citizenship.

A successful commander in the war against the Italian Federate allies *Sulla* was Lucius Cornelius Sulla (138-78 B.C.), a soldier from an obscure family who had served as a cavalry officer under Marius. He was rewarded for his services in the war by election to the consulship, and the Senate went on to give him an important command in the East. Marius, jealous of Sulla's appointment, intrigued to secure it for himself. Stung into retaliating, the enraged Sulla marched on Rome with his army and the Marians fled or were murdered.

Once again the army had been a deciding factor in politics. Now Sulla, secure in his command, left for the East; but in his absence from Rome the inevitable occurred. Back from Africa came a man bent on a horrible revenge—Marius, the great Marius, a pathetic sight in his degeneracy. "Filthy and long-haired he marched through the towns,"

The Roman legionary's armour (1) was simpler and less ornamented than that of the Greeks, the *cuirass,* for example, being made of loops of metal so that it was much more flexible. The light-armed infantryman (2) wore a leather tunic in place of armour, and carried a sword, light spears, and a sling provided with lead bolts (3)—often inscribed with insulting messages to the enemy. The legionary's sword (4), about 22 inches long, and his heavy spear (5) are also shown. The Romans possessed an extensive arsenal of siege engines, including the catapult (6), which could fire a javelin about 500 yards. A simpler contraption was the *onager* ("donkey") (7), which hurled large stones out through a sling when the arm reached the correct position—and had a kick like a mule!

says an ancient historian, "presenting a pitiable appearance, descanting on his battles . . . and his six consulships."

For the next four years there was a blood bath in Rome, although Marius himself died peacefully in 86 B.C. during his seventh consulship. When Sulla finally returned in 83 B.C. another civil war broke out. There could be little doubt about Sulla's course of action, backed as he was by 40,000 hardened veterans who looked for rewards, not to the state, but to him. In a savage reign of terror (see pages 338-339) daily lists of "the proscribed" were posted in the Forum, and anyone who hunted them down was suitably rewarded. The victims—5000 in Rome alone, and uncounted thousands throughout Italy — were ruthlessly butchered, often after torture, and their estates confiscated in order to provide pensions and farms for Sulla's veterans. Altogether it is calculated that the civil wars, along with the strife with the Italian allies, cost about half a million Roman and Italian lives.

❖ *Turning Back the Clock* Although Sulla was appointed dictator for an unlimited period in 81 B.C., his main concern remained the restoration of the Senate to a position of pre-eminence in the state. War and massacres had cut its membership in half; Sulla now brought its numbers up to 600. He also increased the number of certain magistracies. Rome had already acquired an eighth and ninth province, Narbonese Gaul (121 B.C.) and Cilicia (102 B.C.). In 81 B.C., Sulla added a tenth: Cisalpine Gaul, in the fertile region between the Apennines and the Alps.

Sulla introduced other legislation to curb the power of the people. Then, satisfied that he had given the Senate a fresh chance to govern Rome, he voluntarily retired in 79 B.C. In this last remaining year of his life he settled down on his country estate, married a young divorcee (his fifth wife), and wrote his autobiography. His epitaph, which he composed himself, was inscribed on his tomb: "No friend has ever done me a kindness and no enemy a wrong without being fully repaid." It is, as has been said, a boast that every gangster would like to make his own.

Sulla had made a concerted effort to restore the Senate to power. But his actions in turning his army loose on Rome and Romans had a more lasting effect than his constitutional changes. What he wanted was to prevent future generals from doing what he himself had done. In this he failed.

❖ *The General and the Capitalist* Even as Sulla died, Cisalpine Gaul and Spain were already causing trouble. The man the Senate sent to

Spain with sweeping powers to quell the disturbances was Gnaeus Pompeius (106-48 B.C.), a young Equestrian who, at twenty-three, had raised an army for Sulla and been jokingly given the title *Magnus* ("The Great"). Pompey was an indifferent public speaker, but a good athlete and swordsman and a fine soldier.

Pompey soon succeeded in pacifying the hot-headed Spaniards, and on his return from Spain he became associated with Marcus Licinius Crassus (112-53 B.C.). Crassus was a financier of great means shrewdly come by. He had been a veteran Sullan officer, and had been first in line to snap up the property of Sulla's proscription victims. He also gained great fame for being on hand at fires that broke out in the crowded city of Rome, where he would stand idly by with his own private fire department and refuse to do anything until the owner had signed an agreement to sell the property to him for a song. He was soon a very wealthy man.

In addition to his financial wizardry, Crassus had some military ability. Just at this time a violent slave revolt led by a former gladiator, a Thracian named Spartacus, was sweeping Italy. Although many Roman slaves led bearable and even comfortable lives serving humane masters, the lot of thousands of others was intolerable. They were human livestock, completely at their master's disposal, with nothing to prevent their brutal treatment but the fact that it sometimes cost a great deal of money to replace them. Harsh custom discouraged any insubordination on their part: if a master was assassinated all his slaves were executed. And they lived under the ever-present fear of a slave's final punishment, crucifixion. "I know that the cross will be my tomb," says a slave in a popular play. "There are laid my forefathers, my father, grandfather, great-grandfather, great-great-grandfather." Under such circumstances it is understandable that, once organized in revolt, the slaves would fight fanatically for their freedom, and one Roman legion after another fell before their army of 70,000. Finally the Senate appointed Crassus commander-in-chief, and with six legions he was able to kill Spartacus (who at one point, when hard pressed by Crassus, took refuge with his men in the crater of Vesuvius), crush the revolt, and crucify 6000 slaves along the Appian Way. It can scarcely have pleased Crassus when Pompey, who caught some of the remnants of the tattered slave army fleeing north through Etruria, boastfully claimed the credit for ending the war.

THE FALL OF THE REPUBLIC/267

Now Pompey and Crassus both approached Rome at the head of their armies. Each proclaimed his desire to be elected to a consulship, even though Pompey had not held the prerequisite offices and at thirty-seven was some six years under the legal age limit for the consulship. The Senate opposed both candidates, but armies spoke louder than laws. Pompey was granted a dispensation, and both men became consuls in 70 B.C. So ignominiously ended the Sullan attempt to restore the prestige and influence of the Senate, erased by the first hand of force that was raised against it.

After their consulship both Pompey and Crassus retired to private life—though only briefly. In 67 B.C. the Senate sent Pompey to the East to clean out the pirates from the Mediterranean and to break once and for all the power of the king of Pontus. By the time Pompey had completed his campaigns in the Middle East, he had extended the Roman Empire from the Mediterranean to the Euphrates. The Middle East had not seen such peace and security since the days of Alexander the Great.

Julius Caesar

While Pompey had been absent in the East, however, his friend Crassus had not been idle. Once more eager for political recognition, he had formed a coalition with a young man who, some said, had escaped the Sullan proscriptions only because he was judged too wild and unstable to merit liquidation. The dissolute young man was Gaius Julius Caesar.

❖ *A Rising Star*   Julius Caesar was born about 102 B.C., and grew into a magnetic youth whose charming eloquence was only matched by his genius for managing people. He seemed destined for politics: his uncle was a consul, his father a praetor, and his aunt had married the famous Marius. Hence it was natural that he should become a member of the Marian party, and though he escaped the Sullan dagger he did not escape Sulla's misgivings. The dictator saw in this disorderly young man "many a Marius"—and Caesar wisely fled Rome.

Caesar served in the army in Asia until Sulla's death. Then in 68 B.C. his star began to rise rapidly. He served as quaestor in Farther Spain, and after his return to Rome became closely associated with Crassus. Borrowing up to $1,000,000 from his patron, he staged lavish entertainments for the Roman people in order to win his election to the usual magistracies.

The First Triumvirate

In 62 B.C. Pompey returned to Italy from the East, bent on obtaining three things: a *triumph* (that is, a victory parade granted by the Senate),

This head of a colossal statue now in the Palazzo di Conservatori in Rome undoubtedly flatters Julius Caesar. Yet we can still see in the sculpture the tall, well-formed physique, the dark, piercing eyes, and the fair complexion and somewhat full face that an ancient Roman historian described. Also evident, and perhaps more significant in a man born to lead, is a certain haughtiness, an aristocratic exclusiveness which won the respect — if not the love — of his fellow Romans.

senatorial ratification of his actions in the East, and rewards for his veterans. But instead of becoming a second Sulla he disbanded his army, and only then did he press the Senate to provide land for his 40,000 veterans. The Senate refused. In desperation Pompey turned to Crassus and Caesar, and the three of them, in 60 B.C., formed the so-called First Triumvirate. Caesar wanted to be a consul with a chance at future military glory; Crassus wanted a share of the Asian taxes; Pompey wanted land for his veterans. These things, as consul in 59 B.C., Caesar was able to arrange.

The triumvirs, of course, had no intention of giving up power once Caesar's consulship was over. So they made sure that two of their supporters were elected as consuls, banished some political opponents (including that famous man of letters, Marcus Tullius Cicero [106-43 B.C.], though he was recalled the next year), and appointed Caesar governor of Gaul for five years. They also ensured the support of the mob by providing free grain to all who requested it, with the result that before long the state found itself distributing over 123,000 tons of wheat a year. Thus was the cheap grain of the Gracchi converted into an unashamed dole, a powerful device for buying city votes.

In 56 B.C. the triumvirs further agreed to extend Caesar's command for another five years, to make Pompey and Crassus consuls in 55

B.C., and then to give Pompey the western command and Crassus the eastern. Of the three generals, Caesar alone had great success. By conquering Gaul, he expanded Roman control to the Rhine and the North Sea.

Unfortunately the deeds accompanying his conquest are not all heroic. During the eight years of Caesar's Gallic Wars it has been calculated that about 400,000 Gauls were slaughtered and as many more sold into slavery. The country was looted and the booty used either to pay off the army or to bribe politicians in Rome—wherever it went, it did not find its way into the Roman treasury. Julius Caesar was one of the first (and best) of the memoir-writing generals of history, but these unsavoury aspects of his wars are naturally not emphasized in the superb account of his campaigns that he wrote under the title of the *Gallic War*. The fluency of his Latin and the spare clarity of his descriptions should not, however, blind later readers to his ruthless attitude. It is said that he made the equivalent of $40,000,000 out of the conquest of Gaul. When even so scrupulous a man as Cicero cleared $110,000 in a single year as an honest provincial governor, it is obvious that the acquisition of empire was a very lucrative business.

While Caesar was busy in Gaul, Crassus, who had always aspired to military glory, met an unhappy end. He had the misfortune to pick as his adversaries the Parthians, the most skilful archers in the world, one of whom treacherously terminated his turbulent career. Since, with the death of Crassus, Pompey became sole consul, the Senate worked to buy his support—probably hoping to eliminate Caesar and perhaps Pompey himself.

Caesar had many enemies in Rome, and as his term drew to a close there were those who worked avidly to have him prosecuted before the courts for waging unauthorized war in Gaul. Pompey now threw in his lot with Caesar's enemies. Caesar said that if Pompey would disband his troops he would do likewise, a proposal acceptable to neither the Senate nor Pompey. Pompey was put in command of all forces in Italy, and on January 1, 49 B.C., the Senate decreed that unless Caesar surrendered his command he would be declared a public enemy.

❖ *Crossing the Rubicon* While Rome debated, Caesar had been waiting in his winter camp in Cisalpine Gaul, just across the Rubicon River which formed the northern border of Italy. He must have gone through some agonizing deliberation when he received the news that on January 7 the Senate had actually pronounced him a public enemy. But now there was no turning back: it was Caesar or the Republic.

On January 10 Caesar led his army across the Rubicon and marched on Rome. Contrary to the expectations of the Senate, the citizens did not look upon Caesar's invasion of Italy as treason but hailed him as a great patriot. And behind him stood the formidable legions of the Gallic Wars.

Pompey and his army, accompanied by many senators, fled to Greece where they were defeated by Caesar at Pharsalus in 48 B.C. Pompey himself was subsequently killed in Egypt three days before Caesar reached Alexandria. But the Pompeians were given a chance to group for further action in Asia Minor, Africa, and Spain, while Caesar, fascinated with the twenty-one-year-old Cleopatra, dallied in Egypt. When the dust of battle cleared in 45 B.C., Caesar was the undisputed master of the Roman world.

CHAPTER 27

From Caesar to Augustus

Ah friend, I fear the Ides of March have given us nothing beyond the pleasure and satisfaction of our hatred and indignation.

CICERO, to Atticus

The power of Rome was now completely in the hands of one man. What would he do with it? Surely, thought the citizens, those who had opposed him would be doomed.

They were wrong. Caesar was a different sort of dictator. There was no slaughter of his political enemies in Rome. "I am not moved," he wrote to Cicero, "by the fact that those whom I have let off free are said to have gone away to make war on me anew; I like nothing better than to be like myself and to let them be like themselves." To two of his political agents he wrote even more pointedly: "Let this be the new thing in our victory, that we justify ourselves by mercy and generosity." The transformation of Julius Caesar from a thoroughly unscrupulous politician into a great statesman is one of the most interesting studies in history.

Plutarch wrote that Cleopatra's beauty was "not so remarkable that none could be compared with her," and this sculpture certainly would support his verdict. It was rather, said Plutarch, her irresistible personality that made her "bewitching." So fascinating was her charm that 1600 years after her death Shakespeare still sought to fathom its magic:

Age cannot wither her, nor custom stale
Her infinite variety.

❖ *The Dictator in Action*   To carry out his policies Caesar had to have power. This his armies gave him. But to cloak the power in legality Caesar accumulated a cluster of offices, titles, and honours—dictator, consul, tribune, Pontifex Maximus (high priest), censor, and so on. Only one title he dared not take: that of king.

Some of the awe inspired by the dictator Caesar comes out in a letter of Cicero's describing how he had entertained the great man (but was spared his entourage of 2000!) in 45 B.C. Cicero, who now lived in political retirement, had been a Pompeian whom Caesar forgave. He must have been more than a little uncomfortable as Caesar's host.

Everything was good and well served . . . and I think I made a good host. But the guest was not the sort to whom you would say, "Do stop in again on your way back"; once is plenty. Our talk was not serious but mainly literary. In a word, he was pleased and seemed to enjoy himself. . . . There you have the story of his visit or, if I may call it, his billeting.

P.S. When he was passing Dolabella's house, he mounted and paraded the whole of his armed guard to right and left, a thing he did nowhere else. I had this from Nicias.

Caesar's reforms   Caesar's programme for Rome was both far-reaching and far-sighted. His greatest service was to rid her of the cancer of civil war. He did not, however, restore the Republican constitution; it was paralyzed in any case, crippled long before he came to power. In fact the Assemblies and the Senate had so little power that his acts were ratified in advance. There were, however, some reforms. The numbers of praetors, aediles, and quaestors were increased, partly to speed up municipal business and partly to provide rewards for Caesar's followers, and the Senate's membership was again raised, this time to 900.

In the city of Rome itself he began extensive building projects, which not only provided relief for unemployment but enhanced the beauty of Italy's capital city. He also cut the number of those receiving the grain dole by over one-half, bringing it down to 150,000. To take care of landless Romans, and his veterans as well, Caesar planned at least twenty colonies that were to provide homes for 100,000 citizens—a continuation of the work of overseas settlement that Gaius Gracchus had begun. Caesar well knew that the transplanting of citizens was the surest means of spreading the Roman way of life throughout the provinces.

In imperial affairs, Caesar came to realize that generous grants of responsibility bred loyalty. Hence Roman citizenship was extended to Cisalpine Gaul and to certain provincial towns, while Latin rights were granted many others. In addition, the city of Rome attracted intellectuals to herself by granting full rights of citizenship to doctors, teachers, librarians, and scholars who came from the provinces to settle in Rome. Not least important, the system of farming out provincial taxes was abolished and honest governors were appointed—a noteworthy step in establishing goodwill towards Rome.

Perhaps the most lasting and practical of all Caesar's reforms was his revision of the calendar. In place of the old lunar calendar of 355 days a new solar calendar of 365¼ days was introduced. This Julian calendar (as it came to be called) was introduced on January 1, 45 B.C., was slightly revised by Pope Gregory XIII in 1582, and is still the calendar we use today.

❖ *The Ides of March* All these reforms were initiated in the brief sixteen months Caesar spent in Rome between 49 and 44 B.C., and he envisaged even bolder undertakings for the whole peninsula. But his schemes were cut short. For despite all that he did for the common people of Rome there were those who took offence at his ways. Members of the old guard seethed with each new honour that was showered on him: the month Quinctilis was renamed Julius (July); his head appeared on coins; he was called "father of his country"; the dictatorship was

Caesar's enemies

Was there ever such a mixture of pride and humiliation as in a Roman triumph? This victorious general has just passed through a triumphal arch on his way to offer a sacrifice at the Temple of Jupiter on the Capitoline Hill. The chief prisoners trudge in chains before the general's chariot, jeered at by a coarse crowd, while the rejoicing legions

follow. Cleopatra so dreaded the debasement of having to grace Octavian's triumph that she committed suicide. But her children did not escape. They were forced to parade in Rome—marched along beside a litter that bore an image of their dead mother.

granted him for life. And some of Caesar's utterances were not such as to reassure them.

The Republic [he said] was nothing—a mere name without form or substance; . . . Sulla had proved himself a dunce by resigning his dictatorship; and . . . now his own word was law, people ought to be more careful how they approached him. Once when a soothsayer reported that a sacrificial beast had been found to have no heart—an unlucky omen indeed—Caesar told him arrogantly: "The omens will be as favourable as I wish them to be; meanwhile I am not at all surprised that a beast should lack the organ which inspired our finer feelings." . . . During one of his Triumphs, he had ridden past the benches reserved for the tribunes of the people, and shouted in fury at a certain Pontius Aquila, who had kept his seat: "Hey there, Aquila the tribune. Do you want me to restore the Republic?" For several days after this incident he added to every undertaking he gave: "With the kind consent of Pontius Aquila."

The Ides of March

Soon the resentment boiled over. A conspiracy of 60 senators, jealous of Caesar's honours and particularly of his assumption of the dictatorship for life, plotted to assassinate him. Without any real plan of their own for the future, the conspirators stabbed the great statesman to death on the Ides of March (the 15th), 44 B.C.

We shall never know whether or not Caesar's plans for reforming the state would have been successful. We shall never know the full extent of those plans. It is a reasonable guess, however, that the dictator realized that only through one-man rule could the complex problems facing Rome be dealt with efficiently. His death left the great question of who would succeed to his power. As one of Caesar's friends remarked to Cicero, "If Caesar, with all his genius, could not find a way out, who will now?"

❖ *Partners in Proscription* Within hours of Caesar's death a bluff, unprincipled man moved forward, determined to seize the initiative. He was Marcus Antonius (82-30 B.C.), consul and lieutenant of the dead dictator. The Roman historian Suetonius (A.D. 69-150) describes Antony's part in Caesar's funeral:

Mark Antony

Instead of a eulogy the consul Antony caused a herald to recite the decree of the Senate in which it had voted Caesar all divine and human honours at once, and likewise the oath with which they had all pledged themselves to watch over his personal safety; to which he added a few words of his own.

Whatever the "few words" were, the populace of the city became so inflamed that the conspirators fled for their lives. For the moment, Antony held the power.

Antony had, however, reckoned without a certain handsome eighteen-year-old, Caesar's great-nephew Octavius (63 B.C.-A.D. 14). Octavius was in Illyricum at the time of Caesar's murder, and when the news reached him he decided to cross to Italy. Not until he landed at Brundisium did he learn that, according to Caesar's will, he had been adopted and designated as his heir.

Octavian

The news galvanized Octavius into action. As soon as he arrived in Rome he identified himself as Caesar's legal heir by changing his name to Gaius Julius Caesar Octavianus, and demanded his share of Caesar's estate from Antony. Antony was evasive—and perhaps with good reason, for some say he had already embezzled the inheritance. When Octavian asked why the conspirators had not been punished he again hedged. Antony underestimated the lad. He possessed wisdom beyond his years, and set to work like a seasoned politician to win the loyalty of his great uncle's troops. Cicero and the Senate also underestimated him. They planned to use him to get rid of Antony, who had meanwhile gone to Cisalpine Gaul and been declared a public enemy. But Octavian was playing for the highest stakes. He demanded the consulship. When the Senate refused it, he marched on Rome at the head of eight legions of Caesar's veterans.

The Senate's plans for Antony also went awry. Marcus Aemilius Lepidus, the governor of Nearer Spain, now chose to back Antony. The combined forces of Antony and Lepidus could easily overwhelm Octavian—but would their men fight against Caesar's heir? It was safer to parley. So it was that in 43 B.C. these three—Octavian, Antony, and Lepidus—formed the Second Triumvirate. In complete cold blood the triumvirs sat down in Rome to chart their course. Caesar's ghost must have wept to see his adopted son reject his idealism for the brutal tactics of Marius and Sulla.

The Second Triumvirate

As soon as the triumvirs were together alone they wrote the names of those to be killed. . . . They traded their own relatives and friends for liquidation, both then and later when they made new lists, one after another, proscribing some for enmity or mere friction, some because they were friends of enemies or enemies of friends, or very wealthy. . . . The number of senators condemned to death and confiscation was about 300, and of the Equestrians about 2000. . . . twelve (some say seventeen) of the most powerful they decided to send men to kill at once. Among these was Cicero.

Octavian had courted Cicero's favour when he came to Italy to claim his inheritance. ("The young man must be flattered, used, and pushed aside," was Cicero's monumental misjudgment of him.) But Cicero had come out of retirement to attack Antony in a slashing series of speeches called the *Philippics*. His death, then, was assured, and Octavian cynically assented to it. He had become a mature terrorist.

The first task was accomplished; resistance was wiped out in Italy. Now the triumvirs turned to Caesar's murderers, the conspirators, who had fled to Greece. They were defeated by Antony and Octavian at Philippi in 42 B.C. Then the triumphant three carved up the empire. Octavian took the West, Antony the East, and Lepidus Africa.

Partnerships sealed with blood are not often long-lived, and the triumvirate was no exception. Octavian had to find land in Italy for 100,000 veterans. But he also had to defeat Pompey the Great's son, who had seized Sicily and Sardinia. This he did. Lepidus, however, now stepped up to claim Sicily and ordered Octavian to leave, whereupon his own troops began to desert to Octavian. And so this hapless triumvir, a high-born but ineffective man, was shunted into retirement in 36 B.C. Octavian spared his life, but kept a close eye on him until his death twenty-four years later.

❖ *A Fatal Fascination*   Octavian had no other rivals in the West—but there was still Mark Antony. After Philippi, Antony had gone to the East to raise money, and amongst other treasures wanted that of the Ptolemies of Egypt. Undoubtedly Antony had already met the famous
Cleopatra   Cleopatra (69-31 B.C.) when he visited Egypt with Caesar. Besides, Caesar had brought her to Rome, though she returned to Alexandria after the assassination. It was in 41 B.C. that she came at the triumvir's summons to Tarsus, and there occurred one of the most famous encounters in all history.

[She sailed] up the river Cydnus in a barge with gilded poop, its sails spread purple, its rowers urging it on with silver oars to the sound of the flute blended with pipes and lutes. She herself reclined beneath a canopy spangled with gold, adorned like Venus in a painting, while boys like Loves in paintings stood on either side and fanned her. Likewise also the fairest of her serving-maidens, attired like Nereïds and Graces, were stationed, some at the rudder-sweeps, and others at the reefing-ropes. Wondrous odours from countless incense-offerings diffused themselves along the river-banks. Of the inhabitants, some accompanied her on either bank of the river from its very mouth, while others went down from the city to behold the sight. The throng in the market-place gradually streamed away, until at last Antony himself, seated on his tribunal, was left alone. And a rumour spread on every hand that Venus was come to revel with Bacchus for the good of Asia.

This majestic marble statue of Augustus, found in the villa of his wife Livia at Prima Porta, well sums up what the Princeps meant to the Roman world. The Greek sculptor who carved it in 20 B.C. made one set of symbols on the ornate breastplate (originally gilded and enamelled) portray Earth rejoicing in the blessings of peace and prosperity, while the emperor stands with sceptre and oustretched arm as if addressing the troops who assured that peace. The baby at Augustus' feet is Cupid, indicating the emperor's alleged descent from the goddess Venus.

Antony was to fall completely under the spell of this Venus, and small wonder. Not that she was incomparably beautiful, for there is evidence that she was not. But, says Plutarch,

converse with her had an irresistible charm, and her presence, combined with the persuasiveness of her discourse and the character which was somehow diffused about her behaviour towards others, had something stimulating about it. There was sweetness also in the tones of her voice, and her tongue, like an instrument of many strings, she could readily turn to whatever language she pleased, so that in her interviews with Barbarians she very seldom had need of an interpreter, but made her replies to most of them herself and unassisted, whether they were Ethiopians, Troglodytes, Hebrews, Arabians, Syrians, Medes or Parthians. Nay, it is said that she knew the speech of many other peoples also, although the kings of Egypt before her had not even made an effort to learn the native language, and some actually gave up their Macedonian dialect.

Antony and Cleopatra planned to create an eastern empire apart from Rome. But the plans foundered. First the propaganda of Octavian blackened the reputations of the pair for all time: if Romans were to be persuaded to fight against the popular Mark Antony it would be necessary to portray him as a dupe of an Oriental sorceress bent on world conquest. Then when the Roman fleet blockaded Antony's army near Actium his troops, unhappy at the prospect of fighting fellow Romans for the queen of Egypt, began to desert in droves.

Finally early in September (31 B.C.) a naval battle took place. It was not much of a battle. Only a few ships were engaged, and Cleopatra's squadron fled to Egypt, followed by Antony with 40 ships. The rest of the fleet surrendered, as did the land army. The next year Antony and Cleopatra committed suicide. Octavian ruled the world.

In the early summer of 29 B.C. Octavian returned to Rome and celebrated a magnificent three-day triumph. The wars were over at last.

❖ *An Awful Dilemma* Up until 29 B.C. Octavian had shared his power with others, having served as consul seven times. But now as the sole surviving triumvir he faced an awful dilemma.

He had three choices. He could retire, as Sulla had, in which case there would likely be a flare-up of civil war. Or he could wield complete power openly, in which case he might suffer his great-uncle's fate. Or he might do neither. He could, by a slow process of trial and error, feel out the degree to which public opinion would tolerate his exercise of power.

In 27 B.C., at the age of thirty-five, Octavian appeared before the Senate, surrendered his supreme powers, and asked that the Republic be restored. The Senate responded by voting him powers equal to those of a consul and bestowing on him the title "Augustus"—the revered or consecrated one. The month Sextilis was also renamed Augustus (August) in his honour.

Yet despite appearances, Augustus did not really restore the Republic—although he was anxious to have Romans *believe* he was restoring republican government. By his control of the armed forces, by his management of public finance, and by his absolute powers of veto the *Princeps* (First Citizen), as he was now called, was in reality supreme.

❖ *Something for Everybody* Augustus had four main groups to please. The citizens of Rome wanted peace and prosperity; the aristocracy wanted a share in government; the Equestrians wanted to become more prosperous; and the army wanted to have some guarantee of grants of land and money when its veterans were discharged. To win over the populace, Augustus set up a governmental department in Rome to supervise the collection, storage, and distribution of provincial grain. Employment was provided by a programme of public works which included new docks, granaries, baths, theatres, libraries, and aqueducts. And, perhaps best of all, he gave the city a long overdue fire department and police force.

Rome badly needed such protection. As might be expected in a slave-ridden society where life was cheap, many crimes of violence went virtually unchecked in the city. After all, what was one slave more or less—or freedman, for that matter? The satirist Juvenal (A.D. 50-130) tells us that the lurking thugs and robbers did not dare tackle the wealthy man with his "scarlet cloak and long retinue of attendants, carrying torches and brass lamps," whereas the poor man "escorted by the moon or by the feeble light of a candle whose wick has to be made to last" was easy prey for an attack in the dark.

Fire was another constant threat. Juvenal was so afraid of it that he was prepared to leave Rome: "No, no, I must live where there is no fire and the night is free from alarms!" Many of the fires that devastated Rome started in the top floors of those flimsily built apartment houses so disgracefully skimped on by builders and so tall that Augustus had to limit their height to 70 feet. Tenants paid dearly for a dark room on the crowded 6th floor where there was no water (it had to be carried from the nearest fountain), no bathroom (a passer-by in the narrow alley below might consider himself fortunate to be merely doused by the slops and not killed by the vessel itself), and no heat. It was the portable braziers used by these miserable tenants that were responsible for many a fire—and, if the building had not collapsed first, many a fire thus wiped out filth, bugs, sordidness unbelievable, and made homeless countless penniless wretches in a Rome which had no charitable societies, no unemployment insurance, no compassion.

When it came to the work of the government Augustus attempted to mollify the senators by allowing them a greater share in it, turning over to them, for example, the administration of the more highly civilized provinces that were farther removed from invasion. Less important provinces were governed by Equestrians. Henceforth governors were paid salaries—the most practical incentive to conscientious conduct—and all provincial officials were expected to govern efficiently.

Finally, having learned well the lessons of the civil wars, Augustus chose to make up his army by voluntary enlistments. The first step he took was to cut the total armed strength from over 60 legions to 28, the discharged veterans being settled in Italy or the provinces. Some twenty-eight new colonies were founded for them in Italy alone. At the same

HIBERNIA

Hadrian's Wall

BRITTANIA
Londinium

GERMANIA

ATLANTIC

OCEAN

BELGICA

Rhine R.

Danube R.

GAUL

Rhone R.

ADRIA

CORSICA

Rome

SPAIN

SARDINIA

MEDITERR

Carthage

44 B.C.

14 A.D.

180 A.D.

THE ROMAN EMPIRE'S EXPANSION
(44 B.C.-180 A.D.)

time conditions of service and pay were improved for those still in the army. Non-citizens were granted citizenship on enlisting in the legions, and a regular pension was provided on discharge to ensure that generals would no longer have to enter politics to secure rewards for their men at the end of a campaign. Of particular importance in the Augustan military organization was the imperial bodyguard, the so-called Praetorian Guard of 9000 men recruited exclusively from Italy.

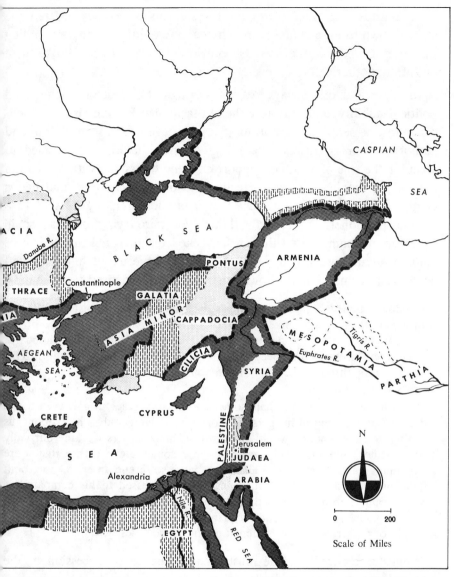

Perhaps the deepest concern of Augustus was the need for Rome's moral regeneration. To this end the ancient temples were repaired and cults were revived (there was even worship of the Princeps himself). In an attempt to restore a sound family life, Augustus had laws passed to encourage marriage and families. Nor was he oblivious of the plight of slaves. The story goes that one day a slave of Vedius Pollio dropped and broke a costly cup of myrrh at a banquet being given by his master for Augustus. As punishment for his clumsiness, Vedius ordered the slave thrown to man-eating carp; whereupon Augustus, countermanding the order, called for all of Vedius's precious cups and calmly broke them one after another before his eyes.

In these and other ways Augustus sought to create efficiency and political stability, and to restore the old-fashioned Roman virtues of self-discipline, a sense of responsibility, and a respect for tradition and authority. For Augustus, like his great-uncle before him, seemed to abandon the role of a ruthless opportunist and to assume with dedication that of philosopher-emperor. He liked to be with children, and had a delightful sense of humour. Once at a public ceremony he said to a nervous petitioner, "You look as though you were trying to offer a small tip to an elephant." And though he lacked the personal magnetism of Julius Caesar there was a touch of homely virtue about him. He had come from a small country town, and all his life practised frugal habits.

He seldom touched wine between meals; instead, he would moisten his throat with a morsel of bread dunked in cold water; or a slice of cucumber or the heart of a young lettuce; or a sour apple off the tree, or from a store cupboard. . . . He often needed more sleep than he got, and would doze off during his litter journeys through the City, if anything delayed his progress and the bearers set the litter down.

Augustus was remarkably handsome, and of very graceful gait even as an old man; but negligent of his personal appearance. He cared so little about his hair that, to save time, he would have two or three barbers working hurriedly on it together, and meanwhile read or write something, whether they were giving him a haircut or a shave. He always wore so serene an expression, both talking or in repose, that a Gallic chief once confessed to his compatriots: "When granted an audience with the Emperor during his passage across the Alps, I would have carried out my plan of hurling him over a cliff, had not the sight of that tranquil face softened my heart; so I desisted."

Augustus realized that he must secure a peaceful succession to the imperial power; so he designated members of his family, one after another as they predeceased him, to carry on. After a number of disappointments—the relatives he chose to succeed him had a habit of dying —he came at last to his stepson, Tiberius. Accordingly, when the old emperor died at the age of seventy-six in A.D. 14, Tiberius was granted for life the powers that his stepfather had held. One of his first acts was to arrange for the deification of his great predecessor.

TIME CHART FOR ROME AND GREECE

DATES B.C.	ROME	GREECE
1400	Bronze Age Indo-Europeans in Po valley	Mycenae conquers Crete
1300		
1200		Siege of Troy
1100		Dorian invasions Fall of Mycenae
1000	Latins settle on site of Rome	Greek migrations to Asia Minor
900	Villanovans at Bologna	City-states
800	Etruscans in Etruria	Homer in Chios
700	Greeks in Sicily and southern Italy Traditional founding of Rome	Colonization around Mediterranean and Black Seas
600	Etruscans at Rome	Age of Tyranny Draco codifies Athenian law
500	Expulsion of Kings	Solon's reforms at Athens Pisistratus becomes tyrant Cleisthenes and the triumph of democracy
400	Plebeians begin opposition to patricians	Persian Wars Themistocles and Confederacy of Delos Pericles and Peloponnesian War
300	Rome entered by Gauls Twelve Tables Final victory of the Plebs	Philip II of Macedon conquers Greece Alexander the Great conquers the East The Hellenistic Age
200	Rome supreme in Italy Rome conquers Carthage Rome turns to eastern Mediterranean	Philip V of Macedon
100	Destruction of Corinth and Carthage A Century of Revolution: Gracchi, Marius	Macedonia becomes a Roman province
30	Revolt of Italian allies Sulla The Triumvirates Octavian triumphant	
27	Octavian given the title "Augustus"	

CHAPTER 28

The Roman Peace

Others, doubtless, will mould lifelike bronze with greater delicacy, will win from marble the look of life, will plead cases better, chart the motions of the sky with the rod and foretell the risings of the stars. You, O Roman, remember to rule the nations with might. This will be your genius—to impose the way of peace, to spare the conquered and crush the proud.

VIRGIL, *Aeneid*

The Roman emperors who followed Augustus are a fascinating lot, touched, as some of them were, by scandal if not by madness. Now that the Republic was gone, free discussion and political parties were no more. Hence ancient Roman historians tended to concentrate on a few themes: the emperor's character, his relations with the Senate, and especially gossip and intrigue connected with the court. But however interesting these emperors may be, it should be remembered that individually they were less important than the system over which they presided.

❖ *Sudden Deaths*   When Tiberius (14-37) became emperor at fifty-two, *Tiberius* he was a completely embittered man. He had had to wait a long time for power; yet he lacked Augustus' gifts for winning support, and probably felt inadequate to exercise it when it was finally his. He tried to do what he thought Augustus would have done as new circumstances arose, but he was never very comfortable, as is shown by the fact that he reserved the right to abdicate.

As Tiberius's reign went on he became increasingly moody, and when his adopted nephew died during an eastern campaign it was rumoured that he had been poisoned at the emperor's command. Finally at the age of seventy-eight he died of a stroke. There was much rejoicing in Rome, and the Senate absolutely refused to vote him divine honours.

Caligula   Tiberius was succeeded by his great-nephew, who was nicknamed Caligula ("Little Boots"). Caligula had been brought up as a child in army camps, suffered from epilepsy, and probably had spells of insanity. As time went on he became pathologically suspicious of anyone who seemed to be at all eminent, and made it plain to the Senate that he could do nicely without them. Finally the Praetorian Guard assassinated him. Thus died an emperor who had been heard to remark morosely that if only humanity had one neck it could be severed in a single blow!

As the Praetorian Guard ransacked the royal palace after Caligula's murder, one of them saw a pair of feet sticking out from beneath a curtain. The gentleman-in-hiding turned out to be no less than the dead emperor's uncle, Claudius. This unprepossessing man, who had suffered poliomyelitis in childhood, was forthwith proclaimed emperor by the Guard. *Claudius*

During his reign (41-54) which began so inauspiciously, the Empire was extended in the East and in Africa. Most famous of all Claudius's campaigns was the invasion of Britain in A.D. 43. In the government of the Empire, Claudius sincerely tried to co-operate with the Senate after the fashion of Augustus and to treat it with deference. But the fact was that the Senate had become increasingly inadequate, with the result that the emperor overshadowed and overruled it.

Claudius carried out two projects originally envisaged by Julius Caesar —the construction of a harbour at Ostia and the draining of some of Italy's marshy areas. Moreover, he copied the illustrious Julius in making generous grants of citizenship to certain parts of the Empire. For Claudius knew his history (he had in fact written some before becoming emperor), and was convinced that in the past Rome had flourished

This delicate Roman pitcher (only 5½ inches high) was fashioned of semi-transparent greenish glass about A.D. 200. The Romans so perfected the Egyptian art of glass-making that glassware came to replace pottery in the home. Glass-blowers took a special pride in their art, as can be seen in this charming creation where tiny blue and white threads of semi-liquid glass have been applied to form a dainty pattern against the blown form.

because she had constantly readjusted her constitution and had not been afraid to admit foreign elements into the citizen body.

Claudius may have known his history, but he did not know much about women. His third and fourth wives proved such unfortunate choices that he finally executed one. The other, the notorious Agrippina, was his own niece (he was her third husband). She persuaded Claudius to adopt her son by a previous marriage, Nero, and began to intrigue to get him the throne. Then in 54 Claudius died very suddenly, after—so it was said—eating a dish of mushrooms prepared by his loving wife.

Nero

❖ *One Man's Savagery* Agrippina now had what she wanted: her son emperor (54-68), and at an early enough age (he was sixteen) for her to influence him. Now she could become mistress of the world. But matters did not turn out quite as she had planned. Nero's advisers encouraged him to be independent of her, and for a few years he gave over the management of affairs to the Senate.

As time went on Nero began to hate his dominating mother, and eventually to plot her death. At this he was nothing if not persistent. He began by depriving her of her bodyguard and so harassing her with lawsuits that she left Rome. Three times he tried poison, and three times she escaped its effects. Then the floor above her bedchamber was made to collapse while she was asleep; yet still she survived. Finally an ingenious ship was built, a ship that would disintegrate and drown her. But Agrippina swam ashore. When news of her miraculous escape was brought to Nero he thought of the perfect solution. He pretended that the messenger had come to assassinate him and ordered Agrippina put to death. Even so, the records tell us, he was not rid of his ambitious mother. It is said that thereafter her ghost haunted him.

When news of the murder reached Rome, it was accepted as having been forced on the emperor. Now Nero felt free to indulge his every whim. He made public appearances as a poet, musician, actor, and charioteer, and posted men to flog the audiences if they did not applaud loudly enough. Hollywood notwithstanding, Nero did not fiddle while Rome burned. It is true that Rome burned in 64; but the emperor was away when the fire started, and he hurried back to take energetic steps to bring it under control and to provide relief for those who had been burned out of house and home. Even so, public suspicion had been aroused by Nero's conduct, and when the rumour flew that the emperor himself was responsible for the fire he thought it prudent, as Tacitus records, to provide a scapegoat.

To allay the rumour Nero fastened the guilt and inflicted exquisite tortures upon a people hated for their wickedness, vulgarly called Christians. The name was derived from Christ, who was executed by Pontius Pilate in the reign of Tiberius. Checked for the moment, the mischievous superstition broke out again, not only in Judaea, the source of the evil, but even in Rome, into which everything infamous and abominable from all quarters flows and flourishes. First some were seized and made confession, and then upon their information a huge multitude were convicted, not so much for the crime of arson as for their hatred of the human race. Mockery was added to their deaths. They were covered with animals skins and torn to pieces by dogs, many were crucified or burned, and some were set afire at nightfall to serve for illumination. For the spectacle Nero offered his gardens, and he presented horse races in addition. In the dress of a charioteer he himself mingled with the crowd or stood up in his sulky. Hence, though the victims were guilty and deserved extreme punishment, nevertheless they aroused compassion, for it was not for the public good but for one man's savagery that they were being destroyed.

Nero rebuilt Rome on a grand scale. The magnificence of his "Golden House" has been recorded in all its opulent extravagance:

Its size and elegance can be sufficiently indicated by the following details. Its vestibule was of a size to contain a colossal statue of himself 120 feet high. It was so spacious that it had a colonnade of three rows a mile long. There was a pond, more like a sea, surrounded by structures to represent cities, and there were rustic stretches with alternating ploughland, vineyards, pastures, woodland, with numerous animals of all kinds, wild and domestic. In the rest of the house everything was overlaid with gold picked out with gems and mother-of-pearl. The dining rooms had ceilings coffered with ivory panels which revolved to scatter flowers and tubes to sprinkle perfume. The main dining hall was round and revolved constantly day and night, like the heavens. His baths had running sea water and sulphur water. When the building was finished and he dedicated it, he expressed his approval only by remarking that at last his house was fit for a human being.

So unpopular did Nero become as a result of his growing despotism that he decided to get away from it all for a while and to visit the birthplace of Hellenic culture. Accordingly, in 66, he undertook a tour of Greece. It was a triumphal tour too: the Greeks awarded him no fewer than 1808 first prizes in artistic and athletic competitions! By the time Nero arrived back in Rome, however, rebellion was brewing, and in 68 the Praetorian Guard and the armies revolted. Wailing "What an artist is lost!" the emperor committed suicide—or rather had one of his own freedmen finish him off when he lost his nerve.

❖ *The Problem of Succession* Now ensued a frantic grab for power as the year 69 saw four men bid for the imperial throne. Civil war once *Vespasian* more erupted in Italy. But in June 70 Titus Flavius Vespasianus arrived in Rome, bringing peace with the sword. The fact that Vespasian (69-79) had two sons, Titus and Domitian, meant that for the time being the troublesome problem of succession was solved.

Vespasian was from a country family, and throughout his life exhibited the traits of solid plebeian stock. For one thing he was somewhat tight-fisted—a timely blessing for a Rome whose coffers had been rifled by the wanton prodigalities of Nero. Vespasian overhauled the tax system, increased provincial tributes, and insisted on honesty in financial affairs. The peace and prosperity of Vespasian's later years were well symbolized by the Colosseum, that vast amphitheatre built on the site of Nero's Golden House and capable of accommodating 50,000 spectators. But what a sad contrast there was between the tastes of Greek and Roman audiences. The Greeks had sat for hours to watch the plays of their leading dramatists. The Romans went quite literally for blood, as this account by a spectator clearly shows.

Chance had led me to the Amphitheatre at midday; I was expecting games, jokes, those interludes in which the spectator's eye is rested from seeing human blood flow. But the opposite happened: the morning's contests had by comparison been humane. Now, no more trifling: these were sheer slaughters. The gladiator had nothing with which to cover himself; all parts of his body were exposed to blows, and no encounter failed to leave its wounds. Did the majority of spectators prefer this kind of combat to that which the usual or extra pairs of gladiators undertook? How could they but prefer it? No helmet, no shield against the sword. What need of protective armament or of a struggle according to rules? These are only ways of delaying the kill. In the morning, men had been delivered to lions and bears; at midday it was to the spectators that they were thrown. After having killed, the combatant must fight again to be killed in his turn; even the victor was earmarked for death. For the contestants there was one outcome only, death, carried out by fire and sword. And all this occurred during the intermission.

Titus   You will be reading about a day in the reign of Vespasian's son Titus (79-81) at the end of this Part. So handsome and popular was this forty-year-old emperor that he was nicknamed "the love and delight of mankind." His generosity seemed to know no bounds. "He reckoned the day lost when he did not bestow a princely gift on someone," says a modern historian. Yet his short reign was marked by several tragedies, including the famous eruption of Mount Vesuvius which buried the cities of Pompeii and Herculaneum in August 79. A graphic eye-witness account of this catastrophe may be read on pages 342-343.

Domitian (81-96), who became emperor at thirty, was a sadistic man who, like Tiberius, was full of resentment at being held back. He dominated the state more and more, ignoring the Senate completely in the latter part of his reign. He put Equestrians into positions hitherto reserved for senators, and tried to uplift the moral tone of Roman society by restoring the old gods—though this last involved persecuting minority religions. His final years were nothing short of a reign of terror, as nobles were accused, executed, and dispossessed on the flimsiest charges of trea-

Domitian

This eloquent plaster cast from Pompeii is the mould of a victim in the very throes of being smothered during the eruption of Vesuvius in A.D. 79. The process by which such moulds have come down to us is an interesting one. Actually most of the volcano's victims were killed, not by the initial hail of pumice, but by deadly carbonic acid fumes which accompanied the dense black cloud of ash and condensed steam. As the victims fell the ashes continued to sift down on them, eventually mixing with steam or rain to harden into a mud shell around the corpse. Thus when the bodies decomposed they left empty moulds that have graphically preserved their death struggles, and which, when filled with plaster, form casts. By this method excavators have preserved countless mute testimonies to the agonies suffered by men, women, children—even dogs—on that August day. When the sky cleared three days later, a city had disappeared, buried in a volcanic mantle 20 feet deep.

son. Again violent means bred a violent end. Domitian was murdered by palace conspirators.

Trajan
Domitian's assassins selected a sixty-six-year-old senator as the new emperor, and this man set a wise precedent. Since he had no son of his own he adopted a successor, a distinguished soldier named Trajan. This adoption was one of the most significant events in the history of the Empire, for it inaugurated a system that provided an orderly and able succession for almost a century. Trajan (98-117) was a Spaniard, the first emperor of provincial origin, and one of the very best to occupy the imperial throne. This great warrior-emperor extended Roman territory north across the Danube and east to Mesopotamia. Yet he was also a fine administrator. In Italy, for example, he set up a sort of family allowance arrangement, while in the provinces he refused to tolerate any misgovernment, personally scrutinizing public expenditures. An example of the careful attention he devoted to provincial affairs can be read on page 341.

Trajan was admired by every class. He won the citizens by vast building projects and the plebs by lavish spectacles. He won the legionaries by his endurance. (Who could help worshipping an emperor who tore up his own clothes to bind your wounds?) And he won the Senate by treating them with respect, always sending back to them reports on his campaigns and insisting that any peace terms with an enemy must be ratified by them. When he died of a stroke at the age of sixty-four while returning from his Parthian campaigns he had not formally adopted a successor, but his wife said that on his death-bed he had indicated his choice: his second cousin, Hadrian.

Hadrian
Hadrian (117-138) was also a remarkably good emperor. He went on the army's route marches, disdaining the use of a vehicle, and was an accomplished architect, builder, and surveyor. He did not wish to expand the Empire; indeed he allowed it to shrink in the Middle East. Yet he believed he had to keep the frontier armies at a keen fighting pitch so that outsiders would not be tempted to attack, and to this end he spent at least half of his reign touring the Empire. It was to prevent raids along Britain's northern frontier that Hadrian's famous Wall was built, a splendidly engineered structure 73 miles long running from the Tyne to the Solway.

The next emperor ruled wisely and reasonably well. But it was the calm before the storm. The army was being allowed to grow lax, and at the very gates of the Empire seethed masses of barbarian tribes awaiting the day of Roman weakness. By the reign of Marcus Aurelius (161-180)

Marcus Aurelius

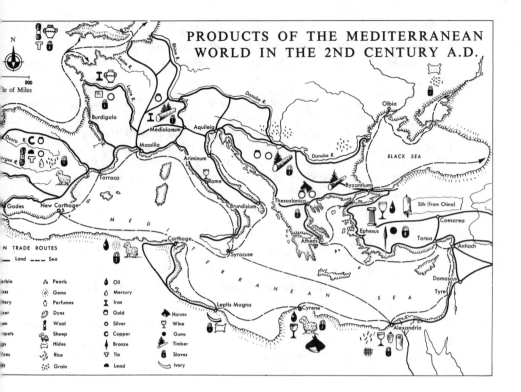

war had once again begun to dominate the affairs of the Empire as
Parthians in the east, barbarians in the north, and a plague all strained
Rome to the utmost.

So ended what one Roman called the "boundless majesty of the
Roman peace." From Augustus to Marcus Aurelius—border wars and
civil conflicts notwithstanding—the lands surrounding the Mediterranean Sea had been united in one political system. It was an era that
had lasted for almost two centuries.

❖ *Diversity under Unity*   The Roman Peace had been protected by an
army of 400,000 men—not a large army considering that the provinces
had increased greatly in number. Under Augustus there were 28 provinces; a century later as a result of conquest and subdivision there were
45; and two centuries after that there were over 100. Rome tolerated
diversity under the unity she imposed on the Mediterranean, and trade
and industry flourished under the efficient and beneficial imperial government bequeathed by Augustus.

About the year 150 a Greek rhetorician delivered an enthusiastic oration in praise of Rome. The Roman peace was not as ideal as this man would have us believe; nevertheless, the world has not seen its like again.

The whole world, as on a holiday, has doffed its old costume—of iron—and turned to finery and all festivities without restraint. . . . Greek and barbarian can now readily go wherever they please with their property or without it. It is just like going from their own to their own country. Neither the Cilician Gates nor the narrow, sandy approaches through Arabia to Egypt present any danger. Nor do impassable mountains, vast stretches of river, or inhospitable barbarian tribes. For safety, it is enough to be a Roman, or rather, one of your subjects. . . .

Yet there is another side to all this. It is true that the Roman solution to the political problems of the ancient world was an advance on the Greek—but at a cost. The tragedy was Rome's loss of personal liberties. There is something terrifyingly prophetic of 20th century dictators in a statement by a Stoic philosopher whom the emperor expelled from Rome.

A soldier, dressed like a civilian, sits down by your side and begins to speak ill of Caesar, and then you too, just as though you had received from him some guarantee of good faith in the fact he began the abuse, tell likewise everything you think, and the next thing is—you are led off to prison in chains.

CHAPTER 29

Civilization Under the Empire

You have surveyed the whole world, built bridges of all sorts across rivers, cut down mountains to make paths for chariots, filled the deserts with hostels, and civilized it all with system and order. . . .

AELIUS ARISTIDES, *To Rome*

The Romans' conquest of the Mediterranean world meant that the cultures of the many peoples they conquered were to be assimilated by them and hence to become widespread. This was particularly true, of course, of Greek culture, with the result that Greek philosophy, art, science, and literature were to become, thanks to the Romans, the basis of European civilization.

❖ *Imported Gods* The Roman culture that resulted from this mix- *Stoicism*
ture, though inferior to the Greek, was no mean product. It evolved
against a background of Hellenistic philosophy, and Epicureanism and
Stoicism both had adherents in Rome. Stoicism, however, became by
far the more important of the two, until by the end of the 1st century
after Christ it was justly famous as the "religion" of educated Romans.
One of its chief prophets was Seneca the Younger, a Spaniard.
Seneca maintained that "the soul's entire struggle is with the
flesh that oppresses it." And he proceeded, in all seriousness, to de-
nounce the heating of houses with furnaces, to declare that taking a
bath was violating nature, and to say that no one should use feather
pillows or bother to shade his head from the sun. But Seneca was
mostly concerned with the moral problems of the noble class. He deplored the riotous living of his day, and did not hesitate to condemn the
Roman games (see page 290) with their bloodshed and their appeal
to the baser instincts. Even in the intermissions, he protested, "men
were strangled lest people be bored."

Stoicism, with its emphasis on self-discipline, made a particular appeal
to the emperor Marcus Aurelius. But the emperor's philosophy was of
a gloomier, more pessimistic kind—and with good reason. By nature
quiet, shy, and a gentle scholar, Marcus Aurelius was forced to spend
most of his life in hard frontier fighting. His *Meditations,* often written
in his tent after a long day of marching or battle, were an expression of
his Stoic creed and a reminder to himself of his exacting duty as
emperor.

Nowhere was the Greek influence more evident than in Roman *Roman religion*
religion. The Greek gods and goddesses were imported and given
Roman names: Zeus became Jupiter; Aphrodite, Venus; Poseidon,
Neptune; and so on. Superstition abounded and was firmly embedded
in Roman beliefs. Trees, brooks, even sewers, had their deities, while
shrines to the protecting spirits (*lares*) were found in every household,
and at city street corners and country crossroads.

All family occasions from birth to death were accompanied by proper
ceremonies, with the father or head of the *familia* officiating as the
household priest. The Roman word *familia* does not have our meaning
of "family," but means rather a household or clan, consisting of the
head of the house, his wife, his unmarried daughters, and his sons and
their wives and families. The spirits of the ancestors were also a very
real part of this household, since the Romans believed that they hovered

near their homes and burial places. It was very important that the family perform regular offerings in order that the souls of the departed would not become unhappy, or even turn into spirits of evil. Consequently ancestor veneration became a very important part of Roman religion, and a childless man might adopt a son to perpetuate his own family in order that his spirit might not be neglected after his death.

At first Roman holidays were closely connected with religious festivals, but in the days of the Empire these holidays became very frequent —as many as 132 days a year in the time of Augustus. Probably schoolboys were especially pleased with this arrangement, since during school term they had only market days (every 9th day) and holidays off, besides their five days in March and in December, and of course the hot summer season. Indeed, the citizens of Rome as a whole were

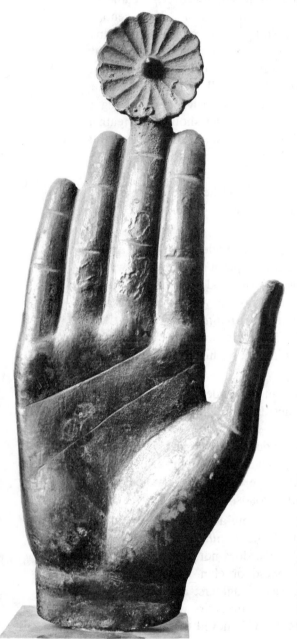

The influence of magic upon the Roman people—both lowly and great—provides a pathetic picture of a fear-ridden society in which countless charlatans and quacks found hosts of gullible clients. Magic, they believed, would protect them. The bronze hand on this page, for example, represents an all-powerful God, and its symbols were supposed to guarantee protection to the faithful. But more often magic was called upon in the service of hate. It may be that deformed hands such as the ones on the facing page, which represent some of the many Roman gods of nature, were used by bitter individuals to inflict a curse upon their enemies.

far from overworked, considering that their working day lasted only from dawn till midday—six hours. With such a surplus of leisure time it is not surprising that Romans came to crave heady entertainment on holidays and gradually lost sight of their religious significance.

As the Empire expanded there were foreign gods to be placated and oracles to be consulted. Many cults found their way into Rome from the East—from Egypt, Asia Minor, Syria, or Persia. Of all these foreign imports the most popular was the Persian sun-god Mithras, because Mithraism adopted Zoroaster's eternal struggle between good and evil and made a powerful appeal to the soldiers of the Empire.

No objection was raised by the government to this multiplicity of cults. A citizen might worship as he pleased, provided, of course, that there was nothing subversive in his religion—in other words, provided his religion did not affect his loyalty to the state. But men and women whose religion was practised in secret gatherings, usually at night, were naturally subject to suspicion. So was a religion that seemed to be narrowly nationalistic. Thus it followed that the Romans suspected the Jews, a tightly knit people who clung exclusively to one God, and the religion that appeared to the Romans to be an offshoot of Judaism, Christianity. The adherents of both these religions refused to worship Caesar; hence they represented a dangerous challenge to the imperial power.

❖ *Practical Feats of Art* Augustus boasted that he found Rome brick and left it marble, and it is true that before his time brick, cement, and wood had been the chief building materials. Of these, cement ought to be specially noted, because it was a characteristic Roman material made from volcanic residue found near Rome and mixed with lime. Roman art was a blend of Etruscan, Greek, and Oriental traditions. The use of the arch was learned from the Etruscans, and permitted the Romans to construct huge buildings which became more immense as the Empire continued. Whereas Greek architecture had striven for harmony and balance, the Roman aim was grandness.

Many of the colossal structures of the Romans were merely monuments to the vanity of the emperors. Yet some were highly practical. They originated at least two types of such buildings, those great palaces called the "baths," and the aqueducts. The baths were magnificent edifices, on whose evidence alone we can state that the Romans were the cleanest people in antiquity. Although every conceivable type of bath was available—hot, cold, swimming, steam, tub, and so on—these establishments were much more than bathing places. Enclosed gardens, promenades, gymnasia, lounges, libraries, and museums enhanced the interior of the greatest ones, such as those of the emperor Caracalla. They were really a Turkish bath, an athletic centre, and a club, all under one roof. And what a roof! The central hall looked like the high, vast concourses of our North American railway stations. Even greater spaciousness was added by the fact that the Romans avoided using a forest of columns, solving the formidable engineering problem involved in enclosing and roofing such a grandiose structure by means of the arch and vaulting.

Roman aqueducts, too, were built solidly and well (the one called the Pont du Gard near Nîmes, France, is still in a wonderful state of preservation), and by the end of the 1st century A.D. they were supplying Rome, then a city of over 1,000,000, with 100 gallons of water per person per day. The very rich might have running water (on the main floor only) in their kitchen and nearby lavatory, and paid for this luxury according to the size of the pipes leading into their house. Sometimes, however, tight-fisted citizens bribed waterworks' labourers to have water surreptitiously piped into their homes!

Sculpture   In their sculpture the Romans attempted to portray real persons rather than the idealized types of the Greeks. They also excelled in a new kind of sculpture, the equestrian statue. But as the Empire grew older the trend was, as in architecture, to the immense. A good example of this is the huge head of Constantine now set up in the Palazzo dei Conservatori in Rome. It towers some eight feet high by itself. Can you imagine the sheer mass of the whole colossal statue? Though it does show a certain force, most of us would prefer the graceful beauty of the *Discus Thrower* to the ungainly bulk of the *Constantine*.

As you can see if you look at pictures of restored Pompeiian houses, murals painted on stucco were a favourite Roman wall decoration. They were often intended to create the illusion of space, and those recovered seem to be mostly copies of Greek or Hellenistic pictures.

The Roman mastery of the arch is nowhere more evident than in this fine granite bridge built during the reign of the emperor Trajan. The graceful structure, which stands 150 feet high, stretches for 630 feet as it spans the Tagus River near Alcantara (the Arabic word for "bridge") in Spain.

The Romans also seemed very fond of having pictures of themselves—almost as fond as we are today. The art of portraiture was widely practised, whether the subject be an emperor, a wanted criminal, or a lover who hoped his picture would be carried next someone's heart.

In the field of science, Romans showed great practical skill. They were outstanding engineers. Their surveying was accurate, and in tunnelling, mining, and drainage no other ancient people can bear comparison with them. Their remarkable road system, too, bears testimony to their meticulous surveying methods, and their construction techniques were amazingly advanced. Most road-beds had large stones in the bottom and worked up to smaller stones on the top, sometimes with a middle layer of hard gravel covered by a layer of fine limed gravel. On the surface, closely fitted limestone slabs sloped slightly to the edges, with drains at both sides. Roman road-beds were at least 40 inches deep—somewhat deeper than modern ones—and the surfaces varied in width from 5 to 23 feet. In all, over 47,000 miles of roads were constructed. How many of us who use "highways" realize that they are

Science

named for those majestic causeways which the Romans raised up above the level of the surrounding land?

When it came to scientific theory, however, the practical Romans had once again to turn to the speculative Greeks. The two greatest scientific treatises of the Roman era were written by Greeks who lived in the 2nd century Empire, Ptolemy of Alexandria (90-168) and Galen of Pergamum (130-200). Ptolemy summarized all ancient knowledge of astronomy and geography. He also formulated independent theories of his own, among them one which (contrary to the beliefs of many other scientists of the day) maintained that the earth was stationary at the centre of the universe—a theory which was to hold up further astronomical progress for some time. More important, however, is the fact that Ptolemy was the first to locate places on the earth's surface by latitude and longitude. Galen, on the other hand, was a doctor in Rome who treated as many as 3000 patients a year. His dissections of apes led him into some errors when he assumed that human anatomy was the same, but even so he made important contributions to the knowledge of the structure and functions of the human body and formulated a theory as to what causes disease.

Literature

❖ *Classics Fit for a Queen*   We have already come across several famous literary figures—Julius Caesar writing of his campaigns in Gaul, Cicero defending the Republic in his political treatises and letters, Tacitus writing his history of the first century of the Empire. But although it is to be hoped that many of you will study some Latin, probably few of you will ever read Latin authors extensively. Still, all of us should remember that not only have the tongues of England, France, Spain, and Italy evolved from the Latin language, but their literatures are solidly rooted in the Latin literary tradition.

It was in the age of Cicero and Augustus that literary production was at its height. To the Romans the most important part of formal education was rhetoric, and when Julius Caesar said of Cicero that he had advanced the boundaries of the Latin genius he meant that Cicero had attained perfection in the art of public speaking. Throughout Roman schools, therefore, emphasis was laid on oratory, the pupils being taught both to write and speak discourses based on Cicero's models. Probably the aim of many a schoolboy was to star—through oratorical skill—in the law courts, and so start up the golden ladder to a political career.

Cicero also wrote essays on literary criticism and philosophy, essays that drew heavily on Greek sources. Perhaps most interesting of all are his private letters (more than 800 of which survive), because, not being intended for publication, they throw a candid light on his times. Cicero's literary creations became classics for generations to come. Centuries later a young English princess, who was to become Queen Elizabeth I, had read nearly all his works before she was sixteen.

With the Augustan Age three poets came to the fore—Virgil (70-19 B.C.), Horace (65-8 B.C.), and Ovid (43 B.C.-A.D. 18). Virgil was a gentleman farmer until his estates were confiscated by Octavian in 42 B.C. to provide land for the veterans of Philippi. The poet was to spend the rest of his life in Rome or Naples in the literary circle of the wealthy Maecenas, a man who may be described as Augustus' minister of propaganda, and the patron of many a struggling artist. Although he wrote pastoral poems as well as an agricultural handbook in verse, Virgil's greatest work was the *Aeneid*, the story of the founding of Rome by Aeneas. This magnificent epic in twelve books weaves together fiction and fact in Homeric fashion in order to demonstrate that all the events of the Roman past formed a logical prologue to the peaceful and prosperous age of Augustus. The *Aeneid* established Virgil as one of the world's master poets, and posterity has always been grateful to Augustus for disregarding the poet's death-bed request that the epic, which had not received its finishing touches, be burned. *Virgil*

Another poet in Maecenas' circle was Horace, the son of a freedman. *Horace* Despite his lowly beginnings Horace received an excellent education, and although he fought at Philippi against Octavian and Mark Antony he was pardoned. Indeed, after Virgil's death he became poet laureate. Horace is most famous for his four books called *Odes*, lyric poems which use Greek metres and deal with an astonishing variety of subjects ranging from a banquet to the defeat of Cleopatra.

Ovid is the least important of the three. Although he is chiefly remem- *Ovid* bered for his *Metamorphoses,* a Roman *Arabian Nights* consisting of a collection of myths and legends about miraculous transformations, his specialty was gay elegies. These finally got him into trouble with Augustus. He died in exile on the Black Sea, banished for "a poem and a mistake."

❖ *One Law for All* One non-literary branch of writing must also be singled out for some emphasis. This is the body of law that the Romans originated and wrote down. We have already seen how some early laws, the *Twelve Tables,* protected the plebs by preventing the upper classes from adjusting the laws to suit themselves. Now under the Empire one

Every sizeable city throughout the Empire (except in Greece) had its amphitheatre, and in this vast Colosseum in Rome as many as 50,000 spectators would crowd in, eager to watch men fight it out to the death. Gladiators were often condemned criminals, prisoners of war, or slaves, and for the successful contestant there was far greater fame and adulation than for a modern prize-fighter. Here an armed Samnite advances on a Gaul, who is equipped only with a net and trident. When one man was finally downed, the crowd shouted "Habet!" ("That's got him!") and indicated their pleasure: waving handkerchiefs meant mercy; thumbs down, death.

Very few Romans protested against these bloody spectacles, or the even bloodier beast shows in which hundreds of wild animals tore each other to pieces. The ultimate in depravity was finally reached in 107 when the Emperor Trajan held an orgy of games that ran through 11,000 gladiators—in 123 days besting Augustus' record for his whole reign.

wise universal system of law, built up through the centuries, was worked out and enforced. This law gave equal justice to all Roman citizens and yet made allowance for local custom. As one emperor wrote to his ambassador, "When in doubt follow the law of the local city."

The law also tended increasingly to protect the poorer and weaker against the stronger and richer. Even in the provinces poor men who could not obtain anyone to advocate their cause were provided for: "No man must be overborne by the influence of his opponents, for that would merely bring discredit on the governor." What was said on behalf of St. Paul at Jerusalem is eloquent testimony to the fairness of Roman law: "It is not the custom of the Romans to hand over any man before the accused prisoner has met his accusers face to face, and has had an opportunity of defending himself upon the charge laid against him."

Roman law is still a vital force. While 70 million people lived under it in the days of the Empire, some 870 million today have legal systems directly traceable to it. Roman law attempted to dispense justice without prejudice, and worked on the principle that the spirit is more important than the letter of the law. Of all the ancient people we have studied, those who lived under this noble system had the best guarantee of securing justice. Perhaps, then, Rome's law was her most enduring achievement.

But the world owes Rome a greater debt. She provided the environment in which Christianity could be born and could grow. In this, as in many other ways, she proved to be the civilizer of Europe.

CHAPTER 30

The Triumph of Christianity

This is the fruit of the triumphs of Rome; they opened the doors for Christ to enter.

PRUDENTIUS, *Against Symmachus*

On a hill outside Jerusalem, about the year 30, there occurred a crucifixion. The Roman legionaries whose job it was to nail up the condemned criminals probably soon forgot the grim incident. But the world never did. For one of the three men crucified that day was the founder of Christianity, a carpenter named Jesus of Nazareth.

❖ *A Mightier than Caesar* Aside from a few references by ancient Roman historians writing long after the events, our evidence for this man's life and deeds comes from the New Testament, and almost entirely from four of its books written in the second half of the 1st century: the Gospels according to Matthew, Mark, Luke, and John. These Gospels tell us that Jesus of Nazareth went up and down his native Galilean countryside preaching to crowds and performing miracles of healing. He taught the common people in a language they would understand, by means of parables—simple stories that enshrined great moral or spiritual truths such as the equality of *all* men before God.

Behold a sower went forth to sow ....*Matthew* 13: 3
If a man have an hundred sheep,
and one of them be gone astray ....*Matthew* 18: 12
A certain man went down from Jerusalem to Jericho,
and fell among thieves ....*Luke* 10: 30
Consider the lilies how they grow ....*Luke* 12: 27
A certain man had two sons ....*Luke* 15: 11
Two men went up into the temple to pray ....*Luke* 18: 10
I am the true vine, and my Father is the husbandman ....*John* 15: 1

In time some of his followers believed that he was God's anointed king, the long-awaited Messiah, sent to unshackle them from Rome, and Jesus himself said that he had come not to destroy the Law but to fulfil it. But he went further in his insistence on a "new commandment . . . that you love one another."

You have heard that it was said, "An eye for an eye and a tooth for a tooth." But I say to you, Do not resist one who is evil. But if any one strikes you on the right cheek, turn to him the other also; and if any one would sue you and take your coat, let him have your cloak as well; and if any one forces you to go one mile, go with him two miles. Give to him who begs from you, and do not refuse him who would borrow from you.

You have heard that it was said, "You shall love your neighbour and hate your enemy." But I say to you, Love your enemies and pray for those who persecute you, so that you may be sons of your Father who is in heaven; for he makes his sun rise on the evil and on the good, and sends rain on the just and on the unjust. For if you love those who love you, what reward have you? Do not even the tax collectors do the same? And if you salute only your brethren, what more are you doing than others? Do not even the Gentiles do the same? You, therefore, must be perfect, as your heavenly Father is perfect.

It is a life-long task to seek after perfection. This master teacher was making soul-consuming demands on his followers.

The ministry of Jesus appeared to be short-lived. Certain religious authorities in Jerusalem accused him of sedition against Rome and had him brought before Pontius Pilate, the Roman procurator of Judaea. After a farce of a trial, he was condemned to die like a common criminal, by the slow torture of crucifixion. And so he died on the gallows of that day, the cross, his agony shared only by one lone disciple and some sorrowing women. Despite all the hope of a Messiah, the great mission was apparently over, ended in the ultimate defeat of the tomb.

Three days later the body was missing, and shortly thereafter the disciples became convinced that they had witnessed their risen master. Cowards were transformed into dauntless missionaries as these rough men proclaimed that it had been a divine Messiah, no less than the Son of God Himself, who had walked with them during his earthly life.

From such an unlikely beginning, in a backward part of the Roman Empire, sprang the Christian church. Its earliest meeting is described in the first chapter of the book of *Acts*.

Then they returned to Jerusalem from the mount called Olivet, which is near Jerusalem, a sabbath day's journey away; and when they had entered, they went up to the upper room, where they were staying. . . . In those days Peter stood up among the brethren (the company of persons was in all about a hundred and twenty). . . .

❖ *An Apostle to the Gentiles* Within a few years of the crucifixion a man named Paul, a Roman citizen born in Tarsus, joined the church. *St. Paul* This Jew, whose Aramaic name was Saul, was certainly not an imposing looking figure, a "man of small stature, thin-haired upon the head, crooked in the legs, of good condition of body with eyebrows joining. . . ." Nor was he a likely candidate for the ministry of Christ. At first he was a violent opponent of Christianity, and led persecutions of Christians in Jerusalem. But one day while on his way from Jerusalem to Damascus to institute fresh persecutions he saw a vision of Jesus and was converted. Soon he himself began to preach the gospel of Christ to fellow Jews.

Some three years later (about the year 36) Paul met Peter, one of Jesus' original twelve disciples and the leading figure in the church in Jerusalem. At this time the members of the church were mainly converted Jews, but at Antioch there had grown up a Christian group which included both Jews and Gentiles. In fact it was at Antioch that the word *Christian* was first coined to describe a follower of Jesus.

The Antioch church commissioned Paul and Barnabas to preach the *Paul's* gospel, and in the ten years between 48 and 58 three great missionary *missionary* journeys were undertaken. Paul and his fellow preachers travelled some *journeys* 8000 miles, founding churches and preaching and writing in Greek. As they passed through the leading cities of Asia Minor, however, they dis-

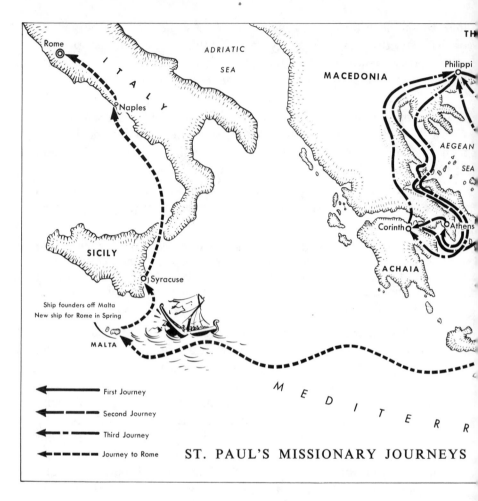

Rome

ADRIATIC

SEA

ITALY

MACEDONIA

Philippi

Naples

AEGEAN

SEA

SICILY

Corinth

Athens

Syracuse

ACHAIA

Ship founders off Malta
New ship for Rome in Spring

MALTA

M E D I T E R R

First Journey

Second Journey

Third Journey

Journey to Rome

ST. PAUL'S MISSIONARY JOURNEYS

covered that despite the fact that Jesus had been a Jew, it was not the
Jews but the Gentiles who welcomed their teachings. Jew though he
was himself, Paul came to believe that to be a Christian it was not first
essential to observe all the requirements of Jewish ritual and the Law.
A council of the church at Jerusalem accepted this suggestion, and
henceforth Paul preached that "there is neither Jew nor Gentile, there is
neither bond nor free . . . for all are one in Christ Jesus." He had become
the "Apostle to the Gentiles."

On his second missionary journey through Asia Minor, Paul came at
length to Troas. Here he had another vision: "There stood a man of
Macedonia, and prayed him, saying, 'Come over into Macedonia, and
help us.'" Paul answered the call. Few decisions can have been as

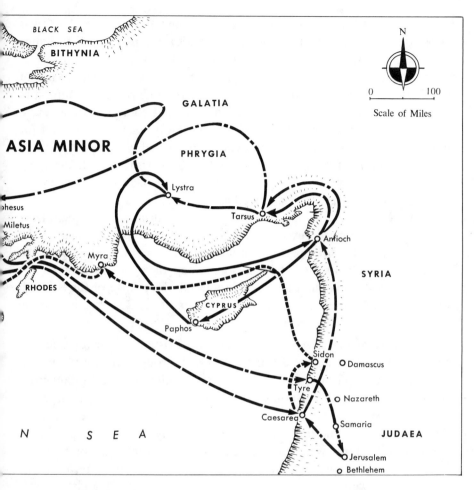

fateful. Now the gospel was going overseas; Christianity was passing from the Orient into Europe.

In both Macedonia and Greece Paul had notable successes, though at Athens, where he preached one of his most quoted sermons (*Acts* 17: 22-31), he was not well received. A few years later a third missionary journey was taken. It was the culmination of a career of hardships.

Five times I have received at the hands of the Jews forty lashes less one; three times I have been beaten with rods; once I was stoned; three times I have been shipwrecked; a night and a day I have been adrift at sea; on frequent journeys, in danger from rivers, danger from robbers, danger from my own people, danger from Gentiles, danger in the city, danger in the wilderness, danger at sea, danger from false brethren; in toil and hardship, through many a sleepless night, in hunger and thirst, often without food, in cold and exposure.

And the hardships were not yet over. About the year 58, Paul was arrested in Jerusalem by the Roman authorities because of a disturbance that broke out when he was in the Temple. He was imprisoned, first at Caesarea in Judaea, and later in Rome, where he was under a kind of house arrest which allowed him to write letters to Christian communities outside Italy. Then, possibly because no one had come from Judaea to Rome in order to accuse him, he was mysteriously released—but not for long. He was soon rearrested and executed, probably during the Neronian persecutions following the fire of 64. So perished Paul, the great apostle who had felt himself called to be the light of the Gentiles and to spread Christianity in Europe as well as in Asia.

A few years later the Jerusalem church itself disappeared when Titus suppressed the Jewish revolt of 67-70. From this point onwards the church became predominantly Gentile. Christians continued to obey the Ten Commandments, but they no longer felt they had to observe the intricate Jewish law, and they slowly replaced observance of the Sabbath on the last day of the week by commemoration of the Resurrection on the first day, Sunday.

❖ *The Blood of the Martyrs*　At first the Christians were regarded by the Roman authorities as just another Jewish group. But by the 60's it was recognized that here was an entirely new religion—and a dangerous one. One of the earliest non-Christian historians to mention the existence of the new faith is Tacitus, who has already been quoted on page 289. About the same time the governor of Bithynia, the younger Pliny, expressed his alarm when he learned that this "crazy and unrestrained superstition" had spread to the villages of the Empire. Why, even the country folk were beginning to forsake the old Roman gods! Pliny's letter asking for the advice of the Emperor Trajan, together with the emperor's reply, is printed at the end of this Part, and shows that there was no organized persecution of Christians at this time (though if you admitted you were one you might be executed). Such persecutions as there were usually resulted from discontent caused by bad harvests, a flood, or an unpopular governor. The Christians were convenient scapegoats.

It is perhaps natural that Christianity, with its message of love and hope and equality, should have made its earliest conversions amongst the humble and downtrodden of the Empire—slaves, poor city workers, and women. By the 2nd century, however, Christianity had penetrated the middle and upper classes as well. Christians had even served in the army under Marcus Aurelius, though they were never very numerous in the legions and must often have had qualms about rendering military service unto Caesar. There was, for instance, the case in 298 of a certain Marcellus.

On October 30, at Tingis [Tangier], Marcellus . . . was brought into court, and it was officially stated: "Marcellus, a centurion, has been referred to your authority by the governor Fortunatus. There is at hand a letter dealing with his case, which at your command I shall read."

When this was read, Agricolanus [the deputy prefect] said, "Did you say what appears in the official records of the governor?" Marcellus answered, "I did." Agricolanus said, "Were you in service with the rank of centurion first class?" Marcellus answered, "I was." Agricolanus said, "What madness possessed you to renounce your oath of allegiance and to speak as you did?" Marcellus answered, "There is no madness in those who fear God." Agricolanus said, "Did you say each of the things contained in the official records of the governor?" Marcellus answered, "I did." Agricolanus said, "Did you throw away your arms?" Marcellus answered, "I did. For a Christian, who is in the service of the Lord Christ, ought not to serve the cares of this world."

Agricolanus said, "The acts of Marcellus are such that they must receive disciplinary punishment. Accordingly, Marcellus, who was in service with the rank of centurion first class, having declared that he has degraded himself by publicly renouncing his oath of allegiance, and having, moreover, put on record insane statements, it is my pleasure that he be put to death by the sword."

This sombre burial room, guarded by the images of revered saints, formed the last resting place of a martyred 3rd century pope whose name you can still see on the wall—"Cornelius." A lamp was kept constantly burning on the short pillar before the cubicle, and oil from it was regarded as a precious relic by medieval sovereigns. Behind the grave stretch out the great dark tunnels of the catacomb, one of many where the early Christians of Rome buried their dead in niches rising in tiers and closed by inscribed marble tablets. These Christians, who believed so joyously in life after death, were often to find themselves near their departed ones during the reign of the emperor Diocletian, when savage persecutions drove the Christians to seek refuge among the tombs of the dead.

When he was being led to execution, Marcellus said, "Agricolanus, may God be kind to you!" And after he said these words he was killed by the sword, and obtained the glory of martyrdom he desired.

Edict of Toleration   Strangely enough, the greater the persecution the more converts there were to Christianity. "The blood of the martyrs," it has been written, "is the seed of the church." The 3rd century saw savage persecutions— and still the number of Christians increased, increased so greatly, in fact, that at a meeting in Milan in 313 the Emperor Constantine granted Christianity toleration and an equal status with other religions. Christianity was still a minority religion, but its triumph was assured. Constantine went on in 321 to declare Sunday, the day originally dedicated to the sun-god, a legal holiday and a day of prayer. Christians in the army were permitted to attend religious services, and the army was even to recite a prescribed prayer suitable for both Christians and pagans.

Christianity had been allowed to come out into the open, but it was still not the state religion, nor did it enjoy any monopoly. It was not until the year 380 that the Emperor Theodosius the Great (379-395) banned pagan worship as a menace to the official religion of the Empire, Christianity, and enjoined all subjects to embrace "the religion delivered by the Apostle Peter to the Romans."

❖ *A Union of Strengths* What factors were responsible for this wide and rapid spread of Christianity?

To begin with, the new religion combined the special strengths and aptitudes of Jews, Greeks, and Romans. From the Jews came monotheism and the over-ruling idea of religion not just as the observance of ritual but as a whole way of life. There was little in the Roman world that provided the spiritual satisfaction Christianity offered. Oriental cults, or Caesar-worship, or philosophical speculation were no match for the impelling message

CHRISTIANITY
—a combination of special strengths—

which instilled such a strong social conscience that Christians actually tried to love their neighbours as themselves. Indeed the very joy with which Christians faced death in the arena must have given many a Roman pause to think.

Christianity was born into a world saturated with Greek philosophy. It is hardly surprising, then, that soon Christian thinkers tried to work out a logical outline of their beliefs in the form of a *theology*. Paul began this process when he had to use Greek translations to express Hebrew ideas in his preaching to the Gentiles. Then as time went on and the Christians realized that their first hopes of Christ's soon reappearing on earth to set up a kingdom were mistaken, they became less antagonistic toward their pagan neighbours and more willing to try to work out a reasoned statement of beliefs that would appeal to intellectuals. As early as a century after the crucifixion there were those who set about proving that Christianity was not a danger to the Roman Empire.

Finally, from the Romans came a magnificent organization: the Empire. The church modelled its administrative units on Roman political subdivisions, and in time the successors of St. Peter, the bishops of Rome, came to exercise a certain authority so that the church, like the Empire, had its chain of command and carefully linked administrations. No other religion could boast such a complete and efficient organization. Moreover, in the beginning Rome had allowed a reasonable amount of religious toleration, and—more important—had provided a single state which facilitated ease of communication. It has been said that travel in the 2nd century A.D. was safer, more rapid, and more comfortable than it was to be again until the age of steamships and railways.

Thus in four short centuries a remarkable thing had happened. Who could have predicted that when "a decree went out from Caesar Augustus that all the world should be taxed," ensuing events, like the everyday occurrence of the birth of a baby, would raise up a force mightier than all of Caesar's legions?

CHAPTER 31

Chaos in the West

. . . who could believe that Rome on her own soil fights no longer for her glory, but for her existence, and no longer even fights, but purchases her life with gold and precious things?

ST. JEROME

In the 2nd century the Empire appeared to be thriving, but already there were signs of strain. Cities were beginning to go downhill economically, taxes mounted, epidemics raged, famines were widespread. And still the expenses of the state mounted. Marcus Aurelius was even forced to auction the crown jewels to raise war funds. A long decline had set in that was to last from 180 to 476.

❖ *Stress and Strain* With the 3rd century, military absolutism triumphed. The army made and unmade a bewildering succession of brutal "Barracks Emperors." In a series of twenty-six emperors only one died a natural death. The ruling emperor in the year 260 faced no fewer than eighteen rivals. Blood drenched the Roman Peace.

So depleted had the legions become in these dark days that the emperors had even begun to hire Germans and Persians to do their fighting for them. The imperial government imposed crushing burdens on an already impoverished middle class, and town councils were ordered to pay up back taxes on deserted farms. Municipal offices had to be forced on unwilling citizens. "Shall I have to be a member of the local council?" was a stock question put to an oracle in these years.

Diocletian   Temporary relief came with Diocletian and Constantine in the late 3rd and early 4th centuries. It was Diocletian who divided the Empire into two parts, the East and the West. This scheme, however, did not work well, and on his abdication after he had suffered a stroke in 305

Constantine   civil war raged. In 306 Constantine was proclaimed emperor by his troops in Britain; but it was to take him another sixteen years to become sole ruler. In the course of his campaigns he won his most memorable victory near Rome at the Milvian Bridge in 312. According to a contemporary historian, on a day sometime before the battle, "about the hour of noon . . . the Emperor had seen with his own eyes, so he said, the victorious emblem of the Cross formed out of light, up in the sky above the

sun, and near it the words: 'Through this sign you will conquer.' "
Though he was not baptized a Christian until he lay on his deathbed a
quarter of a century later, there can be little doubt that Constantine was
a believer from that epoch-making day when his troops went forth to
battle with the name of Christ emblazoned on their shields.

Once he had made himself supreme in the Empire, this outstanding
general, administrator, and legislator became more and more like an
Oriental monarch and less and less like a Roman emperor. Henceforth
he was not *Princeps,* First Citizen, but *Dominus,* absolute lord and
master, and those granted audiences had to kiss the hem of his robe.
The army was increased to 650,000, many warriors from barbarian
tribes being hired along the frontier to replenish ebbing voluntary manpower. Wages were controlled and price ceilings set, with death the
penalty for evasion, although it proved impossible to enforce these
regulations.

Such recovery as there was under Diocletian and Constantine was *Byzantium*
bought at too high a price. The state controlled everything; the state
was absolute. Most significant of all, in 330 Constantine transferred
his capital from Rome to Byzantium, to that New Rome he called
"Constantinople." There were at least three reasons for this move.
First of all there was the need for a headquarters from which it would
be more convenient to direct the defence of the eastern frontiers. Then
there was the indisputable fact that Byzantium, not Rome, lay at the
heart of that day's civilization—at the commercial crossroads of the
East. And finally, the East was the birthplace of Christianity. Constantine probably wanted to establish a Christian capital, as well as to
be free to build up his absolute power. At Byzantium, hundreds of
miles away from the old pagan Roman aristocracy, both of these aims
could be realized.

And so the capital was moved. The Empire remained united in
theory, but the final split between the West and the East had begun.

❖ *The Gate Is Forced* After Constantine's death civil war festered in
the Empire for sixteen years. Even more serious, however, was the fact
that the Mongolian Huns were now on the move westward, pushing
other barbarians before them as they came. These fierce Orientals inspired sheer terror in all who lay in their path. Here is what they were
like according to Gothic and Roman historians of the time.

They have . . . a shapeless lump rather than a head, and pinholes rather than
eyes. They are short in stature, broad-shouldered . . . and have large, thick

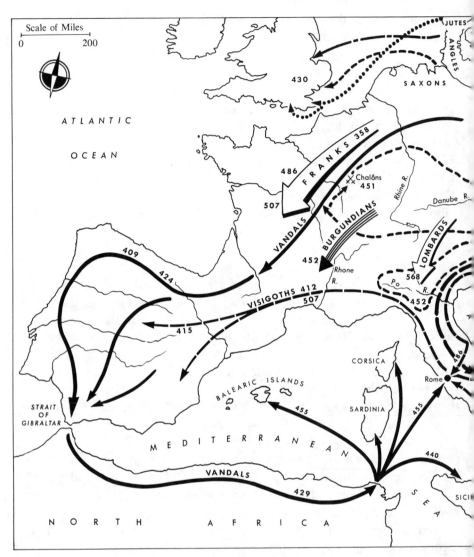

necks, always stretched in pride. Their limbs are compact and strong; they are quick in bodily movement, and bow-legged so that you might imagine them to be beasts with two legs. At birth the faces of male children are disfigured with a sword. They grow up, therefore, with no comeliness, a stunted and foul race, scarcely human, their very language having little resemblance to human speech. . . . They never shelter themselves under roofed houses and have no settled abode, but are homeless and lawless, perpetually wandering with their wagons, which they make their homes. . . . They wear . . . garments of the skins of field-mice . . . and a sort of helmet made of the skins of wild-rats patched together. . . . After a tunic is once put around their necks, how-

314/ROME

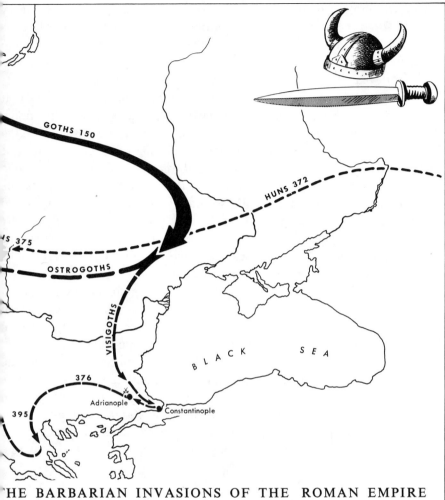

GOTHS 150

HUNS 372

~S 375

OSTROGOTHS

VISIGOTHS

376

Adrianople

Constantinople

395

B L A C K   S E A

THE BARBARIAN INVASIONS OF THE ROMAN EMPIRE
IN THE 4TH AND 5TH CENTURIES

ever worn it becomes, it is never taken off or changed until, from long decay,
it becomes so ragged as to fall to pieces. . . . There is not a person who cannot
remain on his horse day and night. . . . These men, in short, live in the form
of humans, but with the savagery of beasts.

The first to be swallowed up by the Huns were the Ostrogoths (East
Goths), who lived north of the Black Sea. Terrified, their neighbours
the Visigoths (West Goths), north of the Danube, now desperately petitioned the Roman emperor to be allowed to cross the Danube and

settle within the Empire. Their very desperation made it clear that they would force the frontier if their petition were refused. And so it was granted. For days they passed before the wondering gaze of the Roman outposts, men, women, children, cattle, on rafts, in canoes, some hanging on to planks or barrels—an entire people on the move.

Adrianople   The Romans now had a new nation on their hands, a people that could not be dispersed but would have to be allowed to settle down under their own king and their own laws. To give the Visigothic king a place in the imperial administration the Romans proclaimed him one of their own generals. But the Visigoths were treacherously mistreated by their hosts, and eventually turned on them. In a surprise attack the barbarian cavalry conquered the Roman infantry at Adrianople, and both the Emperor Valens (364-378) and his army of the East were destroyed. The gate had been forced open. The barbarians whom the Romans had been holding back for centuries on the Rhine-Danube frontier finally burst in upon the Empire.

Before these mass invasions occurred, however an insidious infiltration had been taking place. For some time barbarians had been hired as mercenaries by Rome to bolster up the armies for which her own citizens would no longer volunteer. These Germanic troops often served under their own kings or generals, so that they formed virtually private armies within the Roman ranks. And should their leader be killed, they were as often tempted to fight against Rome as for her. Thus though Rome's armed forces may have totalled some 400,000 troops as contrasted with the largest opposing German tribal army of 40,000, the Roman armies were spread thin along the frontiers and their loyalty was, in many cases, highly dubious.

Valens' successor, the Emperor Theodosius the Great, did manage for a while to buy peace at a heavy price. The Goths were settled within the Empire, but as self-governing allies who, for pay, would furnish troops for Rome's army. And although Theodosius finally succeeded in controlling the whole Empire, when he died the next year it split apart for good.

❖ *The Final Collapse*   Upon Theodosius' death the Visigothic prince, *Alaric*   Alaric, felt that he was being cheated out of what he had assumed would be his place in the Empire. Enraged and humiliated, he ravaged Thrace and marched to the very walls of Constantinople. There he was bought off by the title of commander of the army and told to move westward into the rugged Balkan country of Illyria. But Italy was too tantalizingly near. In 410, for the first time since the Gallic invasion of the 4th century B.C., barbarians entered Rome as Alaric and his hordes pillaged that great city. In far away Bethlehem a Roman-educated monk mourned the shattered capital: "The lamp of the world is extinguished, and it is the whole world which has perished in the ruins of this one city."

Alaric marched south, but died shortly afterwards. Eventually his people settled down in Spain, forcing another Germanic group, the Vandals, to migrate to North Africa. These Vandals preyed on Mediterranean shipping and even made a famous raid on Rome in 455. For two weeks they sacked the city—an act of vandalism which history has never forgotten. *The Vandals*

Meanwhile the pressure that began this whole juggling of nations, the migrations of the Huns, continued. Steadily, relentlessly they swept westward under their mighty leader Attila (434-453), "the Scourge of God." He was, says a historian of the time, *Attila*

. . a man born to shake the races of the world, a terror to all lands, who in some way or other frightened everyone by the dread report noised abroad about him, for he was haughty in his carriage, casting his eyes about him on all sides so that the proud man's power was to be seen in the very movements of his body. A lover of war, he was personally restrained in action, most impressive in counsel, gracious to suppliants, and generous to those to whom he had once given his trust. He was short of stature with a broad chest, massive head, and small eyes. His beard was thin and sprinkled with grey, his nose flat, and his complexion swarthy, showing thus the signs of his origins.

Attila forced the East Roman emperor to pay a large sum of gold and promise an annual tribute before he would move on westward. Finally, however, the Hun chieftain was checked in Gaul in the summer of 451 at the battle of Chalôns near Troyes and turned his hordes southward into Italy. Here Pope Leo I managed to persuade him to withdraw without attacking Rome—doubtless partly because the Huns were suffering from disease and famine at the time. Actually, despite the terror it instilled, the Hunnish menace had already passed its peak by Attila's day, so much so that when he died in 453 his "empire" fell to bits. Fierce though their sudden ravages had been, the Huns had, in point of fact, never been a very serious threat to European civilization.

The Huns might depart, but Germanic barbarians remained in Italy. Just as their cousins to the north, the Franks and Anglo-Saxons, had established kingdoms for themselves during these years, so in Italy it was the barbarians who were the real rulers. Those who control the army control the state, and it was now barbarian generals who, by

The Huns, whose strange Oriental features struck such terror into their Roman foes, probably looked much like the modern, nomadic Mongols pictured here. The early Mongoloids have been described by a contemporary Roman historian as people who "never shelter themselves under roofed houses, but avoid them as people ordinarily avoid sepulchres . . .; in fact they seem to be a people always in flight."

commanding the barbarian troops that Rome had hired to fight for her, called the tune. Little was left of Rome's greatness. When in 476 a German, Odoacer, became ruler of West Rome in place of a Roman youth, the Western Roman Empire had ended in all but name.

From that day to this historians have asked why it happened.

❖ *Seeds of Destruction*   In the last quarter of the 18th century one of the most famous English historians, Edward Gibbon, wrote his *History of the Decline and Fall of the Roman Empire* in six fat volumes. He was only one, though the best known, of many who have tried to puzzle out the reasons for Rome's fall.

For such a complex and controversial subject as the decline of this mighty empire it is natural that many explanations should be suggested.

One of the persistent themes in Rome's long story is the failure of the government to control the army. The rivalry of the great soldiers of the late Republic led inexorably to the fateful days when the troops themselves made and unmade emperors. Was this trend towards military dictatorship caused by Roman imperialism? Did her very rise cause her to fall?

In a sense it did. Rome eventually held a world empire, yet Rome herself had only a city-state government. When this comparatively elementary type of administration broke down under the weight of empire, the Republic gave way to the military dictatorship of one man. Imperialism cost Romans their republican institutions. And unfortunately the new citizens that Rome acquired through her Empire were less than eager to serve in the army. They preferred to enjoy the fruits of their new status in peaceful pursuits.

For a time the army had been recruited largely from the provinces, where the provincials were tempted by the offer of citizenship on enlistment. But, ironically enough, when the Emperor Caracalla (211-217) ultimately granted citizenship to all freeborn men within the Empire in 212, the chief inducement for enlistment, at least for the better class of men, was removed. At the same time a marked decline in the population of the Empire (from 70 to 50 million) aggravated the problem of obtaining recruits.

It is not surprising, then, to find a Roman historian of the 3rd century writing that the army was coming to consist of those "most vigorous and violent elements who are usually obliged to make a living by banditry." The once proud Roman army began to look like a collection of thugs, making and unmaking "Barracks Emperors." The inferior Roman armies, riddled with foreign mercenaries, must have been regarded with increasing contempt by the hardy barbarians watching and waiting across the frontiers.

Another basic factor in Rome's decline was her failure to industrialize her economy, and thus keep it expanding along with her Empire. We have seen how Romans were a very practical people, given to action rather than theory, to oratory rather than invention. Their education was lopsided; undue emphasis on rhetoric aimed at producing lawyers, administrators, and more teachers of rhetoric. Indeed, the man who worked with his hands was looked down upon. "All mechanics," sneered Cicero, echoing Aristotle, "are engaged in vulgar trades; for no workshop can have anything liberal about it." Perhaps it is not so surprising that no Roman ever, for instance, invented an efficient system of harnessing horses, or made the logical transition from stamping coins in a mint to inventing a printing press. He would probably not have been hailed as a hero if he had.

At first, then, the Romans relied on their slaves instead of inventing machines—a demoralizing and crippling situation which helped strangle the economy. When the supply of slaves declined after the wars of the Republic and the use of freed labour increased, an odd thing happened. Instead of setting up large factories and instituting their own industrial revolution, the Romans simply exported their industries rather than their products. That is, industries moved from the cities out to the villages or large country estates where workers and raw materials were more plentiful. The result was that trade became local rather than international— again a stifling influence on the economy. Then too, capitalists now invested heavily in land and parcelled out their vast country estates to tenant farmers who paid rent in produce and managed a bare existence on these self-sufficient "manors." Such a system hardly encouraged personal initiative, the life-blood of a healthy economy.

Finally, even if the Romans had been technically capable of an industrial revolution the masses within the Empire were too poor to purchase enough goods to stimulate a machine industry. The coinage was increasingly debased; heavier taxation hindered rather than helped recovery; and large western landowners, who were the high imperial officials, made matters worse by granting their own class certain tax exemptions. It was a vicious circle. The more expensive the Empire became the more repressive and hence the more complicated and expensive the machinery of government had to be to grind out the needed taxes.

One last question remains. Why did the Western Empire collapse while the Eastern one survived?

The survival of the East Roman Empire

First, the East was able to recruit citizen armies from the stalwart hillsmen of Asia Minor whereas, as we have seen, the western army came to be made up largely of toughs and barbarians of questionable loyalty. Secondly, in the East senior officials were often middle-class lawyers who did not play favourites, whereas the high imperial officials of the West exempted their own class from taxes. Perhaps most important, while some of the richest areas of the East—Asia Minor, Syria, and Egypt—were virtually sealed off from invasion, the lush farmlands of Gaul and the Po valley were easily accessible to marauding tribes. And when the West had its strongest members—Africa, Spain, and Gaul—systematically lopped off one after another by the barbarians, only impoverished Italy remained, woefully lacking in both manpower and natural resources.

The unkindest cut of all was that the East used its reservoirs of men and money to shove and bribe the barbarians westward. The West, therefore, could not escape the brunt of the invasions, and the disintegration of the Western Empire is hardly to be wondered at.

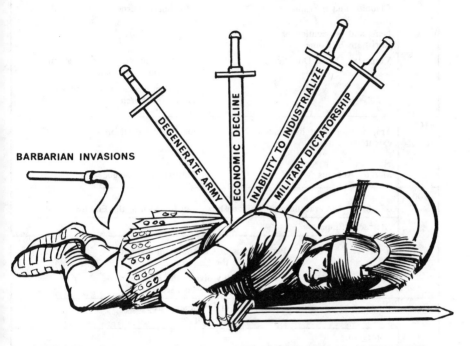

DEATH OF THE WESTERN ROMAN EMPIRE

TIME CHART FOR ROMAN EMPIRE

	WEST	EAST
27 B.C.	Octavian given the title Augustus	
A.D.	Tiberius	Crucifixion of Jesus of Nazareth
	Caligula	
	Claudius and invasion of Britain	Missionary journeys of Paul and others
	Nero and persecution of Christians in Rome	
	Vespasian, Titus, Domitian	Jewish revolt culminating in Roman destruction of Jerusalem
		Jerusalem ceases to be centre of Christian Church
100	Trajan; Empire at its greatest extent	Dacian and Parthian Wars
	Hadrian	
	Marcus Aurelius	Parthian War; plague
200	Caracalla grants citizenship to all freeborn of the Empire	
	"Barracks Emperors"	
	Persecutions of Christians throughout the Empire	
	Diocletian formally divides the Empire into Western and Eastern sections	
300	Persecutions of Christians throughout the Empire	
	Constantine	
	Victory of the Milvian Bridge followed by toleration of Christianity throughout the Empire	
	Constantine reunites Empire and founds new capital at Constantinople	
		Romans defeated at Adrianople
	Empire permanently divided after death of Theodosius the Great	
400	Romans evacuate Britain	East Roman Empire manages to shove and bribe the barbarians to the West and so survives
	Visigoths sack Rome and establish kingdom in Spain	
	Huns under Attila invade Italy	
	Vandals establish kingdom in N. Africa and sack Rome	
476	Odoacer rules Italy on behalf of Emperor at Constantinople	

CHAPTER 32

A Day in the Life of a Roman Matron

To hunt, to play, to laugh, this is to live.

INSCRIPTION FROM THE ROMAN CITY OF TIMGAD, NORTH AFRICA

It was past time to get up: the first streaks of dawn had reddened the sky. Yet the figure in bed did not move. The late feasting the night before had left Racilia glutted and weary, and besides there was something—something she could not remember—that she dreaded, and it seemed safer to stay in bed.

The room was almost totally dark, which was just as well since our worthy matron's face was smeared with a paste of flour and milk and she was hardly a thing of beauty. The shutters remained closed tight against the bright rays of the morning sun, as well as against a host of mosquitoes. Because glass was still rare and expensive, Romans had to choose semi-darkness if they were to shut out the scorching sun of summer or the damp cold and rain of winter. Such cracks of light as ventured in revealed a typical Roman room, scantily furnished and the very antithesis of cosiness. Even the bed of this rich Roman lady left much to be desired in comfort. Set high in a kind of niche, it had a raised foot and head and was provided with a stuffed wool mattress, pillows, and coverlets. There was a footstool by it to help one climb up, but no easy chair: the Romans did not possess such a thing. Nor did this second floor boudoir boast a basin with taps. Romans had no running water on their second floors. After all, with twenty or so slaves in the household to fetch water, what need was there for it?

Racilia moved to climb down from her lofty perch, but as she sat up she felt suddenly sick. It had been quite a banquet—an ostentatious affair provided by one of the newly-rich merchants of Pompeii. And in this bustling metropolis (a third-rate town, the snobbish citizens of Rome would remind you) there were many newcomers to wealth, for the city boasted a thriving textile industry, salt works, mineral baths, and a copious production of wine, the most excellent fish-sauce in the Empire, and all the products of their famous market gardens—fruit, vegetables, especially cabbage, and of course the all-important olive.

Racilia lay back on her pillows to let the nausea subside. No wonder she felt sick. The banquet had gone on from mid-afternoon until midnight and had included everything from eggs to apples (or, as we would say, from soup to nuts). In fact it had turned into one of those disgusting orgies of which Seneca had written scornfully that Romans "ate to vomit and vomited to eat"—literally. Racilia had not been as gluttonous as some, but even so the menu prepared by Publius' high-priced chef had been enough to challenge any digestive system. Although private Roman dinners were often light and simple, the usual three-course formal feast consisted of appetizers (such as fresh oysters, onions, lettuce, and invariably eggs with piquant sauces), dinner proper (several courses of fish, meat—usually the Roman favourite, pork—fowls, and vegetables), and dessert (pastry, sweets, nuts, and fruits such as apples). Wine was served with each course, and just before dessert everyone paused in silence while wine, salt, and meal were offered to the household *lares*. Finally, when the feasting was ended, the guests lingered for hours at the ceremonial drinking match, all of them garlanded with flowers in the ancient belief that they would thereby delay the effects of intoxication.

No "usual" feast would satisfy the vain Publius. He was determined to impress his visitors—although he was known to be mean, and was one of those who made a practice of providing much poorer fare for any humbler guests who might be present. His sideboard last night had displayed his most ornate silver; his dining couches were the most elegant in Pompeii; his guests' hands were washed between courses with wine instead of water; and he served so many courses that Racilia lost count. There were fresh fish, caught, he was proud to tell you, from his own privately stocked pond just an hour before, and such exotic dishes as peacocks garnished with their gorgeous plumes, livers of fish, tongues of songbirds, plus those favourite Roman delicacies, roasted dormice. The guests were duly appreciative. They belched loudly to show their enjoyment, and applauded enthusiastically when the clowns and Spanish dancers provided after-dinner entertainment.

Racilia clasped her aching head at the memory of it all. The laughter had become more and more boisterous, especially since the guest of honour, Marcus Casellius, had brought along a "shadow," an uninvited guest whose role it was to laugh at Marcus's jokes and flatter him. This he did not wisely but too well. The conversation seemed to centre around the chariot races at Pompeii's mighty amphitheatre (built to hold the city's 20,000 inhabitants), and two of the matrons had betrayed, quite unashamedly, more than a passing interest in their favourite charioteers, the matinée idols of that day. Many of these slaves eventually earned their freedom and acquired great riches. The male guests, too, were interested in this conversation—but for different reasons. Romans loved to gamble, and these rich playboys would stake a fortune (and the freedman his last *denarius*) on a chariot race or a gladiatorial combat. As for Racilia, she did not admit even to herself how eagerly she listened for any mention of a certain gladiator, Actius, known throughout the city as "the answer to a maiden's prayer."

Suddenly Racilia felt very much annoyed with that sedate husband of hers, Caius Sallustius. Like many a multiple divorcee, she looked back through rose-coloured glasses to her first two husbands, especially the one to whom she had first plighted her troth seventeen years ago. In the old days of the Republic marriage was a very solemn, very religious affair. Racilia's had been arranged for her by her parents, but she had also been deeply in love—or so she thought—with her fiancé. They had been betrothed in front of witnesses, and Marcus had given her an engagement ring of iron and gold which she immediately slipped on the third finger of her left hand, that finger which every Roman believed to be connected with the heart by a delicate nerve. Racilia had been only fourteen (two years over the minimum age for marriage for a girl; once she had reached the ripe old age of 19 all hope of a husband was gone), and her betrothed 17, only one year over the male minimum marriage age. But then Marcus was very mature. He had exchanged his crimson bordered toga for the white *toga virilis* and cut off his long flowing hair at the age of 14. Henceforth he was considered a responsible Roman citizen, even though his education was not finished (Romans were only half through their education at an age when many Greeks had completed theirs) and he had yet to go off to acquire further learning in Athens.

Little did Racilia realize what a difference her wedding day would make in her life. She remembered how lovely her mother had looked in a pale green tunic of finest Egyptian linen fastened with gorgeous brooches and a gold belt, her arms and ankles adorned with bracelets. She remembered Uncle Sextus (who, like Racilia herself, had a passion for jewellery) sporting on his knuckle an official seal ring so large that a satirist had advised him to wear it on his leg! She remembered Marcus, Marcus with a wreath of flowers in his hair, so young and so dignified in his white toga, that peculiar garment which no other people at no other time had ever worn. It marked Romans out, said Virgil, as "lords

of the world, the race that wears the toga." And she remembered her
father, looking a little sadly at this mischievous daughter of his who had
so suddenly grown up. For with marriage the Roman daughter left her
family, her home, and the household gods and the spirits of her ancestors, and exchanged all these for those of her husband. It was a serious
and, we would hope, a final step.

Racilia herself had been a vision of loveliness in her old-fashioned
straight white tunic with a woollen sash, her saffron coloured cloak, and
her matching yellow shoes. Her hair, an unusually beautiful mass of
auburn curls, had been combed into six locks separated by ribbons, and
over it her veil fell softly, modestly, a flaming orange mist held in place
by orange blossoms. The wedding ceremony began in the atrium with
a sacrifice to the gods, after which the animal's entrails were examined
and the auspices declared favourable. Solemnly, shyly, the young couple
joined hands and repeated together *"Ubi tu Gaius, ego Gaia"* ("Where

you are Gaius, I am Gaia"—"Whither thou goest I will go"), and then the joyful babble of congratulations burst upon them. The wedding feast, provided by Racilia's parents, was a happy occasion which ended with the distribution among the guests of the wedding cake, after which the young couple received presents from everyone. Even Racilia's poor old nurse, like all the family slaves, was expected to give her young mistress some token out of her meagre savings toward freedom. Then it was nightfall and Marcus had, following tradition, playfully torn Racilia from her mother's embrace. It was a gay wedding procession that wended its way to their new home, the flute-players tootling and the torch-bearers grinning and the crowd cheering as the groom scattered nuts among them.

Soon it was all over. Marcus had carried Racilia over the threshold, the crowd had been shut out, and the invited guests watched Marcus offer fire and water to his new wife in token of the life they were to live together. Then the bride kindled the fire on the hearth of her new home and, amidst much scuffling and hilarity, tossed the marriage torch—the Roman "bride's bouquet"—to the guests. After the laughter subsided the bride recited her prayer, and the guests departed leaving the young couple alone. Racilia had become a Roman matron.

How unlike her stay-at-home Greek cousins was this independent young woman! She lacked formal education only because she usually married too young to make it worthwhile. But her mother had taught her, along with her brothers, to speak Latin correctly and do elementary reading, writing, and arithmetic; and when the boys were seven years old and went on to regular school Racilia was launched on her training in home management. She learned to spin a little, to weave and sew a little, in preparation for this day when she would become a Roman matron, the most dignified position held by any women of any race in the ancient world. But most of all she observed how her mother directed the many slaves in their duties. For things had changed since the days of the Republic. Then Roman women had had a great deal of real work to do; but now manual labour had come to be considered dishonourable. Aristocratic Romans had become too wealthy and too dependent on slaves.

Racilia was to find this was the case even more so in her generation. She needed to do no real housework: the steward took charge of that. She never did the household marketing: her husband or a slave looked after that. She probably would not even rear her own children: a slave nurse and tutor assumed that precious duty. What, then, was left for her to do? She might become an intellectual and immerse herself in studies. But she observed that such matrons were scarcely popular among the male population—and they were considered a positive menace to motherhood. Little did they deserve gifts from their families when the first day of March brought around *Matronalia* (Mother's Day). Nor could the society matron enter most feminine professions: the seamstress, the hairdresser, the midwife, the nurse, all these came from the lower classes. There were, however, some occupations open. Women were forbidden to engage in banking operations, but some delighted in taking part in legal frays and politics, and many a one was an astute business magnate. Racilia's closest friend, Julia Felix, rented premises in a section quite near the amphitheatre. Indeed, she had just posted a new notice there which read, "To let, in the property of Julia Felix, shops with rooms above, baths fit for Venus, a first floor."

Racilia, then, entered matrimony with all the proper training. But from the beginning something had gone wrong. Perhaps the evil eye had been on her and Marcus. There had been several signs of bad luck on the very day of the marriage: Marcus's little brother had upset a bottle of oil, and, even worse than that, Uncle Sextus had been so unlucky as to sneeze at the very moment a dish was being offered to him—a very bad sign. Worse still, the poor old gentleman had stumbled over the door-sill on his way out. *Had* an evil spell been cast over their new household?

It would seem so. They had been married on February 4, well in advance of the Memorial Days from February 13 to 21 when weddings were forbidden. But the very next day all the gods of the universe seemed to conspire to show their displeasure with them. Just as the newly-weds had begun their lunch a ghastly noise was heard. The sun still shone brightly, the breezes were benign and fresh, but the couches in the dining room were sliding across the floor, the plaster on the walls was cracking, and there was a tremendous thundering roar. Just in time, Marcus seized his dazed bride's hand and rushed her out of doors. A split second later the candelabra (a heavy stand holding half a dozen little oil lamps) crashed down just where Racilia had been reclining. The furniture rattled around as if a giant hand were shaking it, and then the roof crumpled and the house collapsed like a deck of cards. The seas bucked and churned. Floods broke loose. All was havoc. Stunned, the young couple left Pompeii for Rome, where earthquakes could not follow.

But Rome, with its clamouring plebs, its worldly, immoral social sets, its wild banquets, its many religious sects, and above all its sickening, bloodthirsty spectacles where man murdered man and beast, and beasts tore to pieces beasts and men—all this proved too much for Racilia. From being a sheltered child she was suddenly thrust into a world of temptation, of licentious theatre shows, of endless holidays with wild gambling and brutal exhibitions. She became one of the smart set who dined out almost nightly; she dabbled in current politics and affected an overwhelming passion for Greek and Latin poetry; she could not be bothered with her two children and virtually handed them over to a Greek slave; and finally she could not be bothered with her husband either. In a time when there was a real epidemic of divorce the disease was easy to catch. In five years she was divorced twice.

And then she met Caius Sallustius, a man twice her age. She had so depleted her own dowry and inheritances that this sedate Roman magistrate, a trusted Pompeiian banker whose honest practice of lending out money at 2% interest had gained him a gradual fortune, looked like a safe bet for a secure marriage. Perhaps, too, she was homesick for that small town where she had grown up, a town blessed by long summers and balmy breezes—a far cry from the terrific hubbub of the crowded Roman streets where her slaves could hardly make their way with her litter, so jostled were they by beggars, spattered by horseback riders, and trod upon by the hobnail boots of platoons of soldiers. Nor did the noise stop at dusk, for only then were carts allowed on the streets, and all night long pedlars' and merchants' wagons rumbled through Rome. Somehow, after all this, the earthquake seventeen years ago seemed almost unimportant.

At the thought of that earthquake Racilia sat bolt upright. *Now* she remembered why she had this sense of foreboding, and the feeling gave way to relief. Four days ago she and Caius had nearly repeated the flight she and Marcus had made when the old dreaded roaring once again was heard, the ground shook, cracks appeared in the plaster, and the sea billowed and foamed. It had been the climax to a succession of slight tremors which had started six weeks after Titus, that charming and beloved emperor, had ascended the throne. Caius, who had spent the best years of his life helping repair the ravages of the first quake in A.D. 63, had thought it wise to order the shops which he leased on the front and side walls of his house (he might disdain tradesmen, but not their money!) to be closed, and to move out to his country villa for a

"Then he would stroll over to the Forum to chat with the tradesmen working on the thresholds of their open-air shops. . . ."

couple of days. But now, praise be to Venus the patron goddess of Pompeii, things had settled down again; so they had returned to their city residence. Caius was anxious to get back. Much was expected of the official class in imperial days, and he had a great deal to do regarding a temple which he planned to build as a gift to the Pompeiians.

How good it was on this morning of the 24th of August, A.D. 79, to feel the countryside at peace and the sun, as Racilia found on opening the shutters, shining brightly. The sea was blue and Mount Vesuvius was a kindly blob of mauve on the horizon. Only the birds were strangely quiet, the dogs were apt to bark without any apparent reason, and cattle lowed and strained against their chains. "Perhaps we'll have a hail storm some time today," thought Racilia. At any rate, she was profoundly glad that the tremors had ceased. She did not care to have another house fall down around her ears!

It was only a matter of moments until Racilia had dressed—a simple process for the Romans, since they wore their tunics to bed and hence

had only to slip on some sandals to be fully clothed. Nor was any prolonged washing necessary. She, like Caius, would later be going to the Stabian Thermae (baths) where there was a smaller women's quarters along with the men's. All Racilia had to do, then, was have a slave wash the flour off her face (while her parrot saucily squawked "Pretty girl!"), clean her teeth with powdered pumice stone and rinse off her false ones of special cement paste, and she was ready for her breakfast. All she could face this morning was a glass of water, although sometimes she joined Caius for bread dipped in wine or eaten with honey or cheese.

At this point there was a brisk rap on her door, and an army of slaves descended upon the room with buckets, cloths, ladders, and sponge mops, while another crew set the dust flying with feather dusters and green palm brooms. Sawdust was scattered on the floor and swept up again, all of this accomplished under the eagle eye of Caius's trusted steward, Simonides. Tonight there were to be important guests, and this beautiful mansion with its shining marble and glowing frescoes must be spotless.

The human vacuum cleaners hustled on to the next room, one encouraged by a smart clout, and Racilia was ready to summon her servants for the main occupation of every morning: her beautification and costuming. First came Nerissa, her favourite maid whom she had picked up as a bargain one day at the slave market in the Forum. Racilia had taken good care to have poor Nerissa trotted about, naked, at the end of her chain, while she pinched and prodded her to make sure she was making a good purchase. Nerissa was an Egyptian who was especially deft at making up her mistress's face. And Racilia was a kind mistress. Seldom did she need to have Nerissa whipped to ensure her complete devotion.

Nerissa scuttled about noiselessly getting out the wash-basins, mirrors, combs, pins, brooches, unguents, and dyes, to say nothing of switches of false hair and the numerous straight hairpins that were so difficult to keep in. Then came the hairdresser, Archias, a handsome Greek who skilfully heaped Racilia's hair up to make her look taller, and mercilessly pulled out the gray hairs which kept relentlessly appearing of late. Next she was painted—white on brow and arms, red on cheeks and lips, black on eyebrows and round the eyes. It was quite a business—and to think all these pots would have to be taken to the baths and the whole procedure repeated later on in the day! Finally Racilia was advised regarding a choice of jewellery and assisted on with her long upper tunic, the sign of her exalted rank, a brilliantly embroidered garment of finest blue linen. With a diadem fixed in her hair and a multicoloured shawl around her shoulders she called for her serving-maid to inquire if it was too windy for her green parasol (it was not collapsible). The sun was hot, and she intended to stroll down to the Forum and visit the dressmakers' shops, perhaps to pick up some ready-made garments, or the novelty shops to look at some of the new mirrors made of glass with lead (not mercury) backing.

Racilia bade goodbye to her husband and paused a moment to enjoy the mass of colour in their garden before going out the front gate. Caius was in the atrium interviewing the last of a horde of clients, those hangers-on whom the upper class Roman considered essential for his prestige. He handed out a cast-off toga to one, an invitation to another, and money to most of the others. Then he made his way—accompanied, as was expected of any important citizen, by a train of slaves and clients —to his own private torture chamber, the barber's. So agonizing could the hours spent under a rude iron razor be that some men had their beards plucked, and still others resorted to depilatory methods. Pliny the Elder recommended spiders' webs soaked in oil and vinegar to stop bleeding!

Once Caius had survived the lengthy ordeal he intended to proceed to the fuller's to have his togas cleaned and blocked, an expensive but necessary process for these heavy white garments. Then he would stroll over to the Forum to chat with the tradesmen working on the thresholds of their open-air shops, to gamble a bit, and most of all to discuss the recent elections. Elections were always a subject for avid conversation. Pompeiians waged violent electoral campaigns. The porters, muleteers, and bath-stokers supported their candidates as vehemently as did the members of the powerful trade guilds, the fullers, physicians, bakers, and innkeepers. The Forum walls still blazed with election slogans which would presently be whitewashed over to make way for new advertisements and notices.

Caius was not pleased with the election. He was part of the small minority of rich and influential citizens who were used to monopolizing the administration of municipal affairs. But slowly and surely the newly-rich were pushing their way into the aristocrat's jealous preserve. Who would have thought Caius would live to see the day when a fuller would be elected duumvir? Yet the support of his fellow tradesmen, the most active and important group of workers in Pompeii, had won Marcus Vesonius Primus this office.

Racilia, too, was making her way to the Forum with her retinue of maids, one to hold her parasol over her head, one to fan her with peacock feathers, one to clear the way. Carefully she crossed over the huge stepping-stones so necessary in a climate where torrential downpours were apt to flood the streets, or street-cleaning slave crews might come along to slosh water all over the paving stones. As she left the narrow (10 foot) one-way street for the broad main thoroughfare she bumped into her friend Julia, and they fell to discussing two items of interest: a newsletter which Julia had received from Rome (Racilia made a mental note that she must get her husband to subscribe to this Roman substitute for a newspaper), and the ultra-modern baths now under construction. How luxurious this new clubhouse of the Romans was to be, with games and lecture rooms, drawing-rooms for conversation, a library, and a restaurant. Its many windows would make it so much lighter than the old Stabian Thermae. And although Romans as a whole despised professional athletes, here even she and Julia would be able to don tights or a tunic and roll metal hoops or swing dumb-bells.

It was just past noon, and Racilia must go home for lunch. No respectable women would visit the snack bars so temptingly near. As she turned to go she noticed a theatre poster announcing the performance of a tragedy of Seneca's by a group of actors from Rome. Awnings would be used, it said, and there would be sprinklings of perfumed water on the audience—how delightful! The walls of the houses she passed were covered with scrawled messages, for everyone in Pompeii, it seems, could read and write. She smiled to herself as she noticed such pieces of nonsense as "Everyone writes on the walls but me," or the couplet

> I wonder, O wall, that your stones do not fall,
> So scribbled upon by the nonsense of all.

Some residents resented their walls being used for electioneering: "Painter, I beg of you not to write anything here; if you inscribe a candidate's name, may he fail in the elections and be excluded from all office." But who, thought Racilia, could resist a lover who wrote "Hail, Victoria. May you, where'er you go, sneeze merrily!" Racilia laughed out loud. How beautiful the day was! How busy the hot drink stands, the taverns, the bakeries, the market stalls were! How good life was!

Suddenly she stopped, transfixed, her hands stretched out in horror as a thunderclap resounded that seemed to rend the very heavens. Everyone stood rooted to the ground, but all eyes turned towards one object: Vesuvius. Fiendishly it spewed out a great mouthful of fire, then belched forth a cloud of smoke which blotted out the sun. More crashes came, and with them, as from nowhere but from everywhere, a bruising rain of stones, some the size of tennis balls, some huge and crushing. Then complete blackness descended, pierced now and then by a flash of lightning.

A bird, stunned by a stone, struck Racilia as it fell. The shock seemed to give wings to her feet, and she turned to her three maids. "Run, Nerissa! Run, Psecas! Run, run, run!" She could hear herself screaming hysterically as she joined the mob in a frantic race for the west of Pompeii, where lay the Gate of Herculaneum and their beautiful villa on Mercury Street. If she could only force her way through this sea of humanity to her home, Caius—kindly, steady Caius—would help her escape. But her jewels! Her beautiful jewels! She must take them with her.

Somehow, amidst the screaming, praying, clutching mob of men and animals (anything that could be ridden was in motion) the four women reached the villa. But—her heart sank—Caius was not there. The jewels, and then escape! Nerissa found a torch and the four women began feverishly to gather them up. There was not much time. A fine ash mixed with rain was fast blocking up the doorways, and sulphur fumes stung the eyes and clawed at the throat. "Come! Leave the rest!" cried Racilia, and out into the street they plunged again, floundering now in drifts of ash up to six feet high. Heavier and heavier it weighed on their shoulders. Kerchiefs were of little avail to shut out the poisonous gas, and walking became agony. First one serving maid, then another collapsed. Racilia stumbled and sank down, and Nerissa, faithful to the last, bent over to help her. . . .

Nearly nineteen hundred years later their forms, immortalized in plaster casts, can still be seen, and archaeologists make this note of their fate:

Only the mistress of the house seems to have lost too much time in the gathering of her valuables; she collapsed in the damp and sticky ash of the street, not far from her home; strewn around her were her jewellery, her money, and her silver mirror, and near her were her three serving-women.[1]

SOURCE READINGS

(a)

LIVY (59 B.C.-A.D. 17) wrote a voluminous history of Rome in 142 "books", 107 of which have been lost. (The expression "book" as applied to ancient literature really means a roll of papyrus. Each papyrus roll contained a text that would amount to thirty to fifty pages in modern print.) The history is a patriotic account of Rome, written to glorify the Roman past. The following selection from the second book describes events traditionally attributed to the year 494 B.C. when the plebs, on returning from a campaign, refused to enter Rome.

Without orders from the consuls the plebeians withdrew to the Sacred Mountain beyond the river Anio, three miles from the city. . . . In the city there was great panic; everything was at a standstill because of mutual apprehensions. The plebeians left behind feared violence from the senators, who in turn feared the plebeians remaining in the city, uncertain whether they should prefer them to stay or leave. "How long," they asked, "will the crowd of

[1]E. C. Corti, *The Destruction and Resurrection of Pompeii and Herculaneum* (Routledge and Kegan Paul, 1951), p. 71.

seceders remain quiet? What will happen if foreign war should break out in the meanwhile? Certainly the only remaining hope is harmony in the citizen body, and harmony must be achieved by fair means or foul." They decided to make their advocate Menenius Agrippa, an eloquent man, and a favourite of the plebeians because he was himself a plebeian born. When he was admitted into the camp he is said merely to have told this tale, in the unpolished old-fashioned style:

"Once when a man's parts did not, as now, agree together but each had its own program and style, the other parts were indignant that their worry and trouble and diligence procured everything for the belly, which remained idle in the middle of the body and only enjoyed what the others provided. Accordingly they conspired that the hands should not carry food to the mouth, nor the mouth accept it, nor the teeth chew it. But while they angrily tried to subdue the belly by starvation the members themselves and the whole body became dangerously emaciated. Hence it became evident that the belly's service was no sinecure, that it nourished the rest as well as itself, supplying the whole body with the source of life and energy by turning food into blood and distributing it through the veins." By thus showing that the plebeians' anger against the senators was like internal sedition in a body, he swayed the men's minds. Negotiations for concord were then undertaken. The terms included a provision that the plebeians should have their own magistrates, who should be sacrosanct and possess power to aid the common people against the consuls; it would not be lawful, moreover, for a patrician to hold this magistracy. In this way tribunes of the people were created.

A History of Rome from Its Origins to A.D. 529 as Told by the Roman Historians, prepared by Moses Hadas (Anchor Books, Doubleday, 1956), pp. 17-18.

(b)

THE TWELVE TABLES were a law code of Roman customs drawn up in order that every citizen might know his rights and obligations. This code was inscribed on bronze tablets and exhibited in the Forum until Rome was burned by the Gauls in 390 B.C. The Twelve Tables were, in a sense, the Ten Commandments of the Romans; schoolboys were memorizing them at a time when Greek children were learning their Homer. For a thousand years this code remained the foundation of Roman law.

Table III

When a debt has been acknowledged, or judgment about the matter has been pronounced in court, thirty days must be the legitimate time of grace. . . .

Unless they make a settlement, debtors shall be held in bonds for sixty days. During that time they shall be brought before the praetor's court in the meeting place on three successive market days, and the third market day they shall suffer capital punishment or be delivered up for sale abroad, across the Tiber.

Table IV

Quickly kill . . . a dreadfully deformed child.

If a father thrice surrender a son for sale, the son shall be free from the father.

Table VIII

If any person has sung or composed against another person a song such as was causing slander or insult to another, he shall be clubbed to death.

If a person has maimed another's limb, let there be retaliation in kind unless he makes agreement for settlement with him.

If he has broken or bruised a freeman's bone with his hand or a club, he shall undergo penalty of 300 *as* [bronze money pieces]; if a slave's, 150.

Any person who destroys by burning any building or heap of corn deposited alongside a house shall be bound, scourged, and put to death by burning at the stake, provided that he has committed the said misdeed with malice afore-thought; but if he shall have committed it by accident, that is, by negligence, it is ordained that he repair the damage, or, if he be too poor to be competent for such punishment, he shall receive a lighter chastisement.

If theft has been done by night, if the owner kill the thief, the thief shall be held lawfully killed.

It is forbidden that a thief be killed by day . . . unless he defend himself with a weapon; even though he has come with a weapon, unless he use his weapon and fight back, you shall not kill him. And even if he resists, first call out.

No person shall practise usury at a rate more than one twelfth [probably 8½%] . . . A usurer is condemned for a quadruple amount.

. . . a person who has been found guilty of giving false witness shall be hurled down from the Tarpeian Rock. . . .

Table X

A dead man shall not be buried or burned within the city.

Women must not tear cheeks or hold chorus of "Alas!" on account of funeral.

When a man is dead one must not gather his bones in order to make a second funeral. An exception [in the case of] death in war or in a foreign land. . . .

Anointing by slaves is abolished, and every kind of drinking bout.

Table XI

Intermarriage shall not take place between plebeians and patricians.

N. Lewis and M. Reinhold, editors, *Roman Civilization: Selected Readings,* Vol. I, *The Republic* (Columbia University Press, 1951), pp. 104-109.

(c)

PLUTARCH (see page 215), in his life of the Roman dictator Fabius Maximus, describes the stratagem Hannibal used in 217 B.C. to slip out of a mountain pass where Fabius thought he had him trapped. Hannibal's plunder included thousands of head of cattle. Plutarch tells us how he used these to escape Fabius's trap.

He gave orders to take about two thousand of the cattle which they had captured, fasten to each of their horns a torch consisting of a bundle of withes or faggots, and then, in the night, at a given signal, to light the torches and drive the cattle towards the passes, along the defiles guarded by the enemy. As soon as his orders had been obeyed, he decamped with the rest of his army, in the darkness which had now come, and led it slowly along. The cattle, as long as the fire was slight, and consumed only the wood, went on quietly, as they were driven, towards the slopes of the mountains, and the shepherds and herdsmen who looked down from the heights were amazed at the flames gleaming on the tips of their horns. They thought an army was marching in close array by the light of many torches. But when the horns had been burned down to the roots, and the live flesh felt the flames, and the cattle, at the pain, shook and tossed their heads, and so covered one another with quantities of fire, then they kept no order in their going, but in terror and anguish, went dashing down the mountains, their foreheads and tails ablaze, and setting fire also to much of the forest through which they fled. It was, of course, a fearful spectacle to the Romans guarding the passes. For the flames seemed to come from torches in the hands of men who were running hither and thither with them. They were therefore in great commotion and fear, believing that the enemy were advancing upon them from all quarters and surrounding them on every side. Therefore they had not the courage to hold their posts, but withdrew to the main body of their army on the heights, and abandoned the defiles. Instantly the light-armed troops of Hannibal came up and took possession of the passes, and the rest of his forces presently joined them without any fear, although heavily encumbered with much spoil.

Plutarch's Lives, translated by B. Perrin, Loeb Classical Library (Heinemann, 1915), III, 137-138.

(d)

PLUTARCH, in the following selection from his life of Sulla, describes the dictator's methods on his return to Italy in 83 B.C.

When Sulla learned that the greater part of the enemy had been destroyed and the remainder had fled to Antemnae, he came to Antemnae at dawn. When 300 of the inhabitants sent a herald, he promised them safety if they would do some mischief to his other enemies before coming over. They took him at his word, attacked their fellows, and many on both sides were cut down. Nevertheless Sulla collected these and other survivors to the number of 6000 in the hippodrome, and convoked the senate in the nearby temple of Bellona. As he began to speak, those assigned to the task began to butcher the 6000. Naturally the shrieks of such a multitude being slaughtered in so small a space carried, and the senators were startled. Sulla continued his speech with a calm and unconcerned expression, and bade the senators pay attention to his speech and not busy themselves with what was going on outside: some naughty people were being admonished at his orders. Even the stupidest Roman could now realize that they had changed tyrants, not escaped tyranny. . . .

Slaughter now became Sulla's business, and murders without number or limit filled the city. Private animosities doomed many who had no relations with Sulla; he consented to gratify his associates. Young Gaius Metellus made bold to ask Sulla in the senate what end there would be to these evils and at what point he might be expected to stop. "We do not ask you," he said, "to free from punishment those you are resolved to kill, but to free from suspense those you are resolved to save." Sulla said he did not yet know whom he would spare, whereupon Metellus said, "Then tell us whom you are going to kill."

. . . At once, without communicating with any official, Sulla proscribed 80 persons. Despite general indignation he proscribed 220 more on the following day, and as many again on the third day. In a public address on the subject he said he was proscribing as many as he could remember; those who escaped his memory for the present he would proscribe another time. Further, he penalized humanity with death, proscribing any who harboured or protected a proscribed person, making no exception of brother, son, or parents: the prize for killing a proscribed person was two talents, if a slave murdered his master or a son his father. What seemed the greatest injustice of all, he cancelled the civil rights of sons and grandsons of proscribed persons and confiscated their property. Proscriptions were the rule not only in Rome but in every city of Italy; neither temple of god nor hearth of hospitality nor ancestral hall was unstained by bloodshed; husbands were slaughtered in the arms of their wives, sons in the arms of their mothers. The victims of political passion or private animosity were nothing compared to those slaughtered for their property. Even the executioners were moved to say that his fine house killed this man, his garden that, his warm baths the other. Quintus Aurelius, who had no political connections but thought that his only concern with the misfortune was to condole with those affected by it, walked into the Forum and read the list of the proscribed. He saw his own name, and said, "Too bad. My Alban farm has condemned me." He had not gone far before he was overtaken and massacred. . . .

Hadas, *History of Rome . . . as Told by the Roman Historians*, pp. 58-60.

(e)

In 70 B.C. CICERO (106-43 B.C.), as an up-and-coming Equestrian and a brilliant lawyer, was appointed prosecutor of Gaius Verres, who from 73 to 71 B.C. had been the infamously cruel and dishonest governor of Sicily. Verres openly boasted that he had amassed three fortunes: one for himself, a second to repay his friends and patrons, and a third (the largest) to bribe the jury that tried him for extortion. The following selection from Cicero's *Second Speech against Verres* makes clear the collusion between Verres and Carpinatius, the manager of a tax-collecting company in Sicily, as well as Verres' attempt to make certain that the company's records contained nothing incriminating. Cicero's masterly indictment was so damning that Verres went into exile without waiting for the trial to end. Nemesis, however, finally caught up with him in 43 B.C. when he was proscribed by Mark Antony, who coveted the works of art this rogue had stolen from Sicily.

I was at Syracuse looking through the company's accounts kept by Carpinatius. . . . With the accounts open in my hands, I suddenly caught sight of some erasures that suggested recent injuries to the tablets. As soon as this suspicion struck me, I transferred my eyes and attention to these special items. There were sums entered as received from *Gaius Verrucius son of Gaius*; but whereas up to the second *r* the letters were plainly untouched, all after that were written over an erasure; and there was a second, a third, a fourth, a large number of items of the same character.

Since these erasures on the tablets manifestly indicated some conspicuously villainous and dirty proceeding, I proceeded to ask Carpinatius who this Verrucius was with whom he had such extensive money transactions. The man hesitated, shuffled, went red in the face. . . .

I stated my charge before Metellus [Verres' successor as governor of Sicily], saying that I had inspected the company's accounts; that they included a large one, with a great many entries, under the name of Gaius Verrucius; and that by comparing the months and years I had discovered that this Verrucius had had no account with Carpinatius either before the arrival of Gaius Verres or after his departure. I demanded therefore that Carpinatius should tell me who this Verrucius was . . . where he was, where he came from, and why the company's slave who wrote up the accounts always went wrong at one particular point when he wrote the name Verrucius. . . .

If Carpinatius would not answer me then, will you answer me now, Verres, and say who you suppose this Verrucius is who is almost one of your own clan? I see the man was in Sicily during your praetorship, and the account is enough to show me that he was rich, so it is out of the question that you in your own province were not acquainted with him. Or rather, for the sake of brevity and clearness, step forward, gentlemen, and unroll this facsimile transcript of the accounts, so that instead of following the tracks of his veracity the world may now see it at home in its lair. Do you see the word *Verrucius*? Do you see how the first letters are all right? Do you see the last part of the name, the tail-bit of *Verres* there sunk in the erasure like a pig's tail in the mud? Well, gentlemen, the accounts are what you see they are; what are you waiting for, what more would you have? You yourself, Verres, why are you sitting there doing nothing? Either you must show us Verrucius, you know, or you must confess that Verrucius is you.

Lewis and Reinhold, *Roman Civilization: Selected Readings,* Vol. I, *The Republic,* pp. 363-364.

(f)

PLINY THE YOUNGER (A.D. 61-113) was sent as governor to Bithynia by the emperor TRAJAN (98-117). From Pliny's letters we have an excellent picture of provincial administration under a good emperor. The letter that follows, together with Trajan's answer, is self-explanatory. It was written about the year 112.

Pliny to Trajan

It is my habit to refer to you, Sire, all matters on which I am in doubt. Who can better guide my hesitation or instruct my ignorance? I have never been present at the hearing of legal cases concerned with Christians; and I am therefore ignorant of what it is that is usually punished or investigated, and to what extent this is done. I have hesitated greatly about several problems. Is there any distinction to be made on the ground of age, or are even the youngest to be dealt with in just the same way as the older? Is pardon to be granted to repentance, or does a man who has once been a Christian derive no benefit from having ceased to be one? Is the name of Christian itself to be punished, even if it is not attended by any crime, or is it the crimes that go with the name that are to be punished?

Meanwhile, and for the time being, this is the line which I have followed in dealing with persons who were brought before me as Christians. I have asked them, "Are you Christians?" If they confessed that they were, I have asked them the question a second and a third time, threatening them as I did so with punishment; and then, if they persisted in their confession, I have ordered them to be executed. I had no doubt in my mind that—apart from their belief, and whatever it might be—such inflexible pertinacity and obstinacy ought in any case to be punished. There were also others who showed a similar folly, but whom, as they were Roman citizens, I remitted for trial in Rome.

Eventually, as the proceedings continued, and the range of offences, as usually happens, grew wider, a number of different problems arose. An anonymous list was put before me which contained the names of many persons who denied that they were or had been Christians, and who, repeating the words I dictated to them, invoked the gods, made their supplication . . . to your image (which I had ordered to be brought into court for the purpose along with the statues of the deities), and cursed the name of Christ; none of which things, I am told, any real Christian can be made to do. I therefore thought that these persons ought to be acquitted. Others, who had been named by an informer, first said that they were Christians and then denied that they were; they *had* been, they said, but they had ceased to be—some of them three years back, some of them many years ago, and some even as far back as twenty years. All of them venerated your image and the statues of the gods; and they, too, cursed the name of Christ. They stated that the whole of their fault, or error, had consisted in their habit of meeting before dawn on an appointed day, and singing in turn among themselves a hymn to Christ as their God; they had also bound themselves by oath not to the commission of any crime, but to refrain

341

from theft or larceny or adultery, from any breach of faith, and from refusing to acknowledge a debt to a creditor; after which it was their habit to depart and then to meet again for the purpose of taking food—but food of an ordinary sort and an innocent character; but they had ceased to do even this after the issue of the edict in which, acting under your instructions, I had forbidden the meetings of clubs, and brotherhoods. This made me think it all the more necessary to discover what truth there was in their statement, and I even used torture for the purpose on two of their serving maids, called deaconesses, but I found no evidence of anything except a crazy and unrestrained superstition, and so I postponed the hearing of the case and proceeded at once to consult you.

The matter seemed to me to be important enough for such consultation, especially in view of the number of the persons who were involved. There are many of all ages and every rank, and also of both sexes, who already are, or will be, implicated. The contagion of the superstition has spread not only in cities, but also through villages and the countryside; and yet it still seems possible to arrest and correct it. Certainly it is a fact that the temples, which had been almost deserted, have begun to be attended again, and that the regular services, which had not been held for a long time, are being revived; animals for sacrifice, which had previously found very few purchasers, are now on sale in abundance. This makes it easy to guess what a number of persons can be brought back to the right path if the way is eased for repentance.

Trajan to Pliny

You have followed, my dear Pliny, the right line of action in trying the cases of the Christians who had been brought before you. No general rule can be laid down in any definite terms. Christians are not to be sought out; if they are brought into court and found guilty, they are to be punished—but with this reservation, that any person who has denied that he is a Christian, and has given actual proof by making supplication to our gods, should be pardoned as a penitent even if he is under suspicion in regard to the past. Anonymous lists ought not to be regarded in dealing with any offence: they are the worst of precedents, and they do not agree with the spirit of our age.

From Alexander to Constantine: Passages and Documents Illustrating the History of Social and Political Ideas, 336 B.C.—A.D. 337, translated by E. Barker (Clarendon Press, 1956), pp. 249-252, slightly adapted.

(g)

PLINY THE YOUNGER, in this letter to the historian Tacitus, describes the escape of his mother and himself from Misenum the day after the celebrated eruption of Vesuvius on August 24, A.D. 79. Misenum was a naval base on the bay of Naples, and was situated about twenty miles from the volcano.

It was now the first hour of day, but the light was still faint and doubtful. The adjacent buildings now began to collapse. . . . Then at last we decided to leave the town. The dismayed crowd came after us; it preferred following someone else's decision rather than its own; in panic that is practically the same as wisdom. So as we went off we were crowded and shoved along by a huge mob of followers. When we got out beyond the buildings we halted. We saw many strange and fearful sights there. For the carriages we had ordered brought for us, though on perfectly level ground, kept rolling back and forth; even when the wheels were chocked with stones they would not stand still. Moreover the sea appeared to be sucked back and to be repelled by the vibration of the earth; the shoreline was much farther out than usual, and many specimens of marine life were caught on the dry sands. On the other side a black and frightful cloud, rent by twisting and quivering paths of fire, gaped open in huge patterns of flames; it was like sheet lightning, but far worse. . . .

Soon thereafter the cloud I have described began to descend to the earth and to cover the sea; it had encircled Capri and hidden it from view, and had blotted out the promontory of Misenum. Then my mother began to plead, urge, and order me to make my escape as best I could, for I could, being young; she, weighed down with years and weakness, would die happy if she had not been the cause of death to me. I replied that I would not find safety except in her company; then I took her hand and made her walk faster. She obeyed with difficulty and scolded herself for slowing me. Now ashes, though thin as yet, began to fall. I looked back; a dense fog was looming up behind us; it poured over the ground like a river as it followed. "Let us turn aside," said I, "lest, if we should fall on the road, we should be trampled in the darkness by the throng of those going our way." We barely had time to consider the thought, when night was upon us, not such a night as when there is no moon or there are clouds, but such as in a closed place with the lights put out. One could hear the wailing of women, the crying of children, the shouting of men; they called each other, some their parents, others their children, still others their mates, and sought to recognize each other by their voices. Some lamented their own fate, others the fate of their loved ones. There were even those who in fear of death prayed for death. Many raised their hands to the gods; more held that there were nowhere gods any more and that this was that eternal and final night of the universe. . . .

P. MacKendrick and H. M. Howe, editors, *Classics in Translation,* Vol. II, *Roman Literature* (University of Wisconsin Press, 1952), pp. 365-366.

343

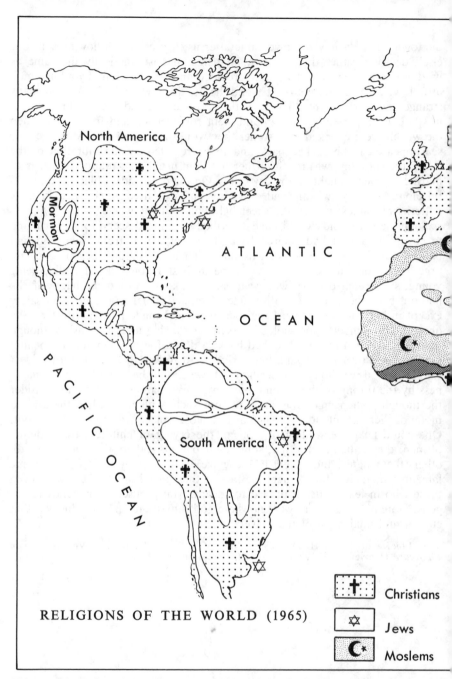

RELIGIONS OF THE WORLD (1965)

	Christians
☆	Jews
☾	Moslems

This map is only intended to give a general idea of the distribution of the world's major religions. It is impossible, for example, to indicate every area where there may be a Christian community. Similarly, Jews are scattered throughout the globe, although significant concentrations are in Israel and in heavily populated areas of Europe and

Asia

PACIFIC OCEAN

INDIAN OCEAN

Australia

Buddhists, Taoist, Confucian, Shinto Sects

Hindus

Tribal Religions

North America. Finally, in the Orient, and particularly in China, there is a mixture of religions. Three religions share predominance there and, indeed, sometimes become intermingled.

345

BOOKS TO READ

1. GENERAL

Cowell, F. R., *Everyday Life in Ancient Rome* (Batsford)
Duggan, A., *The Romans* (World)
Grant, M. and Pottinger, D., *Romans* (Nelson)
Johnston, M., *Roman Life* (Scott, Foresman)
Milliken, E. K., *The Roman People* (Harrap)
Mills, D., *The Book of the Ancient Romans* (Putnam)
Sherwin-White, A. N., *Ancient Rome* (Longmans)
Taylor, D., *Ancient Rome* (Methuen)

2. ROME AND HER CONQUESTS

Charles-Picard, G. and C., *Daily Life in Carthage at the Time of Hannibal* (Allen and Unwin)
Cottrell, L., *Enemy of Rome* (Pan paperback)
Lamb, H., *Hannibal* (Bantam paperback)
Mellersh, H. E. L., *Carthage* (Weidenfeld and Nicolson)

3. A CENTURY OF REVOLUTION: THE GRACCHI TO OCTAVIAN

Buchan, J., *Augustus* (Hodder and Stoughton)
Coolidge, O., *Caesar's Gallice War* (Houghton Mifflin)
Duggan, A., *Julius Caesar* (Knopf)
Haskell, H. J., *This Was Cicero* (Premier paperback)
Pike, E. R., *Republican Rome* (Weidenfeld and Nicolson)

4. THE EMPIRE

Carcopino, J., *Daily Life in Ancient Rome* (Penguin paperback)
Davis, W. S., *A Day in Old Rome* (Allyn and Bacon)
Foster, G., *Augustus Caesar's World* (Scribner)
Lissner, I., *Power and Folly: The Story of the Caesars* (Cape)
Mellersh, H. E. L., *Imperial Rome* (Weidenfeld and Nicolson)

5. CHRISTIANITY

Bouquet, A. C., *Everyday Life in New Testament Times* (Scribner)
Daniel-Rops, H., *Daily Life in the Time of Jesus* (Mentor paperback)
Johnston, G., *The Secrets of the Kingdom* (Westminster)
Smith, E. A., *Men Called Him Master* (Westminster)
Williams, A. N., *Paul, The World's First Missionary* (Association Press)

6. HISTORICAL FICTION

Baumann, H., *I Marched with Hannibal* (Walk) [second Carthaginian war]

Coolidge, O., *Caesar's Gallic War* (Houghton Mifflin)
age of Augustus]

Davis, W. S., *A Friend of Caesar* (Collier-Macmillan) [a young officer
under Julius Caesar's command]

Mitchison, N., *The Conquered* (Cape) [Caesar's conquest of Gaul]

Mitchison, N., *The Blood of the Martyrs* (Constable) [Christian
persecution under Nero]

Powers, A., *Hannibal's Elephants* (McKay) [second Carthaginian war]

Snedeker, C. D., *The Forgotten Daughter* (Doubleday) [slavery at the time
of the Gracchi]

Sutcliff, R., *The Eagle of the Ninth* (Oxford) [Roman Britain]

Sutcliff, R., *The Silver Branch* (Oxford) [Roman Britain]

PART VI

THE EARLY MIDDLE AGES

CHAPTER 33

Recreating Civilization in Europe

It was in this age of universal ruin and destruction that the foundations of the new Europe were being laid.

CHRISTOPHER DAWSON, *The Making of Europe*

Now that the West was ruled by a German, the whole complexion of the Roman Empire changed once and for all. The Western Roman Empire was, of course, ended in fact. Yet in theory it continued, and such a situation had its compensations. The German kings were pleased to associate their rule with the lustre of ancient Rome, and moreover they were soon to win the approval of the Christian Church.

Western Europe, then, found itself under three distinct influences: Christian, Germanic, and Roman. These elements merged to form an entirely new type of civilization, one which received the name *European*.

❖ *The Church Organizes* The Christian Church had enjoyed certain securities and advantages from being born within the framework of the mighty Roman Empire. Yet that same Empire might have proved its undoing. So strong were the secular pressures within the Empire that the Church soon realized that if it were to preserve its unity—indeed, if it were to survive at all—it would have to create a vast organization that would embrace all branches of the Church everywhere.

Already there were heads of the Church in every important city of the Empire, officials called *bishops*. With so many separate churches, there was danger that differences in belief would arise, and in 325 the Emperor Constantine called these bishops—over 300 of them—together at Nicaea to work out a unifying statement of the Church's beliefs. This was the first universal Church council. It was natural that the bishops of the oldest and largest Christian communities should exercise special

---

This fearsome looking helmet was once worn by a 7th century Anglian king. It was discovered, disintegrated, in an untouched funeral mound where a vast horde of treasure was unearthed at Sutton Hoo in Suffolk, England in 1939. Once the helmet had been patiently reconstructed from hundreds of tiny fragments of metal, it was found to have been made of iron, with a silver-plated crest and a covering of thin sheets of silvered bronze.

authority, and the bishops of Rome came to assume the headship of the Church. For they asserted that since Christ had designated the first bishop of Rome, Peter, as His successor on earth with unlimited power in matters of faith and morals, each succeeding bishop of Rome must fall heir to this same power. The bishops of Rome came to call themselves *papa* (father) or "pope."

The supremacy of the popes was not universally accepted. Certain Eastern bishops broke with Rome in 1054 to form the Greek Orthodox Church. Nevertheless the Roman Church was supreme in the West. Christianity became fashionable. The Church grew powerful and wealthy, and some voices were raised against its increasing worldliness. St. Jerome (340-419), for instance, wrote bitterly of a certain type of priest:

All their care is for their clothing, their scents and odours, the close and even fitting of their shoes. The curling iron has left its traces in their crisp locks, their fingers flash with rings, and they scarce venture to go a-tiptoe lest the puddles in the street should soil their feet.

Such criticisms as this came from Christians who often wanted to shut out all the comfortable temptations of the world. In their search for seclusion some of them became hermits and monks.

❖ *Rules for Salvation*   One of the more picturesque of these early ascetics was St. Simeon Stylites (395-461), who carried self-denial to such lengths that he spent thirty years living on a top of a pillar some sixty feet high. Sometimes he fasted for forty days at a time, even tying himself to his pillar in order not to sit or lie down. Less continuous was the bodily punishment practised by a certain Northumbrian hermit.

Since his cell stood upon a river's side, he was wont to dip and plunge himself in the flowing water oftentimes, and continue there singing psalms as long as he could abide for cold, the water now and then coming up to his hips, and now and then to his chin. In the winter season, when pieces of ice half-broken dropped down on every side of him, which he had broken to plunge into the river, diverse men seeing him said; "It is a marvellous matter and a strange case, brother Birthelm (for so he was called), that you can possibly suffer such bitter and sharp cold." Whereupon he answered simply (for he was but a simple and sober-spirited man), "I have known places colder than this."

You must realize, of course, that such extreme behaviour was not general. A more reasonable type of meditative life had been instituted in Egypt in the 4th century, when an establishment was built there with bare rooms in which a number of men might live together under strict regulations of obedience, silence, manual labour, and religious exercises. Such an institution came to be called a monastery. Monasticism was introduced into Italy, and during the 4th and 5th centuries it spread throughout western Europe. But in time the monasteries, like the Church they had protested against, became successful, wealthy, and worldly. Soon the reformers themselves were in need of reform.

The greatest figure in the history of Western monasticism was St. Benedict of Nursia (480-543). Although he came from a rich family, when he was sent to Rome for his education he was so disgusted with the wickedness he found there that he fled and took to living in a cave in the hills. Many times he was sorely tempted to abandon his holy life, but he persevered; and as his fame spread his following grew. To regulate the lives of these followers he established a monastery at Monte Cassino, a hill between Rome and Naples, and in the year 529 he drew up the *Rule*. The Benedictine Rule was a set of regulations

The cloister was often the place where the younger members of the monastic community attended lectures and the elder monks studied. Here, too, the brethren might be allowed, at certain set hours, to converse together. This Benedictine cloister, which is now part of the Lutheran Church of the Redeemer in Jerusalem, may be as old as the 8th century—in fact it is probably part of one of the monasteries whose construction Charlemagne aided by sending large sums of money to Palestine.

(some of which you may read on page 417) for running a monastery. It was not fanatical. It bound the monk to obey the will of an abbot, who was elected by all the monks to administer the monastery. The monk must observe poverty: he could own no property—"neither a book, nor tablets, nor a pen—nothing at all." He must observe chastity, that is, moral purity. And he must vow not to leave the monastery except at the abbot's command.

Monastic life

What was a monk's life like in a Benedictine monastery? His day began early. In winter, prayers were said at about half past three in the morning, and throughout the day there were other religious services. Since candles cast only the feeblest light, bedtime came shortly after sunset. The time between services was spent in study and manual labour such as working in the fields, the latter being Benedict's answer to the problems of health created by the excessively long periods of meditation and contemplation which had been practised by the early hermits. It was a hushed existence. The monastery lay silent as the monks carried out their daily tasks, for idle chatter was strictly forbidden. One meal a day, simple but adequate, sufficed during the winter. In summer there were two meals, but the schedule was stricter, with more work and less sleep.

The monastery at Monte Cassino became the model for many others. From this time on monks studied, prayed, and led economically productive lives in an effort to save their souls. For it must be noted that the primary purpose of the Rule was not to serve society; it was to provide the monks with a safe and practicable route to salvation.

❖ *"Servant of the Servants of God"* Gregory I, the Great, came to the papal throne in 590, having renounced a brilliant government career to become a simple monk. Gregory tightened up the administration of the Church and established the form and order of church worship. He was also very zealous to convert the heathen, a zeal that prompted him to dispatch missionaries even to the Anglo-Saxons in England.

Gregory the Great

The rivalry between the Greek Orthodox Church and the Roman Catholic Church remained acute, and when the head of the church in Constantinople (the *patriarch*) took the high-sounding title of "Bishop of Bishops," Gregory countered with the title "Servant of the Servants of God." Nevertheless Gregory was anything but meek. He summed up in his person and programme the high claims of papal supremacy, and he is chiefly remembered for his assertion of that supremacy. For this reason, and because he checked the papacy's decline in political power, Gregory has often been called the "Father of the Medieval Papacy."

By the 6th century, then, the Church in the West was a highly organized, efficiently managed institution centred in Rome and thoroughly Roman, with Latin its official tongue. In both the Church and the monasteries there was a respect for authority as strong as that accorded any emperor. But unlike the Empire, the Church was not decaying. In fact it was confidently asserting high political claims.

Let us now examine the Germanic element of European civilization up to the 6th century. Was it, too, forged on the Roman anvil?

❖ *Government to the Clash of Spears* Although the Germans were divided into tribes, they were not mere nomads. They pursued settled agriculture and had definite class distinctions: there was a noble class, a class of freemen, and a class of slaves. Public discussions on important matters affecting the entire tribe were decided by a general assembly of men of military age. "If a proposal displeases them," Tacitus records, "the people roar out their dissent; if they approve, they clash their spears." Usually the matter so decided involved a declaration of war. Other public business was considered unimportant.

Two features of Germanic society left lasting impressions on the Middle Ages. These were the element of personal attachment and the administration of justice. *Germanic society*

German warriors were divided into war bands, each of which chose its own chieftain. This chief swore to lead his "companions" well, to share booty with them, and never to desert them; in return his warriors swore undying allegiance to him. This bond of personal attachment is the most important Germanic element of the entire Middle Ages.

In administering justice, the Germans made extensive use of the oath. If the crime was not too serious, the accused could clear himself by having his oath of innocence supported by men who swore, with him, that he was honest. If, on the other hand, guilt was decided, damages could be inflicted through a fine, the cost depending on the value placed by Germanic society on the injured individual. For example, a Roman was fined more for robbing a German than a German for robbing a Roman.

If a major crime had been committed, the accused had to prove his innocence by undergoing the Judgment of God through the *ordeal*. The ordeal might consist of such trials as walking through fire, carrying a red-hot iron in the bare hand, or plunging an arm into a pot of boiling water, after which the wounded limb was bandaged. If the wounds were healing when the bandages were removed a few days later (and remember all this was before antiseptics), the man was innocent. If they were fester-

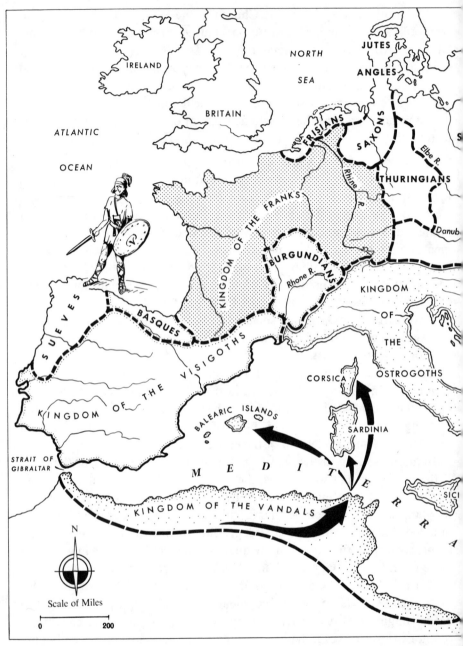

THE GERMANIC KINGDOMS

BYZANTINE EMPIRE IN 527 A.D.

ing he was guilty, and might be beheaded, hanged, or exiled. In this way, the Germans believed, God protected the innocent and revealed the guilty.

There were several refinements of these ordeals. The suspect could, for instance, be bound hand and foot and thrown into cold water. Since water was supposed to cast out impure substances, he was guilty ("impure") if he floated. If he drowned, he at least died innocent! Later in the Middle Ages trial by battle became a popular form of ordeal. A duel was an exciting way to settle guilt, and provided a good show to boot.

❖ *Despotism Tempered with Assassination*   None of the Germanic kingdoms were destined to be long lived. The Ostrogoths were able to establish a kingdom in Italy, but it soon disintegrated. The Visigothic state in Spain perished after some three centuries, and in North Africa the Vandal kingdom lasted only a century.

Arianism

Why did these barbarian states pass away so quickly? Partly because they were a minority—military overlords, thousands of Germans among the Roman millions. And partly because one other factor prevented them from forming a single society with the Romans. They were opposed to the Church of the Empire. The Germans had been converted to Christianity, but a brand of Christianity known as Arianism that was, by the 5th century, condemned by Rome and detested by the bishops. Thus it was that the conquered Romans looked to these bishops—and not to their Germanic overlords—as their leaders.

The Franks

There was one Germanic kingdom which was far more important than the others—the Frankish state. Unlike the other Germans, the Franks did not abandon their homeland. They had originally settled along the North Sea and Rhine River, and now they expanded their holdings to take in Gaul, an area that stretched from the Pyrenees Mountains to the Rhine, and which included modern Belgium, part of Holland, and western Germany. The Frankish kingdom was, therefore, much larger than modern France. Both French and Germans can and do claim the Franks as their ancestors.

Clovis

In 481 a youth of fifteen, Clovis by name, became king of one Frankish tribe. A few years later this shrewd ruler began a career of conquest to round out the Frankish kingdom in Gaul. In the beginning he was not a Christian, but he became a convert to the orthodox brand of Christianity championed by Rome and the bishops. Now his wars became crusades, aimed not only at conquering Gaul but also at blotting out Arianism. But Clovis was no saintly Christian conqueror. He became king of the Franks through murder and treachery (see pages 418-419). Indeed, it has been said of Clovis's descendants, as it might be said of Clovis himself, that their rule was "despotism tempered with assassination."

The Merovingians

Clovis founded the Merovingian dynasty, and before he died in 511 he arranged for all four of his sons to succeed him by dividing Greater Gaul into four portions to be ruled by them. The sons, on their succession, play-acted at being Roman deputies. They took Roman titles as their father before them had done, stamped their coins with the Roman emperor's profile, and pretended to be regents for an emperor in faraway Constantinople. As might have been expected, however, the sons quarrelled over the division of the kingdom. So drastically did these civil wars weaken the authority of the crown that the Merovingian rulers are known as the "do-nothing kings."

❖ *A Roman Veneer* Strangely enough, the ancient Roman traditions were not destroyed in Merovingian Gaul. Rather they became intertwined with Germanic ones. The long-haired Frankish king was elected by his warriors, elevated on their shields, and called *Princeps,* while his court officials also assumed Roman titles. The unwritten German customary laws were set down in codes alongside the written Roman law. The "city" (that is, a town plus its surrounding area) continued to be the unit of local government under a count or duke who collected the old Roman taxes, dispensed justice, and led the troops of his city to war. Each city also had a bishop, usually the descendant of a Roman senatorial family. Thus the Church provided a further link between old Rome and new Frankland.

The society of the Frankish state was mainly agricultural, and as trade within Gaul petered out easy communication broke down and travel became nearly impossible. The ordinary man lived and died without having ventured more than twenty miles from home. The people led such circumscribed existences that the brutal world of high politics scarcely affected them. They were far more concerned with the count's local government than with which Frankish murderer was at the moment occupying the throne.

❖ *From Old Rome to the New* We have now studied both the Christian and the German elements of the new Europe, and in so doing noted how Roman traditions persisted in each. Just what had happened to the Roman Empire since a German assumed command in the West?

After 476 the Western Roman Empire in effect disappeared; the two Roman Empires dwindled into one. That one empire was in the East, and it revolved around a glamorous capital—Byzantium (Constantinople), the "New Rome" founded by Constantine in 330. This remnant of Rome still pretended to exercise authority over both East and West. Germanic kings claimed to be the deputies of the Byzantine emperor, and Roman emperors continued to reign at Constantinople from the time of Constantine until 1453.

A characteristic Byzantine civilization gradually developed, made up of a combination of Hellenistic and Oriental influences and western Roman traditions. Whereas in the West the culture of the barbarians tended to overlay that of the Romans, Roman laws and institutions were preserved in the East. And while a long economic decline destroyed western wealth, the adjective "Byzantine" became synonymous with richness and opulence. The port of Constantinople was the New York and London of its day rolled into one.

❖ *A Greater than Solomon*   By the 6th century the Byzantine Empire was in its golden age, and the emperor, Justinian the Great (527-565), was prepared to use all its rich resources to establish himself as a Christian Caesar. No longer was there to be a variety of rival Christian sects; all of the old empire was to conform to a uniform Christianity. Assisting him was his wife Theodora, an ex-showgirl of great strength of character. At a crucial moment early in his reign, Theodora saved Justinian's throne for him by this ringing declaration that she, at least, would stay and face the rioting citizens.

If there were left me no safety but in flight, I would not fly. Those who have worn the crown should never survive its loss. Never will I see the day when I am not hailed Empress. If you wish to fly, Caesar, well and good, you have money, the ships are ready, the sea is clear; but I shall stay. For I love the old proverb that says "The purple is the best winding-sheet."

The emperor stayed, put down the riot, and went on to rule for another 33 years.

Justinian's first ambition was to reconquer the western provinces from German rule. North Africa was snatched back from the Vandals, Italy from the Ostrogoths, and part of Spain from the Visigoths. Although he was not able to regain all of Spain or Gaul, Justinian created himself an empire so huge that he could boast that the Mediterranean was once more a Roman lake. But while Justinian reconquered the West, the eastern frontiers were in danger as trouble arose with the Persians, the middlemen in the great silk trade between China and Constantinople, and pressure began to be exerted by the Slavs and Bulgars across the Danube. Hence in the long run it would have been better had Justinian concentrated on stemming the tide of invaders from the East rather than wasting his resources in a vain attempt to turn back the clock in the West.

Actually Justianian's conquests are not his greatest accomplishments. History regards his legal reforms and legislative work as far more important. For this enterprising emperor decided to compile and edit all the ancient Roman laws and legal opinions, a task which required the appointment of a great commission. Through his *Corpus Juris Civilis* (The Body of Civil Law), Justinian preserved the legal genius of Rome in the East. It was to take the West much longer—until the 12th century—before it would Romanize its Germanic law.

Justinian's legal reforms

The emperor was an autocratic ruler, supreme in his realm—the elect of God, head of the Church and the state. Elaborate costumes, rich court ritual, and a huge imperial civil service all contributed to an administration whose staggering expenses crippled the Empire's feeble economy in later days. Immense sums of money went into Justinian's ambitious building programme, so much so that the fame of Justinian the builder rivals that of Justinian the lawmaker. And incredible though it may seem, 1400 years later the most famous of his beautiful architectural works still stands in Constantinople—the huge basilica of Hagia Sophia (Holy Wisdom), built in the short space of five years at enormous cost. From the outside it appears plain, almost shabby; but inside, its walls glitter with mosaics—the Byzantine equivalent of painting—small pieces of coloured glass or stone fitted together to make designs and pictures. To give the huge dome height and allow it to enclose a square space, it is raised up on yet another dome from which the top has been sliced off to leave only corner supports called "pendentives." Forty arched windows around the lower lip of the great dome

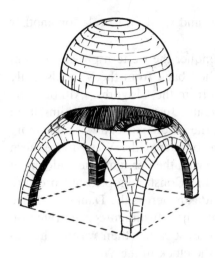

give, from inside, the impression that it is floating on air.

This brilliant solution to the problem of erecting a dome over a square has inspired architects ever since. On the day of the mighty temple's dedication Justinian is said to have exclaimed, "Glory be to God who deemed me worthy of this deed! I have outdone thee, Solomon."

Hagia Sophia symbolized the Byzantine Empire at its zenith. The following centuries were to see that empire's gradual dismemberment, until by the 8th century it had been stripped of all its western possessions. But though this second Rome lost control of the West it was to bequeath a priceless gift to western civilization. It preserved the cultural traditions of both Rome and Greece against the day when they would be returned to a West that had forgotten them.

CHAPTER 34

Islam and the Hammer

Mohammed is the Messenger of God, and those who are with him are hard against the unbelievers, merciful one to another.

THE *Koran*

Europe was soon to go through her own trial by ordeal.

Mohammed   About the year 570, some twenty years before Gregory the Great came to the papal throne, there was born in the Arabian city of Mecca a boy named Mohammed. He was orphaned at an early age, but somehow received enough knowledge of writing and reckoning to become the commercial agent for the caravan business of a wealthy widow. Doubtless on his journeys through the Arabian peninsula he became familiar with both Jewish and Christian teachings, and perhaps he began to contrast them with the many gods and idols of his fellow tribesmen. At any rate, when he subsequently married his employer and became a man of means he devoted his leisure to religious speculation and study.

❖ *Messenger of Allah* Mohammed was a retiring, sensitive person who required nothing of a servant that he could not do himself (all his life he mended his own clothes). According to his adopted son he was

of middle stature, neither tall nor short. His complexion was rosy white; his eyes black; his hair, thick, brilliant, and beautiful, fell to his shoulders. His profuse beard fell to his breast. . . . There was such sweetness in his visage that no one, once in his presence, could leave him.

For ages, Hagia Sophia has been considered the outstanding monument of Byzantine art. The great dome is 107 feet in diameter and rises 180 feet above the floor, the present one being the third to be built since two earlier ones collapsed. The Moslem conquerors of Constantinople turned the great church into a mosque and added the minarets. Today it is a Turkish museum.

Mohammed was, as you can see from this description, idolized by his followers, to whom he was kindness personified. Yet to his enemies he could be cruel and vengeful. He suffered frequent fits of depression and wild hysteria, and had since childhood been subject to mysterious seizures during which he seemed to be struggling to express religious ideas. Gradually he came to believe that this was God's way of trying to speak to him, and one day he had a vision of the angel Gabriel. Twice Gabriel called to him, and twice repeated these words: "O Mohammed! thou art the messenger of Allah, and I am Gabriel."

Mohammed's wife believed in his visions, and he himself become convinced that he was a prophet, the last and greatest of all the prophets (Jesus was one) whom God had sent to save mankind. "I am nothing more than a man," he insisted—but nevertheless the man who, alone of all men, had received the complete message of the true religion. All other prophets had been granted only glimpses of the truth.

At first Mohammed had little success converting his countrymen. After all, Mecca was the centre of worship for all the many gods of Arabia, and the merchants believed that their trade depended on the traffic related to these shrines. Mohammed and his followers were so persecuted that finally in 622 the Prophet fled north with his disciples to the city of Medina. This migration is known as the *Hegira* (flight). It was regarded as such a crucial event in the Prophet's life that the *Moslems,* as his followers are called, date the beginning of their calendar from it, just as we date ours from the birth of Christ.

From now on Mohammed's reputation and power increased steadily. He became the virtual ruler of Medina and a successful commander. Eight years later he returned in triumph to capture Mecca, destroy the idols, and make that city the religious centre of the new faith. When he died in 632 he was the acknowledged spiritual and political leader of most of the Arabian tribes.

The Koran

❖ *The Whirlwind of Islam*   Mohammed's revelations were collected in the *Koran*, a book somewhat shorter than the New Testament. Mohammed believed that the Koran had always existed in heaven, and that only he had been worthy of receiving this, God's divine guide for the human race. It came to him during his spells, in bits and pieces and from time to time, and it was to be followed without question. "Let the Koran always be your guide," said Mohammed. "Do what it commands or permits; shun what it forbids." Among the things that it forbade were wine-drinking and gambling and the eating of certain foods such as pork.

Strands of both Judaism and Christianity appear in Mohammed's teaching of this new religion which he called *Islam* (Islam means "submission to God," while Moslem means "he who submits"). From the beginning, Islam enjoyed fantastic success; even today it is spreading more rapidly in Asia and Africa than is Christianity. This success has been due, in the main, to the simple beliefs of the faith. It is a faith that needs no priesthood or church, for it has no sacraments. Each individual is responsible for his own right belief and conduct; a man can be a good Moslem all by himself in the middle of the desert.

Here is no elaborate theology. At the centre is an uncompromising monotheism: "There is only one God and Mohammed is His Prophet." The Moslem paradise is far from a mystical hereafter. It is one whose delights the thirsty desert-wanderer will not find hard to comprehend. The Koran promises the faithful that he will find himself

> In gardens of delight . . .
> Amid thornless date-trees
> And bananas laden with fruit
> And shade outspread
> And water flowing
> And fruit abundant,
> Never failing nor forbidden.

The Moslem has certain simple duties. He must pray five times daily, kneeling and facing Mecca. Yet this does not win salvation. Says the Koran,

> It is not piety, that you turn your faces
>   to the East and to the West.
>   True piety is this:
> to believe in God, and the Last Day,
> the angels, the Book, and the Prophets,
> to give of one's substance, however cherished,
>   to kinsmen, and orphans,
> the needy, the traveller, the beggars,
>   and to ransom the slave,
> to perform the prayer, to pay the alms. . . .

One of Mohammed's successors said, "Prayer carries us halfway to God, fasting brings us to his palace, and alms gain us admission." The Moslem must also fast daily during the holy month of Ramadan, and, if at all possible, he must make at least one pilgrimage to Mecca.

Mohammed had created a religion vastly superior to the polytheism of the desert tribes; yet it was a man's religion. His acceptance of polygamy and his insistence that the Koran was the final *unchanging* authority on such matters prevented women and girls from advancing from the inferior—and often despised—status in which their society had placed them.

Moslem expansion

The amazingly rapid adoption of the new faith was followed by an

COMPARATIVE EMPIRES

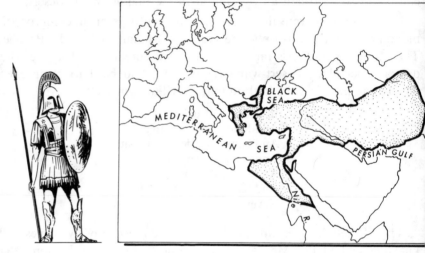

ALEXANDRIAN (323 B.C.

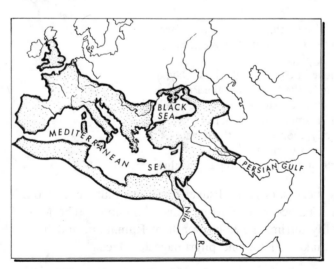

ROMAN (A.D. 180)

even more amazing drive for territory—a drive that turned into a whirlwind. Soon the poverty-stricken Arabian peninsula was feared by the whole Christian world. By 634 Palestine and Syria had been invaded. The Persian Empire fell shortly afterwards, and to the west fierce Arab horsemen galloped out across the North African desert to take Carthage. In 711 they passed Gibraltar on their way into Spain. And still they swept on, not to be checked in Europe until 733, when they were turned

COMPARATIVE EMPIRES

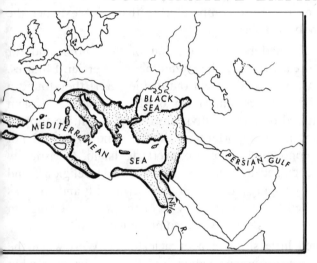

BYZANTINE (565)

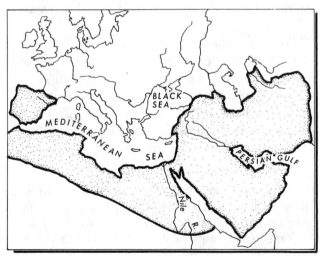

MOSLEM (733)

back by the heavy hand of Charles Martel (see page 367) at the Battle of Tours, near Poitiers in modern France.

Meanwhile Moslem forces had pushed eastward from Persia to penetrate India, and even, by the early 8th century, to probe into the western areas of China. Actually the most decisive check to Moslem expansion came probably not at Tours, but some 2000 miles to the east when, in 718, the siege of Constantinople was lifted and the Moslems were eventually driven out of Asia Minor. Nevertheless, even though checked at Poitiers and Constantinople, Islam had conquered from one end of the Mediterranean to the other. With insignificant armies, these ragged sons of the desert had won an empire comparable to that of Alexander the Great. How had they been able to do it?

For one thing, Arabs had been moving out of their homeland for centuries, and many already lived in the Byzantine and Persian Empires. Thus when a new wave of nomads swept out of the desert they found a ready-made network of fifth columnists in bordering states. Moslem chances were also bettered by internal divisions in the Byzantine Empire and in Spain. Perhaps most important of all, the conquerors did not insist that those they conquered become converts to Islam. Christianity and Judaism were recognized as genuine (if misguided) religions, and their adherents could, by paying a tax, retain their own faith and customs —although if one wished to rise in the service of the state or engage in business and commerce, conversion was recommended.

It must have seemed little short of a miracle to the West when the Moslem raiding parties were at last halted in 733. To discover what stopped them, we must return to the Franks and the Merovingians.

❖ *From the Hammer to the Crown* The "do-nothing kings" of 7th century Gaul were, as their name suggests, an uninspiring lot. Although one lived to the ripe old age of thirty-eight, others barely survived their teens. The real power in the country was an official known as the "mayor of the palace." He was a household official of the king, and his control of administration, taxes, and lands made him the one indispensable man. This situation is clearly described by the secretary and friend of a later Frankish king:

Mayors of the Palace

There was nothing left for the King to do but to be content with his name of King, his flowing hair and long beard; to sit on his throne and play the ruler; to give ear to the ambassadors that came from all quarters, and to dismiss them, as if on his own responsibility, in words that were, in fact, suggested to him, or even imposed upon him. . . . When he had to go abroad, he used to ride in a cart, drawn by a yoke of oxen, driven, peasant-fashion, by a ploughman; he rode in this way to the palace and to the general assembly of the people. . . . The Mayor of the Palace took charge of the government, and of everything that had to be planned or executed at home or abroad.

In 714 a mayor of the palace named Charles Martel defeated various rivals and became leader of all the Franks. Charles faced grave threats: in the south the Frankish dominions were being invaded by the Moslems; in the north loomed the Saxons. What sort of Merovingian army could be called on to stem the tide? Charles could summon the mounted nobles —but they were few; and he could supplement them by a general levy of all able-bodied men—but they were unequipped and undisciplined. What he needed was a new and effective army. But how should it be made up, and where could he get it? *Charles Martel*

Charles's first step was to make the backbone of his army the cavalry. Stirrups had just recently been introduced into western Europe, and they were immensely important. For they allowed a mounted man to stand, so that he could wield lance and sword while riding. Such cavalry, well armoured, could make short work of infantry. But there was a flaw in Charles's plan. A horse, armour, and equipment were all expensive, and their proper use required considerable practice. How could Charles get sufficient numbers of men with wealth and free time for such service?

Charles had decided the kind of army he needed, and he was determined to get it. To this end he enlisted warriors who swore fidelity to him. Then he gave estates to these *vassals,* estates that would be worked by *serfs* (from the Latin *servus,* a slave) in order that the vassals might be free to fight. Each estate was called a *benefice.* Charles even forced the Church to grant benefices so that there would be a large enough fighting force.

How soon Charles used his heavy-armed Frankish cavalry is not known. With or without it, he won everlasting fame and the name of Martel ("Hammer") by turning back the Moslems at the Battle of Tours; likely it played a vital role in his later campaigns when he conquered part of Saxony. At any rate, Charles was without doubt a military genius, and probably the first in the West to realize the possibilities inherent in stirrups. The fact that his method of recruitment was based on a new system of landholding was of monumental significance. Charles Martel created thereby the mould for the whole of medieval society. *Tours*

ISLAM AND THE HAMMER/367

Charles was succeeded as mayor of the palace by his son Pepin the Short (741-768). Pepin decided to end the farce of the monarchy in the Frankish state by making the actual rulers—the mayors of the palace—the kings. Accordingly he appealed to the pope to end the Merovingian dynasty and make him, in fact, king of the Franks. Assured of the Church's support, Pepin was elected king by his subjects and was duly consecrated by the Pope in 754. In return, the Papacy was granted new territory by Pepin, the so-called Papal States of central Italy.

The new Carolingian dynasty had been sanctioned by the Church. The Christian and Germanic traditions had come together.

CHAPTER 35

Charlemagne and The Carolingian Empire

Then all the faithful Romans, seeing what a pillar of defence he was, and what love he had for the holy Roman Church and its vicar, unanimously, at the will of God, and of St. Peter, the doorkeeper of the Kingdom of Heaven, cried out with a great shout: "To Charles, most pious Augustus, crowned by God, great and pacific emperor, Life and Victory!"

THE CORONATION OF CHARLEMAGNE AS REPORTED
BY THE *Liber Pontificalis,* WRITTEN ABOUT 816.

On Pepin's death his two sons, Charles and Carloman, divided the kingdom. Within a few years Carloman died, and Charles, setting aside other claimants, took the whole domain for his own. So illustrious was the rule of this progressive monarch that he is known to history as
Charle-
magne
Charlemagne (Charles the Great).

Charlemagne was a born leader and a talented general. We have an intimate picture of the great man from the biography written by his close friend, Einhard, who gives us such delightful details as the fact that

. . . Physicians . . . were almost hateful to him, because they wanted him to give up roasts, to which he was accustomed, and to eat boiled meat instead. . . . He was temperate in eating and particularly so in drinking . . . but he could not easily abstain from food, and often complained that fasts injured his health. . . . He had the gift of ready and fluent speech and . . . was such a master of Latin that he could speak it as well as his native tongue; but he could understand Greek better than he could speak it. . . . He took lessons in grammar . . .

and other branches of learning. He also tried to write, and used to keep tablets and blanks in bed under his pillow, that at leisure hours he might accustom his hand to form the letters; however, as he did not begin his efforts in due season, but later in life, they met with ill success.

So convinced was Charlemagne of the value of education that he made a genuine attempt to revive the spiritual and cultural life of western Europe.

❖ *A Master Campaigner*   From 771 to 814 Charlemagne waged a series of highly successful wars involving no fewer than 54 military campaigns, many of which he led in person. That Charlemagne could manage to muster large armies at distant frontiers and keep them supplied during lengthy and difficult campaigns was in itself an amazing feat. Almost as impressive was his success at exacting obedience from the officials scattered over his vast realm. He was indeed a man of outstanding ability and unusual force of character.

First Charlemagne overran the Lombard kingdom of northern Italy. Then Bavaria was treated likewise, and finally after 32 years of bitter campaigning he managed to incorporate Saxony within the Empire. The Saxons were particularly stubborn foes, and here Charlemagne's methods were thorough and brutal. His edict gave the Saxons a clear choice:

If any one of the race of Saxons . . . shall have wished to hide himself unbaptized and shall have scorned to come to baptism, and shall have wished to remain a pagan, let him be punished by death. . . . If any one, out of contempt for Christianity, shall have despised the holy Lenten fast and shall have eaten flesh, let him be punished by death.

As you can see, Charlemagne was a fervent, if sometimes misguided, Christian, and he anticipated the Crusades when he crossed the Pyrenees into Spain to do battle for his faith.

The secret of Charlemagne's military success was the organization of his army. Each summer there was a campaign, the starting date of which was determined by the earliest time at which pasture could be found along the route of march. Over the rough roads moved the proud armed horsemen followed by lumbering oxen pulling the baggage wagons laden with armour, clothes, and food. The sun glinted on the heavy two-edged swords of the cavalrymen as they rode along bearing their lances and bucklers. These hardy fighters could shoot arrows without dismounting as they thundered down upon the enemy. Then on foot came the infantrymen, by now greatly outnumbered by the horsemen but still a vital part of a mighty army. Service in the infantry was a heavy burden to poor

Charle-magne's army

Scale of Miles
0
100
200
KINGDOM OF CHARLES THE BALD
KINGDOM OF LOTHAIR
KINGDOM OF LOUIS
KINGDOM OF DENMARK
BALTIC SEA
ANGLO-SAXON KINGDOMS
SAXONY
Elbe R.
Oder R.
SLAVIC
Cologne
Aachen
Rhine R.
BOHEMIA
BRITTANY
Seine R.
Paris
Strasbourg
Danube R.
MORAVIA
Danube R.
Loire R.
BAVARIA
PANNONIA
AQUITAINE
LOMBARDY
Lyons
Geneva
Pavia
Venice
Po R.
Rhone R.
BURGUNDY
ADRIATIC SEA
Arles
Marseilles
PAPAL STATES
SPANISH MARCH
CALIPHATE OF CORDOVA
CORSICA
Rome
Barcelona
DUCHY OF BENEVENTO
Naples
BALEARIC IS.
SARDINIA
Kingdom of Charlemagne, 768
Charlemagne's Conquests to 814
Tributaries of Charlemagne's Empire
SICILY

THE CAROLINGIAN EMPIRE

freemen, particularly so because they were expected to provide their own weapons and food for two months—the usual duration of a campaign, since after that time the king himself had to provide for his men.

Charlemagne was a master strategist and campaigner. Before beginning an operation, he collected information about the countryside through which his army would pass—what food and water there would be, what the climate was like, what rivers there were to cross, how strong the enemy was, and so on. Once an area such as Saxony was finally conquered, he found it advantageous to build forts, which kept the peace and served as outposts for further expansion. Charlemagne even sent naval expeditions into the Mediterranean against the Moslems. No great victories were won there, but Frankish fleets did prevent Moslem raiders from attacking the coastlines of France and Italy.

Charlemagne eventually ruled over an empire that included modern France, Belgium, Holland, Switzerland, most of western Germany, a large part of Italy, a small part of northern Spain, and the island of Corsica. Only Rome had ever boasted a larger and more stable political unit in the West.

❖ *A Meticulous Administrator* Charlemagne was a fervent supporter of everything Frankish. Perhaps for this reason (and to make sure no one would plead ignorance of their contents) he commanded his officials to read his decrees in the town square in the native tongue, and ordered priests to translate their sermons into German. He even began a German grammar. Since he claimed to be God's anointed representative he also felt quite capable of exercising authority over the minutest details of Church administration. Indeed, he thought nothing of telling parish priests what to preach and congregations how to sing.

The king divided up his realm like a private estate, each division being managed by one of his personal servants known as a "count." Charlemagne feared—and with good reason—that the counts, who administered the outlying "counties" and who came from the strongest local families, might come to regard their positions as hereditary and set up private states in opposition to his central government. He therefore created a new official, the *missus dominicus,* or royal messenger, to supervise the counts. Travelling in pairs, the *missi dominici* were, like the ancient Persian agents, the "eyes and ears of the king." They made a yearly circuit of their particular district of the empire and submitted a report to the emperor; and each year they had their circuit changed to prevent collusion with the counts. Charlemagne was well aware of the danger of rebellion in his empire.

Charlemagne did not develop a permanent army or navy, but relied, as we have noted, on the general levy of freemen. A benefice went to the freeman who could afford the horse and equipment required to belong in the cavalry—but how many could afford them? All too often, as you will be reading in the *Daily Life* at the end of this Part, the freeman was forced to become the serf of the rich landowner.

Charlemagne was well aware of the inherent dangers of this situation, and attempted in various ways to preserve free status. For example, he allowed small farmers to band together and send one mounted representative to the wars. The trouble was that the one man on horseback became more important than the four or more who sent him off, and the ones who stayed at home found themselves free in name only. Even after the campaign ended they continued to work the land for their mounted lord, and in time there came to be little difference between the poor freeman and the serf. Thus it came about under the Carolingians that the mounted fighters developed into a small noble class, while the poorer freeman tended to be downgraded into serfdom.

Agrarian policy

Charlemagne himself was thoroughly convinced of the value to the state of a healthy agriculture. Unlike many rulers, he did not ruin peasant holdings by riding roughshod over the fields in his love of hunting. On the contrary, he cut down some of his cherished forests in order to make further land available for cultivation. He devoted by far the greatest portion of his attention to the management of his royal estates, and in his decrees (see page 419) laid down instructions full of the minutest (and for the superintendents, we can be sure, the most annoying) detail.

Economic policy

Finally, Charlemagne tried valiantly to revive the sagging economy. He improved roads and issued a standard silver coinage. He also managed to foster a limited trade with the Frisians, Saxons, and Slavs. But the Europe he inherited had already collapsed economically. Even before the Moslem invasions, Western cities had fallen on evil days; and along with their decay went a decline in their sea trade. Exports dwindled, industries became mere local businesses in the shells of the old cities, and money no longer circulated freely. Henceforth the crumbling towns sheltered only a bishop or a count with his household, while the majority of the people lived off the land in the country.

❖ *New Emperor of the West* The climax of Charlemagne's career came on Christmas Day in the year 800 when he was crowned by the pope in

St. Peter's Basilica in Rome. Thus symbolically was completed the 8th century fusion of traditions when a *German* king was crowned by a *Christian* pope as *Roman* emperor. A new European civilization made up of these three elements was at last fully formed.

But what was undoubtedly Charlemagne's ultimate ambition was not to be realized until two years before his death. In 812 the Byzantine emperor gave him the satisfaction of finally recognizing him as emperor of the West. In 814 the great Charles died.

❖ *The Steel of the Heathen Glistens* Charlemagne's death was followed by two centuries of attack from without, while at the same time civil war between the rival claimants for the Carolingian Empire gnawed at the realm from within. Here are eight sentences taken from contemporary chronicles of the time which describe Europe after Charlemagne.

It was doughty Frankish warriors such as this who won Charlemagne an empire. A characteristic weapon of the Frank was the throwing axe shown here, and he also used an iron-tipped spear, an iron sword, and a wooden shield — often iron rimmed. The iron was, however, of poor quality, for though the Franks had learned how to use the metal they did not discover how to harden it until the 9th century.

CHARLEMAGNE AND THE CAROLINGIAN EMPIRE/373

The steel of the heathen glistened. . . . A hundred and twenty ships of the Northmen ravaged all the country on both sides of the Seine and advanced to Paris without meeting any opposition. . . . The Saracens . . . slaughtered all the Christians whom they found outside the walls of Rome. . . . Michael, bishop of Regensburg . . . gathered his troops and joined the other Bavarian nobles in resisting an invasion of the Hungarians. . . . The cities are depopulated, the monasteries ruined and burned, the country reduced to solitude. . . . Every man does what seems good in his own eyes. . . . The strong oppress the weak; the world is full of violence against the poor and of the plunder of ecclesiastical goods. . . . Men devour one another like the fishes in the sea.

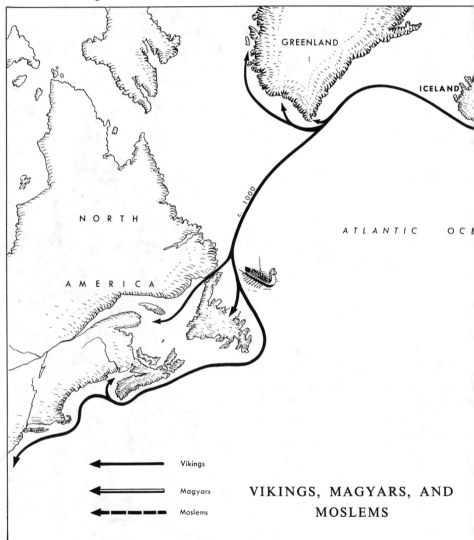

VIKINGS, MAGYARS, AND
MOSLEMS

To anyone with a knowledge of the past, the 9th and 10th centuries must have looked like the 4th and 5th centuries all over again. But there was this difference. Whereas the earlier barbarians had been tolerated, the later invaders were resisted desperately.

The most terrifying of these new marauders were the Vikings or *The Vikings* Norsemen of Scandinavia—the ancestors of the Danes, Swedes, and Norwegians. About the 9th century a combination of circumstances drove the Vikings out of their homeland. Sailing their long graceful ships

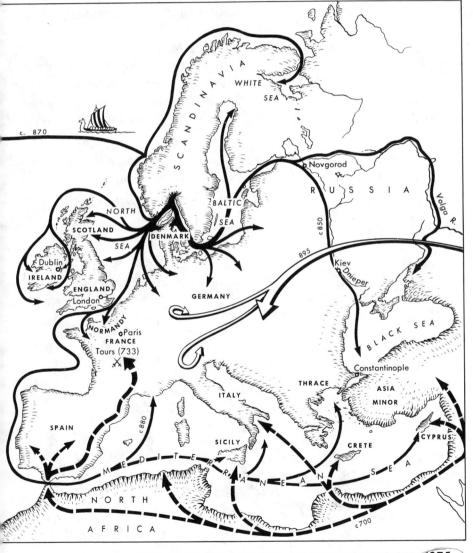

across seas and along Europe's coasts and rivers, they attacked vulnerable settlements, looting and burning towns and monasteries. They also swept the northern seas, eventually going as far as Iceland, Greenland, and even the coast of North America. (Remains of Viking settlements were found in our own country in 1962 when eight house sites and a smithy were discovered on the northern tip of Newfoundland.) It was against such intrepid raiders that the Anglo-Saxon king Alfred the Great of Wessex (871-899) won everlasting fame.

In 885 a large Viking fleet besieged Paris. But they were bought off, and settled down along the Channel coast in an area eventually known as Normandy. Harassed by the Vikings in the north, Europe was also being attacked in the east and south. The Magyars, a Turkish people, were sweeping westward, and eventually got as far as western Germany and the Rhine valley. Meanwhile Moslems conquered Sicily and southern Italy, and forced their way into the Rhone valley of southern France. Violence seemed to burst in on Europe's young civilization from every side.

❖ *A Sorry Lot* Why were these latest barbarians able to raid almost at will? Where was the strength of Charlemagne's Empire?

THE BAITING OF YOUNG EUROPE

It had taken a superman to weld and hold together the great expanse of the Carolingian Empire, and Charlemagne's successors were anything but strong. His son Louis the Pious (814-840) found his later years saddened by quarrels among his four heirs, quarrels which, as it turned out, were to rend the kingdom asunder. For in 842 an event occurred that destroyed any pretence by the eldest son, Lothair, to be sole emperor: Lothair's brother, Louis the German, and his half-brother, Charles the Bald, met to seal an alliance. Each leader swore a solemn oath in the tongue of the other's army—Louis in Old French, Charles in Old High German—so that all might understand. Thus, in their use of two distinct languages, these Strasbourg Oaths provided the first symbolic appearance of the French and German nations. A year later Lothair agreed with Louis and Charles to partition the empire by the Treaty of

What an impressive sight the graceful Viking vessels must have made as they glided about the northern coasts of Europe eleven centuries ago. The ship pictured here was built at the beginning of the 9th century, and had been drawn ashore and used as the final resting place of a Viking queen. Constructed of solid oak, it is 64 feet long and 16½ feet wide at its broadest part. When it was excavated in 1904 it was found to contain an iron anchor, some large wooden water casks, quantities of grave furnishings, and, of course, the remains of the queen—and of the young maidservant who had been buried with her. Good Queen Asa was only in her 30's, but in her short life she had attained at least one distinction, that of murdering her husband.

Verdun. The political unity of Western Christendom had finally been destroyed.

Yet even this three-way division did not prevent further wars, and the Carolingian line proved to be a sorry lot. In place of "the Hammer" and "the Great," we now hear of "the Pious," "the Bald," "the Fat," "the Stammerer," "the Simple." In the face of weak rulers and division from within, attack from without could hardly be resisted. Now the old idea of a great new empire on the foundations of Rome was a mockery; henceforth each man gave his loyalty to the man who could protect him. In such circumstances the strong held the whip hand, and kings and emperors might count for very little.

CHAPTER 36

Castle and Manor

It is seemly that the men should plough and dig and work hard in order that the earth may yield the fruits from which the knight and his horse will live; and that the knight, who rides and does a lord's work, should get his wealth from the things on which his men are to spend much toil and fatigue.

RAYMOND LÛLL, *Book of the Order of Chivalry*

It has been said that if Al Capone, the notorious Chicago gangster of the 1920's, had lived in the 10th instead of the 20th century, he would probably have ended up as a count—if not a duke. If we can imagine the armoured car as a mailed horse and the tommy-gun as a lance, then we are well on the way to understanding the outward trappings of society in the Middle Ages.

❖ *The Feudal Pyramid* In the Roman Empire it had been customary for a humble man to secure the protection of a powerful lord by *commending* himself to him as his client. At first these clients were, like those in the story of Caius Sallustius and his wife Racilia, mere hangers-on. But in the late Empire the client came to place his person and goods at the disposal of his patron, who would grant him land and protection in return for his services. These services might include work as a household servant, or some more exalted administrative position such as a stewardship. And there were specially picked clients who were expected to perform military service for their patron.

In Germanic society the warriors were strongly attached to their chieftain through a war band. Then, as we have seen, Charles Martel began the custom of raising a strong cavalry force by granting benefices to certain cavalrymen who became his vassals. Under Charlemagne some freemen became cavalrymen, while many peasants were downgraded into serfdom.

Thus we can trace the beginnings of the medieval pattern of allegiance *Feudalism* in both the Roman and German traditions, while Charles Martel's method of recruiting grew into a whole new system of landholding known as *feudalism*. Two features of this system are important. In the first place, to belong to a rank above the peasantry a man had to be rich enough to own a horse. This is why the French gave the name *chevalier* to a knight: he was the man who could afford a *cheval* (horse). Second, the lowliest knight who had just enough property to support himself could not hope to protect it unless he surrendered it to another more powerful man. The knight now became a *vassal* of the stronger man, from whom, in return for his services, he would receive his former land

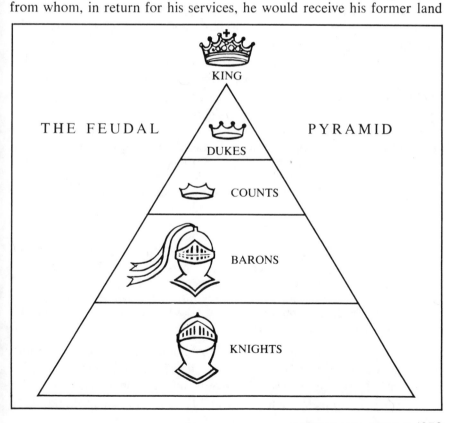

THE FEUDAL PYRAMID

KING

DUKES

COUNTS

BARONS

KNIGHTS

back as a benefice. Thus there developed a regular feudal pyramid. At the top was the king, at the bottom the simple knight, and in between a hierarchy of knights, barons, counts, and dukes.

You will notice that the peasants are not in the pyramid. That is because they did not owe any military service for land, and hence are quite below and apart from the lords. They came in a bewildering variety of gradations from free to slave, and will be discussed when we talk about the manor.

❖ *Mutual Obligations*   At first a lord granted his vassal a benefice only *in trust* as long as the vassal lived. But in time sons came to regard their fathers' estates as their rightful inheritance, and by the 10th century the benefice, now fully hereditary, came to be known as a *fief*. The land-holding relationship in which fiefs play an essential part is called the *feudal system*—although countries and even regions differed so much in their feudal practices that it really ought not to be called a "system."

Homage and fealty

Under feudalism the lord and his vassal were each parties to a con-tract, that is each owed something to the other. This contract was duly solemnized by the ceremony of *homage* and the oath of *fealty*. The ceremony that took place in 1127 at the court of William, count of Flanders, was typical, and may be read in one of the Source Readings. Less typical (we would hope!) was the manner in which Rollo, Duke of Normandy, paid his homage to King Charles the Simple:

King Charles quickly sent Franco, the archbishop of Rouen, to Rollo, the chief of the Normans, and when Franco came to him, he spoke as follows. . . . "If you are willing to become a Christian, you can enjoy peace . . . and you can settle on this land and be a very rich man, for the long-suffering King Charles, influenced by the advice of his followers, is willing to grant you this whole coast . . . which you have devastated too much already. But that there may be peace . . . he will give you his daughter Gisela for a wife. . . ."

Charles and Rollo came together at the place which had been decided upon. . . . The bishops said to Rollo, who was unwilling to kiss the king's foot: "Who-ever receives such a gift should salute the king's foot with a kiss." Rollo replied: "I will never bend my knee to anyone's knee, and I will never kiss anyone's foot." But moved by the entreaties of the Franks, he ordered one of his warriors to kiss the king's foot. The warrior immediately lifted up the king's foot, threw the king on his back, and kissed the foot, while he was stand-ing up and the king was flat on his back.

Mutual obligations of lord and vassal

Just what were the mutual obligations of lord and vassal?   The lord owed the vassal protection from foes and a hearing in his court.   He was also supposed to respect the family and personal interests of his vassal when it came to such lordly rights as naming a husband for a

Even the noble had little privacy in the Middle Ages. His great hall, the main room of his castle or manor house, was the centre of activity, and here he received his vassals, presided over his court, and ate with his family and retainers. The hall itself was, by modern standards, more picturesque than luxurious. A large open fire supplied heat, the grimy smoke staining the rafters as it slowly seeped out through a hole in the roof. The walls were usually hung with pennants and shields, along with trophies won in battle, tournaments, or the hunt. In Spain and southern France contact with the Moslems suggested the idea of laying carpets on the floor, but in the north rushes were more common. Besides, they provided a convenient place to dump the left-overs after a meal—scraps soon ferreted out by the ever-present dogs. Dinner entertainment is being presented in the hall pictured here, as musicians on an open gallery accompany the juggler who is balancing a pair of banners.

CASTLE AND MANOR/381

vassal's daughter who had inherited a fief, or acting as the guardian of an heir who was under age. These rather general obligations of the lord were more than balanced by the quite specific duties that each vassal owed his lord.

First and foremost the vassal owed his lord military service, usually forty days every year. In addition he must be prepared to garrison his lord's castle. He must attend his lord's court when summoned. And last but not least, he owed a whole series of payments. When his lord was captured he must help pay any ransom. When his lord's eldest son was knighted or the eldest daughter married he must make a contribution to the celebrations. If his lord went on crusade, or undertook to remodel his castle, or to do anything else requiring money, the vassal was again expected to contribute. When the lord visited the vassal's fief the vassal owed his lord hospitality, that is, food and lodging. And finally, when the vassal died his heir owed the lord a payment before he could inherit the fief.

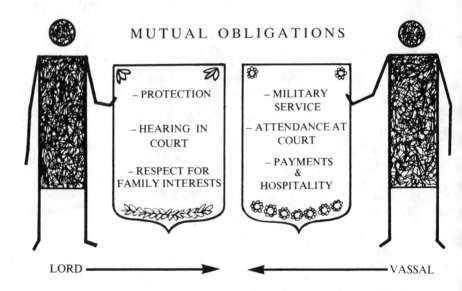

MUTUAL OBLIGATIONS

– PROTECTION

– HEARING IN COURT

– RESPECT FOR FAMILY INTERESTS

– MILITARY SERVICE

– ATTENDANCE AT COURT

– PAYMENTS & HOSPITALITY

LORD ⟶   ⟵ VASSAL

Of course these provisions of the feudal contract were not written down, and hence were much disputed. Moreover the vassal might well owe allegiance to two or more lords, or the lord himself be the vassal of other lords. The king of England, though supreme lord in his own land, was a vassal of the king of France for the duchy of Normandy; while the

French count of Champagne was famous because as lord he was owed the service of 2036 knights, yet was himself the vassal of nine lords.

What would happen if a vassal holding land of two lords found them at war with one another? To whom would he owe allegiance? In such circumstances a vassal chose between *liege* homage and ordinary homage, the liege lord being the one to whom his obligations were more binding. The complications that could still arise even after such distinctions were drawn are well illustrated by the perplexed John of Toul, who, in the early 13th century, took his oath of homage to Beatrice, countess of Troyes, in the following terms:

Liege homage

I, John of Toul, make it known that I am the liege man of the lady Beatrice, Countess of Troyes, and of my most dear lord, Theobald, count of Champagne, her son, against all persons living or dead, except for my allegiance to lord Enjorand of Coucy, lord John of Arcis and the count of Grandpré. If it should happen that the count of Grandpré should be at war with the countess and count of Champagne on his own quarrel, I will aid the count of Grandpré in my own person, and will send to the count and the countess of Champagne the knights whose service I owe them for the fief which I hold of them. But if the count of Grandpré shall make war on the countess and the count of Champagne on behalf of his friends and not in his own quarrel, I will aid in my own person the countess and count of Champagne, and will send one knight to the count of Grandpré for the service which I owe him for the fief which I hold of him, but I will not go myself into the territory of the count of Grandpré to make war on him.

With such conflicting claims as these, and we have given only a single example, you can readily see that many lords could virtually ignore their allegiances and assert a large degree of independence. A lord with a strong, well garrisoned castle could probably hold out against even his king for five or six weeks, by which time the attacking army's forty days' military service would have run out and the besiegers would melt away. In this way the noble with a strong castle became practically independent.

❖ *When Knights Were Bold*   Fighting was a knight's sole occupation. But war was a sport in which dead knights were dead losses: captive ones could be ransomed. Hence even serious wars were not very bloody during a great part of the Middle Ages. When 600 knights fought against 800 others at the Battle of Lincoln (1217), one knight was unfortunate enough to be killed!

Since there could not always be a good rousing war to pass the time, the knights had to think up some way of keeping in fighting trim. The ideal solution was a tournament. It provided an outlet for the warring instincts of the seasoned knight, while at the same time it provided the best possible proving-ground for the fledgling.

A knight cannot shine in war if he has not been prepared for it in tourneys. He must have seen his own blood flow, have had his teeth crackle under the blow of his adversary, have been dashed to the earth with such force as to feel the weight of his opponent, and been disarmed twenty times. He must twenty times have retrieved his failures before he ever set out on combat.

Castles Even the gayest blade, however, had to stay home sometimes, and when the tournament season was over and there was no campaign being waged there was always his lady awaiting him in his uncomfortable castle. In the beginning the castle was far from being a palatial mansion. It usually consisted of only two rooms, the hall in which the knight administered his fief and ate his meals, and the chamber, which was the family's private room and bedchamber. Most castles before the 12th century were wooden and windowless. If the castle was stone there might be a roaring fire, but as chimneys were often non-existent, keeping warm must have been a choking experience.

On an ordinary day the knight rose about dawn or even earlier to get the day's business (such as judging cases or consulting his manorial officials) out of the way early so as to be able to go hunting. About two or three o'clock in the afternoon came the main meal of the day—not a balanced menu of proteins and carbohydrates, but a combination of meat, poultry, and pastry, the whole washed down with gallons of beer, ale, and wine. The extensive use of spices and pepper covered up the rank flavour of tainted meat before the days of refrigeration. Table manners were hardly genteel. One was not supposed to pick one's teeth with a knife, to spit, or to put one's feet on the table—until the meal was over.

After-dinner recreation was simple, consisting of songs by wandering minstrels or the antics of tumblers or dancing bears. The knight usually went to bed soon after darkness, his eyes smarting from the smoky torches which provided the only lamps of that day. "It seems likely," writes a modern medievalist, "that if one of us were offered the choice between spending a winter night with the lord or his serf, we would choose the comparatively tight mud hut with the nice warm pigs on the floor."

You may well ask how the noble class found time for such a comparatively useless existence. Did no one work for a living? The answer is, of course, that the noble class was a very small minority supported, quite literally, on the bent backs of the peasants. These humble folk formed about 90% of the population living on manors.

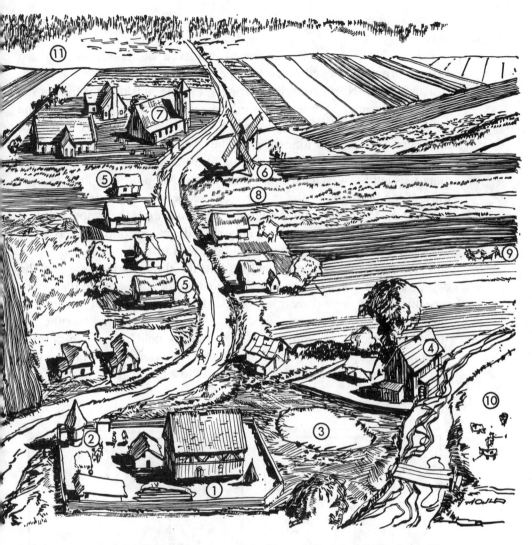

Imagine you are a pilot flying over a manorial village of the late Middle Ages. You can see the following: (1) manor house and enclosed yard, (2) lord's pigeon cote, (3) hollow where open air manor court was held, (4) water-mill, (5) serfs' huts, (6) wind-mill, (7) church, (8) fallow land, (9) serf ploughing, (10) common pasture, (11) woodland. It was in such villages as this that 90% of the people of Europe lived during the Middle Ages.

❖ *Self-sufficient Estates*   In the feudal system each knight was the lord of at least one manor. The manor was really a country estate, a self-sufficient unit consisting of the peasant village and its surrounding fields. Like feudalism, manorialism had Roman and Germanic roots. And also like feudalism, it differed widely from area to area and from century to century.

The manor   About the year 1000 the most usual type of manor in northern Europe probably looked much like the one in the diagram on page 385. Unlike modern North American farmers, the peasants did not live on the fields they farmed but went out to them each day from their huts in the village. The fields of the Middle Ages were often "open," that is, unfenced, and were divided into long strips. The average peasant's strips, which were scattered, made up a total of about 30 acres, while the lord of the manor usually reserved, also in scattered strips, about one-sixth to one-third of the best land of the manor. The scattering of the strips seems to have arisen from two considerations. It meant, first, that good and bad land on the manor would be equally shared; and second, that as more land was cleared every peasant would get his fair portion.

There were two systems of cultivation, the three-field system and the two-field system. Under the three-field system the total area of the manor was divided up into three main sections which were really *groups* of fields. One was the spring "field," planted in the spring; one the fall "field," planted in the autumn; one the fallow "field", in which nothing was planted that year. The three-field system had distinct advantages, as you can figure out for yourself from the following diagrams.

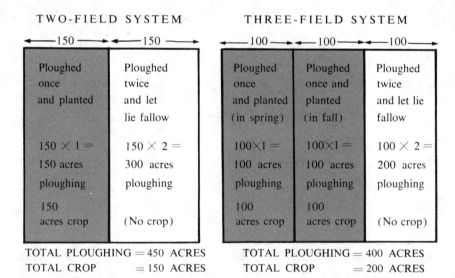

TWO-FIELD SYSTEM

←—150—→	←—150—→
Ploughed once and planted	Ploughed twice and let lie fallow
150 × 1 = 150 acres ploughing	150 × 2 = 300 acres ploughing
150 acres crop	(No crop)

TOTAL PLOUGHING = 450 ACRES
TOTAL CROP   = 150 ACRES

THREE-FIELD SYSTEM

←—100—→	←—100—→	←—100—→
Ploughed once and planted (in spring)	Ploughed once and planted (in fall)	Ploughed twice and let lie fallow
100×1 = 100 acres ploughing	100×1 = 100 acres ploughing	100 × 2 = 200 acres ploughing
100 acres crop	100 acres crop	(No crop)

TOTAL PLOUGHING = 400 ACRES
TOTAL CROP   = 200 ACRES

You can see how much more efficient the three-field system was.

❖ *The Discovery of Horsepower*   Thanks to the Germanic invaders of Europe, a number of epoch-making agricultural "inventions" came into western Europe during the so-called "Dark Ages." One of these was the heavy wheeled plough.

The Roman plough had been suited to the lighter, drier Mediterranean soils and could not cultivate the heavier soils found in northern Europe. But this new plough, mounted on wheels, was sturdier and well suited to the rich northern river valleys. In southern Europe the Roman farmer had worked the fields in one direction and then cross-ploughed them at right angles to the first furrows, in order to scratch deep enough into the soil. But with the heavy wheeled northern plough only one direction of cultivation was required—and for this reason the long strips of land developed on northern manors.

Agricultural "innovations"

Here you can see, side by side, the ancient and modern methods of harnessing horses. The two straps encircling the horse on the left will tend to strangle him when he begins to pull because they press on his windpipe, as well as on his jugular vein. But the other horse, with his modern padded collar resting firmly on his shoulders and attached to the load by lateral shafts, can throw his whole weight into pulling without restricting either his breathing or his circulation.

Perhaps most revolutionary of all was the substitution of horses for oxen in plough teams. This change resulted in an increase in the speed of cultivation comparable only to that brought about by the 20th century replacement of horses by machines. Since horses were faster animals, fewer teams were needed to plough the same area; and because less time was required in the operation, changing weather conditions were not such a hazard.

Before the full strength of horses could be drawn on, however, certain inventions were necessary. The Romans had not used horseshoes, with the result that many a broken hoof had rendered an animal useless. Previously, too, there had been only a yoke system of harness, and teams had been hitched side by side. But by about the year 900 three valuable inventions—the horseshoe, the modern tandem harness, and the horse collar—had been put into use in northern Europe. Horses could now get better traction on stony soil (which would hurt the oxen's feet) and could combine their power by being harnessed one behind the other, while the horse collar allowed them to pull without being strangled by a yoke strap across their windpipe. A team that could pull only 1000 pounds with the antique yoke could pull three or four times that weight when harnessed with the horse collar.

Horses never entirely replaced oxen. They were not as strong and were more susceptible to disease. Moreover they were more expensive to keep because they were grain-fed animals as opposed to the hay-fed oxen—and in the Middle Ages it was difficult enough to provide winter fodder for even an ox. Sometimes the poor creatures were so starved that they could barely stagger out to pasture in the spring. If horses were to be used, then, some surplus grain would have to be grown. This could only be done in northern Europe where the summers were wet enough to allow a spring planting (harvested in the late summer) as well as a fall planting (harvested early the next summer). In southern Europe no more than one crop a year could be produced. Hence horsepower was suited to northern Europe, as was the three-field system, while oxen survived mainly in the two-field areas of the south.

A great new source of power had been discovered. The horseshoe, tandem harness, and horse collar "did for the 11th and 12th centuries what the steam-engine did for the 19th." Truly a medieval agricultural revolution had occurred.

❖ *Much Toil and Fatigue*   The manor's staple crops were wheat, rye, and oats. The peasant could usually supplement his own meagre harvests by the use of the common pasture land, his access to the vineyards and orchards, and his small vegetable plot beside his cottage. He might also own an animal, a few fowls, and a beehive or two. In fact in all things except such commodities as salt (which came from mines, or from marshes along the sea coast) or luxury goods from the East, the manor formed its own self-sufficient community.

Yet despite these few homely privileges the serf was in effect almost a slave. He could not leave his lord's manor for another, nor could he *A serf's life* move to a town. Under a ruthless lord he might be treated with less consideration than the cattle of the fields. Under a kindly lord he might be protected, in some measure, by local custom, which decreed that he could not be dispossessed of his land. Since the lord was himself a vassal he probably spent considerable time away from the manor, which consequently was administered by his *bailiff* or *steward,* assisted by a *provost* or *reeve* chosen from among the peasants. The serfs laboured so that their lord could fight on behalf of his own particular lord, from whom he held the manor as a fief.

The lord owed his serf good government according to local custom,

8. Court duty
7. Tolls
6. Fees
5. Heriot
4. Taxes
3. Corvée
2. Cartage
1. Work on lord's land

Good government
Justice
Fair treatment

LORD'S OBLIGATIONS

SERF'S OBLIGATIONS

1) 3 days' work each week, plus extra work at harvest
2) Bringing firewood to manor house, harvest to granaries, etc.
3) Road repair work
4) Marriage tax, general annual tax, payments of farm produce at Easter and Christmas, etc.
5) Death duty when serf died: best piece of furniture or best beast
6) For use of lord's mill, bake-oven, etc.
7) For use of lord's bridges, roads, markets, etc.
8) Attendance at manor court

justice in the manorial court, and fair treatment according to the Church's teachings. But the serf, in his turn, bore such a heavy burden of obligations to his lord that he was to remain bent under them for centuries.

It will readily be seen that the serf, unlike the vassal, was in no position to oppose his lord. Even although it is doubtful that any individual serf bore *all* these obligations, we must remember that he owed taxes to the Church as well, and that he could escape neither of these—the *tithe* (one-tenth of his produce) and the *mortuary tax* (death duty of second-best beast or piece of furniture). All told, a serf's life must have been dreary in the extreme. The Church might tell the serf that God had ordained his lowly estate: "Are you a serf? Do not be sad; if you have faithfully served your lord, you will be a freedman of the Lord of all men." But the world saw all too clearly the virtual hopelessness of his lot: "All the peasant amasses in a year by stubborn work the noble devours in an hour." Perhaps the most poignant portrayal of the serf's bleak existence is given us by a 14th-century English poet.

As I went by the way, weeping for sorrow, I saw a poor man hanging on to the plough. His coat was of a coarse stuff which was called cary; his hood was full of holes and his hair stuck out of it. As he trod the soil his toes peered out of his worn shoes with their thick soles; his hose hung about his hocks on all sides, and he was all bedaubed with mud as he followed the plough. He had two mittens, made scantily of rough stuff, with worn-out fingers and thick with muck. This man bemired himself in the mud almost to the ankle, and drove four heifers before him that had become feeble, so that men might count their every rib so sorry looking they were.

His wife walked beside him with a long goad in a shortened cote-hardy looped up full high and wrapped in a winnowing-sheet to protect her from the weather. She went barefoot on the ice so that the blood flowed. And at the end of the row lay a little crumb-bowl, and therein a little child covered with rags, and two two-year-olds were on the other side, and they all sang one song that was pitiful to hear: they all cried the same cry—a miserable note. The poor man sighed sorely, and said "Children be still!"[1]

And so the serf grovelled at the bottom of the feudal heap. The one thing—the only thing—that made his life bearable was that it was the only life he knew.

[1]H. S. Bennett, *Life on the English Manor: A Study of Peasant Conditions, 1150-1400* (Cambridge University Press, 1948), pp. 185-186, slightly adapted.

CHAPTER 37

Three Feudal Monarchies

The great theme of European political history in the Middle Ages, once government had become feudalistic, was the attempt of the monarchs to re-assert their lost authority and to reduce the evil of continuous war.

J. W. THOMPSON AND E. N. JOHNSON
An Introduction to Medieval Europe

Now that feudal society has been described, let us examine three great feudal monarchies: France, England, and the German Empire.

❖ *A Stroke of Good Fortune*   Because the mighty feudal lords preferred to indulge in private wars, they were unwilling to accept the overriding authority of kings. In fact, a king was often actually weaker than his great vassals. At the end of the 10th century the king of France, who founded the Capetian dynasty, ruled only one small portion of that country, and was completely cowed by his mighty vassals, as the following account demonstrates. *The Capetians*

... Aldebert, count of Périgord ... carried on war against the town of Poitiers and, through a great slaughter, came out the winner, especially because its citizens rashly attacked him before they should have. He also took by siege the town of Tours. . . . And while Aldebert was besieging the town, King Hugh and his son Robert did not in any wise dare to provoke him to war, but they sent him this message: "Who appointed you count?" they said. And Aldebert replied to them: "Who appointed you kings?"

Yet the monarchy survived, and in time the king of France had a stroke of good fortune. He managed to marry his son to the heiress of the great duchy of Aquitaine—a territory comprising one-third of the area of medieval France. Now the Capetians became the greatest of French feudal lords.

The lady who had brought her land and good fortune with her was Eleanor of Aquitaine. This remarkable and spirited woman eventually divorced her French husband and proceeded, two months later, to marry the young Henry of Anjou, the future Henry II (1154-89) of England. With her went her lands. It was inevitable that the weakened Capetians should regard the English with jealous eyes.

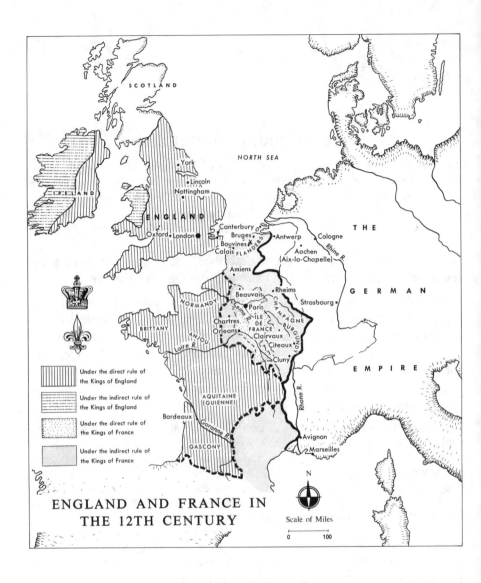

ENGLAND AND FRANCE IN
THE 12TH CENTURY

Scale of Miles

0   100

When Philip II (1180-1223), known in history as Philip Augustus, came to the French throne, he realized that England was now the chief threat to his power. Accordingly he spent much of his life stirring up trouble for the kings of England, finally succeeding in engaging both Richard the Lionheart and the notorious King John (sons of Eleanor of Aquitaine) in warfare. By 1204 Normandy itself had been lost to Philip Augustus, a defeat that earned John of England the reputation of a poor king and a poor fighter.

Thus the history of Capetian France became intertwined with that of England.

❖ *England Turns Towards France*   In the 5th and 6th centuries Germanic invaders had overrun Britain just as they had overrun Europe. These invaders, the Jutes, Angles, and Saxons, at first split up the old Roman province of Britain into a score of petty kingdoms. It took the wars of resistance against the Vikings to unify England under King Alfred the Great, and even he never really exercised authority over the whole country.

Then in the 11th century the Danes took over England when Canute *Hastings* (1016-35) conquered the island. And finally in 1066 the Normans under Duke William defeated Harold, the last Saxon king. At the battle of Hastings, about 7000 English, using methods of the 7th century, fought without cavalry and with few archers against about the same number of Normans using 11th century methods—that is, archers and mounted knights. Thanks to the Norman Conquest, England was to rapidly experience a revolution in military equipment and techniques that had taken three centuries to accomplish across the Channel.

Because William the Conqueror had come from a great French fief, he proceeded to turn England, too, into a thoroughly feudal state. His 5000 knights insisted on their share of the conquest, and as each county was taken over William was forced to allot fiefs in that district. This meant that the fiefs were scattered about, and that England, unlike France, was not divided up among the great nobles into compact blocks —a factor which turned out to be greatly to the crown's advantage. Although both the king and his vassals built many great castles, William had no intention of letting his knights get the upper hand. To ensure his control the Conqueror made all the landholders of England take a solemn oath to him as liege lord. Thus in various ways William built up a strongly feudal English state.

But the barons were a headstrong lot, and not even William the Conqueror was able to prevent a revolt. Such rebellions continued after his death (1087), and finally resulted in chaos under the weak king Stephen (1135-54).

❖ *The Greatest English King*   In 1154, however, there came to the throne the greatest of all English kings, Henry II, the great-grandson of *Henry II* the Conqueror. Henry spent much of his reign fighting against his four sons, particularly Richard and John, whom Philip Augustus was not at all averse to turning against their father. Perhaps the sons were justified

THREE FEUDAL MONARCHIES/393

in their resentment, for Henry, who ruled England, a section of Ireland, and about two-thirds of France, refused to trust them with any part of his so-called "Angevin Empire."

The dust of Henry's wars has long since settled down, until the very names of his battles are remembered by few. What is far more important is the way in which Henry II increased the royal power in England. Under Stephen it had reached its lowest point since the Conquest. Now Henry set about revitalizing it—and he was just the man for the job. The energy and restlessness of this short, barrel-chested man knew no bounds, as a distracted member of Henry's entourage well knew:

If the king has promised to remain in a place for a day—and particularly if he has announced his intention publicly by the mouth of a herald—he is sure to upset all the arrangements by departing early in the morning. As a result you see men dashing around as if they were mad, beating their packhorses, running their carts into one another—in short giving a lively imitation of Hell. If, on the other hand, the king orders an early start, he is certain to change his mind, and you can take it for granted that he will sleep until midday. Then you will see the packhorses loaded and waiting, the carts prepared, the courtiers dozing, traders fretting, and everyone grumbling. People go to ask the maids and the doorkeepers what the king's plans are, for they are the only people likely to know the secrets of the court. Many a time when the king was sleeping a message would be passed from his chamber about the city or town he planned to go to, and though there was nothing certain about it, it would rouse us all up. After hanging about aimlessly for so long we would be comforted by the prospect of good lodgings. . . . But when our courtiers had gone ahead almost the whole day's ride, the king would turn aside to some other place where he had, it might be, just a single house with accommodation for himself and no one else. I hardly dare say it, but I believe that in truth he took a delight in seeing what a fix he put us in. After wandering some three or four miles in an unknown wood, and often in the dark, we thought ourselves lucky if we stumbled upon some filthy little hovel. There was often a sharp and bitter argument about a mere hut, and swords were drawn for possession of lodgings that pigs would have shunned.

Henry was a man of no mean education. He could speak French and Latin and could understand most of the other west European languages. Foreign scholars were encouraged to come to his court, and we are reminded of Charlemagne when we read the words of Henry's secretary: "With the king of England there is school every day, constant conversation of the best scholars and discussion of questions."

Henry's legal reforms   This brilliant ruler undertook a far-reaching organization of his realm. In particular he turned his attention to a reform of England's legal system. Up until now the only way to bring a criminal to trial was through a formal accusation by the injured party or by one of his friends or relatives. Naturally people were slow to accuse a powerful man, and if a murdered man had no friends or relatives an accusation could not be brought. Henry changed this system by ordering twelve men in each district to appear before the royal justices and inform them whether anyone in their district was suspected of committing a crime. Because these men had to swear (French *jurer* = to swear) to the truth of their statements they were called *jurors.*

The cause of justice had been furthered, it is true. Yet still the procedures were very crude. The accused was tried by the ordeal of water —but even if he sank and did not drown, Henry was not completely convinced of his innocence. Henceforth such a man, if still suspected by the jury, was exiled and his property confiscated by the king.

In this way, it should be noted, Henry's legal innovations were the source of welcome revenue for the Crown. Nevertheless we should remember that this great English king showed his suspicion of trial by ordeal a half century before the Church moved to abolish it in 1215.

By this so-called *jury of presentment,* the ancestor of the grand jury, and by other reforms, Henry II pruned away the power of the baronial courts and made the Crown the stronghold of justice. He gave us the beginning of what is called *common law,* that is a law common to all men and applied throughout the whole kingdom. Now, instead of the great variety of feudal custom being applied helter-skelter, the judges in the expanded royal courts began to apply the king's law, and this common law began to supplant all other varieties of law. The birth and development of the common law is one of the proudest accomplishments traceable to Henry II and England in the Middle Ages.

Henry II was without doubt a talented administrator. Yet he was a violent man, and anything but a likeable person. He and his successors, Richard and John, bore down hard on their English nobles, collecting feudal dues up to the limit and doing everything they could to increase the royal power and to clip the barons' wings. Henry also, as we shall read later, came into conflict with the Church, and especially with the Archbishop of Canterbury, Thomas Becket.

The great monarch wore himself out at fifty-six and died in 1189, an embittered man because his sons and his queen were all in revolt against him. When Henry was brought the list of traitors and the name of his youngest son and favourite, John, led all the rest, it almost broke his heart. Two days later he died, having been forced to agree that the

1

1066

2

1200

4

1346

3

1300

5

1415

Y. MOULD.

rebellious Richard should succeed him. His last words were, "Shame, shame on a conquered king!"

The new king, Richard (nicknamed *Coeur-de-Lion*), was a magnificent warrior. But as a ruler he was far from outstanding, mostly because his absence on the Third Crusade and various French campaigns kept him away from England for all but six months of his ten-year reign. Indeed, had his father not laid such sure administrative foundations for him, it is doubtful if the realm would have continued along peacefully while this son, "the least English of all the kings of England," sought military glory abroad.

Richard the Lionheart

When Richard died in 1199—not in the glorious crash of combat but from a chance wound inflicted during a petty siege in France—his younger brother John ascended the throne. John was a conscientious ruler, but a hateful man and an unsuccessful warrior. Consequently his reputation has been permanently blackened. You will be learning more about this most interesting king, however, in the next Part.

❖ *The Collapse of a Perfect Pyramid*　When the Carolingian Empire was split up in 843 by the Treaty of Verdun (see page 377), one of the three remnants became the East Frankish kingdom. The kingdom proved to be a weak one, riddled by nobles' rebellions and Magyar invasions, and was loosely ruled by the duke of Saxony.

Finally the Saxon king Otto I (936-973) defeated the Magyars once and for all and was crowned emperor by the pope in 962. His central

---

Here we may trace the development of armour in the Middle Ages. At the time of the Conquest, Norman battle armour (1) consisted mainly of the knee-length chain mail shirt, split front and back to make riding easier. The large, elongated shields, decorated with simple non-heraldic patterns, were ideal for horsemen. In 1200 (2) mail still covered the body, including the hands, and the surcoat had been adopted from the Moslems to protect armour from both sun and dampness. The surcoat here is emblazoned with one of the many versions of the Cross worn by crusaders. By 1300 (3) mail was giving additional protection to vulnerable places. There were solid or plate armour knee-caps and small shoulder shields, while the head was completely enclosed, first in mail, then in a helmet. Heraldry had by now become an intricate science of symbols and markings, and each knight had his own special crest. By the time of Crécy (4), plate covered the mail over much of the body, the surcoat had become shortened, and the helmet had begun to acquire a movable visor for better sight and breathing. In another half century (5) plate armour was virtually complete, the full weight of the helmet resting squarely on the shoulders so that the head could not turn independently of the body.

Because a fine suit of mail such as (2) would cost about $12,000 at today's values, it would be hopelessly beyond the reach of all but the very wealthy. Common soldiers, archers, and pikemen were protected only by hardened leather or quilting, with perhaps a metal headpiece. It is an eloquent commentary on the value of medieval armour that in the celebrated Bayeux Tapestry depicting the Norman Conquest, unarmoured soldiers may be seen stripping mail shirts from the fallen while the battle rages on!

German states formed the nucleus of a shifting, expanding group of territories which by the 13th century came to be labelled the "Holy Roman Empire" (see map page 392), or, as we shall call it, the German Empire.

Unfortunately for their power, the German emperors were to become involved, in the 11th century, in a long and bitter dispute with the Church. The German nobles were not slow to take advantage of the monarch's preoccupation with this struggle, and increased their collective strength against him. At length a man emerged who looked as if he might be able to end the struggle—Frederick I (1152-1190), nicknamed Barbarossa because of his red beard.

Barbarossa proved to be the last of the great medieval emperors. Like Henry II of England, he set about restoring the rights of the monarchy, rights shattered by the preceding century of conflict with the Church. But he was also ambitious to extend his rule over wider territories. In fact he tried to build up a compact royal domain which he dreamed of using as a base for a great new empire, modelled on that of Charlemagne.

It was only a dream. Six separate expeditions into Italy did not finally re-establish the imperial power there, and sapped the strength needed to consolidate his control of Germany and to keep the Empire from falling apart. Moreover, Frederick was hampered by an obsession with his own personal version of feudalism. This version involved a perfect pyramid with himself at the top and all the princes of Germany as his vassals. In order to put his theories into practice, he attempted (and with considerable success) to make all German bishops and princes his vassals. But instead of increasing his own power by adding all confiscated lands to his royal domain, as English and French monarchs were doing, he tried to keep the pyramid from becoming top-heavy by parcelling them out again to other princes. The result was that the princes' power increased while the emperor's decreased.

Even so, Barbarossa never lost control of Germany. In 1190 he was drowned while participating in the Third Crusade.

Germany needed to be ruled by a hand of iron, and when succeeding emperors proved to be only flesh and blood, confusion prevailed. Under Frederick II (1215-50) the monarchy lost almost entirely its power over the German princes, and within a few years the shadowy German Empire had crumbled into a maze of bickering states.

❖ *Three Feudal Monarchies*   The history of the three feudal monarchies that dominated medieval Europe until the 13th century shows that feudalism could take one of two roads. It could lead to a strongly centralized state under a vigorous king-overlord (as in France and England), or it could lead to a collection of semi-independent states in which the vassals called the tune (as in Germany).

It was in England that a strong monarchy developed most rapidly. In France, only gradually did the king's might match that of the great barons. And in Germany, where the emperors never succeeded in becoming much more powerful than their vassals, the development of a strong central government lagged perhaps 500 years behind France. Of the three feudal monarchies that attempted to build up their power, then, the English was the most successful, its strength born of a line of brilliant kings who made feudalism serve them first and their barons second.

CHAPTER 38

The Church and Learning

The night of barbarism had descended on the Latin world, a darkness in which no light was visible other than that of the tapers of the Church and the homely student-lamp of the monk brooding in his cloister.

FERDINAND GREGOROVIUS,
History of Rome in the Middle Ages

It may seem to you that medieval men poured all of their energies into warfare and politics. Many did; but during the early Middle Ages, from the 5th to the 12th centuries, there were others—for the most part dedicated churchmen—who kept the light of learning flickering in Europe during some of this youthful civilization's darkest moments.

❖ *Beacons in the Gloom*   In the tottering Roman Empire of the 4th and 5th centuries, there lived in the North African city of Hippo a most remarkable man. His name was Augustine (354-430). Augustine had *St.* been a follower of the pagan philosophers, but he turned from them to *Augustine* Christianity and eventually became bishop of Hippo. The learned bishop earned such a reputation for his theology that he is today the most famous of what are called the Church Fathers.

Monks observed the vow of silence as they copied and illuminated their manuscripts. But sometimes they wrote each other notes on the margins, notes we can still read today! Often it took years to complete a single book. We can realize, then, how great was the misfortune that befell a certain monastery when, after a hard winter, a hungry bear broke into the library and devoured some leather parchments—including, alas, the monastery's only Bible.

Faced as he was with the political disintegration of his world (even as he died the Vandals were at the gates of the city), St. Augustine searched for some explanation for the catastrophe. The pagans blamed Rome's fall on Christianity, but Augustine answered the accusation in his profound book, *The City of God*. The truth is rather, says Augustine, that Rome fell because she clung to false gods. God has a plan for mankind, and all history is the story of the conflict between the City of God (composed of good and faithful Christians) and the City of Man (weak Christians and pagans). In so reasoning, Augustine furnished Christians with sound answers to the questions raised by the pagans.

As you know, the monasteries of the Benedictine Rule filled an important role by preserving knowledge during the collapse of organized society in western Europe. In a day when most people were indifferent to learning, monks spent long hours, often in dim light and freezing cold, copying ancient manuscripts. Scholars such as Bishop Gregory of Tours stood out in sharp contrast to the ignorance of their age, as did also the Northumbrian monk, the Venerable Bede (673-735). Bede *Bede* wrote Latin and could read Greek. He not only composed a history of England, but also wrote commentaries on the Bible and corrected St. Jerome's 4th century Latin translation of the Bible, the so-called *Vulgate*.

It is, in fact, from Bede that we get our most vivid portrayal of how the Benedictines brought Christianity to northern England in the 7th century. The missionaries, he tells us, were invited to preach, and after they had had their say an aged councillor addressed his Northumbrian king thus:

So seems the life of man, O King, as a sparrow's flight through the hall when a man is sitting at meat in wintertide, with a warm fire burning on the hearth but the chill rain storm without. The sparrow flies in at one door and tarries for a moment in the light and heat of the hearth-fire, and then, flying forth from the other, vanishes into the wintry darkness whence it came. So tarries for a moment the life of man in our sight, but what goes before, or what comes after, we know not. If this new teaching tells us aught certainly of these, let us follow it.

The names of St. Jerome, St. Augustine, and Bede are only three among many that might be chosen to illustrate the intellectual life of the years between the fall of Rome and the era of Charlemagne. Yet these three alone remind us that it is hardly fair to call these centuries the "Dark Ages," if by that sober label we mean centuries when *all* intellectual activity died. To be sure, the standard of achievement was far below what it had been in the days of Greece or Rome. Gregory of Tours, for example, wrote his Frankish history in ungrammatical Latin unsure of both genders and cases, and, true to his day, accepted without question all sorts of superstitions and legends. And even the methods of some 9th century historians were not too exacting, as you can see from the frank admission of a bishop of Ravenna regarding the biographies of his predecessors:

Where I have not found any history of any of these bishops, and have not been able by conversation with aged men, or inspection of the monuments, or from any other authentic source, to obtain information concerning them, in such a case, in order that there might not be a break in the series, I have composed the life myself, with the help of God and the prayers of the brethren.

THE CHURCH AND LEARNING/401

The Bayeux Tapestry is a famous work of art—an embroidered strip of linen 20 inches wide and 231 feet long—which was created to commemorate the Norman victory at Hastings in 1066. Here are two scenes from the tapestry. The one above depicts part of William the Conqueror's invasion fleet (notice how the ships resemble Viking ones) transporting men and horses across the English Channel. The second scene, in the thick of the fray, shows the mounted Norman knights bearing down on the English, who fought on foot and are clearly getting the worst of the battle. Nevertheless, English battle-axes are wielded bravely against Norman swords and lances. The tapestry is an early portrayal of the use of saddles, stirrups, bridles, and even horseshoes.

The Carolingian Renaissance

Under Charlemagne a significant renaissance (rebirth) of learning occurred. The Merovingians had had palace schools for the nobles' sons; Charlemagne's school affected his whole empire. He imported leading scholars to his palace school at Aachen (Aix-la-Chapelle), and it was his ambition alone that was in large measure responsible for the Carolingian Renaissance.

Alcuin

The foremost teacher in Charlemagne's great educational experiment was the famous Anglo-Saxon scholar, Alcuin of York (735-804). Alcuin wrote Bible commentaries, collected and supervised the copying of manuscripts, and ran the palace school. One of the most important results of this revival of learning was a clearer form of handwriting called Caroline minuscule, which replaced the cramped and crabbed Merovingian script. Caroline minuscule is the ancestor of the modern roman type which you are reading at this moment. So successful was Charlemagne's work that a century after he had sent to England for Alcuin to educate Gaul, King Alfred the Great sent to Gaul for teachers to re-educate England.

The most learned man of the 10th century was Gerbert, who stands out like a beacon in the gloom of the crumbling Carolingian Empire.

Vnſer druhtan ntchiumin·

Here is an example of that graceful script developed during the reign of Charlemagne —Caroline minuscule.

Gerbert, who died as Pope Sylvester II in 1003, was educated in France and Spain and became especially noteworthy for his mathematical skill. He was a great teacher, inventing various mechanical aids with which to instruct his students. Among his famous inventions were a sphere representing the earth and surrounded by metal bands depicting the orbits of the planets, a hydraulic organ, a water clock, and an abacus for solving numerical problems. He also wrote textbooks and introduced his students to the great authors of Rome.

Gerbert

❖ *Light from the Infidels* Actually, however, the greatest cultural developments between the 7th and 12th centuries we owe, not to the Christians, but to the Moslems. For by their conquests they passed on the classical heritage of the East, and in this way it came to the West. Moreover, the Moslems handed on their own culture to us. Their contributions in commerce, industry, geography, and astronomy can easily be seen simply by making a list of some Arabic words now used in English.

muslin	admiral	monsoon	calibre	zenith
damask	cable	traffic	magazine	nadir
tabby	sloop	tariff	check	zero
bazaar	barque	risk	average	cipher

The Moslems also made important contributions in mathematics, chemistry, and medicine. Their mathematicians did the Western world a great service in displacing the clumsy Roman numerals by adopting from India the Hindu numerals which we call "Arabic." It was the Moslems, too, who introduced the science of algebra in the 9th century and invented the zero, "one of the greatest inventions of the human mind."

Moslem mathematics

Moslem chemistry (*al chemie* in Arabic) was rather primitive, much

Chemistry

time and thought being spent on alchemy, the attempt to convert base metals into gold. Still, a great deal was learned from the experiments performed in this search. As has been said, "the failure of the alchemist was the success of the chemist."

Moslem medicine   The most interesting Moslem accomplishments were in the field of medicine. The Moslems translated the medical works of the Greek physicians Hippocrates and Galen, and wrote treatises of their own on ophthalmology (diseases of the eye). In fact their doctors laid the foundations of many modern medical practices—the first clinical account of smallpox was written by a Moslem—and their skill contrasted sharply with Christian superstitions of the time, as you will see on pages 421-422. It is remarkable that at a time when westerners believed in demon possession and thought that plague was some form of divine punishment, Moslem physicians had already discovered how diseases spread. One Arab physician writes:

The existence of contagion is established by experience, study, and the evidence of the senses, by trustworthy reports on transmission by garments, vessels, ear-rings; by the spread of it by persons from one house, by infection of a healthy sea-port by an arrival from an infected land . . . by the immunity of isolated individuals. . . .

Another reiterates:

The result of my long experience is that if a person comes into contact with a patient, he is immediately attacked by the disease with the same symptoms.

This is a far cry from superstition, magic, and witchcraft.

CHAPTER 39

A Day in the Life of a Carolingian Student

Be it known, therefore . . . that we, together with our faithful, have considered it to be useful that the bishoprics and monasteries . . . ought to be zealous in the culture of letters, teaching those who by the gift of God are able to learn, according to the capacity of each individual.

CHARLEMAGNE, *Edict on Education*

Ricolf sat very quietly at the great banquet table, observing those around him with awe and fascination. He was a long way from home. A long, long way.

The centre of the animated group, of course, the sun around whom they all revolved, was the king, the great Charlemagne himself. As usual he was wearing the plain national garb—a silk-fringed tunic, an ornate belt such as the Franks loved to wear, cross-gartered hose, and the sign of his noble birth, a handsome sword whose hilt was encrusted with jewels. How impressive he must appear on those solemn occasions when he wore his glittering diadem, jewelled boots, and cloth of gold!

But Charlemagne despised formal or foreign dress. He was a Frank, and proud of it. Nevertheless, many of his noblemen were eagerly availing themselves of the rich Eastern finery that was now making its way across the border from Italy, and Ricolf had heard the story of how the king once gave his courtiers a lesson on the virtues of simple dress. One day when they were visiting his court in their silks and pheasant skins and ermine wraps he took them on a hunt. Through the thickets they raced until, torn by branches, clawed by thorns and briers, drenched by rain, and finally smeared with blood, they captured the boar. You can imagine what they looked like on their return. By contrast, Charlemagne's sheepskin needed only a brisk brushing to be clean and white again. "Oh most foolish of all men!" he chided them. "Which of these furs is more valuable and more useful, this one of mine which I bought for a single shilling, or yours which you bought for many pounds?"

The king gave the impression of being handsome, and it was something of a shock to Ricolf to discover, on seeing him so near, that the regal nose was too large, the neck was too short and thick, and the strong six-foot figure was marred by a slight paunch. But nothing could lessen the dignity of that proud bearing, and the kindly beauty of the merry face was undeniable. Right now the king's large, clear eyes were shining with excitement as he argued a point with his trusted friend and adviser, the learned Alcuin. Charlemagne sorely missed the sage counsel of his old tutor, who had just recently retired to a position as abbot of Tours and now returned only rarely to Aachen for brief visits. Perhaps Alcuin had been the first to recognize the remarkable intellectual agility of this amazing monarch, born 700 years ahead of his time. He and the king had enjoyed such complete accord when it came to the dream of a cultured Frankland. "I loved so much in you," wrote Alcuin, "what I saw you were seeking in me." And so an English scholar had become "Minister of Education" for the realm, and the king his willing pupil.

It was easy to see how the assemblage here tonight loved Charlemagne, and with good reason. Laughter and warm hospitality always surrounded him, and he had the gift of living with his countrymen rather than above them. Yet his obsession for efficiency could spell disaster for the laggard who crossed his path. And though he was loyal to his friends and affectionate to his wives, there were those who said his love for his daughters was selfish and possessive. As Ricolf watched them hovering near their father at the table, waiting on his every whim, he saw that the reports of their beauty had not been in the least exaggerated. But why did their father never allow them to marry? Was it, as some said, because he could not bear them away from his side? Or was it rather that he knew too well how the brides of foreign rulers were sometimes mistreated? One Frankish ruler had had his wife strangled when she displeased him, and another was sent home minus her ears.

Only one of Charlemagne's sons sat with him at the table—Charles, a handsome lad, the image of his father and the apple of his eye. The delicate Louis, that ascetic youth whom the king found so hard to understand, was absent, and Ricolf had never seen Pepin, the hunchbacked son, who had been sent from court, rumour had it, because of family trouble. The members of Charlemagne's famous inner circle, however, were almost all gathered tonight. Ricolf had been seated next to one of the guests of honour—his adored sponsor, Theodulf. This erstwhile Goth from Spain was, as usual, engaged in a heated debate with Paul the Deacon (a Lombard), and Peter of Pisa (an Italian), while a bustling little Frank named Einhard—"a small body which houses a great spirit," Theodulf described him—listened attentively. Some day Einhard would immortalize this whole company in a biography that was to be the masterpiece of the age.

There was a clattering at the back of the great banquet hall and a delicious aroma foretold the imminent arrival of the main feature of the feast, a great roast of venison. The amiable chief steward, surrounded by a squadron of chefs, fussed about the roast as if it had been an honoured guest, until Ricolf almost felt that the royal treasurer and chamberlain, who ushered people to their proper places, should announce the name of the deer as it was borne in! All looked at the meat with relish except Alcuin, who quietly went on with his porridge and cheese.

It seemed to Ricolf that that immense roast, side by side with Alcuin's humble porridge, symbolized more vividly than anything else could do the contrast between his own past and present. What a long way he had come! He had entered a new world.

Ricolf had been born near Orléans, the son of a poor Frankish free-man. He was the youngest of seven. His mother had died in childbirth, and his father's sister, herself a widow, had raised him. In all his child-hood he had never known a day when he had had quite enough to eat, nor the faintest whiff of luxury.

Aside from the fact that Ricolf's father, Wolfar, paid a set rent for his small landholding, his position differed little from his neighbours who were serfs. The manor, with its church, mill, forge, and bakery, was their whole world. The peasants would live out their lives there and die there, their days an unending succession of dues to the lord and work on the land. It was as if they had been bound to the seasons by chains, to be dragged inexorably after them forever. The work, the battle against the land, was unending. The autumn was the worst. Then every-one—even Ricolf's aunt—had to go out into the fields to reap the harvest before it was too late; the fruit and nuts had to be gathered; firewood had to be collected; the cottage had to be made a little more weather-proof and the lean-to for the ox strengthened; tools had to be repaired, grain ground, cheeses made. The tasks took every minute of daylight, and required the peasant to be jack-of-all trades.

Yet what was the harvest but the signal for autumn ploughing? And what was the autumn ploughing but the signal for winter sowing? Dawn to dusk, dawn to dusk, the days broken only by the plainest of meals—

"The autumn was the worst. . . . Dawn to dusk, dawn to dusk. . . ."

a hunk of dark rye bread and a mug of ale, some cheese and an onion or two, a thick soup for supper. In the fall the puny cattle were usually slaughtered for lack of winter feed, but their meat was so tough that one wag said he'd rather eat the leather. It was more sensible to keep pigs anyway: they could root for themselves. Once in a while Ricolf's aunt, on a very special occasion like his birthday (which they happened to remember only because he had been born on a Church Feast Day), boiled a fowl, and occasionally they all guiltily enjoyed a poached fish or rabbit. After all, argued Aunt Hildigard, why shouldn't they? The rabbits—if not the doves from the lord's dovecote—seemed to eat up half the peasants' meagre crops. Then there had been the time when they had been so overjoyed to be presented by the lord with a cut of mutton—until they found it was tainted, dead of the plague. Such was the lord's generosity!

So the little family inched its way along from one harvest to the next, penniless but cherishing a priceless possession, *freedom*. And then Ricolf's father, like many another small landowner, lost even the slim margin of independence he had: he gave himself up as a serf to his lord. What had forced him to such a drastic step?

The medieval man lived under two great curses, famine and war. Transportation was so slow that it was impossible to bring food in sufficient quantities to alleviate a famine, and Wolfar had fought to keep body and soul together through three of them—one, in 791, so dreadful that it had reduced some of his countrymen to cannibalism. He had also seen plague carry off his only daughter and eldest son. Then, as if the struggle for existence were not bitter enough, Wolfar, being a free man, was liable to compulsory military service from which serfs were exempt. If he went his gear and provisions were expensive, and he could not harvest his crops; if he stayed he was subject to a fine so large that he might not be able to pay it, in which case his land would fall forfeit to the collector. In addition, every Frankish freeman had to attend courts when summoned, and this duty plus the increased calls for military aid against the fearful Saxons forced many a freeman to accept the yoke of serfdom. At least, thought Wolfar miserably, if he should die a serf his sister and children would be looked after in some fashion by the lord.

Wolfar had hung on tenaciously to his freedom, and Charlemagne himself, who was always concerned that the poor not be abused and that widows should be protected, strove to prevent the freeman's exploitation. The king adopted a sliding scale of fines, and decreed that "our judges, counts, or *missi* must not extort payments of a fine from those poor persons to whom the emperor has in his mercy forgiven what they ought to pay."

The *missi dominici,* too, tried to enforce justice. But in too many cases it was a losing battle. There were lords who were just; but there were also lords like Wolfar's. Such a villain could be persuaded by a fat bribe to release certain prosperous freemen from military service, and then would draft only the poor wretches who were left. He would impose forced labour on his freemen, pasture his animals on their land, and collect contributions not demanded by custom. All knew how useless it was to bring complaints against him in his own court. On one occasion he simply seized the land of a frail and senile freeman, and then insisted he had bought it.

By all these abuses the lord wore down the small remaining nucleus of poor landholders in his domain. But he had one especially refined, and perfectly legal, method of bending a freeman to serfdom. He ordered him to attend court so frequently that he had no time, after the labour demanded of him by his lord in lieu of additional rent, to look after his own property. Such was the special treatment meted out to Wolfar. And it worked. After he had been subjected to repeated summonses to court he went, a beaten man, to his lord. Solemnly he performed the outward and symbolic acts which accompanied this descent into serfdom: he put a bell-rope around his neck to denote his abject dependence on his lord, and four coins on his head to signify his servile condition. No longer would he tender his taxes by hand like a free man. Henceforth he, and his children, and his children's children would be swallowed up in the nameless ranks of serfdom, for ever and ever.

By accepting serfdom, Wolfar had transferred his intolerable military duties to his lord and attained a measure of security. The lord did not consider it good economics to let either his cattle or his serfs starve. But Wolfar had exchanged old burdens for new. Now the lord's claim upon his time increased enormously: the serf owed him three days out of every week, besides the fact that he could be called upon at almost any time to work on other projects on the manor. Suddenly Ricolf's whole family was hemmed about with restrictions. The serf's daughter could not marry out of the village unless he paid a fee; he was not allowed to grind his own corn, to sell his own beast, to brew or bake or even gather firewood without a series of fees or permissions. For pasturing cattle the serf paid cheeses. For letting swine roam in the woods he paid a certain number of pigs. He was constantly forced to put his lord's affairs first and his own second. All told, the serf was treated with little more consideration—and sometimes with less kindness—than the cattle of the fields. Yet even at that there was one, in these harsh medieval years, who fared worse—the wanderer, the displaced person who was utterly free, completely miserable, and heartily despised and distrusted by the villagers with whom he mixed. Such a person would gladly have changed places with Ricolf's father just to work a small holding and *belong* somewhere.

Of course life held some pleasures, too. The days when the peasants all worked together on the lord's fields were usually full of good companionship (despite the fact that one of their fellows was assigned a club to keep them at work), and the lord's food was ravenously devoured. And there were marriages and funerals and drinking bouts, and festivities and dancing in the churchyard on holy days. At Christmas time the peasants went to the manor house for a feast, each bearing his own faggot of brushwood lest the cook serve his meat raw, and each his own dish and mug. How delicious the fine wheat bread was, and how luxurious the good helping of meat—and how nice to pretend one was the lord as one sat drinking after dinner at his table! How far away, for the moment, was the small windowless hut with the packed dirt floor that got so slippery when the rain or snow came in through the hole in the roof! And how quickly it was time to go home to the dark little two-roomed abode, to grope about for a candle amidst the chickens, pigs, cats, and dogs, and then to settle down, blissfully unaware of how the straw scratched through the pallet and the wooden bolster numbed the ears. It was all very well for Charlemagne to talk of cleanliness (he even tried to prevent the peasants from treading grapes with their feet —imagine!); but how was the serf to keep warm, short of burning himself up, without his animals in his hut?

How good it was in the spring to get out of the crowded little huts into the open air. The cooking fire on the floor gave scant heat and much smoke, and the stench was unbearable. So many people—why, Ricolf did not understand—died in the winter time, babies, old folks, often whole families. But the sun seemed to bring happiness. With the summer the women could cook and spin outside and tend their chickens and their gardens, and sometimes little children stopped coughing and grew rosy-cheeked again.

One of the peasant's diversions was to go to church. Ricolf was very musical, and he thrilled to the chanting of the Mass. Indeed, he loved everything about the church—its many-hued windows, its heavy carvings, its mysterious Book. This love was not shared by his father, who had struggled too often to pay its dues, a burden that was even heavier now that the emperor had decreed that the tax should be doubled from 10% to 20% of their income. Poor serfs. What the lord did not take the church demanded.

Ricolf, too, put many long hours into the earning of the tithe; yet the Church remained his special source of joy. He could not have told you why. He knew vaguely that it was concerned for the lowly and the weak; it limited, for example, the size of stick a wife could be beaten with. And in some dim way he believed that it protected him from all the charms and devils that his Frankish ancestors had bequeathed him. To the superstitious peasant the earth was a living creature. One magic rite (which Charlemagne, realizing its waste, tried to forbid) required that a part of the seed for sowing should be buried deep in the ground as a sacrificial offering to Erda, the goddess of the earth, who might otherwise be offended by having a plough rudely driven into her body. A sick person was not permitted to approach cultivated fields, and a funeral procession must bypass them on its way to the grave. There was a village magician, and he had been called in once when Ricolf was very ill to provide a healing potion and break the evil spell over him.

Like the other peasants, Ricolf performed rites and believed in the evil eye. But somehow when he entered the church he felt he had a refuge from the malicious spirits that inhabited groves and gnarled tree trunks. Besides, the priests had other magic. They baptized bells and attached slips of paper to them in order to prevent hail, they themselves had sacred trees, groves, and springs, and they acted as soothsayers with the aid of the Bible. In vain did King Charles fight against such superstition. Once again he was ahead of his times.

It was Ricolf's delight at being inside the church on every possible occasion that first drew him to the priest's attention. When Theodulf had been made Bishop of Orléans he had organized four major schools in his diocese, open not just to priests but to all who wished to enter. He also ordered his parish priests to organize free schools for the village children, both serf and free. Convinced of the boy's intelligence, the priest managed to persuade the lord to allow Ricolf to attend one of these schools, and soon he was receiving rudimentary training (as, indeed, were some of the unlettered priests themselves) and was being taught to read. The priests also, at the royal command, began laboriously to correct their woefully inaccurate copies of the scriptures, and would have assigned some of this drudgery to their pupils had the king not added anxiously to his dictum, "And do not allow your boys to corrupt the books by their own reading or writing. If a copy be needed of the Gospel, or Psalter, or Missal, let men of ripe age write it out with all diligence."

Ricolf learned quickly and well, and had an unusual artistic gift which soon showed itself in his fine illuminations of his boyish copies of the Psalter. One day the great Bishop Theodulf himself visited the school, and when he saw Ricolf's work and talked to him he was so impressed by the boy's abilities that he decided to take him to the renowned Palace School at Aachen, which Alcuin had made famous, for advanced training. That was two years ago. Now Theodulf, like Alcuin, had a new position. He had been made one of the king's *missi,* and had come to visit Charlemagne at the end of one of his tours. The king, knowing Theodulf's fondness for his protégé, had invited Ricolf to dine with the royal party tonight in order that he might talk with Theodulf. That was how it had come about that Ricolf, son of a serf, dined with the great Emperor Charlemagne.

Although the king himself never learned, try as he might, to read or write, he was surrounded by literate men who kept him well informed. Once, in his burning desire that all should thirst after knowledge as he himself did, he cried to Alcuin, "Oh, if only I had twelve such clerics, so learned and perfectly versed in all wisdom as were Jerome and Augustine!" Whereupon the pious Alcuin, always respectful but never afraid of his beloved master, answered tartly, "The Creator of Heaven and earth Himself had but few such men, and you want *twelve* of them!" This evening, as usual, the company was treated to readings from St. Augustine's *City of God,* and then Theodulf was asked to recite one of his poems. He chose one which he knew Charlemagne liked especially (it may even be a favourite hymn of yours today):

> All glory, laud, and honour
> To Thee, Redeemer, King,
> To whom the lips of children
> Made sweet hosannas ring!

The poem went on for several stanzas and was enjoyed by most of the party. Ricolf noted, however, that one of the warriors named Wibod was not exactly moved to ecstasy. First his head nodded, and then he sat fiercely awake, clapping his hand to his thick black hair in despair and glaring at the reciting Theodulf until Charlemagne noticed him and froze him with a glance.

The reproving look reminded Ricolf of the first time he had seen the great king. A Latin lesson was in progress in the palace school when the king, accompanied by his fifth wife, the gentle and intellectual Luitgard (who loved to sit in on some of the classes), entered the room. The lesson was from a textbook that Alcuin himself had written, and went like this:

What is life? The joy of the good, the sorrow of the wicked, the waiting for death.

What is man? The bondsman of death, a passing wayfarer, a guest upon earth.

What is the sun? The splendour of the universe, the beauty of the sky, the glory of the day, the divider of the hours.

What is winter? The exile of summer.

What is spring? The painter of the earth.

And so on.

The lower-class children answered beautifully and their work was admirable. "My children," said the king, "you have found much favour with me because you have tried with all your might to carry out my orders. Now study to attain perfection and I will give you bishoprics and splendid monasteries and will always honour you." But the upper-class children, the darlings of the Frankish nobility, had stammered out incorrect answers and presented messy notebooks, and they felt the full force of the royal wrath. "You nobles," he thundered at them, "you sons of my chiefs, you superfine dandies, you have trusted to your wealth and have set at naught my orders which were for your own good; you have neglected learning and gone in for luxury and sport, idleness and profitless pastimes. By the King of Heaven, I take no account of your noble birth and your fine looks, though others may admire you for them. Know this for certain, that unless you make up for your laziness by vigorous study, you will never get favours from Charles." And with that he stomped out of the room. The king had great ambitions for teaching the high and the low alike and at one time. But he was to find that the high, and not the low, protested against such education. They

Soon after Ricolf joined Alcuin in Tours, Charlemagne reached this climax of his career—his coronation in Rome on Christmas Day, 800.

had no intention of demeaning themselves by letting their children mingle with inferiors.

Although discipline in the school was strict, Alcuin liked his classes to be informal (usually in dialogue form), and the king and his family all received training in them. The king, an eloquent speaker, was especially interested in rhetoric and astronomy. Alcuin strove endlessly to correct the medieval errors that had crept into Latin. "Be very careful," he would say, "of the initial *h*: *ara* means altar, *hara* a pigsty!" He submitted all his textbooks to Charlemagne, who would have his secretary read them to him, for approval. How, wondered Ricolf, did the great king have time, amidst all his campaigns and administrative tasks, to take so much interest in learning?

The banquet was nearing its close, and Charlemagne signalled the minstrels to begin. The royal face beamed with pleasure at the German folksongs, and Alcuin—who disapproved of them, as he disapproved of the whole study of the vernacular—looked very bored in a genteel way. Suddenly Ricolf was electrified as the king turned to him and, with a twinkle in his eye, posed this riddle: "I saw the dead give birth to the living, and the alive consumed unto death by the living's wrath. What did I see?" The whole company, who dearly loved a riddle, had grown quiet. Ricolf felt Theodulf's eyes upon him. Taking a deep breath to quell his nervousness he replied modestly, "I believe, sire, that it is Fire, born from the friction of dead trees." There was applause and laughter, and Ricolf felt his cheeks growing crimson, whereupon the king, always kindly, turned the conversation towards Theodulf and a discussion of his new work as *missus*.

Theodulf needed no second bidding to enumerate some of the abuses he found. Ricolf listened avidly, fascinated to hear him mention some of the very acts that had led his father to give up his freedom. Theodulf also criticized corrupt bishops, and named several lower officials he had discharged. He stressed how he had carried out Charlemagne's wishes by warning the stewards of the royal estates not to force peasant labour on their own holdings, nor to grind these humble folk down into poverty. Finally he described a courthouse at Narbonne where he had presided. The noisy cries of "yea" and "nay" filled the courtroom with barbarous confusion, and Theodulf strongly disapproved of the Germanic principle whereby a life might be paid for in money but theft was punished by the loss of a hand or an eye—or even crucifixion. Most of all, he deplored the bribery attempted in order to gain a favourable verdict. Some officials went about with a great ox-cart laden high with their "gifts"; and even he himself had accepted some timid offerings of fruit and vegetables, cheese and small birds, lest the lowly donors be hurt. But he had angrily refused objects of gold and fine brocade. "With this battering-ram," he cried, "they hope to break down the wall of my soul. But they would not have thought that they could shake *me,* if they had not so shaken other judges before."

The feasting was over now, and the king, who despised drunkenness, did not encourage his guests to linger over their wine. Amidst the patter of conversation Ricolf was astounded to hear the king remark, almost too casually, that Harun-al-Rashid, the caliph of Bagdad, would soon be sending him the gift of an elephant. An elephant! All that

Ricolf knew about these mighty beasts came from medieval lore: they were mountainous in bulk; they could bear young only once in their long lifetime of three centuries; an elephant's hair burned in a house would cause snakes and all poisonous things to leave promptly; and a few other wondrous details which escaped him at the moment. Who would ever have thought that he, a peasant lad, would be in this wonderful palace at Aachen with its golden chapel, its marble pool that held over a hundred men at the king's mammoth swimming parties, and its huge bronze eagle poised on the palace roof for visitors to see from afar. True, Charlemagne had stripped mosaics and marbles from Rome and Ravenna to beautify his chapel, but still he was creating an island of culture in a country of barbarians. And now he was to have an elephant too! No wonder Ricolf was overawed.

As the banqueters rose to go Ricolf bowed respectfully to Father Alcuin, and that worthy looked searchingly into the eager face of the young student. "You copy manuscripts well, my son, and your hand is deft with a brush. We have need of many books in Tours. Perhaps some day you and I will do great things together."

The words, the searching look, the tired, lined face kept coming back to Ricolf. He knew how discouraging the work in Tours was. Occasionally extracts from Alcuin's letters to Charlemagne would be read at school. "Here I am, struggling day by day with the uncultured minds of Tours," he wrote. "I do make some progress, though it isn't much." "You know well what delight there is in arithmetic, how necessary it is for understanding the Bible. How few care about such things! Worse still, they run down those who are keen to learn." The battle against illiteracy was heart-breaking, and the old man was worn down by it. "These boys pester me with their little problems like flies in the summertime at our windows!" Most of all, texts were scarce and inaccurate. It costs too much to buy them from the monasteries, he protests. What is he to do? How can he spread the light of learning without help?

Help was forthcoming. The peasant boy who had done such delicate illuminations and had mastered such fine Caroline minuscule back in Orléans, who had studied so assiduously at Aachen and worked with such joy carving ivory panels in the Palace School workshop, the sensitive scholar who had revered Alcuin all his life, now chose gladly to go to Tours to join him. God willing, they would be granted some time. For a few brief years Alcuin would be spared, so that together they might spread the light of learning a little further into the Frankish gloom.

416/THE EARLY MIDDLE AGES

SOURCE READINGS

(a)

The *Rule* set up by ST. BENEDICT (480-543) for his followers at Monte Cassino has been called "a model of practical and spiritual wisdom." You will see some of this wisdom in the following regulations:

3. *Of calling the Brethren to Council*   As often as any important matters have to be transacted in the monastery, let the Abbot call together the whole community, and himself declare what is the question to be settled. And, having heard the counsel of the brethren, let him consider within himself, and then do what he shall judge most expedient. We have said that all should be called to council, because it is often to the younger that the Lord revealeth what is best. But let the brethren give their advice with all subjection and humility, and not presume stubbornly to defend their own opinion; but rather let the matter rest with the Abbot's discretion. . . .

6. *Of the Practice of Silence*   Let us do as saith the prophet: "I said, I will take heed to my ways, that I sin not with my tongue, I have placed a watch over my mouth; I became dumb and was silent, and held my peace even from good things." Here the prophet sheweth that if we ought at times to refrain even from good words for the sake of silence, how much more ought we to abstain from evil words, on account of the punishment due to sin. Therefore, on account of the importance of silence, let leave to speak be seldom granted even to perfect disciples, although their conversation be good and holy and tending to edification; because it is written: "In much speaking thou shalt not avoid sin"; and elsewhere: "Death and life are in the power of the tongue." . . . But as for buffoonery or idle words, such as move to laughter, we utterly condemn them in every place, nor do we allow the disciple to open his mouth in such discourse.

36. *Of the Sick Brethren*   Before all things and above all things care is to be had of the sick, that they be served in very deed as Christ Himself, for He hath said: "I was sick, and ye visited Me." And, "What ye have done unto one of these little ones, ye have done unto Me." And let the sick themselves remember that they are served for the honour of God, and not grieve the brethren who serve them by unnecessary demands. . . .

48. *Of the daily manual labour*   Idleness is an enemy of the soul; and hence at certain seasons the brethren ought to occupy themselves in the labour of their hands, and at others in holy reading. We think, therefore, that the times for each may be disposed as follows: from Easter to the first of October, let them, in going from Prime in the morning, labour at whatever is required of them until about the fourth hour. From the fourth hour until near the sixth let them apply themselves to reading. And when they rise from table, after the sixth hour, let them rest on their beds in perfect silence; or if any one perchance desire to read, let him do so in such a way as not to disturb any one else. Let None be said in good time, at about the middle of the eighth hour: and then let them again work at whatever has to be done until Vespers. And

if the needs of the place, or their poverty, oblige them to labour themselves at gathering in the crops, let them not be saddened thereat; because then are they truly monks, when they live by the labour of their hands, as did our fathers and the Apostles. . . .

54. *Whether a Monk ought to receive letters, or tokens* By no means let a monk be allowed to receive, either from his parents or any one else, or from his brethren, letters, tokens, or any gifts whatsoever, or to give them to others, without permission of the Abbot. And if anything be sent to him, even by his parents, let him not presume to receive it until it hath been made known to the Abbot. But even if the Abbot order it to be received, it shall be in his power to bid it be given to whom he pleaseth; and let not the brother to whom it may have been sent be grieved, lest occasion be given to the devil. Should any one, however, presume to act otherwise, let him be subjected to the discipline of the Rule.

58. *Of the Discipline of receiving Brethren into Religion* To him that newly cometh to change his life, let not an easy entrance be granted, but, as the Apostle saith, "Try the spirits if they be of God." If, therefore, he that cometh persevere in knocking, and after four or five days seem patiently to endure the wrongs done to him and the difficulty made about his coming in, and to persist in his petition, let entrance be granted him, and let him be in the guest-house for a few days. Afterwards let him go into the Novitiate, where he is to meditate and study, to take his meals and to sleep. Let a senior, one who is skilled in gaining souls, be appointed over him to watch him with the utmost care, and to see whether he is truly seeking God, and is fervent in the Work of God, in obedience and in humiliations. Let all the hard and rugged paths by which we walk towards God be set before him. And if he promise steadfastly to persevere, after the lapse of two months let this Rule be read through to him, with these words: "Behold the law, under which thou desirest to fight. If thou canst observe it, enter in; if thou canst not, freely depart." If he still stand firm, let him be taken back to the aforesaid cell of the Novices, and again tried with all patience. And, after a space of six months, let the Rule be again read to him, that he may know unto what he cometh. Should he still persevere, after four months let the same Rule be read to him once more. And if, having well considered within himself, he promise to keep it in all things, and to observe everything that is commanded him, then let him be received into the community, knowing that he is now bound by the law of the Rule, so that from that day forward he cannot depart from the Monastery, nor shake from off his neck the yoke of the Rule, which after such prolonged deliberation he was free either to refuse or to accept. . . .

    The Rule of St. Benedict, translated by D. O. H. Blair (Abbey Press, Fort Augustus, Scotland, 5th edition, revised and corrected, 1948), pp. 25, 39, 101, 123, 125, 137, 139, 145, 147.

(b)

GREGORY OF TOURS (538-594) was the son of a wealthy Gallo-Roman family, and was made bishop of Tours in 573. He is most famous for his *History of the Kings of the Franks*. The following selection, which describes the methods used by Clovis to become king of all the Franks, seems to condone his many crimes in view of his vigorous support of orthodoxy versus Arianism.

While Clovis was sojourning at Paris, he sent secretly to the son of Sigibert, saying: "Thy father is grown old, and is lame of one foot. If he were to die, his kingdom would fall to thee of right, together with our friendship." The prince, seduced through his ambition, plotted his father's death. One day Sigibert left Cologne and crossed the Rhine, to walk in the forest of Buchau. He was enjoying a midday repose in his tent when his son compassed his death by sending assassins against him, intending so to get possession of the kingdom. But by the judgment of God he fell himself into the pit which he had treacherously digged for his father. He sent messengers to King Clovis announcing his father's death in these terms: "My father hath perished, and his kingdom and treasures are in my power. Come to me, and right gladly will I hand over to thee whatever things may please thee from his treasure." Clovis answered: "I thank thee for thy goodwill, and request of thee that thou show all to my envoys; but thou shalt keep the whole." On the arrival of the envoys, the prince displayed his father's treasure, and while they were inspecting its various contents, said to them: "In this coffer my father used to amass pieces of gold." They answered: "Plunge thy hand to the bottom, to make sure of all." He did so; but as he was stooping, one of them raised his two-edged axe and buried it in his brain; so was his guilt towards his father requited on himself. When Clovis heard that Sigibert was slain, and his son also, he came to Cologne and called all the people together, addressing them in these words: "Here ye what hath befallen. While I was sailing the Scheldt, Chloderic, son of my cousin, was harassing his father, and telling him that I desired his death. When his father fled through the forest of Buchau, he set bandits upon him, delivering him over to death. But he in his turn hath perished, stricken I know not by whom, while he was showing his father's treasure. To all these deeds I was in no wise privy; for I could not bear to shed the blood of my kindred, holding it an impious deed. But since things have so fallen out, I offer you this counsel, which take, if it seemeth good to you: turn ye to me, and live under my protection." At these words the clash of shields vied with their applause; they raised Clovis upon a shield, and recognized him as their king. Thus he became possessed of the kingdom of Sigibert and of his treasures, and submitted the people also to his dominion. For daily the Lord laid his enemies low under his hand, and increased his kingdom, because he walked before Him with an upright heart, and did that which was pleasing in His sight.

The History of the Franks by Gregory of Tours, translated by O. M. Dalton (Clarendon Press, 1927), II, 78-79.

(c)

CHARLEMAGNE (768-814) in his Decree concerning Villas laid down detailed instructions as to what he expected from the stewards on his estates. These villas were combined farms and "factories," and the Emperor took a keen personal interest in checking the efficiency of their superintendents.

34. They must provide with the greatest care, that whatever is prepared or made with the hands, that is, lard, smoked meat, salt meat, partially salted meat, wine, vinegar, mulberry wine, cooked wine, garns, mustard, cheese, butter, malt, beer, mead, honey, wax, flour, all should be prepared and made with the greatest cleanliness.

40. That each steward on each of our domains shall always have, for the sake of ornament, swans, peacocks, pheasants, ducks, pigeons, partridges, turtle-doves.

42. That in each of our estates, the chambers shall be provided with counter-panes, cushions, pillows, bedclothes, coverings for the tables and benches; vessels of brass, lead, iron and wood; andirons, chains, pot-hooks, adzes, axes, augers, cutlasses and all other kinds of tools, so that it shall never be necessary to go elsewhere for them, or to borrow them. And the weapons, which are carried against the enemy, shall be well cared for, so as to keep them in good condition; and when they are brought back they shall be placed in the chamber.

43. For our women's work they are to give at the proper time, as has been ordered, the materials, that is the linen, wool, woad, vermilion, madder, wool-combs, teasels, soap, grease, vessels and the other objects which are necessary.

62. That each steward shall make an annual statement of all our income; an account of our lands cultivated by the oxen which our ploughmen drive and of our lands which the tenants of farms ought to plough; an account of the pigs, of the rents, of the obligations and fines; of the game taken in our forests without our permission; of the various compositions; of the mills, of the forest, of the fields, of the bridges, and ships; of the free-men and the hundreds who are under obligations to our treasury; of markets, vineyards, and those who owe wine to us . . . of the fish-ponds; of the hides, skins, and horns; of the honey, wax; of the fat, tallow and soap . . . of the hens and eggs . . . the number of fishermen, smiths, sword-makers, and shoe-makers . . . of the forges and mines . . . of the colts and fillies; they shall make all these known to us, set forth separately and in order, at Christmas, in order that we may know what and how much of each thing we have.

S. C. Easton and H. Wieruszowski, *The Era of Charlemagne: Frankish State and Society* (Anvil Books, Van Nostrand, 1961), pp. 133-134, 132-133.

(d)

This performance of HOMAGE, FEALTY, and INVESTITURE took place in 1127 at the court of William, count of Flanders, on the death of his father, Charles.

Through the whole remaining part of the day those who had been previously enfeoffed by the most pious count Charles, did homage to the new count, taking up now again their fiefs and offices and whatever they had before right-fully and legitimately obtained. On Thursday, the seventh of April, homages were again made to the count, being completed in the following order of faith and security:

First they did their homage thus. The count asked if he was willing to become completely his man, and the other replied: "I am willing"; and with clasped hands, between the hands of the count, they were bound together by a kiss. Secondly, he who had done homage gave his fealty to the representative of the count in these words, "I promise on my faith that I will in future be faithful to Count William, and will observe my homage to him completely, against all persons, in good faith, and without deceit." Thirdly, he took his oath to this upon the relics of the saints. Afterwards, with a little rod which the count held in his hand, he gave investitures to all who by this agreement had given their security and homage and accompanying oath.

T. C. Mendenhall, B. D. Henning, and A. S. Foord, *Ideas and Institutions in European History, 800-1715: Select Problems in Historical Interpretation* (Henry Holt, 1948), p. 11.

(e)

USAMA was a Syrian prince whose memoirs included stories based on the reports of his Arabic physician Thabit. About 1140 Thabit witnessed the two cases of surgery that are described here.

They brought to me a knight with an abscess in his leg, and a woman troubled with fever. I applied to the knight a little cataplasm; his abscess opened and took a favourable turn. As for the woman, I forbade her to eat certain foods, and I lowered her temperature. I was there when a Frankish doctor arrived, who said, "This man can't cure them!" Then, addressing the knight, he asked, "Which do you prefer, to live with a single leg or to die with both of your legs?" "I prefer," replied the knight, "to live with a single leg." "Then bring," said the doctor, "a strong knight with a sharp axe." The knight and axe were not slow in coming. I was present. The doctor stretched the leg of the patient on a block of wood, and then said to the knight, "Cut off his leg with the axe, detach it with a single blow." Under my eyes, the knight gave a violent blow, but it did not cut the leg off. He gave the unfortunate man a second blow, which caused the marrow to flow from the bone, and the patient died immediately.

As for the woman, the doctor examined her and said, "She is a woman with a devil in her head, by which she is possessed. Shave her hair." They did so, and she began to eat again, like her compatriots, garlic and mustard. Her fever grew worse. The doctor then said, "The devil has gone into her head." Seizing the razor he cut into her head in the form of a cross and excoriated the skin in the middle so deeply that the bones were uncovered. Then he rubbed her head with salt. The woman, in her turn, expired immediately. After asking them if my services were still needed, and after receiving a negative answer,

421

I returned, having learned from their medicine matters of which I had previously been ignorant.

C. H. Haskins, *The Renaissance of the Twelfth Century,* Loeb Classical Library, (Harvard University Press, 1927; reprinted by Meridian Books, 1957), pp. 326-327.

BOOKS TO READ

1. GENERAL

Hartman, G., *Mediaeval Days and Ways* (Macmillan)
Mills, D., *The Middle Ages* (Putnam)
Power, E., *Medieval People* (Anchor paperback)
Strong, C. F., *The World of the Middle Ages* (University of London Press)
Tappan, E. M., *When Knights Were Bold* (Harrap)

2. MEDIEVAL CHRISTIANITY

Baldwin, M. W., *The Mediaeval Church* (Cornell paperback)
Reeves, M. E., *The Medieval Monastery* (Longmans)
Thomson, G. S., *Medieval Pilgrimages* (Longmans)

3. THE BYZANTINE EMPIRE AND ISLAM

Chubb, T. C., *The Byzantines* (World)
Lamb, H., *Theodora and the Emperor* (Bantam paperback)
Pike, E. R., *Mohammed* (Weidenfeld and Nicolson)

4. FROM CHARLEMAGNE TO FEUDALISM

Chubb, T. C., *The Northmen* (World)
Davis, W. S., *Life on a Mediaeval Barony* (Harper)
Lamb, H., *Charlemagne* (Bantam paperback)
Milliken, E. K., *Saxon and Viking* (Harrap)
Mitchell, R. J., *The Medieval Tournament* (Longmans)
Phillips-Birt, D., *Finding Out About the Vikings* (Muller)
Proctor, G. L., *The Vikings* (Longmans)
Quennell, M. and C. H. B., *Everyday Life in Roman and Saxon Times* (Batsford)
Sellman, R. R., *The Vikings* (Methuen)
Sellman, R. R., *Castles and Fortresses* (Methuen)
Winston, R., *Charlemagne: From the Hammer to the Cross* (Vintage paperback)

5. MANORIALISM

Bennett, H. S., *Life on the English Manor* (Cambridge paperback)
Reeves, M. E., *The Medieval Village* (Longmans)

6. FEUDAL MONARCHIES

Churchill, W. S., *A History of the English-Speaking Peoples,* Vol. I, *The Birth of Britain* (Bantam paperback)
Kelly, A., *Eleanor of Aquitaine and the Four Kings* (Vintage paperback)
Milliken, E. K., *Norman and Angevin* (Harrap)
Painter, S., *The Rise of the Feudal Monarchies* (Cornell paperback)
Sellman, R. R., *Norman England* (Methuen)
Stuart, D. M., *The Story of William the Conqueror* (Methuen)

7. HISTORICAL FICTION

De Wohl, L., *The Restless Flame* (Lippincott) [St. Augustine]
O'Faolain, E., *High Sang the Sword* (Oxford) [Vikings]
Scott, Sir Walter, *Ivanhoe* [England in the days of Richard the Lionheart]
Sutcliff, R., *The Shield Ring* (Oxford) [Vikings in England]
Trease, G., *Mist over Athelney* (Macmillan) [Alfred the Great]
Treece, H., *Hounds of the King* (Bodley Head) [Saxons battle Normans]

CHAPTER 40

The Rise of Towns

City air makes a free man.

GERMAN PROVERB

From the 12th century on city life flourished in Europe, the universal Church—rising to its heights in the 13th century—began to lose both power and prestige, nation-states were strengthened, and parliaments sprang to life. Hence although the three centuries between 1100 and 1400 are often called the Later Middle Ages in contrast with the Early Middle Ages between 500 and 1100, a better name for this period would perhaps be the "Age of Transition." These three centuries are really a bridge between medieval and modern times. Our business life, our nation-states, our political institutions, and our universities all stem from the later Middle Ages.

❖ *The Revival of Trade*   In order to understand the revival of trade and the rise of towns we must retrace our steps a bit. After the fall of the Roman Empire in the West trade declined, but did not disappear, and the manorial system came to provide reasonably self-sufficient communities for most people. The difficulties of travel for the few enterprising pedlars can scarcely be imagined in our days of superhighways. By chance an account has survived of a journey made in the 9th century from Rheims to Chartres by a canon of Rheims. After sloshing through rain and floods and getting lost in the forest, the weary traveller came at last to a bridge.

When I reached the bridge it was scarcely light enough to see. Carefully examining the structure I was once more overwhelmed with new misfortunes. For it had so many holes and such great gaps in it that the citizens of the town could scarcely cross it even by daylight in the course of their necessary business. But my quick-witted guide, who was pretty well experienced in travelling,

In the Middle Ages, it was believed that society should consist of three groups: those who prayed (clergy), those who fought (knights), and those who worked (serfs). These groups are well portrayed in this late 13th century illuminated manuscript. Note the absence of representatives of a middle class (merchants and townsmen).

In the Middle Ages heavy goods were often shipped on river boats such as the one seen here. On the shore road, a stout country cart and a pack-horse are followed by a tinker with a square pack on his back, a box of tools, and a pair of bellows for blowing up his charcoal fire, while another traveller carries his children in a kind of shoulder cradle. They are making their way to the town, which has the typical massive medieval walls perhaps 20 feet high and 10 feet thick.

searched about on every side for a skiff. Finding none, he came back to the dangerous task of trying to cross over the bridge. With the aid of heaven he managed to get the horses over safely. Where there were holes he would sometimes lay his shield down for the horses to step on, sometimes place boards across that were lying around, and now bending over, now standing up, first running ahead, then coming back, he finally got safely across with me and the horses. . . .

Is it any wonder that, when the dangers of lurking robbers were added to such hazards, trade did not flourish?

By the 11th century all this was beginning to change. Successful campaigns against the Moslems in the Mediterranean were resulting in the reopening of ancient trade routes between East and West, with the Italian cities first feeling the surge of new markets. Then land and

river routes carried the riches of the East inland as well. But the roads were still terrible and the ships small and dangerous, so that merchants moved in caravans or fleets for protection.

Local merchants could, however, buy goods from foreign traders (though everyone was thoroughly suspicious of most foreigners) at the great international fairs, where wholesale trading was carried on. Since these fairs were spaced throughout the year so that there was almost always at least one being held somewhere in Europe, the merchants travelled from one to another. During a fair, each day was set aside for dealing in a different commodity—for example, wool would be sold one day, and perhaps hides or wine the next—and on the last day foreign money would be exchanged and accounts settled.

Medieval fairs

Fascinating as the great fairs were, it must be remembered that the bulk of business was done in local town markets, where elaborate regulations protected consumers from unscrupulous merchants. No merchant was allowed to corner a market on goods, and the medieval man distrusted anyone who bought simply to sell at a profit.

❖ *A Town Is Born*   Towns usually developed where roads crossed or where goods were unloaded for trans-shipment, which might be where there was a junction of navigable rivers, often near a castle, cathedral, monastery, or the ruin of an old Roman city. The Eastern luxury goods the merchants could provide—sugar, spices, drugs, dyes, perfumes, gems, rugs, and a score of other exotic articles—were much coveted, especially by the local prince who lived in a castle (*burg* in German). For this reason merchants from far and near were apt to congregate near him. When they discovered, however, that the lord wanted a toll to allow them to enter the gate of the burg, they set up their stands outside the walls. The cluster of stalls gradually developed into a well established market with a permanent settlement of traders.

Such a settlement was really a *suburb,* which means "a place in the shadow of the city walls." But it was dangerous in those days of sudden passions to be unprotected, so that the inhabitants of the new communities soon banded together to purchase from the lord the right to build their own protective wall and to have their own government. Now these good people came to be called *burgesses,* a term that simply meant dwellers in the newly fortified suburb. The new settlements grew rapidly, for just as a modern metropolis tends to spread ever wider, absorbing its suburbs, so the medieval town was constantly spilling over its old walls and building new ones.

The men who settled in the new suburbs were often the sons of runaway serfs, landless men who wanted freedom to come and go while at the same time possessing a safe place for their family and their stock of goods. By the 12th century these townsmen were asking their lords if they could purchase certain privileges, privileges which were granted in the form of a *charter*. The charter usually granted freedom to anyone who lived in the town for a year and a day, so that a runaway serf who could escape detection for this period would thereafter be free. Serfdom and the business pursuits of townsmen were incompatible anyway: no townsman could perform the long list of services due a lord. For this reason the charter usually stated that burgesses could rent their land and buildings from the lord for money, and in some instances they could even buy them outright. Men of the town were granted exemption from feudal courts in favour of their own town courts, and the townsman could sell freely in the market of his own town. In exchange for all these rights the lord received money—perhaps to pay for a crusade, perhaps to renovate his castle.

Closed Corporations In the towns almost every citizen had some-thing to do with manufactures and trade, and societies called *guilds* were set up to regulate local businesses. In some ways these guilds were like our modern trade unions because they set up rules and regulations for working. But in many ways they were different. For one thing, whereas in a trade union all members are employees, in the guilds every-one in a certain trade—masters (who were really employers), journey-men (their assistants), and apprentices (youths learning the trade)—belonged to the same guild. For another, not only did these men band together to control and protect their craft, but also to help each other in time of need and to enjoy good fellowship together. In this respect guilds were more like fraternities than trade unions.

How did the guild help its members? It looked after them in sickness and paid for masses for the repose of their souls. If a guildsman died poor, the guild arranged his funeral, provided for his widow, found husbands for his unmarried daughters, and arranged apprenticeships for his sons. And what good times the members had together! Medieval townspeople had an immense capacity for fun, and enjoyed their many Holy Days to the full. Each guild had its feast day once a year or oftener, and each had its own patron saint. The guildsmen would cele-brate such days by dressing in their full livery and marching from their hall to the church for services before embarking on a gay programme of feasts, games, and theatrical presentations. Since the guild halls, like the town hall and the cathedral which towered over all, surrounded the public square at the centre of the town, this colourful procession would make its way through a good portion of the narrow, crooked streets before the day was over. What these streets looked and smelled like (and how they smelled!), however, you will have to find out from the *Daily Life* at the end of this Part.

It was the duty of each guild to put on a religious production called a mystery or miracle play, which was acted out on the cathedral steps or on huge two- and three-storeyed wagons called "pageants" that could be moved about from one part of the town to another for repeat per-formances. The plays dealt with Bible stories such as the Creation or Noah's Ark, and were often replete with a collection of animals. Nor did they hesitate to mix religious instruction with slapstick comedy. Satan, for instance, was usually the clown. The plays grew more and more elaborate until eventually they became so expensive that the guilds tried to get out of having to produce them. At this point, however, the law stepped in and required them to continue them or pay a fine.

Merchant guilds were the first to be established. Their aim was to maintain a jealous monopoly of local trade (anyone outside the town was considered a foreigner), to ensure the good quality of merchandise sold, and to fix prices—although within broad limits, so that there might be some room for bargaining. Alongside the merchant guilds grew up the *craft guilds* for separate professions, the butchers, the bakers, the candlestick makers, and many, many others. There was hardly a man who did not belong to some guild (they were even formed for pilgrims and lepers), and the masterless man was almost as much of a misfit in medieval society as the wanderer. These newer guilds had two special objectives: to make sure that every member had work (and for this reason they limited the number of apprentices permitted to learn any one trade), and to make sure that every member's workmanship was good. Each craftsman had to allow guild officers to examine his materials and finished products, and working on Saturday afternoons, Sundays, holidays, or after dark was strictly forbidden. The guilds also tried to prevent cut-throat competition. No guildsman could underprice or undercut a brother craftsman in any way, and no overlapping of crafts was permitted. For example, the proud cordwainer who made shoes must not mend them, and the humble cobbler who mended them must not make them. You may learn about a few of the regulations governing one guild in the Source Reading.

Apprenticeship

Before a man was allowed to practise a trade he had to be apprenticed, usually at the age of 14, to a master for from three to twelve years. Then he became a day labourer or journeyman (the French *journée* means *day*) for some master until he had saved enough money to pay the entrance fee to the guild and to set up a shop of his own. Finally he was examined by a board of his guild, though even if his skill were found acceptable he might still be required to produce a "masterpiece" before he could become a master. Unfortunately as time went on the masters, who governed the guilds, became more and more restrictive, and ended up by using various means—such as raising the entrance fees so high that many journeymen could never save enough to pay them—to limit the number of masters and hence increase their power even more. Eventually the exclusiveness of the craft guilds and their unreadiness to admit new members forced workers to go to country villages where there were no guilds. As a result, new and prosperous towns grew up in later years that were free from their irritating control.

Here is a good guild member working at his trade. He is a hatter, and when he finishes his creation he will display it in the "window" of his shop. His counter projects into the street, and his premises are long and narrow, with a workroom behind his shop and his living quarters above it. A third-storey attic provided room for storage. What do you suppose the large vat in the background was used for?

❖ *A New Civilization*   With new towns springing up, the lord of the manor found it difficult to hold his serfs on the land. Some did not try. Ready money was scarce, and more than one lord was glad to let a serf settle in town in order to get a lump sum of cash or yearly payments in place of manorial obligations. Other serfs preferred to stay on the lord's land but to pay a money rental and perform no manorial services. As free peasants they could sell their produce in the neighbouring town and lease land from the profits.

Between the middle of the 10th and the end of the 13th centuries the population of Europe rose sharply; in fact it did not again go up at a corresponding rate until after 1800. This increase in population naturally required the production of more food and a need for improved agricultural techniques. The great demand was, of course, for bread. A more widespread use of the heavy wheeled plough produced more grain, while the water-wheel and the newly invented windmill speeded up the milling of flour. As the great forests were cut back more land was brought under cultivation, land which the lords worked, not by serfs, but by hired labour or by renting out new farms.

From the 10th century onwards an ageless institution began to disappear from Christian Europe as slavery tended to decline. The Church had strongly opposed slavery. Now the cumulative effects of the newly available horse-, water-, and wind-power supported this opposition by diminishing the need for slave labour.

. . . from the twelfth and even from the eleventh century there was a rapid replacement of human by non-human energy wherever great quantities of power were needed or where the required motion was so simple and monotonous that a man could be replaced by a mechanism. The chief glory of the later Middle Ages was not its cathedrals or its epics or its scholasticism: it was the building for the first time in history of a complex civilization which rested not on the backs of sweating slaves or coolies but primarily on non-human power.[1]

CHAPTER 41

The Crusades and the Commercial Revolution

Trade followed the cross, and perhaps the cross was guided by trade.

WILL DURANT, *The Age of Faith*

While towns were rising in Europe and trade was reviving, a momentous meeting of churchmen took place at Clermont in France. There, in November 1095, Pope Urban II (1088-99) preached what has been called "the most effective oration in history." You may read part of this amazing speech on page 483. What had prompted it?

❖ *Dieu le veut!* You will recall that after the death of Mohammed the Moslems swept from one end of the Mediterranean to the other. In

[1]Lynn White, Jr., "Technology and Invention in the Middle Ages", as cited in A. F. Havighurst, editor, *The Pirenne Thesis: Analysis, Criticism, and Revision* (D. C. Heath, 1958), p. 83.

1095 a certain group of them had control of Palestine, and it seemed to good Christians a scandal that this sacred land where Jesus Christ was born, lived, and was crucified should be in the hands of unbelievers. Thus the pope was preaching to a sympathetic audience when he urged his hearers at Clermont to take up the Cross and wrest the Holy Land from the infidels. Aroused and inspired by his sermon, the great crowd responded with a shout, *"Dieu le veut!"*—"God wills it!"

There was more than one motive behind Urban's appeal. Doubtless he was sincere in his desire to recover the Holy Land for Christendom. But he must also have known that a successful crusade would greatly increase the prestige and influence of the Church. Moreover, Urban had created problems for himself when, in his anxiety to curb feudal warfare, he had reissued the Peace and Truce of God. These banned warfare against women, children, or clergymen, and prohibited fighting on weekends, on the countless Holy Days, or even during such seasons as Lent and Advent. To try to so restrict the fighting of feudal nobles without providing some outlet for their warlike spirits was, as Urban must have realized, a vain hope. Now, however, there could be unlimited warfare —against the enemies of Christ. Finally, the Pope must have cherished the idea of healing the recent schism between the Eastern and Western churches, a split that had occurred in 1054 when the Patriarch of Constantinople had rejected the claim of papal supremacy and certain other Roman Catholic doctrines. Both East and West would take up the fight against the infidel. Perhaps a war for a common cause would unite them.

The First Crusade

Thus, despite the appearance of spontaneity, it was only after much careful thought and plenty of advance publicity that the First Crusade was launched.

❖ *The Sign of the Cross* Unfortunately the Crusade quickly got out of hand. The emotional enthusiasm of wandering preachers like Peter the Hermit swept many simple people off their feet, and eagerly they flocked to take up the cross. Here is how one chronicler of the time describes the earliest crusaders.

As every one hastened to take the road of God each hurried to change into money everything that was not of use for the journey, and the price was fixed not by the seller but by the buyer. It was strange and marvellous to see every one buying dear and selling cheap: everything that was needed for the journey was very costly, but the rest was sold for nothing. . . . It touched the heart to see these poor crusaders shoeing their oxen as if they had been horses, and harnessing them to two-wheeled carts on which they put their small belongings

In the 11th century the Christian reconquest of Spain from the Moors (Moslems) was taken up by a Castilian noble, Rodrigo Diaz de Vivar, better known as El Cid (Arabic *sid*="master"). The Cid has been glorified as the noble Christian hero of Spain, but actually he was a ruthless freebooter who was banished from Castile and thereafter offered his services, at the head of 300 free lances, to Christians and Moslems alike. Churches and mosques were plundered with equal indifference. He is pictured here as he tackles a Moslem opponent in the throes of his greatest victory — the capture of Valencia in 1094.

and their little children. At each castle and each city they passed on the road they stretched out their hands and asked if they had not yet reached that Jerusalem which all were seeking.

The few from this ignorant and unorganized rabble who did manage to reach Constantinople waited there for the main body of crusaders, the feudal knights and men-at-arms under the command of the barons of

France. By the autumn of 1096 this force had started east, and by the next spring had crossed into Asia. Mutual distrust began to eat into the feudal chieftains from Europe, and, moreover, the Byzantine emperor and his troops soon abandoned the westerners in Palestine and went home. Constantinople thereby handed over all leadership of the Crusade to Rome.

In June 1098 Antioch finally fell to the crusaders. But even in victory there was dissension: the northern French attributed the fall to their superior generalship, and the southern French to the discovery by one of their followers of a sacred relic—the very lance that had pierced Christ's side as he hung on the cross. So bitter did the quarrel become that the question of the authenticity of the relic and the honesty of its discoverer, Peter Bartholomew, had to be settled by the ordeal of fire.

The fire was growing so hot that the flames shot up thirty cubits into the air. . . . Then Peter Bartholomew, clothed only in his tunic, and kneeling before the bishop of Albar, called God to witness that he had seen him face to face on the cross. . . . Then, when the bishop had placed the Lance in his hand, he kneeled and made the sign of the cross, and entered the fire with the Lance, firm and unterrified. For an instant's time he paused in the midst of the flames, and then by the grace of God passed through. . . . But when Peter emerged from the fire so that neither his tunic was burned nor even the thin cloth with which the Lance was wrapped up had shown any sign of damage, the whole people . . . threw themselves upon him and dragged him to the ground and trampled on him, each one wishing to get a piece of his garment, and each thinking him near some one else. . . . Peter had died on the spot, as we believe, had not Raymond Pelet, a brave and noble soldier, broken through the wild crowd with a band of friends and rescued him at the peril of their lives.

Despite such disputes the crusaders did at last capture Jerusalem in 1099 with a force of 2000-3000 knights and 8000-12,000 infantry. Apparently no action against the Moslems was too revolting so long as it contributed to the glory of Christian arms, and an eye-witness has left us the following description of how the Holy City was taken.

The capture of Jerusalem

On the top of Solomon's Temple, to which they [the Moslems] had climbed in fleeing, many were shot to death with arrows and cast down headlong from the roof. Within the Temple about ten thousand were beheaded. If you had been there, your feet would have been stained up to the ankles with the blood of the slain. What more shall I tell? Not one of them was allowed to live. They did not spare the women and children.

It is not hard to see why many modern historians regard the Crusades as a blot on the history of the West. They were, says one scholar, "a

For over one hundred and fifty years this great Crusader castle "stuck like a bone," wrote a Moslem, "in the very throat of the Saracens." Krak des Chevaliers was built by Frankish knights of the 12th and 13th centuries in what is today northern Syria, with the purpose of protecting the Latin Kingdom of Jerusalem. Today the imposing fortress which once rang with the commands of mailed knights stands empty and silent, its towers keeping an eerie vigil over the stark, torrid wastelands where centuries before it was the chief Christian bastion of the Holy Land.

tragic and destructive episode. The historian as he gazes back across the centuries at their gallant story must find his admiration overcast by sorrow at the witness that it bears to the limitations of human nature. There was so much courage and so little honour, so much devotion and so little understanding. High ideals were besmirched by cruelty and greed, enterprise and endurance by a blind and narrow self-righteousness; and the Holy War itself was nothing more than a long act of intolerance in the name of God. . . ."[2]

In 1147-49, 1189-92, and 1202-04 other crusades followed. They were failures; but worse than that, they revealed the depth to which

[2]S. Runciman, *A History of the Crusades*, Vol. III, *The Kingdom of Acre and the Later Crusades* (Cambridge University Press, 1954), p. 480.

unrestricted crusading warfare could sink. And this under the sign of the Cross! The Fourth Crusade never did reach the Holy Land: it veered from its course and ended with the capture and sack of Constantinople in 1204. After this tragic climax the movement fell off ingloriously, though crusades—including two tragic ones undertaken by children— continued to be organized over the next two centuries.

What, finally, did the Crusades accomplish? Historians used to say that practically everything that happened in the 13th century was caused by them, but now they are much more cautious. Today we know, for example, that most of the science and learning of the East was *not* brought back to Europe by the crusaders. Nevertheless the Crusades had the following important results:

RESULTS OF THE CRUSADES

1. Westerners acquired a first-hand geographical acquaintance with the East.
2. Westerners became accustomed to Eastern luxury goods—spices, fabrics, perfumes, etc.—and hence the demand for them increased in Europe.
3. Genoa, Pisa, and especially Venice became practically the exclusive agents for Eastern goods.
4. The need for ready cash for the expenses of the Crusades resulted in a revival of a money economy in the West, and the new trade with the East resulted in the development of international banking.
5. To raise money for crusading, lords sold charters of liberties to their serfs.
6. Many troublesome nobles were killed off.
7. The papacy acquired greater power and prestige.
8. Both the Church and the state imposed special taxes in order to finance the Crusades, thereby becoming accustomed to increased taxing power.
9. Criticism of these taxes, as well as criticism of the perversion of the Crusades, resulted in resentment toward the Church and criticism of it.

❖ *Bursting the Bonds of Feudalism* As you can see from the preceding table, the Crusades were a very important factor in speeding up the revival of trade and commerce that was already sweeping over western Europe. It was the new money economy that, more than anything else, burst the bonds of feudalism. We call all the economic developments that accompanied these changes the "Commercial Revolution."

Commercial Revolution

Under feudalism there had been only two classes, nobles and peasants. Now the townsmen formed a third class midway between the two, that is, a *middle* class. The individual members of this class should not be thought of as all being equals, for there was a world of difference between the rich merchant and the poor apprentice. Nevertheless, they had one thing in common—freedom. All lived beyond the arbitrary will of any lord, free to impose their own restrictions under their own town government.

There was no love lost between nobles and townsmen. The noble was likely to resent the fact that the merchant had more ready cash available, whereas the merchant might envy the noble's lands and titles, even if their cash value was slight. Moreover, where the monarchy was strong there grew up an alliance of town and crown. Kings ceased to depend on their feudal and manorial incomes and developed instead a system of regular taxes paid by all subjects. The townsmen paid a large share of these taxes. Consequently they demanded, and got, an important share in the government.

The 12th and 13th centuries witnessed a change in the knight's way of life. Money made his life softer and more luxurious, while new methods of warfare diminished his military value. To capture the new stone castles that had replaced wooden ones the knight was less vital than the engineer and the sapper. By the 12th century it became the custom to travel unarmed instead of always riding laden down with heavy armour. Then, should enemies meet, each knight would, as a chivalrous gentleman, give the other time to arm properly. Tournaments became more popular and less violent. They were now great social affairs which even the ladies attended. But more important was the convention that knights defeated in tournaments had to pay a ransom and lost their horse and armour to the victor. Private profit became a greater incentive than public glory.

The truth was that the spirit of ancient feudalism was dying, and chivalrous manners sought to compensate for a power that the knight no longer wielded. This changed attitude toward the knight is well illustrated by the *fabliaux,* short humorous verse stories which became popular in the 13th century. The heroes of these stories were not, as of old, knights or nobles. They were shrewd, hard-headed townsmen and merchants who knew what they wanted and had no scruples about how they got it. One of the most famous fabliaux is the *Romance of Reynard,* whose hero, the sly fox, makes fools out of the Lion King and his vassals. All merchants, of course, were not deceitful robbers such as Reynard, but this type of story did indicate an increasingly worldly attitude symbolized by the townsman.

Romance of Reynard

The status of the medieval woman was continually improving. Whereas at the opening of the 12th century a knight who tired of his wife could abandon her for another, by the end of the century this action required the sanction of an ecclesiastical court. Yet the life of the humble peasant's wife remained essentially the same, and something in this description of her harried existence sounds all too familiar to the modern young mother:

And what I ask besides, though it may seem silly, how the wife stands, that heareth, when she cometh in, her child scream, sees the cat at the bacon, and the dog at the hide? Her cake is burning on the stone, and her calf is sucking all the milk up. The pot is boiling over into the fire, and the churl her husband is scolding. Though this be a silly tale, maiden, it ought to deter thee more strongly from marriage, for it seems not silly to her who trieth it.

The impact of town life and an increasing population had struck hard at the very roots of the manor and the fief. And its effect on commerce and industry was nothing short of revolutionary. Originally the Church had condemned usury, so that few except Jews would lend money for interest. The ordinary medieval man, if he were loaned a sum, would expect the lender to be satisfied if he received the capital back intact. There was for many years no idea of investment for profit. It was only during the later Middle Ages that what we call *capitalism* began to grow up when shrewd Italian businessmen, particularly Venetians, accumulated enough wealth so that they could afford to invest it and thus earn more. It was also Italians who made popular a number of modern financial practices and institutions such as banks, letters of credit, bills of exchange, and government bonds. *The growth of capitalism*

❖ *An Astonishing Tale*   One 13th century Italian businessman is worth special notice. He is Marco Polo. Marco's father lived in Constantinople, where he traded on behalf of Venice, and in 1271 he took his son on the long three-and-a-half year overland expedition to the court of the great Mongol ruler of China, Kublai Khan (1257-94). The young Marco stayed in China for 17 years, during which time he won the favour of the Great Khan. After he returned to the West he was captured in a war with Genoa, and while in prison dictated his amazing travel tales of China, that ancient and mysterious land visited by so few Westerners. Marco Polo's account was so accurate and vivid that it completely eclipsed all earlier descriptions of the East. *Marco Polo*

Kublai Khan was the grandson of the mighty Mongol emperor, Genghiz Khan (1206-27). The savage Mongols had swept into North China in the 10th century, murdering, plundering, destroying—and

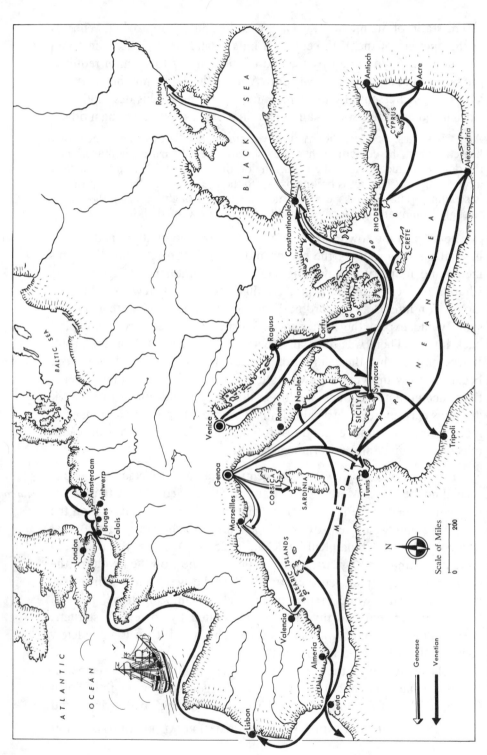

MEDIEVAL COMMERCE: PRINCIPAL SEA ROUTES BY THE 14TH CENTURY

yet in the end partially adopting Chinese civilization. As the ancient proverb has it, "China is a sea that salts all the rivers flowing into it." Finally in the 13th century Genghiz Khan not only conquered several of the northern provinces of China, but also—far to the west—founded a Mongol state close to the modern city of Volgograd (formerly Stalingrad). A few years later these Mongols were so strong that even the powerful Moslem empire asked for French and English aid to stem their expansion. They were curtly rebuffed. "Let us leave these dogs to devour one another," said one English bishop.

It was after the Mongol threat to Europe had receded that the Polos visited the court of Kublai Khan. This great emperor finally united the various Chinese empires, which had shifted shape like an amoeba from dynasty to dynasty. He also sent one of the largest overseas expeditions in world history—140,000 men—to invade Japan. But fate intervened. A typhoon aided the determined Japanese in repulsing the invaders.

Marco Polo swept aside the veil of Oriental mystery that shrouded this ancient empire of Kublai Khan, and revealed to an astonished Europe such wonders as money made of paper:

> In this city of Kanbalu [Peking] is the mint of the Great Khan, who may truly be said to possess the secret of the alchemists, as he has the art of producing money by the following process.
>
> He causes the bark to be stripped from those mulberry-trees the leaves of which are used for feeding silk-worms, and takes from it that thin inner rind which lies between the coarser bark and the wood of the tree. This being steeped, and afterwards pounded in a mortar, until reduced to a pulp, is made into paper. . . . When ready for use, he has it cut into pieces of money of different sizes, nearly square, but somewhat longer than they are wide. . . . The coinage of this paper money is authenticated with as much form and ceremony as if it were actually of pure gold or silver; for to each note a number of officers, specially appointed, not only subscribe their names, but affix their seals also. When this has been regularly done by the whole of them, the principal officer, appointed by his Majesty, having dipped into vermilion the royal seal committed to his custody, stamps with it the piece of paper, so that the form of the seal tinged with the vermilion remains impressed upon it. In this way it receives full authenticity as current money, and the act of counterfeiting it is punished as a capital offence.

❖ *Stagnation and Depression in Europe* Marco Polo's tales of the East, fascinating as they were, fell on sceptical ears (he was nicknamed "Marco Millions"). Hence they did not greatly influence the people of his own time, and actually it was the 15th century before the great trading ventures to the Orient began. For the present, Europeans concentrated

In 1275 an impressionable twenty-year-old came with his father and his uncle to the glittering court of Kublai Khan. Marco Polo was to serve the mighty emperor faithfully for the next seventeen years, and has left us this impressive (if flattering) description of his remarkable employer: "Kublai . . . is of middle stature. . . . His limbs are well formed, and in his whole figure there is a just proportion. His complexion is fair, and occasionally suffused with red, like the bright tint of the rose, which adds much grace to his countenance. His eyes are black and handsome, his nose is well shaped and prominent."

mainly on promoting the large-scale production of woollen cloth in Flanders and Florence, where busy looms wove the wool sheared from the backs of English and Spanish sheep. In fact woollen cloth was the only Western product that the East imported in any quantity.

Apparently 13th century Europe lacked the capital, energy, and technical skill necessary to follow the trail blazed by Marco Polo. Indeed, the overall picture in Europe was of an economy that was becoming stagnant.

By the end of the 13th century the steady expansion of population and production had halted. Guilds became more restrictive in their membership, and an ever-increasing group of journeymen found themselves at loggerheads with the rich merchants. Civil wars often tore rich and poor townsmen apart, and organized strikes by workers in industry became common. Most discontented of all were the peasants, who either found themselves working for fixed wages despite a rise in prices or threatened with a revival of serfdom. So desperate did they become that on three occasions major peasant revolts broke out, in Flanders in 1323-28, northern France 1358, and England in 1381.

As if these economic problems were not serious enough, in 1348-50 a great plague swept westward across Europe, with lesser waves following in 1361-62 and 1369. This was the bubonic plague, the Black Death. It carried off between one- and two-thirds of the town population of Europe, though fewer people died in the country. We now know that fleas infected from plague-stricken rats carried the disease, and the frightful lack of public sanitation certainly promoted its easy and rapid spread. So terrible was the scourge that it completely dislocated life all over Europe, as the following account by an English monk who lived through it clearly shows.

The Black Death

The dreadful pestilence penetrated the seacoast by Southampton and came to Bristol, and there almost the whole population of the town perished, as if it had been seized by sudden death; for few kept their beds more than two or three days, or even half a day. Then this cruel death spread everywhere around, following the course of the sun. And there died at Leicester in the small parish of St. Leonard more than three hundred and eighty persons, in the parish of Holy Cross, four hundred, in the parish of St. Margaret's, Leicester, seven hundred; and so in every parish, a great multitude. . . .

In the same year there was a great murrain [infectious disease] of sheep everywhere in the kingdom, so that in one place in a single pasture more than five thousand sheep died; and they putrefied so that neither bird nor beast would touch them. Everything was low in price because of the fear of death, for very few people took any care of riches or property of any kind. A man could have a horse that had been worth 40s. for half a mark [6s. 8d.]. . . . Sheep and cattle ran at large through the fields and among the crops, and there were none to drive them off or herd them; for lack of care they perished in ditches and hedges in incalculable numbers throughout all districts, and none knew what to do. . . .

The Black Death was followed by economic crises so severe that they were comparable in their gravity to our own Great Depression of the 1930's, during which much of the prairies turned into a giant dustbowl.

After the plague there was little increase in European population for two centuries. Indeed, some of the land that ambitious towns had enclosed within their walls in the 14th and 15th centuries remained open fields right up to modern times.

CHAPTER 42

The Church and the Feudal Monarchies

. . . only the Roman pontiff is rightly called universal . . . his name is unique in the world . . . he is allowed to depose emperors . . . he can absolve subjects from their oaths of fidelity to iniquitous rulers.

GREGORY VII

Even though the early Middle Ages witnessed the rise of feudal monarchies, society continued to be more international than national. And above all states stood the Church. Yet where lines of authority intersected, the tempers of laymen and churchmen might rub raw.

As the Church increased in prestige and influence, dedicated churchmen moved to carry out much needed reforms, including the enforcement of clerical *celibacy* (the non-marriage of clergy) and the prohibition of *simony* (the purchase of church offices). The Church also sought to control the appointment of its personnel, who, too often, had been chosen by kings and emperors and were later merely ratified by Rome. One way to ensure this control was to insist that a new bishop could be invested with his power only in a ceremony at Rome.

❖ *The Road to Canossa*   One of the Church's most vigorous reformers

Gregory VII was Hildebrand, who became Pope Gregory VII in 1073. As pope he was determined to reform and rule, to purify the Church, and to make himself the overlord, under God, of both kings and emperors. He was particularly insistent that he (through his clergy), and not the lay ruler, should perform the ceremony of investiture whereby new church officials were given the symbols of their office.

The Investiture Controversy   It was on this matter of the investiture of bishops that the battle was joined. The quarrel soon turned into a full-blown attempt by the papacy to take over the control of the German church from the Emperor Henry IV (1056-1106), and the sharp letters exchanged between pope and emperor may be read at the end of this Part. Henry persuaded the German bishops to renounce their obedience to the pope, but the pope retaliated by deposing Henry, releasing all his subjects from their allegiance to him, and cutting him off by excommunication from the Church. Finally in 1077 Gregory appeared to have won the victory. Henry journeyed to Italy, and, according to legend, stood for three days barefoot in the snow outside the castle at Canossa where the pope was lodged until Gregory finally forgave him.

The end of Gregory's story was not, however, a happy one, for the great pope was eventually driven from Rome. His famous last words were typical: "I have loved justice and hated iniquity; therefore I die in exile."

Only a generation later (1122) the Concordat of Worms finally settled

The castle of the Counts of Flanders, modelled in the 12th century after Crusader fortresses in Syria, was restored at the end of the last century. Note the moat (formed by the River Lième), the massive walls protected by a watch-tower, the count's house to the left, and the high square keep or donjon in which a last stand could be made if the outer defences were breached. A trading quarter spreading over 200 acres grew up across the river from the castle, and in 1194 was enclosed with a wall. It was thus that the town of Ghent was born.

the Investiture Controversy by providing for a double ceremony of investiture—one by the secular ruler for lands and secular privileges, one by a Church official for spiritual authority. But this compromise was far from ending the contest between the Church and feudal monarchs. It merely shifted it to other grounds.

❖ *Murder in the Cathedral*   Among those who continued to oppose the Church's claims to overriding authority was the redoubtable Henry II of England, whom we have already met in his role of legal reformer. Just as much as the German Emperor Henry IV, Henry II wished to control the Church within his realm. Inevitably his ambitions clashed with those of his Archbishop of Canterbury and former friend, Thomas Becket.

Henry II

Becket insisted that clergy accused of a crime should be tried only in the special courts of the Church. Henry was just as insistent that clergy found guilty in the Church courts should be sent to the royal courts for sentencing. Eventually Becket fled to France, but after six years of exile a compromise was worked out and he was allowed to return. It was soon evident, however, that the stubborn archbishop had no intention of forgiving his enemies, for he proceeded to excommunicate some of the king's friends. Now Henry lost his temper completely. "My subjects are sluggards," he stormed. "They keep no faith with their lord; they allow me to be made a laughing stock of by a low-born cleric." Four of the king's knights overheard him. They needed no second prompting to get rid of the haughty Becket. Post-haste they made their way to Canterbury Cathedral, there to murder the archbishop within the sanctuary of his own church.

Thomas Becket

Henry was horrified and the Christian world was scandalized. The king now had not only to convince the Church of the genuineness of his sorrow, but also to give in to the pope's demands and allow Church courts to have sole jurisdiction over clergy accused of crimes. He had lost this round with the Church.

But Henry II was not the sort of man to take defeat lying down. He continued to dominate church life in England in other ways, insisting, for example, that elections of bishops be strictly in accord with the royal will. Here is the text of a letter he wrote to one group of clergy who were about to elect a new bishop!

Henry, king of the English &c. to his faithful monks of the church of Winchester, greeting.
I order you to hold a free election, but, nevertheless, I forbid you to elect anyone except Richard my clerk, the archdeacon of Poitiers.

Such battles of will between the feudal monarchs of Europe and the Church were to continue until finally, in the 13th century, they reached their climax. This climax was brought about partly because of the strong personalities of determined popes, and partly because of a new reforming zeal which was spreading throughout the Church. Symbolizing this zeal were two new monastic orders.

❖ *Go Forth into the World*   As we learned earlier, the main purpose of the monasteries was to save the souls of the monks, and any social services they provided were accomplished by the sick and the needy coming to the monastery, not by the monks going to them. What was needed was a monastic order that instead of retiring from the world would go out into it. In the 13th century two such orders were founded. They are known as "mendicant" orders (the Latin verb *mendicare* means "to beg") because the friars, as the mendicants were called, were sent forth to serve the common people while living in poverty amongst them, begging their way.

The first order was founded by St. Francis (1181-1226), the son of a *St. Francis* well-to-do cloth merchant of the Italian town of Assisi. St. Francis was *of Assisi* a rather wild young man, but he experienced a conversion and dedicated his life to the service of the poor. He has been described as "probably the most Christlike man that has ever lived." Francis drew up a brief and simple Rule for his followers, and the great Pope Innocent III authorized the new religious order. Its members came in time to be known as Franciscans.

A second mendicant order founded about this time was associated with *The* a cultured Spaniard named Dominic (1170-1221), who had been involved *Dominican* in a mission in France to win back *heretics* (the holders of beliefs that the *Order* Church defined as untrue) to the faith. St. Dominic's concern was to found an order that would combat ignorance by preaching the Church's teachings. As he told his followers: "Henceforth the world is your home: go forth into the whole world, teach and preach." Dominic's new order, too, came to be called after its founder and was known as the Dominican Order. Because of its emphasis on doctrinal learning and preaching, it was natural that the Dominican Order should play a prominent part in the affairs of the Inquisition.

Occasionally the friars incurred the wrath of the local clergy, on whose parishes and jurisdiction they seemed to trespass. (That none too scrupulous associate of Robin Hood, the corpulent Friar Tuck, is a caricature of a certain type of friar.) Yet in reviving the influence of the Church in

One wonders how long this 13th century castle will be able to withstand the concentrated barrage from these great siege engines. The siege tower, a movable platform usually built on the scene and covered with hides to protect it from fire, is being moved close to the castle so that troops can climb up inside it and cross over a bridge on to the walls. The battering ram at the right, operating under the protection of a shelter called a *cat,* may finally succeed in opening a breach in the wall through which the troops will pour. Meanwhile another huge contraption hurls stones at the walls— although it could on occasion throw more imaginative missiles such as a dreadful inflammable liquid known as "Greek fire," or a dead horse.

the new towns and in combating heresy the friars made an inestimable contribution to the strengthening of the medieval Church. That Church was to reach the very pinnacle of its power in the 13th century.

❖ *The Most Efficient Monarchy*　The greatest pope of the Middle Ages

Innocent III was Innocent III (1198-1216). He served at the papal court under five popes before he came to the papal throne at the age of only thirty-seven, and proved to be not only a churchman but a politician and a diplomat as well. Like Gregory VII, Innocent had a very exalted idea of the supremacy of the Church of Rome over all other institutions—an attitude that

naturally brought him into conflict with the rulers of France, England and Germany. Innocent, however, made a practice of winning his disputes.

Under Innocent III the Church became the greatest state in Europe. An army of officials was needed to handle the mass of correspondence dealing with everything from personal moral problems to international affairs, and to administer the wide-flung concerns of the papacy. Often a great council was held in Rome at which the clergy assembled (some 1300 came to the Lateran Council of 1215) to work out Church policies. Thus the papacy had come to be the most efficient of medieval monarchies.

One of Innocent's successors, Gregory IX (1227-1241), is notable *Gregory IX* chiefly for continuing the quarrels with the German Empire and for establishing the court of the Inquisition. Heresy had flourished during the 12th century, especially in the new towns. The Inquisition was created to prevent false beliefs from spreading, and to stamp out any that persisted. The Church believed it was essential to obtain complete obedience and devotion to its teachings.

The Inquisition followed a set procedure. Inquisitors would preach a sermon in the town square; then heretics were granted some time in which to discover the error of their ways and be received back into the true faith. At the end of this period the judges questioned witnesses on oath, that is they conducted a sworn *inquest* (hence the term *inquisition*), and cross-examined the persons still accused of heresy. If they admitted their heresy and desired reconciliation with the Church an appropriate penance was meted out. Most trials ended at this point. But if the heretic refused to recant his heretical beliefs he was handed over to the state to be burned at the stake.

It must be realized, however, that the Inquisition tried very hard to win back souls for the Church. Execution was only the last resort. The cancer had to be cut out before it spread any further, for those who persisted in their heresy might endanger the faith of others. What shocks us today are the methods used—the anonymous accusation, the secret trial, the questioning under torture, the invitation to prove one's repentance by turning informer and denouncing one's past associates. Nevertheless we must remember that for the 13th century heresy was the most dangerous crime imaginable, so vile and insidious that any means to suppress it seemed justifiable.

❖ *The Humiliation of the Papacy*   By the end of the 13th century the prestige and power of the papal monarchy had slipped badly. It is true that in 1302 Pope Boniface VIII (1294-1303) issued a papal pronouncement which declared, among other things, that

> there is one Holy Catholic and Apostolic Church . . . and outside of this there is neither salvation nor remission of sins. . . . We, moreover, proclaim, declare and pronounce that it is altogether necessary to salvation for every human being to be subject to the Roman Pontiff.

Yet the very pope who made this statement was arrested the next year by agents of the French king and died, a broken man, a month later. Thus in a single century the papacy has lost enormous power and prestige. Even so, the next century was to see it still more deeply humiliated.

In 1305 a French archbishop became pope, and, on the pretext of disturbed political conditions in the Papal States, took up what was assumed to be only temporary residence at Avignon on the east bank of the Rhone River. Actually he never did move to Rome, nor did his six French successors. And while Avignon was not technically in France it was surrounded by French lands, so that the papacy could hardly escape

French pressure—to the profound displeasure of the English and the Germans. For this reason historians have used the term "Babylonian Captivity" to describe the years between 1305 and 1378 when the French popes reigned from Avignon.

The popes knew that their position at Avignon created many problems; but it was not until the last years of his pontificate that Gregory XI, the seventh Avignonese pope, moved back to Rome. At his death the rivalry between opposing factions of cardinals was so strong that two popes were elected, one Italian, one French. They proceeded to excommunicate each other, each claiming to be the only true successor to Peter.

It was an unhappy period in the Church's history. The "Great Schism," as it is called, lasted for a generation, and indeed before the controversy was settled in 1417 there were at one time three popes. It is not hard to see how the Babylonian Captivity and the Great Schism would destroy much of the prestige and influence of the popes, and many sincere Christians in the 14th century were harshly critical of both the popes and their office. It was perhaps symptomatic of the Church's decline that, despite the heavy fire it was under, no new reforming orders were created. In fact a new Franciscan or Dominican order might have been frowned upon as dangerous and heretical. But the seeds of unrest had been sown. A Church that would not reform itself might in time have reform thrust upon it.

The Great Schism

THE RISE AND FALL OF PAPAL POWER

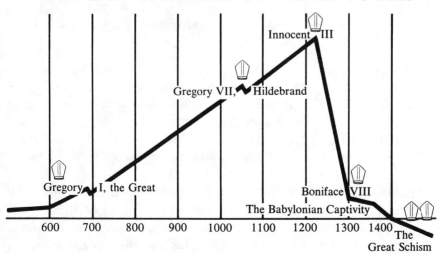

❖ *The Great Charter*   Though the French kings were strong enough to best the papacy, many of the English and German monarchs of this period were indifferent rulers. Even King John of England (1167-1216), who was no weakling, got into serious trouble with his subjects.

When this intelligent but disagreeable man lost out in a dispute with Rome over who should be Archbishop of Canterbury, he retaliated by seizing Church property. Now the clergy joined with the discontented baronage, whose goodwill had already been forfeited by two generations of Angevin heavy-handedness. For in a very real sense, John had to pay the bill for the excessively high financial demands made by his father, Henry II, and his Lionhearted brother. Yet as far as tyranny was concerned John was little worse than his predecessors; like them, he was merely trying to develop the royal power to the full. He was unfortunate enough to be caught with a nearly static royal revenue in a time of increasing costs, whereas the incomes of the barons were rising. John saw it, then, as only logical that he should even out the situation by exacting more money from his barons in order to balance his budget.

Magna Carta   All this is clear to us now, but King John's barons could only see that he was going too far too fast. On June 15, 1215, they forced him to set his seal to their demands, which were edited and published four days later as the famous Magna Carta. Magna Carta did not give rights to the common people of England, nor was it a great monument to national liberty. Rather it was a feudal document reciting the grievances of the barons and defining the rights and obligations of John as their feudal overlord. Nevertheless the Great Charter was of enduring importance because it insisted that the king was and ought to be below the law— something English barons were to remind English kings of many times over.

❖ *A Unique Institution*   John's successors, too, quarrelled with the barons. And even though two of them, Edward I (1272-1307) and Edward III (1327-77), were famous knights and generals, their foreign wars left England heavily burdened with debt. Consequently when weak kings like Henry III (1216-72), Edward II (1307-27), or Richard II (1377-99) inherited the crown they were faced with a seething baronage that had no intention of granting tax after tax.

Parliament   The baronial discontent of the 13th and 14th centuries was to result in the creation of an institution that was unique in all of Europe, the English parliament. In a solemn meeting of King, Lords, and Commons (the latter made up of the ordinary knights and the representatives of

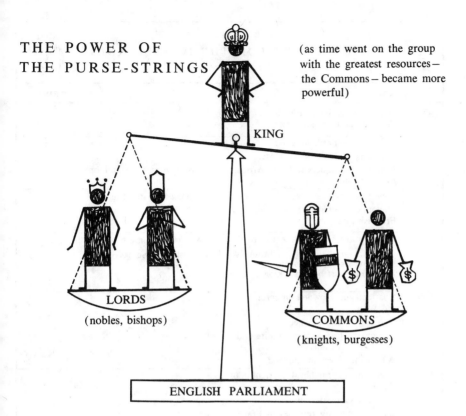

THE POWER OF
THE PURSE-STRINGS

(as time went on the group
with the greatest resources —
the Commons — became more
powerful)

KING

LORDS
(nobles, bishops)

COMMONS
(knights, burgesses)

ENGLISH PARLIAMENT

the towns), Englishmen learned to govern themselves by balancing off their opinions in a sort of great national debate. Even the strongest English kings were forced to engage in this collective national bargaining, for parliament had discovered the secret of strength: to hold the state purse-strings. If the kings were to have enough money for their wars they would have to submit to the will of parliament. This was especially true of King Edward III, who in 1337 began the long series of campaigns in France known as the Hundred Years' War.

Only England developed parliament. The strong French monarchs simply overrode the objections of both their nobles and the Church and ruled as they pleased. Their very efficiency as administrators delayed representative government in France until the Revolution of 1789. On the other hand, the weak German emperors were never able to fully control their strong nobles or to create more than a figurehead monarchy. As a result the Germans were not to become acquainted with constitutional democracy until the 19th century.

TIME CHART FOR THE MIDDLE AGES

	WEST	EAST
476	Odoacer rules Italy on behalf of Emperor at Constantinople	
500	Clovis in Frankish kingdom Founding of Benedictine Order Justinian reconquers Italy, N. Africa, part of Spain	Justinian at Constantinople (Byzantium)
600	Pope Gregory the Great Mayors of the palace rule Frankish kingdom	Mohammed in Arabia
700	Moslems cross from N. Africa to Europe Charles Martel turns back Moslems at Tours; rise of feudalism Pepin the Short becomes king of the Franks	Moslem expansion in Middle East Constantinople saved from the Moslems
800	Charlemagne crowned emperor in the West Carolingian Renaissance Collapse of Carolingian Empire and barbarian invasions Alfred the Great in England	
900	Beginning of Medieval Agricultural Revolution Otto I in Germany and Italy Capetian dynasty founded in France	
1000	Rise of Towns; feudalism declining Norman Conquest of England; Henry IV and Gregory VII quarrel over investiture	Schism between Papacy and Eastern Orthodox Church at Constantinople
1100	First Crusade Renaissance of the 12th century; rise of Universities Henry II in England; Frederick Barbarossa in Germany	Second Crusade fails Third Crusade fails
1200	John of England quarrels with Pope Innocent III Commercial Revolution Capitalism in Italy	Fourth Crusade captures Constantinople Kublai Khan rules Mongol Empire; Marco Polo travels to China
1300	Pope Boniface VIII humiliated by French King Papacy at Avignon Outbreak of Hundred Years' War; the Black Death Growth of English parliament under Edward III	The Black Death
1378	The Great Schism in the Church	

By the end of the 14th century, then, the most significant political developments in Europe were taking place in the day-to-day government of medieval England. You may read more about this apprenticeship in democratic government in the Source Reading on pages 485-486.

CHAPTER 43

The Medieval Mind

I do not want to be a philosopher if it means resisting St. Paul; I do not wish to be Aristotle, if it must separate me from Christ.

ABELARD

In the 12th century there occurred an upsurge in the cultural life of the West which flooded across the barriers of nations and affected thousands of people—far more than had the Carolingian Renaissance of 300 years earlier. We call this movement the Renaissance of the Twelfth Century. Ironically enough, it was triggered by the West's old foes, the Moslems, when they passed on to Europe the writings of Greece and Rome. To this legacy they added some of their own learning, rich with Eastern lore. Thus it came to pass that a strengthened and awakened West, roused from its lethargy by this intellectual transfusion, began to develop a vigorous cultural life of its own.

❖ *A New Literature and an Old* As the Middle Ages progressed, Latin no longer was written according to the stylistic and grammatical standards of the age of Cicero. This does not mean that it was "bad" Latin. Actually medieval Latin was a new language, not a corruption of an old one. Perhaps a modern writer can help you understand why such a new language was inevitable.

If one is to understand what had been happening to Latin, he should try to say in words known to Shakespeare that "A dive-bomber dropped incendiary bombs on an ammunition dump, creating an explosion which destroyed all telephonic communications, railroad installations, and motor roads, wrecking a large number of tanks, refrigerator cars, and parked aircraft." Obviously the Bard would be hopelessly confused amidst such a vocabulary. It was equally impossible to say in Ciceronian phrase that "The penitent sinner confessed his heresy to the priest, and was given absolution, whereupon, proceeding to the high altar of the cathedral, he received the eucharist and was relieved of the excommunication which had been placed upon him by the bishop." Yet the Middle Ages needed these words as much as we need the technical vocabulary of our own time, and like ourselves, as new conditions arose, they adapted new words to express new ideas.[3]

In the 12th century, then, rules of grammar were simplified, and a great deal of Latin poetry departed from classical models. Some, which celebrated the pleasures of youth, even gave such dangerous advice as this:

> Cast aside dull books and thought;
> Sweet is folly, sweet is play;
> Take the pleasure Spring hath brought
> In youth's opening holiday!

Nevertheless the Greek and Roman classics which had been neglected during certain periods of the Middle Ages were once again being studied avidly. These Greek classics had come to Europe in a very roundabout way: the Moslems translated them into Arabic and brought them to Spain, the Spaniards translated them into their own language or into Hebrew, and finally they were translated once more, this time into Latin. Although a text was apt to become quite garbled in passing from Greek to Arabic to Spanish (or Hebrew) to Latin, this is how most of the Greek scientific classics came to the West.

Vernacular literature

Yet despite this classical revival a new literary age was about to be born, the age of the vernacular. By the 13th century works written in the *vernacular*, that is, in European national languages as opposed to international Latin, were common. And although Latin literature continued to be produced, there sprang up alongside it a luxuriant growth of German, Scandinavian, Irish, and French writings. Autobiographies, travel books, poetry (such as the *fabliaux*), and drama associated with the Church all enjoyed a great vogue.

Especially popular was a long French allegorical poem called the *Roman de la Rose* (*Romance of the Rose*). The Rose symbolizes the lady-love of the poet, and through the poem wander a host of other characters—Idleness, Danger, Evil-Tongue, Fear, Shame, Reason, Youth, and so on—whose intrigues help or hinder the lover's efforts to pluck the Rose. The *Roman de la Rose* expresses the townsman's contempt for the old-fashioned ideals of chivalry when it satirizes courtly manners. It also served as a model for the later morality plays such as

[3] J. L. LaMonte, *The World of the Middle Ages: A Reorientation of Medieval History* (Appleton-Century-Crofts, 1949), p. 555.

Everyman—much more refined and subtle creations than the early *Noah's Ark*.

❖ *From Doubt to Truth*   When Aristotle was rediscovered in the West via the Moslems, many men were disturbed by apparent contradictions between his views and the Bible's.   Medieval churchmen always claimed that there could be no conflict between reason and faith, and therefore many scholars set about trying to make Aristotle's philosophy agree with Christianity by means of an ingenious series of arguments.

Peter Abelard

The most celebrated philosopher of that day, and one of the greatest teachers of all time, was the Frenchman Peter Abelard (1079-1142). Abelard's far-ranging mind soon got him into trouble, particularly when he collected a number of passages from Scripture and from the Church Fathers that seemed contradictory, and published them under the title *Sic et Non* ("Yes and No"). Abelard was not trying to tear down religion, but he did insist that "by doubting we are led to inquiry, and from inquiry we perceive the truth." It is to this brilliant and courageous intellectual that the schools of Paris, from which the University of Paris ultimately sprang, owe their development.

Abelard's extensive studies were prophetic of a movement which was soon to follow, one which attempted to consolidate all knowledge. The movement culminated in the writings of two 13th century Dominicans, Albert the Great (1193-1280) and his pupil Thomas Aquinas (1225-74), both of whom wrote monumental works in an attempt to sum up all knowledge and reconcile it with Christian doctrine.

In the Middle Ages philosophy and theology were essentially one subject, and the student studied them in a *summa* (or "sum total"), that is, a book dealing exhaustively with a particular topic, usually by the method of question and answer. By the 13th century textbooks consisted of the Bible, the writings of the Church Fathers such as St. Augustine, and the various *summae,* which contained 12th century translations of the Greek and Roman philosophers along with commentaries on them.

𝕷etabitur iuftus in Domino

These pointed letters in 13th century Gothic script perhaps reflect Gothic architectural design.

Thomas Aquinas was born in southern Italy and eventually joined the Dominican Order, coming under the influence of Albert the Great at

St. Thomas Aquinas

Cologne and Paris. Aquinas himself taught in Italy and Paris and produced prodigious works in spite of the fact that he died in 1274 before he was fifty. His *Summa Theologica* is the greatest intellectual achievement of the 13th century, and perhaps of the entire Middle Ages—a staggering undertaking which in a modern English translation runs to twenty volumes. In it St. Thomas poses some 631 questions on every imaginable aspect of life and Christianity; then an answer is given to each question; a number of opinions contradicting each answer are presented; and finally St. Thomas disposes of the contrary opinions by stating his own. In all, St. Thomas answers some 10,000 objections to his conclusions. No man before or since has subjected his own philosophy to such a comprehensive and searching logical examination.

For St. Thomas, there could be no conflict between faith and reason. If anyone thought there was a conflict it was only because of faulty reasoning. It was with this conviction that St. Thomas created a comprehensive structure of learning, elaborate, consistent with both Christianity and Aristotelianism according to his own reasoning, and authoritative. And although some of what he wrote was condemned as heretical only three years after his death, by 1323 the Church had canonized him. Today he remains the official philosopher of the Roman Catholic Church.

❖ *Herald of the Renaissance*   A complete contrast to St. Thomas
Dante Aquinas, who embodied the medieval spirit, was Dante Alighieri (1265-1321), a cultured Italian who, in his daring criticism of the Church and his skilful use of the vernacular, heralded the Italian Renaissance. Dante was exiled from Florence after supporting a municipal revolution in which Pope Boniface VIII played a part. But although he was unsuccessful in politics he turned out to be a literary genuius. His most famous work is the epic poem the *Divine Comedy,* in which he relates his adventures as he progressed through Hell, Purgatory, and Paradise. In the poem the German Emperor Henry VII is in Heaven, while Pope Boniface is confidently awaited in Hell—a good example of the boldness of 14th century papal criticism. Dante, however, wrote in Latin as well as Italian, so that he belonged to the Middle Ages just as much as to the Renaissance. As a student once wrote in his examination, "Dante stood with one foot firmly planted in the Middle Ages, and with the other saluted the rising star of the Renaissance"!

❖ *The Lion and the Sheep-dog*   The Moslem stimulus which was felt in almost every area of medieval learning also affected science, a subject which began its revolutionary development in the 13th century. In order to appreciate just how enlightened the new approach was, let us look for a moment at an example from a popular handbook of the early Middle Ages. The following scientific gem appeared under the heading "Lion."

The Lion has three characteristics; as he walks or runs he brushes his footprints with his tail, so that hunters may not track him. This signifies the secrecy of the Incarnation. . . . Secondly, the Lion sleeps with his eyes open; so slept the body of Christ upon the Cross. . . . Thirdly, the lioness brings forth her cub dead; on the third day the father comes and roars in its face, and wakes it to life. This signifies our Lord's resurrection on the third day.

As you can see, science in the early Middle Ages was dominated by religious considerations. It was felt, for example, that animals should be described for the moral they pointed up. By the 13th century, however, the attitude had become very different.

The new outlook is evident in the work of Thomas Aquinas's teacher, *Albert the* Albert the Great, who as well as being a theologian was an outstanding *Great* biologist. Albert disagreed with and criticized some of Aristotle's scientific writings and proceeded to describe plants and animals from his own examinations. His keen powers of observation can be seen in his famous description of sheep-dogs.

The dogs . . . that follow sheep for the sake of guarding them differ in size, but all are habitually trained to run down wolves. The female, especially, is distinguished in this chase. I have seen one of them teach her young to pursue a wolf by running ahead of them to incite them on their course. When the wolf threatened to escape, she would hold it until the young dogs had caught up; then she would let it go again. And if the wolf bit the young dogs, she would not immediately come to their aid; for she wanted them to be provoked against the wolf. These dogs vary in size, some being very large, bigger and stronger than wolves, and some being smaller. All belonging to this breed, however, are larger and fiercer than other dogs.

Now admittedly it is a great deal easier to observe sheep-dogs than lions, but even so note the difference in the observer's attitude. Our early medieval author writes a nonsensical passage on lions in order to prove a religious doctrine, whereas our 13th century author is interested only in describing sheep-dogs as they actually behaved according to his own observations.

Noteworthy scientific works were also produced by two Englishmen: *Robert* Robert Grosseteste and Roger Bacon. Robert Grosseteste (1168-1253), *Grosseteste* the chancellor of Oxford University and bishop of Lincoln, was one of the first to systematically employ experiments for the purpose of discovering scientific laws. He tried, for example, to explain the nature of rainbows by studying refraction in lenses. In his account of mirrors he even added some remarks on perspective lenses, with which, he said, "we may make things a long distance off appear as if placed very close, and large near things appear very small . . . we may make small things placed at a distance appear any size we want, so that it may be possible for us to read the smallest letters at an incredible distance, or to count sand, or grains, or seeds, or any sort of minute objects." Others must have experimented with lenses, for we know that spectacles were in use before the end of the 13th century

Roger Bacon   One of Grosseteste's pupils was the Oxford Franciscan, Roger Bacon (1214-94). Bacon was, however, little more than a theorist who often criticized his predecessors without fully understanding them. Nevertheless his accounts of practical experiments are accurate and valuable, and an interesting one may be read in the Source Reading on pages 486-487.

❖ *A Climate Congenial to Learning*   In the Middle Ages there was, of course, learning that was not "book learning." The fledgling knight was trained as a squire in some baronial castle, just as the apprentice was trained in some master's shop. But although many young ladies and gentlemen of the nobility were taught by clerks and chaplains how to read and write, any real education was limited almost entirely to clergymen. At first monasteries were the chief educational centres; then the cathedral schools were promoted by the Carolingian Renaissance. In both, the main objective was to train men for service in the Church.

Grammar schools   By the 12th century, many free grammar schools—theoretically open to all—had been set up in the towns. This did not mean, however, that everyone was educated. Far from it. In the first place, most boys had to leave school to become apprentices by the age of 14, and in the second, primary education was a most unpleasant experience. The student was not expected to think; but he *was* expected to learn Latin by rote and speak it always, with the teacher meting out incessant punishments to the unfortunate pupils by liberal and often brutal applications of the rod. Perhaps some of them disliked children as actively as this writer of the 13th century:

I have never cared for children, little, medium-sized or big; the little one is hard to rear and does not let the people sleep at night; the middle-sized one runs down the street and must be kept from horses and carts; the big one battles with father and mother to get rich estates, and he has to be brought back continually from the taverns.

It is time now to turn our attention to the big ones.

In the 12th century a more advanced centre of learning, that peculiar institution known as the university, rose to prominence. The University of Bologna, established early in that century, was a centre for the study of Roman law, a subject in which interest had been sharply revived at this time. The University of Paris developed at approximately the same time. And Oxford began its distinguished career a little later.

Although universities were born eight centuries ago, in some ways their organization has not changed greatly since the Middle Ages. These medieval institutions offered a number of courses, but we will concentrate on the so-called "arts " course of a university such as Oxford or Paris. The seven subjects of the curriculum were divided into two groups as shown in the diagram, and were all essential to the work of the clergy.

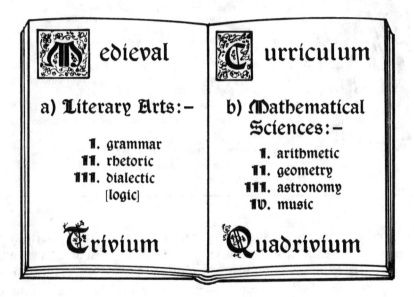

Medieval Curriculum

a) Literary Arts:–

1. grammar
11. rhetoric
111. dialectic
[logic]

Trivium

b) Mathematical Sciences:–

1. arithmetic
11. geometry
111. astronomy
1V. music

Quadrivium

The first three helped the priest prepare his sermons, while he needed arithmetic for keeping parish accounts, geometry (which included surveying) for settling property disputes, astronomy for setting movable dates (such as that of Easter) in the church calendar, and music for chanting the hymns. Hence these subjects provided a "practical" education for that time, and the degree of Master of Arts (M.A.) provided a licence to teach in a university or the necessary grounding for further study in medicine or theology.

Today's modern university campus with its great lecture halls, laboratories, and athletic facilities bears little physical resemblance to its medieval ancestor. Students in the Middle Ages attended lectures in the professors' own rooms or in buildings they rented for the purpose. Once there they were subjected to a lecture delivered at break-neck speed on some standard text such as the works of Aristotle, while they did their best, in an age of few books, to take copious notes. All told, the student led a pretty austere life. Here is a daily timetable:

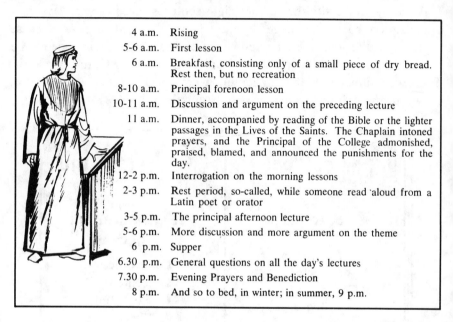

4 a.m.	Rising
5-6 a.m.	First lesson
6 a.m.	Breakfast, consisting only of a small piece of dry bread. Rest then, but no recreation
8-10 a.m.	Principal forenoon lesson
10-11 a.m.	Discussion and argument on the preceding lecture
11 a.m.	Dinner, accompanied by reading of the Bible or the lighter passages in the Lives of the Saints. The Chaplain intoned prayers, and the Principal of the College admonished, praised, blamed, and announced the punishments for the day.
12-2 p.m.	Interrogation on the morning lessons
2-3 p.m.	Rest period, so-called, while someone read aloud from a Latin poet or orator
3-5 p.m.	The principal afternoon lecture
5-6 p.m.	More discussion and more argument on the theme
6 p.m.	Supper
6.30 p.m.	General questions on all the day's lectures
7.30 p.m.	Evening Prayers and Benediction
8 p.m.	And so to bed, in winter; in summer, 9 p.m.

The boy who underwent such a rigorous routine was only fourteen or fifteen when he enrolled. If he survived six years of such an existence he became a Bachelor of Arts (B.A.), and if he pursued his studies for up to ten years more he became a Master. Thus he might spend a total of sixteen years getting a college education.

Of course not all medieval students spent their whole time with books and study, any more than all modern ones do. Freshmen were hazed unmercifully, many students wasted their parents' money (and wrote ingenious letters home for more), and even the teachers could be unacademic, one German master being dismissed for stabbing a colleague to death in a faculty meeting. The fact that the university was not considered part of the town meant that the students often tangled with the law, or (and we can hardly blame them for this) with the merchants who tried to grossly overcharge them. Nevertheless, despite the publicity given

The medieval university often had no regular buildings, classes frequently being held in a room rented by the master with the students sitting literally at his feet. Because the price of books was prohibitive, many a student made up his own "texts" from his lecture notes. A popular test of learning was the debate, which sometimes went on for hours between masters or, as in the illustration, between advanced students.

the exploits of wilder students, the average student—then as now—was law-abiding and fairly inconspicuous.

The medieval universities, of course, trained men for the learned professions—teaching, law, medicine, and theology. But perhaps their greatest contribution was that they provided a climate congenial to learning. If much that they studied seems out of date to us today, and if their methods seem crude, we might well wonder what the historian of the future will say in writing of certain 20th century universities in which it is possible to learn how to ride a horse, how to play golf, or how to apply make-up!

Romanesque churches, as you know, tend to have gloomy interiors. Here is a particularly good example of the way in which some artists attempted to lighten one of them, the 11th century church of Saint-Savin near Poitiers in France. Notice how your eyes are drawn upward by the colourful Old Testament scenes painted on the barrel vaulting, while the heavy supporting columns appear less massive because of their varied designs which imitate marble and onyx.

❖ *Strength and Light* More than anything else, the cathedral symbolizes the Middle Ages. It is a combination of beauty and strength, body and soul, that is typically medieval.

The early churches of the Middle Ages were simple rectangular buildings with wooden roofs. Since these roofs often caught fire and burned, destroying the whole church, builders turned their attention to the erection of a church with a non-inflammable roof, one made of stone. The arched stone "ceiling" that evolved was called a *vault,* and the new style of church architecture that made extensive use of it was called *Romanesque* ("Roman-like") because it resembled the Roman hall of justice.

Romanesque architecture

The Romanesque style was dominant in the 11th and 12th centuries, just when stone castles were beginning to replace wooden ones. Because the long barrel vaults were very heavy, massive stone pillars and thick walls were needed to support them. Nor could these walls be weakened by more than a few narrow windows. Consequently the interior was gloomy. Sculptors often tried to counteract this heavy impression by decorating the outside facing with elaborately fashioned figures representing Bible stories, and by enhancing the great interior pillars with carved capitals. Such carving was not lifelike but stylized, the human figures often being elongated to harmonize with the columns.

Since the gloomy Romanesque style was not suited to the shorter days and long winters of northern Europe, a series of important discoveries in the middle of the 12th century led to the creation in France of a more suitable form called *Gothic.* In the first place it was found that tall slender columns could support considerable weight if they were made to radiate out at the top like the branches of a tree in what was called *ribbed vaulting.* Then *pointed arches* were introduced to give greater height. And finally a decorative device called the *flying buttress,* which was really part of the scaffolding incorporated into the building, was added. The flying buttresses, along with the ribbed vaulting, enabled the slender columns to support the heavy roof without buckling outwards. Consequently the walls of the church did not have to be heavy and could be punctured with large windows to let light flood the interior. The whole impression given by a Gothic cathedral is one of vertical lines constantly striving upward, soaring, as it were, to heaven.

Gothic architecture

Gothic decoration was brilliantly conceived. The large pointed windows were filled with stained glass, while on the façade and surrounding

Amiens Cathedral took nearly two centuries to complete, and is considered the finest example of Gothic architecture in France. This cut-away drawing of the *nave* or body of the church illustrates some of the main features of Gothic cathedrals: (1) ribbed vaulting, (2) clerestory (a wall of windows), (3) pointed arch, (4) flying buttress, (5) timber trussed roof. The peak of the roof at Amiens is approximately 200 feet from the ground, and light from a multitude of tall stained glass windows bathes the interior. Hence the whole effect is one of exalted lightness and richness.

the doorways lifelike sculptures gilded with fresh paint (far different from the grimy gray stone of today) clustered in profusion.

Not all churches were strictly Romanesque or Gothic; some started out in one style and ended up in another. Mostly, however, the contrast

There is an almost mystic blending of delicacy and strength—of heaven and earth—in this magnificent façade of Amiens cathedral. The soaring towers give it a noble dignity, and the profusion of sculptured figures provides a whole museum of religious art. And as the great rose window catches the last rays of the setting sun it forms the crowning glory of a cathedral that has been described as "one of the greatest of man's symphonies in stone."

between the two styles was as marked as in the pictures you have seen, and their chief differences may be summarized as follows:

ROMANESQUE
(11th-12th centuries)

1. barrel vaulting
2. round arches
3. massive pillars
4. narrow windows
5. thick walls
6. gloomy interior
7. horizontal lines
8. stylized sculpture

GOTHIC
(12th-15th centuries)

1. ribbed vaulting
2. higher pointed arches
3. slender columns
4. large stained glass windows
5. thinner walls
6. light-flooded interior
7. vertical lines
8. more lifelike sculpture

❖ *Defying Gravity to Glorify God* "Our civilization has not produced a greater miracle than the Gothic cathedral," writes a modern historian. And it must be admitted that our churches, even though they are stylistically correct, rarely compare with medieval ones. Our stained glass does not match theirs. Our churches are not usually set off by a square, nor do they tower over their surroundings as medieval cathedrals did. In fact our cathedrals are often dwarfed by huge office buildings of plainer style. It requires considerable effort on our part to realize how and why these medieval cathedrals were built, one of the tallest stretching to the height of a modern fifteen-storey building, not counting additional towers and spires. In truth, as has been said, the Gothic cathedral rose "defying gravity to glorify God" in a miracle of medieval engineering.

Something as complex as a cathedral was not built by amateur architects or dabbling masons. Cathedrals required expert plans and swarms of workmen, both specialists and unskilled labourers. The construction was supervised by a master mason, who was a highly skilled and well paid professional. The assisting masons, too, had to be experts, since even a small error in one section of the vaulting could be disastrous. Proficient carpenters were needed to erect the scaffolding and the protective wood covering under which the vaults could be completed, as well as for the more delicate task of fashioning choir stalls and other furniture. Since smiths, plumbers, and glaziers were also required for any major construction job such as a cathedral, great numbers of wage-earning craftsmen must have travelled about from one large building project to another.

Church building was usually not a year-round activity. The work went ahead only during the summer or as money became available, though a skeleton staff was maintained during the off seasons. It is little wonder, then, that a cathedral like Notre-Dame in Paris, begun in 1163, was not finally finished until some time after 1300, or that many cathedrals never were completed up to the last tower or buttress. Yet the overall medieval rate of production was astonishing. In France alone, between 1170 and 1270 some 80 cathedrals and 500 churches of cathedral proportions were begun.

Why were all these cathedrals built? The most obvious motive was, of course, to glorify God. But this is hardly the whole story. The cathedral *The* was the heart of the medieval city—the medieval community centre. *cathedral* Municipal meetings and ceremonies were held in the cathedral square; the Gothic façade provided a dramatic backdrop for medieval miracle plays performed on the church steps; and medieval holidays always began with a religious service. The cathedral was the first object the traveller sighted from afar, and naturally each town was eager to have the greatest church. When, for instance, the citizens of Amiens completed a magnificent cathedral with an interior height in the nave of 141 feet, the men of Beauvais determined that their cathedral should soar even higher. So they built their nave to the incredible height of 154 feet. But they had, alas, succeeded in glorifying God without defying gravity, for the vaulting collapsed twice. And though rebuilding and reinforcing finally did produce the highest choir in Christendom (157 feet), the Beauvais cathedral was never finished.

Medieval men poured all their learning and all their art into these immense sanctuaries, and their carvings and glass reminded high- and low-born alike of the eternal truths of Christianity. "The pictures and ornaments in a church are the text and scriptures of the laity," wrote a 13th century bishop; and a Bible in glass and stone is exactly what the cathedral was for the illiterate masses. Those who could read had the *Summa* of Thomas Aquinas. Those who could not had their *summa* in the cathedral.

CHAPTER 44

A Day in the Life of a Medieval Townswoman

The medieval burgess . . . was a different kind of person from all who lived outside the town walls. Once outside the gates and the moat we are in another world. . . .

HENRI PIRENNE, *Economic and Social History of Medieval Europe*

All over London the bells rang out the Angelus to herald the new day, and devout burgesses, some struggling awake, some already hard at work, paused to say one Paternoster and five Ave's. In an age when only the occasional monastery could boast a mechanical or even a water clock, bells were the time-keepers, the watchdogs, the newscarriers, the messengers of joy and sorrow for every city. Townspeople knew the position and purpose of every bell they heard. They knew whether it warned them of an attack, or clamoured for their assistance at a fire, or summoned them to a guild meeting, or sounded the curfew to say that all shops must close and every man be off the streets and behind the comfortable bolts of his own door—"unless he be of good repute and carry a light." The priest who went to comfort the dying tinkled a small bell to request prayers for the departing soul, and bells tolled after death, often for an hour, finishing with strokes that indicated the age, sex, and social rank of the deceased. Indeed, one John Baret of Bury St. Edmunds willed that the chimes should toll day and night for thirty days after his death!

Anne Brown scuffed through the thick, clean hay on her bedroom floor and opened the casement window. She was the proud mistress of one of the finest houses in London—though not so fine as to incur the rancour of jealous neighbours the way one man had done. When he bedecked his residence with a lofty brick tower the neighbours vowed that he was demonstrating how superior he was by looking down on them. But he got his reward: heaven soon smote him with blindness. A second tower-builder was duly beset with gout so that he could not climb his own stairs. Fortunately Anne's husband, Richard, had not been so vain, but had constructed a fine stone dwelling (a rarity in a city of wooden houses) at the centre of town, where the more prosperous houses had always been constructed so as to be away from enemy fire.

There was little danger of enemy attack in these days of the 1270's, but there were other dangers almost as frightening. These were times of swift and uncontrolled passions, and townsmen were still required to undergo a certain amount of military training. One of Richard Brown's duties as an alderman was to lead the men of his ward into battle, and for this reason he kept a hackney in his stables and his sergeant's light mail near at hand. Londoners took their military power very seriously, and never forgot that they had kept King Stephen on the throne through nearly twenty years of civil war. The knights ignored Henry III's prohibition of tournaments and continued their jousts and tourneys at Smithfield and elsewhere, the combatants' need for thick armour—much heavier than could have been used on the battlefield—bringing London armourers some welcome trade. Even at that, armour had not reached the solid proportions of Henry VIII's suit which may still be seen in the Tower of London and weighs 63 lbs. 11 oz. without the gauntlets!

Richard dearly loved to try his hand with the lance, and, like many a medieval man, bore the marks of one violent encounter—a jagged scar across his left cheek. Richard's younger brother Tom, who lived with them, delighted in wielding an iron-shod stick against his adversaries as he flew over the frozen Moorfields on his bone skates, or, in the summer, in aiming his lance at a shield fastened in midstream, while crowds gathered either to cheer when he shattered his lance on it or hoot with laughter when he missed and got dunked in the river. Wrestling, racing, fighting with sword and buckler, throwing the javelin, all these were the delight of youths of every class. But not all games ended peacefully. When a team of Londoners won a wrestling match against the suburb of Westminster in 1222, the Westminster men turned up for the return match bearing arms. Enraged, the Londoners rushed to Westminster and pulled down the house of the Steward of the Abbey, whereupon the indignant Abbot hastened to London to complain. He was stoned out of the city. Clearly, things had got out of hand. The next morning the ringleader of the rioters and two others were hanged, some lost feet or hands, and the king fined the City heavily for breaking his peace. Londoners were so apt to grab up their arms on any provocation that in 1281 they were prohibited from carrying swords and bucklers in the City at night. Nevertheless insults were still apt to draw blood, and life was never dull.

Sometimes, thought Anne with a shiver, life was not dull enough. London might be surrounded by stout walls 18 feet high, and the watchman might question and exact tolls of all who came and went, but no walls, no watchman could keep out the City's strongest and fiercest enemy: fire. Just a block down from the Browns' substantial residence lay the charred ruins of a row of wooden houses. City regulations had banned thatched roofs after the terrible fire of 1212, but try to get the humble burgesses to change to tile! There were other attempts to prevent wholesale conflagrations: a tub of water was to be set outside every house in summer, and great hooks were available for pulling down a burning roof or even a whole house if necessary. But their benefits must have been more psychological than practical. Fines discouraged carelessness. If the flame of a fire was so high that it could be seen outside, the householder had to pay the sheriff forty shillings. But many roofs still had only smokeholes, and even from the few chimneys that existed sparks were apt to float forth and lodge on a neighbour's thatch.

Rarely did anyone set a fire: the terrible penalty was death by burning. But what could be done about the poor simpleton who pulled his straw mattress near the hearth to keep warm, and in so doing burned up himself and half a city block? And what could be done about the townsfolk who liked to light bonfires on Holy Days and were careless with their torches? So often the results were disastrous. Someone would cry "Fire!" The beadle would blow his horn. The neighbouring church bells would ring. The city authorities would marshal an army of volunteers into a bucket brigade to bring water from a nearby well. Hooks would be fetched from the Guildhall and ladders from the wealthy citizens would be dragged along the street. And all the while the fire leaped higher, reaching across narrow alleyways and licking at the wooden walls, a searing, sneering giant towering over its puny human opponents and ignoring the ineffectual splashes of buckets of water.

It was almost time for Anne to get ready for Mass. Like most people of her time, she tended to value formal worship more than righteous thinking. Had not Henry II dictated letters during the singing of High Mass?—and no one thought the worse of him for it. London housewives usually went to church three times on Sunday and once on holy days, and started every day with Mass. Soon the bells would be ringing for service, but Anne lingered a few moments to watch the activity outside her window. Yesterday she would by no means have lingered. For then the garbage men had not yet come, and the stench was so terrible on a summer's day that an open window was almost beyond endurance. Fortunately London now had official garbage collectors, rakiers, who were supervised by men called scavengers, the latter being honoured street officials despite their title.

The rakiers would bring along their carts (only 12 for the whole city) and shovel up any refuse that the kites and ravens had not been obliging enough to make off with: slops, soiled rushes, offal of every description, feathers, dead cats and dogs, everything imaginable and unimaginable that had collected during the week. The sewer that ran down the middle of the street might bear away some of the waste; but too often it became clogged with items as formidable as a dead horse. In vain was each man directed to keep his section of the street clean. Supremely oblivious to the dangers of dirt, the townsmen required the powerful incentive of a king's visit—or a plague—to spur them on to really ambitious garbage collecting. The people threw their slops on the streets (and often on the courteous gentleman who allowed his lady friend to walk on the inside), shoved their refuse in front of their neighbour's house, or showered garbage over the walls or just outside the gates of the city where the miserable lepers hovered with their bells and alms baskets. Worst of all was the offal deposited by butchers or fishmongers. For a time butchers were allowed to clean carcasses from a special wharf opposite Fleet Street prison, but the stench made the inmates so ill that the privilege was revoked at the end of the 13th century. Poor prisoners! The common offenders such as those who played dice in Newgate's crowded gatehouse room were not so badly off. But the serious offenders who lay in dark dungeons—fed only on mouldy bread and water or bad meat, and terrified, as were all medieval men, of the toads, snakes, and other creeping things that inhabit the damp and the wet—had enough to contend with without being suffocated by stench.

Already the sounds of the city were beginning—the cries of the water carriers (who called regularly at the Brown home) trundling their kegs on carts or shoulder yokes, the clatter of a wagon being driven across the cobbled forecourt of the house, the raucous conversations of serving-maids carrying their water jugs to the nearest conduit, and above all the squeals of pigs hunting through refuse, the barks of dogs snapping at horses' heels, the indignant protests of geese and chickens being given merry chase. The streets of London were never free of this menagerie of barnyard animals who dirtied the roads, blocked the way, and generally made any kind of order impossible—and this in spite of the fact

"The remaining members of the group made their way along the shop-lined streets all
too quickly to suit the maids."

that the scavenger was authorized to kill wandering swine or geese on sight. Any wise citizen either rode on horseback or wore stout, high boots when venturing forth on the streets.

Now the various workmen were hurrying past. Anne could tell the hard-working members of various trades by their tools and their physical characteristics—even deformities. There strode the blacksmith, his arms bulging with muscles, the tanner with his stained fingers, the carpenter with his axe dangling from his neck and his planer and adze draped at his side. . . . Anne jumped guiltily as the maid came in to tidy up the bedroom, and started to dress while the girl made up the large bed. There was a great plumping up of the feather mattress and silk-cased pillows, and a careful smoothing of the fine woollen blankets and silk coverlet. Then the steel mirror was polished and the large chests oiled before the four-poster's canopy (which kept out cold draughts) was smartly spanked to rearrange the dust. The smoky torches in the great main room below might remind Anne of her former home, but nothing in the old castle had approached the comfort of that bed!

Yet the bustling clamour of London still made Anne homesick for her home in the midlands, and she was glad that her father was coming into the city to see her today. Proud, stubborn, lovable Sir John! How loath he had been, moderate though his circumstances were, to see his daughter demean herself by marrying a merchant instead of a fellow knight! But she had two brothers, so that she would be able to bring no land to a future husband, and she was no beauty. To be the answer to a medieval man's prayer her hair should have been blonde but it was brunette; her nose should have been straight but it turned up impertinently; her eyes should have been gray and wide-set but they were black and dancing; and instead of being willowy she was pleasingly plump. Her father offered her the choice of a disagreeable widower, a knight with six children, or the life of a nun—a choice which reduced her to rage and then to tears.

Nevertheless her father was not unkind, and he dearly loved this merry daughter of his. Hence when the sale of his wool brought him in contact with a rich, middle-aged merchant named Richard Brown, and that merchant (who despite his calling and his lack of ancient lineage seemed remarkably genteel) begged for his daughter's hand, he gave his permission provided that the lady was willing. Ten years ago he would not have even considered such a match. But he had heard that a similar alliance had been permitted by a knight of proud (if poor) family two years ago and the skies had not fallen. And after all, Anne was no child: she was fifteen. In those days a boy came of age at fourteen and a girl at twelve, and for reasons of property or security mere babies in cradles were sometimes betrothed and even married. One James Ballard, aged ten, was married without the consent of any of his friends, and the next day told his uncle that his bride, "the said Jane (beyinge a bigge damsell and mariageable at the same tyme) had intised him with two Apples, to go with her to Colne and to marry her."

Anne was willing. Richard was not handsome, but despite the scar he had a good, strong face and a kind one. And to live in London, in a great house with plenty of money to run it—that would be a perfect life. Life, of course, is never perfect, and although Anne was as happy with Richard as she expected to be (it never occurred to her that she should be in love with him) there were other sorrows, deep ones. She had been married now only three years, but already she had lost two infants. For although once a baby had safely arrived it was remarkably well cared for, being kept in swaddling clothes, and fed, bathed, and changed every three hours, there was so little defence against childhood diseases that relatively few children lived to maturity. A man who passed thirty was fortunate. At forty he was aging. At fifty-five he was old. Medieval folk ate few vegetables and too much meat, and, in an age when there was no tea, coffee, or cocoa, and most water was not safe to drink, too much beer and wine. Besides, nothing was known of antiseptics or contagion, and epidemics swept people off like the tide from the sea. One had snatched Anne's babies from her; so Richard still had no heir.

It always seemed odd to Anne that, should she have two sons, it would be the youngest, not the eldest, who would inherit his father's riches. This was because a burgess was usually a craftsman (Richard had originally been a Draper), and by the time he died it was supposed that his elder sons would have set themselves up in their chosen craft and be under the protection of a guild. The youngest, however, might need support until he could learn a trade.

Anne hurried to her garden and dropped by the kitchen (which was isolated in the back yard as a fire precaution) to give the cook some flowers to flavour the day's special dishes. Then, since her husband was still away on a business trip, she hustled to join her brother-in-law and the servants for Mass. Anne liked to go to church. It was one of the few opportunities she had to visit her neighbours, even if the priest did sometimes complain that the women squatting on their heels at the back of the church were busier gossiping than saying their prayers! She walked modestly at the head of the little group, always mindful of the training she had received now and then at her noble aunt's castle. No rich woman's ostentatious display of gold-threaded cloth, no flashy jewels, no vermilion face paint or white powder for her. Nor did she choose the loud, clashing colour combinations so dear to most women of the age. She never overdressed, as her husband tended to do, and had nothing but scorn for those lavishly bedecked women who had prompted the passage in 1281 of a law attempting to prohibit lower class women from dressing themselves "in the guise of their betters." Nevertheless the average burgess would have immediately recognized the excellence of the cloth in her long sleeves and the beautiful fit of her shoes. "See that they fit so close," says the *Roman de la Rose,* "that the low-class fellows will argue how you got into them and how you will get out."

On the way home Anne dispatched a servingman to buy some dainties from the excellent cookshop on the river bank—that distinctive London establishment (the only genuine eating-house this side of Paris) which boasted an infinite variety of food either to eat there or take out. The remaining members of the group made their way along the shop-lined streets all too quickly to suit the maids. Anne, too, loved to "window-shop," even though not one of the streets reserved for each trade contained a dress shop. There was no such thing in London. There were no ready-mades; all clothes and hose, unless they were "hand-me-downs," were made-to-measure. Nevertheless there was plenty to see. The trading was fast and furious, and the noise—between iron-rimmed cart wheels, horses' hooves, poor folk's wooden-soled shoes, and the sounds of the craftsmen ringing out from the back rooms of the shops— was deafening. Add to all this the crying of wares, which, in an age that knew no advertisement, was a raucous, ear-splitting occupation, and you have a complete hubbub.

One eager merchant moved towards the ladies as they paused, ready, although he knew the law forbade him to do so, to clutch his prospective client by the sleeve. Anne had little use for such high-pressure salesmanship and made her way on past a group of bystanders who were shouting with laughter at a drunk trying to help a blind man along. The medieval man loved a good laugh, but he was often crude, if not cruel, in his diversions. The drunkard, the mutilated, even the diseased, who were always to be found on city streets, furnished him with a continual source of amusement. Taunting the one-armed, the one-legged, the spastic, the blind, the half-witted, pitching offending creatures into the water, baiting animals, mocking culprits exposed in the stocks, watching cocks tear each other to pieces, enjoying a good hanging—these were highly amusing and enormously popular pastimes. Even punishments for offences such as selling bad merchandise involved horseplay. When one John Penrose sold bad wine he was condemned "to drink a draught of the same wine and have the rest poured over his head."

As Anne took off her kerchief at home she could picture Sir John, accompanied, like any respectable knight, by his squire, making his way steadily towards the city on his trusty *destrier* (warhorse) at the rate of a good six miles per hour. The roads were terrible, and the woods which came right down to the edge harboured both wild animals and robbers. Perhaps, thought Anne hopefully, he would fall in with some pilgrims going to Canterbury—pilgrimages were so fashionable now —or even with one of those perpetual pilgrims who went about these days journeying hither and yon and being given food and clothing by pious hosts. She could imagine the old man (after all, he was fifty-three) exchanging songs and stories with his fellow travellers in the manner of the true courtier that he was.

Actually Anne was glad to have her father's meal to fuss over with the cook. She got tired of embroidery and playing little girls' games with her neighbours. She got tired of supervising the mending and airing of clothes, the taking out of grease stains, the packing and unpacking of furs in heavy trunks, and of the never-ending battle against fleas, flies, and mosquitoes. The truth was that she was a very intelligent woman. She had been taught to read; but books were non-existent in most medieval homes. She had been taught to embroider, to spin and weave, and to accompany herself on the viol as she sang. Finally, she knew a little astronomy (any doctor's first question was to ask under what constellation the patient had been born), and, like any good knight's daughter, the rudiments of nursing. She knew how to wash a limb in strong vinegar alcohol and sew up a wound with thread, and to aid its healing by applying the white of an egg (which, incidentally, was sterile and hence actually helpful). In the 20th century she might have been a nurse; but she had been born in the 13th. And so she spent her days chasing fleas and distilling the scent of roses and playing hide-and-seek with other ladies.

It was with delight that Anne heard her father arrive, and she ran to greet him affectionately. He was dressed plainly but neatly, and had gone to the trouble of shaving—a real effort since, like most men, he ordinarily shaved only once a week. Somehow he seemed shorter to his daughter than he used to, although he was of average height (just over five feet) for the times. But then she was used to her tall husband who was 5′10″. Sir John responded a trifle grumpily. To tell the truth he was a bit ashamed of his affection for his impish daughter, and so disguised it. He was glad to see her happy, but he still distrusted and made no attempt to understand his son-in-law's career. For Richard was no ordinary merchant. He practised a new profession, wholesale international trade, and ran risks that would strike terror into the heart of the bravest knight.

In these days, everyone knew that the producer really should sell direct to the consumer. Hence someone like Richard, who imported foreign goods (imagine dealing all the time with foreigners!) to resell them was really going against nature. Besides, imports should be kept to a minimum. Most good knights like Sir John kept all their ready cash securely locked up in a strong box, so that there was little in circulation. And surely this was sound practice. Obviously the way to make England rich was to keep her silver in the country. But how could foreign trade be carried on without money? The Jews had been so abused and ruined that there were few who could lend out cash. What, then, did a merchant do? What he did, Richard had discovered, was to sell his merchandise for sealed drafts. Sometimes, it was true, these drafts "bounced"; but so far Richard had been lucky. He had even begun to lend money out himself. He could not accept interest, of course; but what was wrong with accepting bonds at less than face value?

Such intricacies of business were beyond the comprehension of Sir John, even if he had been sympathetic to them, for feudal lords saw wealth as consisting only in silver or land. He could understand his son-in-law's trading in England's time-honoured commodity, wool. But all these dealings in foreign luxuries smacked almost of treason. Anne rarely discussed her husband's work with her father—partly because she only hazily comprehended it as being very chancy but so far very lucrative. Instead she made a practice of cooking his favourite stews, to be eaten with the aid of bread and fingers (no belching, toothpicks, or elbows on the table, please), and boiling fowl until it was ready to fall apart. She had also fashioned some delicate pastries which, in a clockless kitchen, she had timed in the oven by saying a certain number of Paternosters. It was not the dinner Anne would have liked to prepare. Peacocks dressed in their own skins made such an impressive dish at a large dinner party, and she had a special recipe for dressing a swan which she was longing to try:

Make a stiff bed of paste about the thickness of your thumb and colour it green. Comb it out, and it will look like a meadow of green grass. Take your swan and gild him over with gold; then have a kind of loose, flying cloak of a vermilion colour within and painted with arms without; then set the swan upon his bed, cover some part of him with the cloak, stick about him small banners upon little sticks, the banners painted with the arms most agreeable to the people seated at the table.

But this was a private dinner party for two, and she must serve something that the old gentleman's tender teeth could manage. Age brought many infirmities, not the least of them being perpetual toothache.

After dinner there was time for a leisurely chat by the hearth while quinces and pears simmered in honey over the smouldering coal. Anne missed the friendly crackle of wood. But the forests were disappearing, and wood had become so dear that Londoners had taken to using coal. Anne always made a point of inquiring about her father's favourite falcon, which he often brought with him and which merited a special perch in one bedroom. He, in turn, regaled her with a description of his last visit to court, where the barons had lounged about amidst the menagerie of their pets—hawks, falcons, parrots, or ravens fluttering on wrists, monkeys perched on shoulders, dogs underfoot gnawing on bones, spoiling the rushes, and yapping as tails were stepped on. Even a pet badger waddled about, and one of the knights boasted he had tamed a weasel! By contrast, Anne's news that she had a new wooden bath tub seemed rather tame. Nevertheless she was proud of it. It doubled as a table when turned over, and was even furnished with a small stool so that the bather could soak himself at his leisure. Let the peasants be dirty and smelly if they would. The gentry of the 13th century liked a hot bath with soap and water at least once a month; and if the merchant class was not quite so particular Anne did not care to have her father know it.

As Sir John made ready for his departure Anne tucked some ginger and cloves in his pocket for him to munch on the way to quiet his nervous stomach, and he thanked her for her trouble with quaint formality. Grumpy the old gentleman might be, but discourteous never. He was a true knight, whose manners inside the castle were as important to him as his courage outside it. Anne felt a sadness at seeing her father go that she could not quite understand. Perhaps it was because he had

". . . her father's favourite falcon . . ."

begun to move more slowly. He would never fight again. His modest castle had long ceased to need more protection than the bark of a good watchdog, and henceforth he would pay a fee rather than go to war should his king need his services. Indeed, he was a member of a vanishing breed. In his county the time had passed when every village need be defended by a professional man of war, and yeoman landholders were becoming reluctant to take up knighthood. Knightly equipment was becoming costlier, and the burden of local duties was increasing. The knight must act as juryman in the shire court, and there was now talk of two country knights being chosen to confer with the barons in parliament. Sir John would be proud to do this, but he was still of a generation that could not help thinking of itself as a race of fighting men.

Sir John and his squire had gone only a block when a tall, richly dressed figure rode toward them and greeted them. It was Richard, returned from his selling venture a day early. The two men conversed politely but briefly, and then the old knight rode slowly away out of sight. Anne felt a sharp sense of loss. It was almost as if her father, in leaving the noisy jostle of London and returning to his country castle, had gone back to another land, another age. Her husband, with all his daring, all his urbanity, all his skill at money-making, seemed to have no place in Sir John's feudal society. Could he be blazing the path to a new world?

Anne could not know it, but what she had just witnessed was the parting of two ages. The prosperous merchant would take the knight's place before her fire. The Middle Ages were making way for the Renaissance.

SOURCE READINGS

(a)

The ARTICLES OF THE SPURRIERS OF LONDON of 1345 illustrate the controls laid down by the members of a particular craft guild. A few of the articles follow.

In the first place,—that no one of the trade of spurriers shall work longer than from the beginning of the day until curfew . . . by reason that no man can work so neatly by night as by day. And many persons of the said trade, who compass how to practise deception in their work, desire to work by night rather than by day; and then they introduce false iron, and iron that has been cracked, for tin, and also they put gilt on false copper, and cracked. And further,—many of the said trade are wandering about all day, without working at all at their trade; and then, when they have become drunk and frantic, they take to their work, to the annoyance of the sick, and all their neighbourhood, as well by reason of the broils that arise between them and the strange folks who are dwelling among them. And then they blow up their fires so vigorously, that their forges begin all at once to blaze to the great peril of themselves and of all the neighbourhood around. And then, too, all the neighbours are much in dread of the sparks, which so vigorously issue forth in all directions from the mouths of the chimneys in their forges. By reason thereof it seems unto them that working by night should be put an end to, in order such false work and such perils to avoid. . . . And if any person shall be found in the said trade to do the contrary hereof, let him be amerced [fined], the first time in 40d., one-half thereof to go to the use of the Chamber of the Guildhall of London, and the other half to the use of the said trade; the second time, in half a mark, and the third time in 10s., to the use of the same Chamber and trade; and the fourth time, let him forswear the trade forever.

Also that no one of the said trade shall . . . cause to be sold, or expose for sale, any manner of old spurs for new ones, or shall garnish them or change them for new ones. . . .

Also, that no alien of another country, or foreigner of this country, shall follow or use the said trade, unless he is enfranchised before the mayor, alderman, and chamberlain; and that by witness and surety of the good folks of the said trade, who will undertake for him as to his loyalty and his good behaviour.

From *Translations and Reprints,* II, No. 1, pp. 12-17, as quoted in J. H. Dahmus, *A History of Medieval Civilization* (Odyssey Press, 1964), pp. 417-419.

(b)

When Pope URBAN II (1088-1099) preached the Crusade at Clermont in 1095 four contemporary writers reported the address. ROBERT THE MONK, whose version is translated below, claimed to have actually been present when the pope spoke.

"Oh, race of Franks, race from across the mountains, race chosen and beloved by God. . . . To you our discourse is addressed, and for you our exhortation is intended. We wish you to know what a grievous cause has led us to your country, what peril, threatening you and all the faithful, has brought us.

"From the confines of Jerusalem and the city of Constantinople a horrible tale has gone forth and very frequently has been brought to our ears; namely, that a race from the kingdom of the Persians, an accursed race, a race utterly alienated from God, a generation, forsooth, which has neither directed its heart nor entrusted its spirit to God, has invaded the lands of those Christians and has depopulated them by the sword, pillage, and fire; it has led away a part of the captives into its own country, and a part it has destroyed by cruel tortures; it has either entirely destroyed the churches of God or appropriated them for the rites of its own religion. . . .

"Let the deeds of your ancestors move you and incite your minds to manly achievements; likewise, the glory and greatness of King Charles the Great, and his son Louis, and of your other kings, who have destroyed the kingdoms of the pagans, and have extended in these lands the territory of the Holy Church. . . .

"However, if you are hindered by love of children, parents, and wives, remember what the Lord says in the Gospel, 'He that loveth father or mother, more than me, is not worthy of me.' 'Every one that hath forsaken houses, or brethren, or sisters, or father, or mother, or wife, or children, or lands for my name's sake shall receive an hundred-fold and shall inherit everlasting life.' Let none of your possessions detain you, no solicitude for your family affairs, since this land which you inhabit, shut in on all sides by the sea and surrounded by mountain peaks, is too narrow for your large population; nor does it abound in wealth; and it furnishes scarcely food enough for its cultivators. Hence it is that you murder and devour one another, that you wage war, and that frequently you perish by mutual wounds. Let therefore hatred depart from among you, let your quarrels end, let wars cease, and let all dissensions and controversies slumber. Enter upon the road to the Holy Sepulchre; wrest that land from the wicked race, and subject it to yourselves. That land which, as the Scripture says, 'floweth with milk and honey'. . . ."

When Pope Urban had said these and very many similar things in his urbane discourse, he so influenced to one purpose the desires of all who were present that they cried out, "God wills it! God wills it!" When the venerable Roman pontiff heard that, with eyes uplifted to heaven he gave thanks to God and, with his hand commanding silence, said:

"Most beloved brethren. . . . Unless the Lord God had been present in your minds, all of you would not have uttered the same cry. . . . Let this then be your battle-cry in combat. . . . When an armed attack is made upon the enemy, let this one cry be raised by all the soldiers of God: 'God wills it! God wills it!'. . .

"Whoever, therefore, shall determine upon this holy pilgrimage and shall make his vow to God to that effect and shall offer himself to Him as a living sacrifice, holy, acceptable unto God, shall wear the sign of the cross of the Lord on his forehead, or on his breast. When, having truly fulfilled his vow, he wishes to return, let him place the cross on his back between his shoulders. Such, indeed, by two-fold action will fulfil the precept of the Lord, as He commands in the Gospel, 'He that doth not take his cross and follow after me, is not worthy of me'."

K. M. Setton and H. R. Winkler, editors, *Great Problems in European Civilization* (Prentice-Hall, 1954), pp. 106-108.

(c)

Emperor HENRY IV (1056-1106) wrote in the following manner to Pope GREGORY VII (1073-1085), sometime in the year 1076.

Henry king not by usurpation but by the holy ordination of God to Hildebrand at present not the apostle but a false monk. . . . Our Lord Jesus Christ called us to the kingship, but he did not call you to the priesthood. For you ascended by these steps: you have obtained money, which is abhorrent to the monastic vow, by wiles, by money you have obtained favour, by favour you have obtained a sword, and by the sword you have obtained the chair of peace and from the chair of peace you disturb the peace in that you have armed subjects against their rulers, have taught that our bishops called to their office by God are to be spurned, and have usurped for laymen authority over their priests so that these laymen depose or condemn those whom they have received as teachers from the hand of God by the imposition of episcopal hands. On me also who although I am unworthy to be among the anointed have been anointed in the kingship you have lain hands. . . . the true pope St. Peter announces "Fear God, honour the king." You, however, who fear not God, dishonour me his appointed one. Wherefore St. Paul, when he does not spare an angel from heaven if he preaches otherwise, has not excepted you preaching otherwise on earth. For he says: If anyone, either I or an angel from the sky should preach other than is preached to you, he is accursed. You, therefore, damned by this curse and by the judgment of us and all our bishops descend and leave the purchased apostolic seat: let another ascend the throne of St. Peter who does not excuse violence by religion but teaches the true doctrine of St. Peter. I, Henry, king by God's grace with all our bishops say to you: Descend, descend, damned throughout the ages.

Pope Gregory struck back by excommunicating Henry in the same year, and put his answer to the emperor in the form of a letter to St. Peter:

O blessed Peter, prince of the Apostles, mercifully incline thine ear, we pray, and hear me, thy servant, whom thou hast cherished from infancy and hast delivered until now from the hand of the wicked who have hated, and still hate me for my loyalty to thee. Thou art my witness, as are also my Lady, the Mother of God, and the blessed Paul, thy brother among all the saints, that thy Holy Roman Church, forced me against my will to be its ruler. I had no thought of ascending thy throne as a robber, nay, rather would I have chosen to end my life as a pilgrim than to seize upon thy place for earthly glory and by devices of this world. Therefore, by thy favour, not by any works of mine, I believe that it is and has been thy will, that the Christian people especially committed to thee should render obedience to me, thy especially constituted representative. To me is given by thy grace the power of binding and loosing in Heaven and upon earth.

Wherefore, relying upon this commission, and for the honour and defence of thy Church, in the name of Almighty God, Father, Son and Holy Spirit, through thy power and authority, I deprive King Henry, son of the Emperor Henry, who has rebelled against thy Church with unheard-of audacity, of the government over the whole kingdom of Germany and Italy, and I release all Christian men from the allegiance which they have sworn or may swear to him, and I forbid anyone to serve him as king. For it is fitting that he who seeks to diminish the glory of thy Church should lose the glory which he seems to have. . . .

Setton and Winkler, *Great Problems in European Civilization*, pp. 141-142.

(d)

RICHARD THE REDELESS is the title of a satirical poem written in 1399 in criticism of Richard II of England. The following modernized selection is an attack on the parliament of 1398, which was dominated by Richard.

When the day for action arrived, the lords were assembled and also the knights of the shire. According to the usual form, the cause of meeting was first declared and then the king's will. A clerk began with a dignified speech setting forth the main points before them all, and asking above all for money, with flattery to the great men to avert complaints. When the speech was ended, the knights of the commons were commanded to meet on the morrow, before dinner, with the citizens of the shires to go through the articles which they had just heard and grant all that had been asked them. But to save appearances, and in accordance with custom, some of them falsely argued at some length, and said: "We are servants and we draw a salary, we are sent from the shires to make known their grievances, to discuss matters on their behalf and to stick to that, and only make grants of their money to the great men in a regular way, unless there is war. If we are false to the people who pay our wages, we are not earning them."

Some members sat there like a nought in arithmetic, that marks a place but has no value in itself. Some had taken bribes, so that the shire they represented had no advantage from their presence. . . . Some were tattlers, who went to the king and warned him against men who were really good friends of his and deserved no blame either from king, council or commons, if one listened carefully to the very end of their speeches. Some members slumbered and slept and said little. Some stammered and mumbled and did not know what they meant to say. Some were paid dependents, and were afraid to take any step without their masters' orders. Some were so pompous and dull-witted that they got hopelessly involved before they reached the end of their speeches, and no one, whether he sat on the bench or whether he was a burgess, could have made out what they wanted to say, there was so little sense in it. . . .

Some had been got at beforehand by the council and knew well enough how things would have to end, or the assembly would be sorry for it. Some went with the majority, whichever way they went, while some would not commit themselves. Some were quite openly more concerned about the money the king owed them than about the interests of the commons who paid their salaries, and these were promised their reward; if they would vote the taxes, their debts would be paid them. And some were so afraid of great men that they forsook righteousness.

H. M. Cam, *Liberties and Communities in Medieval England* (Merlin Press, London, 1963), pp. 230-231.

(e)

When it was noised about that ROGER BACON (1214-94) was writing a great book on philosophy, Pope Clement IV heard of the project and asked Bacon to send him a copy. But the best Bacon could do was to give the pope an outline of what he intended to write, for the work was never completed. This discussion of the rainbow, quoted from Bacon's outline, the *Opus Maius (Major Work)*, probably originated with his teacher, Robert Grosseteste.

I now wish to unfold the principles of experimental science, since without experience nothing can be sufficiently known. For there are two modes of acquiring knowledge, namely, by reasoning and experience. Reasoning draws a conclusion and makes us grant the conclusion, but does not make the conclusion certain. . . . if a man who has never seen fire should prove by adequate reasoning that fire burns and injures things and destroys them, his mind would not be satisfied thereby, nor would he avoid fire, until he placed his hand or some combustible substance in the fire, so that he might prove by experience that which reasoning taught. . . .

He therefore who wishes to rejoice without doubt in regard to the truths underlying phenomena must know how to devote himself to experiment. For authors write many statements, and people believe them through reasoning which they formulate without experience. Their reasoning is wholly false. For it is generally believed that the diamond cannot be broken except by goat's blood, and philosophers and theologians misuse this idea. But fracture by means of blood of this kind has never been verified, although the effort has been made; and without that blood it can be broken easily. For I have seen this with my own eyes, and this is necessary, because gems cannot be carved except by fragments of this stone. . . .

But if we give our attention to particular and complete experiments and such as are attested wholly by the proper method, we must employ the principles of this science which is called experimental. I give as an example the rainbow and phenomena connected with it. . . .

Let the experimenter first, then, examine visible objects, in order that he may find colours arranged as in the phenomena mentioned above and also the same figure. For let him take hexagonal stones from Ireland or from India. . . . and let him hold these in a solar ray falling through the window, so that he may find all the colours of the rainbow, arranged as in it, in the shadow near the ray. . . . Let the experimenter proceed further, and he will find this same peculiarity in crystalline stones correctly shaped, and in other transparent stones. . . . And further let him observe rowers, and in the drops falling from the raised oars he finds the same colours when the solar rays penetrate drops of this kind. The same phenomenon is seen in water falling from the wheels of a mill; and likewise when one sees on a summer's morning the drops of dew on the grass in meadow or field, he will observe the colours. Likewise when it is raining, if he stands in a dark place and the rays beyond it pass through the falling rain, the colours will appear in the shadow near by; and frequently at night colours appear around a candle. Moreover, if a man in summer, when he rises from sleep and has his eyes only partly open, suddenly looks at a hole through which a ray of the sun enters, he will see colours. Moreover, if seated beyond the sun he draws his cap beyond his eyes, he will see colours; and similarly if he closes an eye the same thing happens under the shade of the eyebrows; and again the same phenomenon appears through a glass vessel filled with water and placed in the sun's rays. Or similarly if one having water in his mouth sprinkles it vigorously into the rays and stands at the side of the rays. So, too, if rays in the required position pass through an oil lamp hanging in the air so that the light falls on the surface of the oil, colours will be produced. Thus in an infinite number of ways colours of this kind appear, which the diligent experimenter knows how to discover. . . .

J. B. Ross and M. M. McLaughlin, editors, *The Portable Medieval Reader* (Viking Press, 1949), pp. 626-627, 629-632.

BOOKS TO READ

1. TOWNS AND CRUSADES

Duggan, A., *The Story of the Crusades* (Faber)
Duggan, A., *Growing Up in the Thirteenth Century* (Faber)
Holmes, U. T., *Daily Living in the Twelfth Century* (Wisconsin paperback)
Komroff, M., *Marco Polo* (Methuen)
Lamb, H., *The Crusades* (Bantam paperback)
Lamb, H., *Genghis Khan* (Bantam paperback)
Reeves, M. E., *The Medieval Town* (Longmans)
Sellman, R. R., *The Crusades* (Methuen)
Treece, H., *Know About the Crusades* (Blackie)

2. THE MEDIEVAL MIND

Haskins, C. H., *The Rise of Universities* (Cornell paperback)
Temko, A., *Notre-Dame of Paris* (Compass paperback)

3. HISTORICAL FICTION

Costain, T. B., *The Black Rose* (Doubleday) [an Englishman in the Mongol Empire]
De Wohl, L., *The Quiet Light* (Lippincott) [St. Thomas Aquinas]
Duggan, A., *God and My Right* (Faber) [Henry II and Becket]
Duggan, A., *Knight with Armour* (Penguin paperback) [First Crusade]
Harnett, C., *The Wool-Pack* (Methuen) [medieval wool merchants]
Hueffer, F. M., *Ladies Whose Bright Eyes* (Lippincott) [14th century England]
Power, R., *Red Cap Runs Away* (Puffin paperback) [wayfaring life]
Scott, Sir Walter, *The Talisman* [Third Crusade]
Simon, E., *The Golden Hand* (Cassell) [building a cathedral]
Treece, H., *The Children's Crusade* (Bodley Head) [the tragic crusade of 1212]
White, H., *Bird of Fire* (Collier-Macmillan) [Francis of Assisi]

TOWARD A BRAVE NEW WORLD

To be ignorant of what happened before you were born is to be ever a child.

CICERO

As we have watched the pageant of the past move across the world's stage we have observed civilization only in its formative years. We have witnessed its birth and have seen its slow growth through ancient and medieval times until, with the later Middle Ages, it came of age. With civilization's coming of age, then, we leave our story—but it is a story that is just beginning to gain exciting momentum. For by 1400 a new spirit was sweeping across Europe, a spirit of independence symbolized by four movements in particular: the rise of towns, the development of capitalism, the decline of the secular power of the Church, and the hardy growth of the English Parliament. Men were beginning to strike out against the very roots of their society: they were questioning authority, and as they did so they looked hopefully forward to what Shakespeare called a "brave new world." Heaven, they believed, could in some measure be brought down to earth.

The first stirrings of this bolder spirit came in Italy with the Renaissance of the 14th and 15th centuries. "Man," declared one Renaissance writer, "can make whatever he will of himself." With such supreme self-confidence, what could man not do? And so Europeans struck out for new horizons, geographical and intellectual. They sailed forth in tiny ships across vast oceans; and they invented, with movable type, the means to send their very words across the continents. Now when a new and daring idea was born how quickly it could spread!

It was inevitable that the transition from the medieval to the modern world should bring strains and stresses. Such pressure, in the 16th century, split the medieval Church wide open into two parts, Roman Catholic and Protestant. Man's complacency was to be shattered even more rudely by the Scientific Revolution of the 17th century, which forced many people to contemplate a new and—to them—infinitely disturbing picture of the universe and of man's place in it.

Nevertheless this explosion of knowledge was merely a puff of smoke compared to the atomic upheaval of ideas which was to uproot modern man. We have been catapulted into a totally new, sometimes totally frightening, stage of civilization. More and more, machines are replacing people, while at the same time the vast unfolding of the cosmic universe has once again shaken man's estimate of his own importance on a planet

489

whose size has proved to be infinitesimal. Is our space age too far removed from the days of Caesar and Charlemagne to have any relation at all to the past?

No, indeed. Even as we can better understand the adult if we have known him as a child, so we may better understand our civilization if we know something about its infancy and adolescence. For the basic problems remain essentially the same in every age—problems of government and of personal and international morality. If we do not make an attempt to learn how the men of the past lived and thought, we cannot have a clear view of what is happening to us in our own century. An American philosopher has written that "when experience is not retained, as among savages, infancy is perpetual. Those who cannot remember the past are condemned to repeat it."

Let us not, then, be savages. Rather let us at least make sure of this: that if we of the 20th century should fail to solve the problems facing modern civilization, it will not be because we were ignorant of how men tried and failed in the past.

GENERAL REFERENCE BOOKS

Fishwick, D., Wilkinson, B., and Cairns, J. C., *The Foundations of the West* (Clarke, Irwin)

Fox, E. W. and Deighton, H. S. (editors), *Atlas of European History* (Oxford)

Hardy, W. G., *Our Heritage from the Past* (McClelland and Stewart)

Lavender, E., Lewis, F. B., and Sheffe, N., *A Thousand Ages* (McGraw-Hill)

New, C. W. and Phillips, C. E., *A World History from Ancient Times to 1500* (Clarke, Irwin and Dent)

Palmer, R. R., editor, *Atlas of World History* (Rand McNally)

McEvedy, C., *The Penguin Atlas of Medieval History* (Penguin paperback)

Speiser, E. A. and others, *Everyday Life in Ancient Times* (National Geographic)

Strong, C. F., *The Ancient and Early Medieval World* (University of London Press)

Trueman, J., *The Enduring Past: Earliest Times to the Sixteenth Century* (Ryerson)

Unstead, R. J., *Looking at Ancient History* (Black)

Van der Heyden, A. A. M. and Scullard, H. H. (editors), *Atlas of the Classical World* (Nelson)

PUBLISHER'S ACKNOWLEDGMENTS

QUOTATIONS

Permission to quote copyrighted material has been sought from the original publishers or as otherwise indicated in the text. Special acknowledgment is made to the following:

DR. HELEN M. CAM for permission to use the excerpt from her book on pages 485 to 486.

CHRIST COLLEGE, CAMBRIDGE, AND UNIVERSITY COLLEGE, OXFORD, for their consent to the use of selections from *The Book of the Dead* on page 90.

DOUBLEDAY AND COMPANY, INC., for the selection on page 289 from *A History of Rome from Its Origins to* A.D. *529 as Told by the Roman Historians* by Moses Hadas (Anchor, 1956).

HOLT, RINEHART AND WINSTON, INC., for the quotation on page 380 from *Ideas and Institutions in European History, 800-1715: Select Problems in Historical Interpretation* by T. C. Mendenhall, B. C. Henning and A. S. Foord, (© 1948).

PHOTOGRAPHS

Grateful acknowledgment is made to the following for permission to reproduce the photographs on the pages indicated:

Aerofilms and Aero Pictorial Limited, London: 436

Alison Frantz, Athens: 139

Art Reference Bureau, Ancram, New York: 57, 189

Alinari; 154, 174, 194-195, 205, 222, 251, 272, 279

Anderson; 269, 291

Marburg; 40

Mas; 299

British Museum: 94, 182, 258, 348, 424

British School of Archaeology in Jerusalem, London: 19

Ewing Galloway, New York: 72, 445

Franciscan Fathers of La Custodie de Terre Sainte, Jerusalem: 351

French Government Tourist Office, New York: 467

Giraudon, Paris: 296, 297, 402, 403

The Louvre, Paris: 43

Matson Photo Service, Los Angeles: 116

Metropolitan Museum of Art, New York: Harry Burton; 57

Dick Fund, 1940; 226

Rogers Fund, 1912; 260

Montreal Museum of Fine Arts: 287

National Geographic Society, Washington: 10

National Tourist Office of Greece, Athens: 187

Oriental Institute, University of Chicago: 45 right, 54, 104

Rijksmuseum, Amsterdam: 69

Jean Roubier, Paris: 464

Charles Scribner's Sons, New York: 2 (Reproduced from *Men of the Old Stone Age* by Henry F. Osborn. Copyright 1915 Charles Scribner's Sons; renewal copyright 1945 A. Perry Osborn.)

Universitetets Oldsaksamling, Oslo: 377

University Museum, University of Pennsylvania: 45 left

Yale University Art Library: 132

Every reasonable care has been taken to trace ownership of copyrighted material used in this book. The authors and publisher will welcome information that will enable them to rectify any reference or credit in succeeding printings.

INDEX

NOTE:

The pronouncing guide incorporated in this index is as accurate as it is possible to make it without using the technical phonetic symbols.

Chaldean, 102
Cretan, 135
Egyptian, 41, 58
Greek, 185, 203
Indian, 67-68
Minoan, 135
Old Stone Age, 3, 13-14, 17, 24
Roman, 298-299
Aryans [air'ee-unz], 68, 69
Ashur [aw'shur], 95, 99, 101, 123, 124
Ashurbanipal [aw-shur-baw'ni-pawl], 99, 100, 101, 122
Asoka [a-soh'kuh], 201
Assembly:
    Greek, 152, 155, 174, 175
    Roman, 232, 272 (*see also* Centuriate, Curiate and Tribal Assemblies)
Assyria, 42, 95-102, 105, 109, 114, 117-119, 123, 127-129, 157
    army, 99, 122-129
    art, 95, 100-101, 104
    Empire, 99-101
    law, 128
    literature, 101
    medicine, 101
    religion, 101
    science, 101
    women, 127
Assyrians, 57, 95
Aswan High Dam, 47
Athena [a-thee'nuh], 170, 186, 187
Athens, 124 ,140, 143, 147, 151, 152, 154, 155, 157, 158, 161, 162, 164, 165, 168-176, 181, 183, 189, 192, 200, 206, 208, 210-212, 214, 218, 258, 307, 325
    Assembly, 174, 175
    courts, 152, 156, 170-171
    democracy, 147, 151, 154, 156-157, 172, 173, 175, 190, 216, 217, 219
    fleet, 162
    law, 151, 152, 169
    Long Walls, 171, 175, 176
    women, 207, 210
Aton, 55, 56
Attica, 151, 152, 154, 156, 158, 173, 174, 178, 188
Attila [at'i-luh], 317
Augustine of Hippo, 399-400, 457
    City of God, 400, 412
Augustus, 275, 277-285, 286, 287, 293, 296, 297, 300-302, 311
Australoids, 24
Avignon, Papacy at, 450-451

B

Baals [baylz], 112, 117, 119
Babylon, 42-43, 95, 98, 99, 120, 130, 198
Babylonia, 43, 114
    language, 28, 46, 98
Babylonian Captivity:
    Church, 451
    Jews, 102, 103, 109, 114-115, 120, 130-131

Bacon, Roger, 459, 486
    Opus Maius, 486
Bactria, 197, 201
Bailiff, 389
Banks, 439
Barbarians (*see* Germans and Huns)
Barnabas, 305
Baron, 380
Barracks Emperors, 312, 319
Bartholomew, Peter, 435
Baths, Roman, 298, 331-333
Bavaria, 369
Bayeux Tapestry, 397, 402
Beauvais, 469
Becket, Thomas, 395, 446
Bede, the Venerable, 401
Behistun [bay-hi-stoon'] inscription, 108, 129
Benedict, St., 351
    Rule, 351-352, 417-418
    Order of, 351-352, 400-401
Benefice, 367, 372
Beyrut, 97
Bible, 401, 457 (*see also* New Testament and Old Testament)
Bills of exchange, 439
Bishops, 349, 356, 357, 444, 446
    Rome, 350 (*see also* Papacy and Pope)
Bithynia [bi-thin'ee-uh], 308
Black Death, 443, 444
Boeotia [bee-oh'shuh], 140, 212, 213
Bologna, 225, 248
    University of, 461
Bonds, 439, 479
Boniface VIII, Pope, 450, 458
Book of the Dead, 57, 90
Boulê [boo'lay], 155, 171
Brahma, 70
Bronze:
    tools, 6
    weapons, 76, 77
Bronze Age, 27, 41, 61, 82-88, 102, 133, 134, 224
    migration, 53, 57, 68
    pottery, 54
Brundisium, 277
Bucephalus [byew-sef'uh-lus], 193, 194, 197
Buddha, 70-72, 78, 79, 90
Buddhism, 70-73, 81, 90, 91, 201
Bulgars, 359
Burgesses, 428, 470
Byblos, 49
Byzantium, 165, 313, 358
    civilization, 358-360
    Emperor, 373, 435
    Empire, 358-360, 366

C

Caesar, (Gaius) Julius, 268-271, 284, 287, 300
    Gallic Wars, 270
Caesarea, 308

EGYPTIANS

SHANG—1400 B.C.

ROMAN

BYZANTINE